T H E
EPISTLES
O F
JOHN

An Expositional Commentary

D. Edmond Hiebert

BOB JONES UNIVERSITY PRESS
Greenville, South Carolina 29614

Library of Congress Cataloging-in-Publication Data

Hiebert, D. Edmond, (David Edmond), 1910-
    The Epistles of John : an expositional commentary / D. Edmond Hiebert.

    Includes bibliographical references and index.
    ISBN 0-89084-588-3
    1. Bible.   N.T.   Epistles of John—Commentaries.   I. Title.
  BS2805.3.H54   1991
  227'.94077—dc20   91-24565
                                                  CIP

The Epistles of John: An Expositional Commentary
by D. Edmond Hiebert

All Scripture quotations, unless otherwise noted, are from the King James Version of the Bible. Quotation from other translations does not necessarily indicate an endorsement by the publisher of all of the contents of such translations.

NOTE:
The fact that materials produced by other publishers are referred to in this volume does not constitute an endorsement by Bob Jones University Press of the content or theological position of materials produced by such publishers. The position of Bob Jones University Press, and the University itself, is well known. Any references and ancillary materials are listed as an aid to the reader and in an attempt to maintain the accepted academic standards of the publishing industry.

ISBN 0-89084-588-3

Cover designed by Jim Hargis
Edited by Mark Sidwell
Text in Times Roman and headings in Optima
Printed in the United States of America

20   19   18   17   16   15   14   13   12   11   10   9   8   7   6

Contents

Assurance Through the Witness of the Spirit (5:6-12)

Part 2: Second and Third John

Abbreviations

For the full publishing information on these versions, see pp. 351-52 of the Bibliography.

ASV	American Standard Version (1901)
Goodspeed	Edgar J. Goodspeed, *The New Testament, An American Translation* (1923)
KJV	King James Version (1611)
NASB	*New American Standard Bible* (1971)
NEB	*New English Bible* (2nd ed. 1979)
NIV	New International Version (1978)
NKJV	*New King James Bible* (1979)
Rotherham	Joseph Bryant Rotherham, *The Emphasized New Testament* (1878)
RSV	Revised Standard Version (1946)
RV	English Revised Version (1881)
TEV	Today's English Version (1966)
T.R.	Textus Receptus

Preface

Throughout the various periods of the Christian era, devout believers have always cherished the Johannine Epistles as a priceless portion of the New Testament. The grand simplicity of their contents has unfailingly nurtured the faith and stimulated the life of the humblest believer, while the profound depths of their teachings have challenged the most scholarly interpreters. They have been the subject of innumerable sermonic expositions and scholarly treatises; yet their inexhaustible contents continue to spur renewed examination of their God-given truths.

This expositional treatment of the Epistles of John seeks to delve into the inspired riches of these letters to aid in their study by the diligent student. The quoted English text is that of the familiar *King James Version,* but the interpretation is based directly on the Greek. Although the commentary is based on a study of the Greek text, it is intended also for students who may not be proficient in their knowledge of that language. The portion under consideration is always first quoted in English with the Greek text, in transliteration,[1] added in parentheses. As needed, the various aspects of the Greek text are treated to bring out the fuller significance of the Johannine message.

A detailed outline of these epistles, setting forth their contents, appears before the beginning of the exposition of each epistle and is inserted throughout the exposition as a guide to the unfolding of the message.

These epistles first captured my attention years ago as a teen-age believer eager to gain a fuller understanding of the Christian faith and life. They have continued to be the object of my personal study and classroom exposition in the years since then. My indebtedness to many sources in the effort to unfold these epistles will be readily evident from the footnotes and the bibliography.

---

[1]In the transliterations the usually adopted equivalents for the Greek letters are used, except in the case of *upsilon,* where I have consistently used *u* instead of the more common *y.*

1

An Introduction to First John

The forceful simplicity of its sentences, the note of finality behind its utterances, the marvelous blending of gentle love and deep-cutting sternness of its contents, and the majesty of its ungarnished thoughts have made 1 John a favorite with Christians everywhere. The plainness of its language makes it intelligible to the simplest saint, while the profundity of its truths challenges the most accomplished scholar. Its grand theological revelations and its unwavering ethical demands have left their enduring impact upon the thought and life of the Christian Church. First John is indeed a singular, irreplaceable gem among the books of the New Testament.

The Form of 1 John

In the various catalogs of the books of the New Testament this writing is always classified as "letter"; yet, unlike 2 and 3 John, it does not display the regular features of a letter as seen in the models of contemporary correspondence. It is like Hebrews in that it begins without an opening salutation, but it lacks entirely the epistolary conclusion of that epistle. It concludes as abruptly as the Epistle of James, but it is without the formal epistolary opening of James. It contains no formal thanksgiving for the readers, as is characteristic of the opening paragraphs of Paul's letters. It does not contain a single personal name beyond a passing reference to Cain (3:12), nor does it offer a single concrete statement–personal, historical, or geographic–concerning either writer or readers. It is destitute of all that is merely local or specific.

The absence of the customary epistolary features has led some writers to regard the title of "epistle" as a misnomer. These writers have suggested several different designations to characterize more closely the nature of this

1

writing.[1] Suggestions that it is a general tractate or a homily are unsatisfactory, however, in view of the intimate relations between the writer and its readers. The author deals with an actual life situation and addresses readers with whom he had intimate relations, knowing their history, attainments, and needs, as well as the dangers they faced. The letter springs out of a definite historical situation and is adapted to meet that situation. It glows with the writer's keen interest in and personal concern for his readers. Although lacking the external epistolary features, the contents of 1 John confirm its epistolary character.

In view of its hortatory and moralistic tone, some have thought of 1 John as a sermon, containing the substance of a sermon, or several sermons, written out, either before or after delivery. Houlden regards it as "a hortatory treatise, directed to an intimately known audience."[2] Martin remarks, "The moralistic and hortatory tone of much of the letter also suggests a baptismal context, as the material belongs to the type of instruction given to new converts ('little children,' as they are called in 2:1, 12; 3:18; 4:4; 5:21; cf. 2:13, 18; 3:2, 10)."[3] While 1 John clearly reflects the author's pastoral concern for those he addresses, the contents make clear that it is not the transcription of a sermon. Repeatedly the author indicates that the form of communication he is using is that of writing (1:4; 2:1, 7, 8, 12, 13, 14, 21, 26; 5:13). Only once does he use the expression "I say" (5:16). The designation "little children" does not establish that the recipients were recent converts needing instruction in the basic elements of the Christian faith. Its contents show that at least some of those addressed had been Christians for a long time and were advanced in their knowledge of Christian truth. The author's manner of address points to an epistolary communication; he refers to himself as "I" or "we" and addresses persons whom he designates as "you." Its contents establish that 1 John arose as a written communication to readers personally known to the writer.

The intimate relationship between the writer and his readers, the pertinence of the hortatory appeals, and the tone and contents of the composition as a whole justify its classification among the New Testament epistles. But the absence of all that is merely local suggests that it was not intended for

---

[1]Donald W. Burdick, *The Letters of John the Apostle* (Chicago: Moody Press, 1985), pp. 68-69, notes that 1 John has been called a treatise, a homiletical essay, a sort of dedicatory epistle for John's gospel, a tract or pastoral manifesto in vague epistolary form, a pastoral rather than a letter, a homiletical epistle, an open letter, an encyclical in epistolary form and a true letter. For further data see Burdick.

[2]J. L. Houlden, *A Commentary on the Johannine Epistles,* Harper's New Testament Commentaries (New York: Harper & Row, 1973), p. 54.

[3]Ralph P. Martin, *New Testament Foundations: A Guide for Christian Students* (Grand Rapids: Eerdmans, 1978), vol. 2, *The Acts, The Letters, The Apocalypse,* p. 368.

a single congregation but rather for a larger circle of congregations within the writer's acquaintance. While accepting the classification of 1 John "as a bona fide New Testament epistle," Burdick rightly holds that "it should be described as encyclical or circular in nature and pastoral in function."[4]

The Authorship of 1 John

1. External Evidence

First John is better attested by external evidence than any of the other general epistles. Eusebius of Caesarea (c. 265–c. 339)[5] in his famous *Historia Ecclesiastica* placed 1 John among the *homologoumena,* the acknowledged books,[6] in his list of the canonical books (3. 25). Only 1 John and 1 Peter among the general epistles were so classified by him.

The earliest definite trace of this epistle is in Polycarp, bishop of Smyrna (c. 70-155/160). In his *Epistle to the Philippians* (c. 115) he writes: "For whosoever does not confess that Jesus Christ has come in the flesh, is antichrist, and whosoever does not confess the testimony of the cross, is of the devil" (7:1). In view of the fact that the word "antichrist" occurs in the New Testament only in 1 and 2 John and does not occur frequently in the subapostolic literature; and that "confess," "witness," and "to be of the devil" are characteristically Johannine expressions; these words clearly seem to have been inspired by 1 John 4:2-3. Irenaeus, who as a youth in Asia Minor had listened to Polycarp preach, informs us that Polycarp in his youth had known the Apostle John.[7] Since Polycarp suffered martyrdom at the age of eighty-six, he must have been a contemporary of the apostle John for some twenty years. The quotation by Polycarp proves the early date of the First Epistle of John and at least suggests, if it does not attest, its Johannine authorship. In view of Polycarp's acquaintance with John, is it possible that he could have been ignorant of its authorship? Would he have appropriated its teaching and its very terminology if he had had any doubts as to it authoritativeness?

Eusebius tells us that Papias, bishop of Hierapolis (c. 60–c. 130), "made use of testimonies from the First Epistle of John" in his work entitled "Interpretations of our Lord's Declarations" (*Eccl. Hist.* 3. 39). He quotes

---

[4]Burdick, p. 70.

[5]The dates are generally those given in J. D. Douglas, ed., *The New International Dictionary of the Christian Church* (Grand Rapids: Zondervan, 1974).

[6]From the standpoint of their canonicity, Eusebius classified Christian documents as the *homologoumena* (the acknowledged), the *antilogomena* (the disputed), and the *nothoi* (the spurious). He added that books put forth by the heretics in the names of the apostles "are to be ranked not only among the spurious writings, but are to be rejected as altogether absurd and impious" (*Eccl. Hist.,* 3. 25).

[7]See Eusebius, *Eccl. Hist.* 5. 20, and Irenaeus, *Against Heresies* 3. 3. 4.

Irenaeus as saying that Papias "was John's hearer and the associate of Polycarp, an ancient writer" (3. 39; Irenaeus, *Against Heresies,* 3. 3. 4).

Thus we have two early witnesses to this epistle, both from the province of Asia, well within the first half of the second century. In view of the scantiness of the literature which has come down to us from that period, it is remarkable indeed to have these two early witnesses.

Irenaeus, bishop of Lyons, is the first known writer to cite the epistle by name as written by John. Eusebius records that Irenaeus, who as a boy listened to Polycarp, apparently in Smyrna, "also mentions the First Epistle of John, extracting many testimonies from it" (*Eccl. Hist.* 5. 8). In his noted work *Against Heresies* Irenaeus quotes 1 John 2:18-19 and expressly remarks that he is quoting from John's epistle (3. 16. 5). He also quotes 1 John 4:1-2 and 5:1 and identifies his quotation as from John's epistle (3. 16. 8).

The Muratorian Canon, a fragmentary Latin list of New Testament books known at Rome, cites this epistle and ascribes it to John. As an obvious translation of a Greek document, it is usually dated somewhere between A.D. 170 and 200. These testimonies by Irenaeus and the Muratorian Canon confirm that by the end of the second century 1 John was accepted both in the East and West as authoritative and as of Johannine authorship. Further testimony to the epistle is found in the writings of Clement of Alexandria (c. 155–c. 220), Tertullian (c. 160–c. 215/20), Origen (c. 185–c. 254), Cyprian (c. 200/10-258), and others. As Guthrie remarks, "This evidence is sufficient to show that from very early times the Epistle was not only treated as Scripture but was assumed to be Johannine, in spite of the fact that no specific claim to this effect is made by the writer himself."[8] It is evident that 1 John, undoubtedly one of the latest of the New Testament books to be written, took an immediate and permanent position as an authoritative, inspired writing.

This strong testimony to the Johannine authorship of the epistle is not weakened by the rejection of it by Marcion, a prominent heretic in the mid-second century, and by the Alogoi. Marcion rejected it, as he did all the gospels except an expurgated Luke and all the epistles except those of Paul, not because he regarded them as spurious, but because they contradicted his peculiar anti-Judaistic views. The obscure sect in Asia Minor, designated the Alogoi by Epiphanius, rejected "the books of John" as spurious and ascribed them to Cerinthus because the group distrusted the Johannine teaching concerning the Logos.[9]

---

[8]Donald Guthrie, *New Testament Introduction,* rev. ed. (Downers Grove, Ill.: Inter-Varsity Press, 1970), p. 865.

[9]Theodor Zahn, *Introduction to the New Testament,* trans. from the 3rd German ed. (Edinburgh: T. & T. Clark, 1909), 3:200.

2. *Evidence from the Epistle*

The internal evidence has ramifications beyond the epistle itself. In considering the internal evidence we begin with whatever information about the author can be gleaned from his actual letter. As an anonymous writing, the epistle offers no information concerning the personal identity of the writer, but it gives us sufficient material whereby we may classify him. His relation to his readers is one of intimacy and recognized authority. Indeed, his relation to the readers was so well known that it was superfluous for the writer to declare his identity; the intimate relationship between writer and readers is taken for granted throughout.

As Westcott points out, "The writer of the Epistle speaks throughout with the authority of an Apostle."[10] But he nowhere makes any passionate claim to apostolic authority; he does not feel it necessary to assert that he possesses such authority. Instead he assumes that his readers recognize and accept his distinctive position. As Guthrie notes,

> He clearly expects not only to be heard, but to be obeyed (cf. iv. 6, as well as the whole impression of the Epistle). He writes in categorical, almost dogmatic, terms. There is no disputing the truth of what he says. He condemns error in no uncertain terms (cf. ii. 18ff., iv. 1ff.), and leaves no opportunity for compromise.[11]

In the opening verses of the epistle (1:1-4), the writer includes himself among those who were personal witnesses of the earthly existence of the incarnate Logos. His use of "we," "us," and "our" appears to be a vivid assertion that he was one of a group of eyewitnesses who saw, heard, and personally touched the incarnate Christ. These eyewitnesses formed a distinct group as over against the "you" to whom his writing was addressed, and the impression that the writer is speaking as an eyewitness is supported by his categorical assertion in 4:14. Feuillet well asks, "Without sufficient proof have we the right to treat lightly so solemn an assertion?"[12] Westcott accepts that "St. John throughout this section uses the plural as speaking in the name of the apostolic body of which he was the last surviving representative."[13]

But the interpreters are not agreed as to the precise import of the writer's first personal pronouns in this Prologue. He may be understood to be using an editorial "we" in an effort to avoid calling attention to himself alone.

---

[10]Brooke Foss Westcott, *The Epistles of St. John, The Greek Text with Notes,* 3rd ed. (1892; reprint ed., Grand Rapids: Eerdmans, 1950), p. xxxi.

[11]Guthrie, p. 866.

[12]A. Feuillet, "The Johannine Epistles," in A. Robert and A. Feuillet, *Introduction to the New Testament,* trans. from the French (New York: Desclee Company, 1965), p. 680.

[13]Westcott, p. 4.

But Kistemaker believes that "the so-called editorial 'we' is too vague to be applicable here."[14] Or he may be viewed as employing "the homiletical *we* in which the speaker identifies himself with Christians in general."[15] Thus Dodd holds that the writer "speaks not exclusively for himself or for a restricted group, but for the whole Church to which the apostolic witness belongs."[16] But this is an unwarranted weakening of the author's language and confuses the distinction between "we" and "you" in this passage. In fact, "it would bring no authentication of his message if the author were referring only to the fact of the incarnation which all Christians generally had 'seen.'"[17] More recently R. E. Brown interprets the writer's "we" to denote not the apostles directly but rather "the tradition-bearers and interpreters who stand in a special relationship to the Beloved Disciple in their attempt to preserve his witness."[18] Brown, well aware that such "tradition-bearers" cannot be said to have personally touched the incarnate Christ with their own hands, seeks to remove the difficulty by insisting that they "participated in the sensation only vicariously."[19] But only one who had been one of Christ's original disciples could truthfully assure his readers in the face of heretical claims that he had personally seen, heard, and touched the incarnate Son of God. As Stott points out,

> The first person plural is used not only of the verbs describing the historical experience, but also of the verbs describing the proclamation of it. The persons who make the announcement are the persons who had the experience. . . . It is they whose eyes have seen, ears heard and hands handled, whose mouths are opened to speak.[20]

The data that can be gleaned from the epistle itself therefore agrees with the external evidence that the writer was the Apostle John.

3. Relation to Fourth Gospel

Any consideration of the internal evidence concerning the authorship of 1 John at once raises the question of its relation to the Fourth Gospel, whose

---

[14]Simon J. Kistemaker, *Exposition of the Epistle of James and the Epistles of John,* New Testament Commentary (Grand Rapids: Baker, 1986), p. 204.

[15]Burdick, p. 28.

[16]C. H. Dodd, *The Johannine Epistles,* Moffatt New Testament Commentary (New York: Harper & Row, 1946), p. 16.

[17]Guthrie, p. 866.

[18]Raymond E. Brown, *The Epistles of John,* The Anchor Bible (Garden City, N.Y.: Doubleday & Co., 1982), pp. 95, 160.

[19]*Ibid.,* p. 160.

[20]J.R.W. Stott, *The Epistles of John,* Tyndale New Testament Commentaries (Grand Rapids: Eerdmans, 1964), pp. 31-32.

authorship early church tradition uniformly ascribed to the Apostle John.[21] The prevailing view within Christendom has been that both writings were produced by the same man, and the internal evidence in favor of identical authorship is strong.

The list of phrases common to both works is striking. Brooke, in his discussion of their relation to each other, lists no less than fifty-one references in the epistle which find a parallel in the Fourth Gospel.[22] The parallels clearly reflect a common terminology, but they are not stereotyped repetition; there are significant variations in the use of the varied expressions. As Brooke points out, the explanation of these similarities lies between either an imitator or a writer who varies his phrases as he desires.[23] The latter is the more probable.

The Fourth Gospel and 1 John also reveal similarities of style. In each there are an infrequent use of the relative, a frequent employment of disconnected sentences, and the union of an affirmative and negative expression of thought. There is a restricted range of vocabulary in both writings, which is identical to an extent without parallel in two independent works. The Greek word *paraklētos,* "paraclete," for example, occurs four times in the Gospel and once in 1 John but nowhere else in the New Testament. The expression "only begotten" *(monogenēs)* as an expression of the Son's uniqueness occurs in John 1:14, 3:16, and 1 John 4:9. Both works use the literary device of contrast: life and death, light and darkness, love and hate, and truth and the lie are examples. This similarity between the two writings is all the more remarkable when it is remembered that the nature of the Fourth Gospel is objective narrative, whereas the epistle is hortatory and polemical. The acceptance of a common authorship for these two writings greatly strengthens the evidence for the Johannine authorship of 1 John because tradition emphatically ascribes the Fourth Gospel to the Apostle John.

But in the twentieth century some modern interpreters have vigorously assailed this view of the common authorship of the Fourth Gospel and the First Epistle of John.[24] While freely admitting the similarities, these interpreters hold that the differences outweigh the resemblances. Instead they hold that the two works are not from the same author but are rather the

---

[21]See D. Edmond Hiebert, *An Introduction to the New Testament* (Chicago: Moody Press, 1975), vol. 1, *The Gospels and Acts,* pp. 192-203.

[22]A. E. Brooke, *A Critical and Exegetical Commentary on the Johannine Epistles,* International Critical Commentary (New York: Scribner's 1912), pp. ii-iv.

[23]*Ibid.,* p. v.

[24]For an impressive list of authors who accept one author for both works and those who do not accept that view, see Brown, p. 20.

compositions of leading members of the "Johannine Community" who adhered to and sought to preserve the teaching of the Apostle John.[25]

Some question common authorship on the basis that the style of the two compositions is different. Thus Dodd says,

> While the rhythm of both is slow and regular, in the Gospel it is subtly varied, within the limits imposed by its general character; but in the Epistle regularity often descends to monotony. The language of the Gospel has an intensity, a kind of inward glow, a controlled excitement, which the reader does not feel, or seldom feels, in the Epistle.[26]

Dodd admits that such a criticism is subjective and that matters of style are differently estimated by different minds. Ross counters the view of Dodd by replying,

> We need only say that we have found, and that not seldom, this intensity, this inward glow, in the language of the Epistle, as in the language of the Gospel, and the fact that such a mental reaction is experienced at all in the reading of the Epistle tends to prove that we are all the time in contact with the same mind. And, if it be the case that in the Gospel we have a richness of language that is wanting in the Epistle, may the explanation not be that the Gospel was composed with greater care, as a book intended to bring home conviction of the truth of Christianity to enquiring minds, while the Epistle, written to believers, is composed with greater freedom and simplicity of language.[27]

Some critics have objected to apostolic authorship for 1 John on the ground of the alleged "feebleness" of the epistle, as evidenced by its frequent repetitions. That there is repetition in the epistle, greater than in the Fourth Gospel, may be allowed. But closer inspection will reveal that these alleged repetitions always result in a progress of thought. This repetition of thought may be due to the old age of the author, as has been suggested, but this point must not delude us into thinking that the underlying thought is not of great value. But even granting that the author's style may be a mark of old age, this fact would not furnish an argument against the traditional

---

[25]See Dodd, pp. xlix-lvi; R. Alan Culpeper, *The Johannine School: An Evaluation of the Johannine-School Hypothesis Based on an Investigation of the Nature of Ancient Schools,* Society of Biblical Literature Dissertation Series, no. 26 (Missoula, Mont.: Scholars Press, 1975); Stephen S. Smalley, *1, 2, 3 John,* Word Biblical Commentary (Waco, Texas: Word Books, 1984), p. xxii; Oscar Cullman, *The Johannine Circle* (Philadelphia: Westminster Press, 1975), pp. 53-87; Raymond E. Brown, *The Community of the Beloved Disciple* (New York: Paulist Press, 1979); Brown, *The Epistles of John,* The Anchor Bible, pp. 69-115.

[26]Dodd, p. xlix.

[27]Alexander Ross, *The Epistles of James and John,* New International Commentary on the New Testament (Grand Rapids: Eerdmans 1954), pp. 110-11.

authorship since it is freely admitted that the Apostle John must have been of quite advanced age when he wrote the epistle.

Brown advances the argument that "there is a marked difference between the two works in terms of clarity of expression" and maintains that "the greater obscurity of the Epistles becomes an argument for differences of authorship."[28] While the Fourth Gospel is not without its difficulties of interpretation, it is well known that 1 John contains its due share of obscurities and ambiguities. In the epistle the author's use of the personal pronoun in reference to deity often leaves undetermined whether the reference is to the Father or to Jesus Christ. In the Fourth Gospel, with its explicit evangelistic aim (20:31), such ambiguities would be undesirable; but in the epistle, addressed to readers who adhered to apostolic Christology, such ambiguities would be significant and challenging. The fact that the epistle was addressed to readers familiar with the writer's teachings, as well as the fact that the work was prompted by a sense of urgency in view of the crisis facing the readers, would help to account for these obscurities of expression.

Advocates of duality of authorship maintain that the theological outlooks of the Gospel and epistle are at variance with each other. It is asserted, for instance, that the eschatological view of the epistle is more primitive than that found in the Fourth Gospel. The epistle, it is held, holds out the prospect of a near advent of Christ and the end of the world (2:17, 28) whereas the Fourth Gospel gives a profound reinterpretation of eschatology by presenting the judgment not as future but as present (3:18) and viewing the coming of Christ as happening in the experience of every believer (14:18). But this assertion is erroneous. The Fourth Gospel also speaks of a final and universal judgment (5:29), refers to "the last day" (6:39, 40, 44, 54; 11:24), and holds to a personal return of Christ (21:22-23). As Burdick points out, "To interpret John 5:28-29 strictly in terms of realized eschatology is to ignore the natural meaning of Christ's claim. This eschatology is as primitive as that of 1 John 3:2."[29]

It is claimed that there is "a real difference in the conception of the Paraclete, who is identified in the epistle (2:1) with Jesus Christ as the Righteous One, whereas, in the gospel, Jesus either sends the Paraclete or is at most a Paraclete himself."[30] But there is no disagreement here. In the Gospel Jesus refers to the Holy Spirit as "*another* Paraclete" (14:16), thus implying His own character as Paraclete. The objection rests upon the mere use of the word rather than its meaning in its context. Brown likewise sup-

---

[28]Brown, *The Epistles of John,* pp. 24-25.

[29]Burdick, p. 21.

[30]James Moffatt, *An Introduction to the Literature of the New Testament,* 3rd ed. (1918; reprint ed., Edinburgh: T. & T. Clark, 1949), p. 592.

ports duality of authorship by asserting that reference to the Spirit is much less specific in 1 John than in the Fourth Gospel and remarks, "The treatment of the Spirit of Truth alongside the Spirit of Deceit in 1 John 4:1-6 is strangely vague about the personal quality of the Spirit."[31] However, 1 John 5:8 presents the Spirit as carrying on the personal work of bearing witness, and 2:20, 27 recognizes the seemingly impersonal term "anointing" as referring to the Spirit's personal activity of teaching. Also, the work of the indwelling Spirit pictured in 1 John 3:24 and 4:13 is in keeping with the presentation of the Spirit's work in Christ's farewell discourse in the Gospel.

It is maintained that the reader notices a modification of the idea of faith between the two writings. Thus Moffatt says, "While in the Gospel faith is equivalent to the coming of a man to the truth and light of God in Christ, or to a reception of the words of Jesus in the heart, the writer of the epistle, though far from being an intellectualist, tends to resolve faith into a confession of Jesus as the Son of God (2:23; 4:2-3; 5:1)."[32] But in the Fourth Gospel there is an equally definite insistence upon the necessity of accepting the deity of Christ (cf. 5:17, 39-40; 8:23-24, 55-58). However, the full development of the christological faith, spurred by later heretical perversions, naturally has no place in the gospel which deals with the period when that faith was first being presented and verified.

Again, it is said that the epistle presents Christ's death as propitiatory (2:1-2) whereas the propitiatory element is absent in the Gospel. Admittedly the Gospel does not use the word propitiation as does the epistle (2:2; 4:10), but the basic idea is there, although not in the developed form of the epistle. The concept is involved in the statement "Behold the Lamb of God, which taketh away the sin of the world" (1:29). This concept is latent in the teaching of the entire Fourth Gospel. However, for the writer to have put all of his own theological expressions into the mouth of Him whose teachings he professes to report would have been an anachronism.

Attempts to establish duality of authorship for these two writings are not convincing. That there are differences between them is clear, but these differences do not cancel out the marked similarities. These differences show only that the writer was a man of enough versatility to alter his phrases and concepts at will as the occasion demanded. A skillful imitator could hardly have combined elements of likeness and unlikeness in such a manner. After a careful consideration of the differences between the two writings, Brooke concludes, "There are no adequate reasons for setting aside the traditional view which attributes the Epistle and Gospel to the same authorship. It

---

[31]Brown, *The Epistles of John,* pp. 26-27.
[32]Moffatt, p. 591.

remains the most probable explanation of the facts known to us.''[33] And Burdick closes his lengthy discussion of the authorship of 1 John with the following conclusions: ''In the light of the current flux and the new view of the fourth gospel that has emerged, it is not unreasonable for a theological conservative to conclude that the arguments decidedly favor John the apostle as the author of both the fourth gospel and the first epistle.''[34] We accept without hesitation the traditional view that the Apostle John was the author of both the Gospel and the First Epistle.

4. John's Ephesian Ministry

The acceptance of the Johannine authorship of 1 John at once raises the problem of John's later years. The Apostle John disappears from the story of Acts after chapter 8. In the Pauline Epistles he is mentioned only in Galatians 2:9. Does extant information about the later life of John agree with the view that he was the author of these writings?

According to persistent Christian tradition, John spent the closing years of his long life at Ephesus, from which he carried out an extensive evangelistic and pastoral ministry to the regions around. Christian apologist Justin Martyr (c. 100-165) writes in his *Dialogue With Trypho* (ch. 81): ''There was a certain man with us, whose name was John, one of the Apostles of Christ, who prophesied, by a revelation that was made to him, that those who believed in our Christ would dwell a thousand years in Jerusalem.'' Eusebius in his *Ecclesiastical History* (4. 18) informs us that this dialogue took place at Ephesus.

Irenaeus (c. 140-203), bishop of Lyons in Gaul but apparently born in Asia Minor, bears explicit testimony to John's Ephesian residence. In his famous work *Against Heresies* he speaks of the testimony of ''all the elders. . . who were conversant in Asia with John, the disciple of the Lord'' and then adds that John ''remained among them up to the times of Trajan'' (2. 22. 5). He also says, ''Afterwards, John, the disciple of the Lord, who also had leaned upon His breast, did himself publish a Gospel during His residence at Ephesus in Asia'' (3. 1. 1).

Polycrates (lived c. 190), bishop of Ephesus, says in his epistle to Victor, bishop of Rome (d. 198), ''And moreover John also that leaned back upon the Lord's breast, who was a priest bearing the plate of gold, and a martyr and a teacher–he lies asleep at Ephesus'' (Eusebius, *Eccl. Hist.* 5:24). Eusebius also quotes Clement of Alexandria (c. 155–c. 220) as saying of John the apostle:

---

[33]Brooke, p. viii.

[34]Burdick, p. 37.

When, after the tyrant's [i.e., the Emperor Domitian's] death, he returned from the isle of Patmos to Ephesus, he went away upon their invitation to the neighboring territories of the Gentiles, to appoint bishops in some places, in other places to set in order whole churches, elsewhere to choose to the ministry some one of those that were pointed out by the Spirit (*Eccl. Hist.* 3. 23).

Further evidence to the same effect might be cited from Origen and Apollonius. Plummer summarizes the evidence for John's residence at Ephesus:

That S. John ended his days in Asia Minor, ruling "the Churches of Asia" from Ephesus as his usual abode, was the uniform belief of Christendom in the second and third centuries, and there is not sufficient reason for doubting its truth. . . . S. John's residence there harmonizes admirably with the tone and contents of these Epistles.[35]

Those who reject the apostolic authorship of the Fourth Gospel and the First Epistle find it necessary to discredit this tradition. Their attack upon the tradition of John's Ephesian residence is made along two lines. There is, first of all, the argument from silence. Critics point out that there is nothing in the New Testament to suggest that the Apostle John went to Asia. Obviously, the Acts and the Pauline Epistles do not do so, but the date for the Johannine residence at Ephesus comes after that time. To those who accept the traditional authorship of the Johannine epistles and the Revelation, the Bible clearly does give such evidence. More serious is the silence of Ignatius (martyred c. 98/116) whose letters to the various Asiatic churches, written within about twenty years of the supposed date of the death of the Apostle John, make no mention of him. Even in his letter to the Ephesians he is silent about John, although he does mention Paul.[36] This silence is admittedly remarkable; why Ignatius did not mention John if he had resided at Ephesus is not known. However a negative argument from silence may be delusive and avails little in the face of the strong testimony to the contrary.

The second point of attack on the tradition of the Ephesian ministry of John is his supposed early martyrdom. Some scholars argue that there is sufficient evidence to show that John was actually martyred at an early age; hence the tradition of his long life and residence at Ephesus must be in error. Moffatt advances three lines of evidence in support of this view.[37]

Advocates of this position call attention to the prophecy by Jesus that the sons of Zebedee would drink of His cup (Matt. 20:23; Mark 10:39). In view of Mark 14:36 it is held that Jesus' prophecy implies the martyrdom

---

[35]Alfred Plummer, *The Epistles of S. John,* Cambridge Bible for Schools and Colleges (1883; reprint ed., London: Cambridge University Press, 1938), p. 11.

[36]See Moffatt, pp. 613-14, for further development of this argument from silence.

[37]*Ibid.,* pp. 602-8.

of both; it is even suggested that John actually died at the same time as his brother James (Acts 12:2). But such an early date for the death of John is in direct conflict with Paul's statement in Galatians 2:9, unless we adopt the improbable hypothesis that the John there mentioned was John Mark. The silence of the New Testament on any martyrdom of John offers a serious obstacle to this contention. The solid tradition of the Ephesian residence is against it. The prophecy of Jesus does not require such a rigid and literal interpretation. Certainly John's experiences of persecution may be accepted as fulfillment of the word of Jesus.

To support this position, scholars also cite the testimony of Papias that John "was killed by the Jews." This quotation is given by George Hamartolos, a Byzantine monk of the ninth century, as found in the second book of Papias. An eighth-century epitome of the History by Philip of Side in Pamphilia says, "Papias says in his second book that John the Divine and James his brother were killed by Jews." This cannot be an accurate quotation from Papias since "John the Divine" is a later expression, nor is Philip's reputation as an accurate historian particularly high. Papias, to be sure, may have made a statement to that effect, but he may well have used the word *martyr* in its wider sense of "witness," or his words may originally have had reference to the martyrdom of John the Baptist. That they prove the actual martyrdom of the apostle John seems improbable. "Many scholars refuse to credit the evidence of these fragments, including Harnack whose opinion in the matter is disinterested, since he denies that St. John lived at Ephesus."[38]

Advocates of an early martyrdom also mention evidence from ancient calendars. A Syriac fourth-century calendar commemorates as martyrs on December 27 "John and James the Apostles at Jerusalem." A Carthaginian calendar of the sixth century reads for the same date "St. John the Baptist and James the Apostle," but this appears to be a confusion of persons because the same calendar also commemorates John the Baptist on June 24. Therefore on the basis of the Syriac calendar and the apparent testimony of the martyrdom of a "John" on the Carthaginian calendar, supporters of the early martyrdom theory argue that here is evidence that John actually suffered martyrdom. But it may well be that these calendars speak of Saint John in a loose sense as a martyr, for they also style Saint Stephen as an apostle.

None of the evidence used to refute the traditional view that John lived at Ephesus rests on very secure ground, and there seems to be no compelling reason to discredit the firm tradition as to such a residence. The fact of John's living to an old age seems definitely to lie behind the statement found

---

[38]Willoughby C. Allen and L. W. Grensted, *Introduction to the Books of the New Testament*, 3rd ed. (Edinburgh: T. & T. Clark, 1936), p. 94.

in John 21:20-23. Without it the circulated report that John would not die is without explanation.

5. The Elder John

The figure of "John the Elder" as a person distinct from John the Apostle looms large in any modern discussion of the authorship of the Johannine literature. Opponents of the traditional view generally hold that the tradition has confused two men by the same name. They think that John the Apostle had been mistaken for another John, resident in Asia, who may have been the real author of the gospel and the epistles.

The only evidence for the actual existence of this second John, whom Renan called "a shadow which has been mistaken for a reality,"[39] rests upon the interpretation which Eusebius placed upon certain words which he quoted from Papias. The passage from Papias reads thus:

> I shall not hesitate also to put down for you along with my interpretations whatsoever things I have at any time learned carefully from the elders and carefully remembered, guaranteeing their truth. . . . If, then, any one came, who had been a follower of the elders, I questioned him in regard to the words of the elders,–what Andrew or what Peter said [*eipen*], or what was said by Philip, or Thomas, or by James, or by John, or by Matthew, or by any other of the disciples of the Lord, and what things Aristion and the presbyter John, the disciple of the Lord, say [*legousin*]. For I did not think what was to be gotten from the books would profit me as much as what came from the living and abiding voice (*Eccl. Hist.* 3. 39).

Eusebius comments on this passage:

> It is worth while observing here that the name John is twice enumerated by him. The first one he mentions in connection with Peter and James and Matthew and the rest of the apostles, clearly meaning the evangelist; but the other John he mentions after an interval, and places him among others outside of the number of the apostles, putting Aristion before him, and he distinctly calls him a presbyter. This shows that the statement of those is true, who say that there were two persons in Asia that bore the same name, and that there were two tombs in Ephesus, each of which, to the present day, is called John's (3:39).

The words of Papias are admittedly open to two interpretations. One interpretation, that followed by Eusebius, holds that he made mention of two different Johns; the other view holds that he made mention of the same John twice, both times referring to the Apostle John. This ambiguity has divided scholarly opinion concerning the actual existence of a second John in Ephesus.

---

[39]Quoted by F. W. Farrar, *The Early Days of Christianity,* author's ed. (New York: Cassell, n.d.), p. 618.

Was Eusebius right in his interpretation that there were two Johns at Ephesus? It is worth noting that he had a theological interest in putting this construction upon the words of Papias. It gave him the desired opportunity to get rid of the apostolic authorship of the Revelation, which he disliked because of its use by the Chiliasts, a feeling which he shared with Dionysius of Alexandria. He seems indeed to have learned this interpretation from Dionysius, bishop of Alexandria (died, c. 264), whose testimony on the matter he preserves in his history (*Eccl. Hist.* 7. 25). Dionysius had difficulty understanding Revelation and believed that it was not written by the Apostle John. He was aware that John Mark did not suit his need to find another John at Ephesus but added "I think that there was a certain other [John] among those that were in Asia, since it is said that there were two tombs at Ephesus, and that each of the two is said to be John's" (*Eccl. Hist.* 7. 25). Eusebius accepted this suggestion of Dionysius and sought to support his interpretation of the ambiguous words of Papias with the remark that Papias was "a man of very little intelligence" because of his millennial views (3. 39).

In his interpretation Eusebius is not quite fair to Papias when he says that Papias called this second John "*a* presbyter." Papias did not call him "a presbyter" but "the presbyter," and that may be an altogether different thing. He also overlooks the fact that the John of the second clause is given exactly the same designation as the John of the first clause, as one of "the presbyters" and as a "disciple of the Lord." Eusebius makes the terms "presbyter" or "elder" mean two different things in the same sentence, which seems very improbable. He also ignores the significance of the change in tense from "said" *(eipen)* to "say" *(legousin)*. The critical interest of Eusebius thus led him to discredit the statement of Irenaeus that Papias "was a hearer of John" the apostle (*Eccl. Hist.* 3. 39). When Eusebius wrote his first book of history, the *Chronicon,* he had all the writings of Papias before him, and there he remarked without hesitation that Papias was a pupil of the apostle. But when he wrote his *Ecclesiastical History,* his critical concerns led him to the conclusion that Papias was only the pupil of "the Presbyter" John, not the apostle. Eusebius did not profess to know anything about this second John but simply adopted the tentative guess of Dionysius that there were two different men named John at Ephesus. Nor does the reference to the two tombs at Ephesus prove the existence of two Johns; they could just as well represent two rival claims being made for the burial place of John. Irenaeus, who likewise knew the writings of Papias, makes no mention of a second John at Ephesus. Zahn summarizes his view of the two interpretations: "It is safe to say that the 'Presbyter John' is a product of the critical and exegetical weakness of Eusebius."[40]

---

[40]T. Zahn, "John the Apostle," in *The New Schaff-Herzog Encyclopedia of Religious Knowledge* (1908; reprint ed., Grand Rapids: Baker, 1950), 6:205b.

Clearly Papias was concerned about gathering the eyewitness testimonies of the historical disciples of the Lord. He first mentioned gathering information from individuals who had known and personally heard various members of the disciples of Jesus, eliciting what these disciples had said *(eipon);* then he mentioned what "Ariston and the presbyter John, disciples of the Lord" were saying *(legousin).* This gave him the advantage of having heard the living voice of those who still survived. Since John apparently outlived all the other apostles, he would still have been alive and ready to give testimony to Papias personally during Papias's early years.

6. Conclusion Concerning Authorship

The question of the authorship of 1 John is admittedly beset with many perplexing problems and difficulties. Yet we believe that all the evidence, external as well as internal, is best accounted for by accepting the traditional view that 1 John is the work of the Apostle John. Many today find the hypothesis of "the Johannine school," which preserved and promoted the tradition emanating from the Apostle John, appealing and acceptable. Barker, while personally holding that "single authorship appears to be the simpler explanation of the date," asserts, "If another author is proposed, this requires a person with a viewpoint so similar to that of the author of the Gospel that it makes little difference in the end whether one holds to one or two authors."[41] Yet we side with the verdict of Guthrie: "In spite of all assertions to the contrary, it must be admitted that these alternative theories do not provide as adequate an explanation of the high regard in which this Epistle was held as the traditional testimony."[42]

The Readers of 1 John

Any information about the original recipients of 1 John must be gleaned from the contents of the epistle. That these recipients were primarily converts from heathenism has been inferred from the fact that the epistle contains no direct quotations from the Old Testament but does carry a definite warning against idolatry (5:21). While consistent with the Gentile origin of the readers, these features do not *prove* the readers' ethnic background but rather provide a description of the author. The scant evidence favors a Gentile origin for most of the readers; yet it is very probable that those addressed also included believers from among Jews of the Diaspora.

It is evident from the epistle that at least some of the recipients had been Christians for a long time and were advanced in their knowledge of Christian

---

[41]Glen W. Barker, "I John" in *The Expositor's Bible Commentary* (Grand Rapids: 1981), 12:303.

[42]Guthrie, p. 869.

truth. Repeatedly the writer declares that he was not offering them anything new in the way of doctrine or exhortation (2:7, 18, 20, 21, 24, 27; 3:11). There is no intimation that the writer had taken any part in their original evangelization; rather he refers to that which they had heard "from the beginning" (2:7, 24). Yet he writes to them as one who has been intimately acquainted with them for a considerable time and has been active in their midst as a teacher and acknowledged leader.

Some have thought that the epistle was directed to a local congregation. Ephesus and Corinth have been suggested. The epistle contains no precise geographical evidence to determine the location of the readers. In view of the tradition about John's ministry in Asia and the fact that the earliest testimonies to the epistle come from that province, it seems most natural to locate the readers there. The scope of John's Asian ministry, as well as the absence of all that which is merely local in the epistle, leads to the conclusion that it was addressed to a group of congregations under the supervision of the writer. This conclusion is in accord with the nature of the writer's relation to the readers as well as the false doctrine combatted in the epistle. Thus, strictly speaking, 1 John is not a general epistle addressed to the Church as a whole but was directed to a group of churches within John's acquaintance.

The view that this epistle was addressed to the Parthians, although it carries the weight of Augustine's name, cannot be accepted as valid. No other writer, preceding or contemporary with him, lends any support to that view; scholars have offered varied conjectures as to the origin of that view.[43] It probably arose from a corruption of the text Augustine had.

The Occasion for 1 John

The basic reason for writing 1 John was the author's deep concern for the spiritual welfare of the readers. There is no explicit reference to persecution in the epistle; words of consolation for those who are suffering for their Christian faith, such as abound in 1 Peter, are entirely absent. Most interpreters have taken this characteristic to mean that pressures from the outside world were not peculiarly pressing at the time of writing.[44] The recipients were indeed familiar with the hatred of the world (3:13), but apparently they were not at the time subjected to an officially prompted hatred against them; it was a hatred which naturally arose out of the moral antagonism between the Church and the world.

---

[43]Brooke, pp. xxx-xxxii; Westcott, p. xxxii.

[44]W. M. Ramsay, *The Church in the Roman Empire Before A.D. 180* (New York: G. P. Putnam's Sons, 1919), holds that it would be a mistake to argue from the absence of any explicit reference to persecution that this epistle was composed in a time of peace, pp. 304-5.

While well aware of the danger facing the readers from the opposition and allurements of the world, John was primarily prompted to write to assure that the readers were equipped to withstand the false teachers. They had already achieved a victory over the false teachers (2:19), but John was concerned that the personal faith of the readers be deepened and established in order to assure their stability. This strengthening of the faith would prepare them to resist the seductions of the world and equip them to detect and refute the speculative false teachings bidding for their acceptance.

Some scholars, such as Brooke, believe that John's concern for his readers was stimulated by a spiritual laxity on the part of the readers, resulting in a slow decline in brotherly love. "The enthusiasm of the early days of the Faith is no longer theirs. . . . Their Christianity had become largely traditional, half-hearted and nominal."[45] This condition made them susceptible to the seduction of worldliness and rendered them more prone to consider elements of speculative philosophy foreign to the Christian faith.

But others, such as Burdick, wonder "whether the idea of the 'loss of their first love' really comes from 1 John or whether it is not, in fact, suggested by the letter of Christ to the Ephesian church found in Revelation 2:1-7."[46] There is little in the epistle that explicitly supports such a condition of a lack of enthusiasm and a loss of love. Instead "John commends his readers for their spiritual condition. He is urging them not to lose the warm vital experience they now enjoy (2:24, 27)."[47] John's pastoral heart taught him that his readers needed to be warned and strengthened against such a spiritual declension.

The Place and Date of 1 John

1. Place

The epistle gives no indication as to the actual place of its composition. In view of the strong tradition that the Apostle John spent the latter years of his life at Ephesus and from there carried on a ministry to the surrounding churches, as well as the explicit testimony of Irenaeus that "John, the disciple of the Lord, who also had leaned upon His breast, did himself publish a Gospel during his residence at Ephesus in Asia" (*Against Heresies,* 3. 1. 1), it seems most natural to hold that 1 John was written there.

2. Date

There are no clear indications in the epistle that would fix a definite date for the composition of 1 John. No inference as to the time can be drawn

---

[45]Brooke, p. xxviii.
[46]Burdick, p. 66.
[47]*Ibid.,* p. 67.

from the statement "it is the last time" (2:18), because it is a note of spiritual, not chronological time. The tone of the epistle and the writer's attitude toward his readers suggest an old man writing to a younger generation. His acquaintance with the readers and the conditions within the churches suggest that John must have been at work in Asia already for a number of years when he wrote, but there is no hint that John arrived in Ephesus before the death of Paul. The fact that the epistle does not mention the destruction of Jerusalem in A.D. 70 seems to suggest that it was written some time after that crucial event. If the breaking up of the Jewish world had but recently taken place, it seems very probable that some reference would have been made to that momentous change. If the absence of any reference to persecution means that the Church was not being actively persecuted by the state, then the time of composition would most likely be either before the reign of Domitian or at the close of his reign, suggesting either an early date around A.D. 80 or a later date of about A.D. 97. The references to the heresy being combatted in 1 John clearly imply a date before the beginning of the second century when Gnosticism came to full bloom. Since most scholars generally accept that 1 John was written after the Fourth Gospel, a date around A.D. 97 is possible. Whatever the precise date assigned to 1 John, it is clear that the epistle originated in the last quarter of the first century.

The Purpose of 1 John

1. Practical Edification and Exhortation

John's basic purpose in writing this epistle was the practical edification of his "children" in the true faith and life as Christians. His purpose is given in several statements: "These things write we unto you, that your joy may be full" (1:4); "My little children, these things write I unto you, that ye sin not" (2:1); "These things have I written unto you that believe on the name of the Son of God; that ye may know that ye have eternal life" (5:13). The author's practical purpose is evident. It is his basic desire to ground them in the assurance of their salvation (5:13). This emphasis is reflected in his repeated use of words such as "knowledge," "assurance," and similar terms. He provides them with a series of tests whereby they may test their own faith and conduct and so reassure their own hearts. He desires to encourage and stimulate their spiritual growth so that the joys of the Christian life may not be dimmed by the allurements of the world or the seductions of doctrinal error. They must firmly realize that their Christian faith is based on positive, demonstrable, proven facts and that the reception of eternal life in Christ Jesus lays upon them the responsibility of a conduct consistent with their position as children of God. This mode of conduct calls for a life motivated by the indwelling power of Christian love. The epistle emphasizes this fact by stressing the strong combination of faith and love. It is not certain whether the exhortations addressed to the readers are intended to be corrective or preventative, but probably both functions are actually involved.

The stated purpose of the epistle, as given in 5:13, stands in interesting relation to the stated purpose of the Fourth Gospel: "Many other signs truly did Jesus in the presence of his disciples, which are not written in this book: But these are written, that ye might believe that Jesus is the Christ, the Son of God; and that believing ye might have life through his name" (20:30-31). The gospel and this epistle are complementary in purpose. The purpose of the Gospel of John is distinctly evangelistic, to lead its readers to a personal saving faith in Jesus Christ the Son of God; the purpose of 1 John is pastoral, to lead believers into a full understanding and assurance of their salvation in Jesus Christ. Both books present the fundamental doctrines of Christianity. "But in the Gospel these are given as the foundation of the Christian's *faith;* in the Epistle they are given as the foundation of the Christian's *life.*"[48] The Christian life that knows the joy of salvation in daily conduct is based upon the assurance of salvation. The contents of the epistle, we believe, are most advantageously studied in the light of the writer's purpose as stated in 5:13.

2. Polemical Purpose

That the epistle also has a polemical purpose is obvious. The author is clearly intent on refuting the doctrinal errors which were exerting their pressures on his readers. But the epistle is not merely polemical; the false teachings confronting them are to be exposed and refuted by the very tests which establish the nature and validity of the Christian faith to which his readers adhere. By their nature the revealed truths of the Christian gospel, which save and assure the true believer, also expose and condemn the errors of the heretic. Thus, as Westcott remarks,

> St. John's method is to confute the error by the exposition of the truth realized in life. His object is polemical only so far as the clear unfolding of the essence of right teaching necessarily shews all error in its real character.[49]

The Graeco-Roman world of the first century was a veritable babble of competing voices, and there were various attempts on the part of some individuals to syncretize these divergent religious and philosophical views. Scholars generally agree that the heresy 1 John confronts was some form or forms of Gnosticism, but it is unwarranted to identify it with the full-blown Gnosticism of the second century. Among the numerous converts won to Christianity in Asia were doubtless professed converts who were former adherents of religious systems marked by Gnostic tendencies. Some of them

---

[48]Plummer, p. 35. Plummer's italics.
[49]Westcott, p. xxxix.

soon sought to syncretize their old views with their newly accepted Christianity. When they sought to propagate their new interpretations in the assemblies, sharp controversy arose and, rebuffed by the adherents of the apostolic message, they withdrew (2:19). But they continued to pressure various members of the congregation through their contacts with them (2:26). These heretics may have promoted a fuller development of their varied Gnostic views after their withdrawal from the churches.[50] At any rate, that the incipient elements of Gnosticism were active in the first century is certain.

First John clearly combats a heresy that was "perverted in its Christology and woefully deficient in its morality."[51] These evils were rooted in the heresy's underlying philosophical and religious assumptions. As a speculative philosophy of religion, Gnosticism was grounded in the basic assumption that spirit is good and matter is inherently evil; Gnostics regarded the two as being in perpetual antagonism. This assumed dualism at once created a gulf between the true God and this material world. The Gnostics, the "knowing ones," as the name implies, laid claim to a superior knowledge which was the privilege of the few. They held that spiritual excellence consisted, not in a holy life, but in their superior knowledge which enabled them to rise above the earthbound chains of matter in their apprehension of the heavenly realities as an esoteric revelation. This knowledge, they claimed, had been made known to them through Christ as the messenger of the true God. Thus "the gnostic Christ was not a savior; he was a revealer. He came for the express purpose of communicating his secret gnosis."[52] Involved was a spurious Christology, rejecting the reality of the incarnation and the atonement. If matter is absolutely evil, it followed that there could be no true incarnation of the Son of God in human form. Since it was unthinkable that spirit and matter could unite in any real and vital union, the incarnation of the holy Son of God was impossible.

These heretics rejected the Christian revelation of the incarnation for a more "reasonable" view; they proposed two solutions. One view was that the Christ did not assume a real human body but only appeared to have one. This view was known as Docetism, from the Greek verb *dokeō,* "to seem, to appear." First John does not explicitly denounce such a Docetic Christology since John merely indicates that the false teachers denied that the Son of God had come in human flesh. As Burdick notes, "The apostle's silence

---

[50]Brown, *The Epistles of John,* suggests that these secessionists played a catalyzing role in the later development of Docetic and Gnostic systems of thought (pp. 59, 104).

[51]Burdick, p. 61.

[52]Ronald H. Nash, *Christianity and the Hellenistic World* (Grand Rapids: Zondervan, 1984), p. 222.

at this point does not prove that a Docetic Christology was not in view; it leaves the door open for either possibility."[53]

The second proposed solution was known as Cerinthianism, whose chief exponent was Cerinthus, a Jewish contemporary of the Apostle John at Ephesus (Irenaeus, *Against Heresies,* 3. 3. 4). Cerinthus distinguished Jesus from the Christ. He held that the man Jesus, the son of Joseph and Mary by natural generation, was pre-eminent in righteousness and wisdom and that the "Christ spirit" came upon him following his baptism and empowered his ministry, but that the Christ departed from him before the crucifixion. The man Jesus suffered, died, and rose again, but the Christ, a pure spirit, remained impassible. In thus splitting the person of Jesus Christ, Cerinthus destroyed the reality of the incarnation and, consequently, His atoning work.

In view of their basic assumption of a dualism between spirit and matter, the Gnostics regarded the human spirit as entrapped in a material body. Deliverance was to be realized through the esoteric knowledge they had attained. This knowledge professedly enabled them to arise above the earth-bound chains of matter into heavenly apprehension of truth. This claim to a superior knowledge influenced their personal attitudes. Moffatt notes,"The superior theosophic insight to which they laid claim led naturally to a sense of pride in themselves as the *elite* of Christendom, which fostered an un-brotherly contempt for the unenlightened members of the church."[54] Their philosophical assumptions not infrequently led to a disregard of the ethical demands of Christianity. In the words of Dodd, "some of the heretics believed themselves to be so far above good and evil that their conduct scandalized even the easygoing censors of Roman Society."[55] In opposition to this dangerous viewpoint, John insists on the intimate connection between Christian faith and conduct. He points out that true Christian knowledge, possessed as the result of the anointing from the Holy One (2:20), is a knowledge which involves holiness of life and conduct as well as intellectual enlightenment (1:5–2:5).

There is no evidence that all Gnostics were guilty of this scandalous disregard for the ethical demands of Christianity. Some held that the evil material dimension in human life was to be transcended through the practice of a rigid asceticism. Even this view, however, was a perversion of the apostolic doctrine of the victory over sin through the risen Christ and the indwelling Spirit.

---

[53]Burdick, p. 63.

[54]Moffatt, p. 586.

[55]Dodd, p. xx.

The Character and Contents of 1 John

1. Language and Style

The style of 1 John is one of artless simplicity yet majestic beauty. As Farrar observes,

> It is a style absolutely unique, supremely original, and full of charm and sweetness. Under the semblance of extreme simplicity, it hides unfathomable depths. It is to a great extent intelligible to the youngest child, to the humblest Christian; yet to enter into its full meaning exceeds the power of the deepest theologian.[56]

There is a sameness of construction which tends to monotony; yet the author's apparent repetitions produce an advance in the thought. Although his language is pure Greek, insofar as it is free from solecisms, yet it is as unlike Greek as possible in its periodic structure. He is not given to those long and complicated sentences which characterize the writings of Paul. John's sentences are coordinated by simple conjunctions after the Hebrew model. He makes frequent use of the parallelistic form so common to the Wisdom Literature of the Old Testament. The thought is frequently pressed home by being expressed both positively and negatively. His statements at times assume a triple form.

The language of John may justly be described as meditative. We feel as though he is engaged in meditation and is allowing us to overhear his thoughts as they arise. His method is not that of formal argument but of categorical affirmation. His "writings may be characterized as intuitive rather than analytic and deductive."[57] He speaks with a tone of authority; he sets forth his pronouncements and passes on without stopping to vindicate them. His words carry a calmness and finality which leave their inevitable impression on the soul. As Moorehead remarks, "There is a dignity, a magisterial gravity, that makes the epistle both apostolic and commanding."[58]

John has a way of developing his thought in terms of its opposite. Light suggests darkness, life is opposed to death, truth to error, love to hate, and God to the Devil. "He thinks in terms of ultimates. His colours are white and black; there is no grey."[59]

---

[56] Farrar, pp. 520-21.

[57] Burdick, p. 85.

[58] William G. Moorehead, *Catholic Epistles–James, I and II Peter, I, II, III John, and Jude,* Outline Studies on the New Testament (New York: Revell, 1908), p. 90.

[59] W. Graham Scroggie, *Know Your Bible, A Brief Introduction to the Scriptures* (London: Pickering & Inglis, n.d.), vol. 2, *The New Testament,* p. 346.

2. Structure

Any hurried attempt to set forth in logical outline the contents of this epistle will inevitably result in frustration, for it is exceedingly difficult to analyze. Indeed some have seriously questioned whether the author had any plan at all in writing the epistle. Some, for example, have viewed the epistle as the ramblings of an old man without system or sequence. Others have thought of it as being merely a series of aphorisms without much sequence of logical connection. Still others have gone so far as to suggest that the present book reveals the work of a redactor or redactors compiling some earlier Johannine materials.

It is a mistake, however, to think that there is confusion and lack of order in its contents. Burdick asserts, "In fact a thorough study of the epistle shows it to be most carefully and intricately organized."[60] The difficulty lies in the nature of its composition. To analyze it is like attempting to analyze the face of a cloudy sky. "There is contrast, and yet harmony; variety and yet order; fixedness, and yet ceaseless change; a monotony which soothes without wearying us, because the frequent repetitions come to us as things that are both new and old."[61]

The attempts of commentators to find the outline of the epistle have produced varied results. Moffatt summarizes these results:

> Little success has attended the attempts to analyze it into a double (*God is Light, God is Love:* Plummer; 1:5–2:27; 2:28–5:5; Findlay), triple (1:1–2:11; 2:12–4:6; 4:7–5:21: Ewald; *God is Light, God is Righteous, God is Love:* Farrar), fourfold (1:5–2:11; 2:12-28; 2:29–3:22; 3:23–5:17: Huther), or five-fold (1:5–2:11; 2:12-27; 2:28–3:24a; 3:24b–4:21; 5:1-21: Hoffman) arrangement.[62]

Plummer frankly says, "Probably few commentators have satisfied themselves with their own analysis of this Epistle: still fewer have satisfied other people."[63]

John's method is not that of syllogistic logic. His thought moves in cycles rather than straight forward. Lenski gives this view of the structure of the epistle:

> John rises above formal divisions and parts. This letter is built like an inverted pyramid or cone. First the basic apex is laid down in 1:1-4; then

---

[60]Burdick, p. 86.

[61]Plummer, pp. 42-43.

[62]Moffatt, p. 584. For a listing of various outlines see Feuillet, pp. 671-72; Brooke, pp. xxxii-viii; I. Howard Marshall, *The Epistles of John,* New International Commentary on the New Testament (Grand Rapids: 1978), pp. 22-26; Burdick, pp. 86-92.

[63]Plummer, pp. 42-43.

the upward broadening begins. Starting with 1:5-10 the base rises and expands, and so continues in ever widening circles, as one new pertinent thought joins the preceding. Here one block is not laid beside the other, so that joints are made. There are really no joints, not even where the new thoughts are first introduced. The line of thought simply spirals in rising widening circles until all is complete. Keeping from idols (5:21) is only the brief, final touch.[64]

It is the point of wisdom to recognize the distinctive character of the structure of 1 John. By its very nature, any systematic outline of it must leave much to be desired. Yet for practical study some outline of it is much to be desired. The analysis used in this study of the epistle is based on the announced purpose in 5:13. It is hoped that it may prove helpful in making clear the basic aim of the epistle. (See the outline on pp. 29-34.)

3. Contents

First John is devoid of all that is merely local; no temporal or individual matters are introduced. Yet, while the epistle is wholly impersonal, it is not abstract. Everything is related to the Christian life in the most intimate way. The coloring of the epistle is moral rather than local. There is a spiritual and universal tone in it which makes it peculiarly adaptable to the present situation in the churches.

One cannot fail to notice the striking fact of the author's gentleness and tenderness of love blended with the most decided sternness and decisive pronouncements of judgment. "The absolute antagonism and incompatibility between the Christian life and sin of whatsoever kind or degree is maintained with a vehemence of utterance that verges at times on the paradoxical."[65] No other writer in the New Testament uses stronger words in denunciation of sin and error than John. Thus we have a remarkable picture of the "son of thunder" (Mark 3:17) blazing forth in judgment against sin but mellowed in love and kindness toward those who yield themselves to our righteous and loving God.

The epistle contains no quotations from the Old Testament, and only one allusion is made to Old Testament history (3:12). There is no mention of any detail of religious ritual or of ecclesiastical organization. There is no mention of circumcision and the controversy which it aroused in the early life of the church, nor any trace of the conflict between the advocates of Law and Grace, between works and faith, nor any mention of the distinction

---

[64]R.C.H. Lenski, *The Interpretation of the Epistles of St. Peter, St. John and St. Jude* (Columbus, Ohio: Wartburg Press, 1945), p. 366.

[65]R. Law, "John, The Epistles of," in *The International Standard Bible Encyclopedia* (Grand Rapids: Eerdmans, 1939), 3:1712.

between Jew and Gentile. All these matters have been superseded in the consciousness of one universal Christian brotherhood. The main questions and considerations of the epistle center around the person and work of Christ Jesus and their implications for Christian living.

This is the epistle of love and brotherhood. The word *love (agapaō)* and its derivatives occur no less than fifty-one times in 1 John. It is also the epistle of experiential knowledge and Christian assurance. The words for knowledge (*ginōskō* and *oida*) occur forty-one times in the epistle. One of the characteristic ideas of the epistle is that of "witness." Since false teachers are questioning the received message of Christianity, the author sets himself to prove that the message which he declares has been fully attested. It is confirmed not only by Christian experience but also by the very testimony of God.

The epistle is rich in doctrinal content, setting forth the essential truth of the Christian faith. Its double assertion, "God is light" (1:5) and "God is love" (4:8), adds to the Biblical teaching concerning the nature of God. Its emphatic portrayal of the nature of Jesus Christ, the Son of God, as both human and divine is central to the Christology of the New Testament. The doctrine of sin is prominent in the epistle; reference is made to sin in every chapter. It sets forth a series of tests which offer a valid ground for assurance of salvation and the knowledge of God; these tests also serve to expose spurious claims to fellowship with God. The work's references to the return of Christ (2:28; 3:2-3) and the future day of judgment (4:17) are valuable touches on the doctrine of eschatology. It presents the reality of eternal life embodied in Christ (5:12), received through faith in Him in this life and extending uninterrupted into eternity (3:2).

4. Famous Interpolation

The Textus Receptus, upon which our King James Version (1611) is based, contains a famous interpolated passage for which there is no valid textual evidence.[66] The passage reads as follows, the italicized words marking the interpolation:

> For there are three that bear record *in heaven, the Father, the Word, and the Holy Ghost: and these three are one. And there are three that bear witness in earth,* the spirit, and the water, and the blood: and *these* three agree in one (5:7-8).

---

[66]For the textual evidence see Kurt Aland et al., ed., *The Greek New Testament,* 3rd ed. (New York: United Bible Societies, 1975); Zane C. Hodges and Arthur L. Farstad, *The Greek New Testament According to the Majority Text* (Nashville: Thomas Nelson Publishers, 1982). See Bruce M. Metzger, *A Textual Commentary on the Greek New Testament* (London, New York: United Bible Societies, 1971), pp. 716-18, for an evaluation of external and internal evidence.

The external evidence is overwhelming against the authenticity of these words, commonly known today as "the Johannine Comma."[67] They are found in no Greek uncial manuscripts; no Greek cursive manuscript before the fifteenth century contains them. Only two known Greek cursives (cursive 629 of the fourteenth century and 61 of the sixteenth century) have the addition in their text; cursive 635 of the eleventh century has it in the margin in a seventeenth-century hand, and 88 of the twelfth century has it in the margin by a modern hand. In these cursives the words are a manifest translation from a late recension of the Latin Vulgate. No ancient version of the first four centuries gives them; nor is it found in the oldest Vulgate manuscripts. None of the Greek Church Fathers quoted the words contained in this interpolation. As Feuillet points out, their failure to cite it is "an inexplicable omission if they knew it: in fact, how could they not have used it in the Trinitarian controversies?"[68]

In Greek texts the words were first printed in the Complutensian Polyglot of 1514. Erasmus did not find them in the Greek manuscripts which he had, and he did not put them into his first two editions of the Greek Testament. Erasmus rashly promised to insert them into his Greek text if they could be found in any Greek manuscript. When he was confronted with Codex Montfort, cursive 61, he inserted them, although he stated that he suspected that the words had been inserted in the Greek to conform to the Latin. He blandly explained that he had inserted the words into the Greek text to avoid calumny! From the text of Erasmus the interpolated words passed into the editions upon which the Authorized King James Version was based.

The earliest certain reference to the Johannine Comma is in the *Liber Apologeticus*, attributed to the Spanish writer Priscillian (d. 385) or to Instantius, one of his followers. The words apparently arose as a marginal allegorical gloss on the Biblical text and were later incorporated into the body of the epistle. Research suggests that this interpolation had its origin as an expansion of the Johannine text stemming at the earliest from the third century in North Africa or Spain.

---

[67]That is, "the Johannine [interpolated] clause," from the Greek *komma* which means a short clause.

[68]Feuillet, p. 683.

2

An Outline of 1 John

Prologue: The Reality of the Incarnation (1:1-4)
- A. The Apostolic Encounter with the Word of Life (1)
- B. The Historical Manifestation of the Eternal Life (2)
- C. The Personal Issues of the Apostolic Proclamation (3-4)
    1. The Summary of the Apostolic Proclamation (3a)
    2. The Aim of the Apostolic Proclamation (3b)
    3. The Goal of the Apostolic Letter (4)

I. Assurance Through the Test of Fellowship (1:5–2:17)
- A. The Basis for Christian Fellowship (1:5)
- B. The Hindrances to Christian Fellowship (1:6-10)
    1. The Denial of the Sinfulness of Sin (6-7)
        a. The view advanced (6a)
        b. The condemnation stated (6b)
        c. The corrective presented (7)
            1) The correct conduct (7a)
            2) The twofold result (7b)
    2. The Denial of Human Sinfulness (8-9)
        a. The view advanced (8a)
        b. The condemnation stated (8b)
        c. The corrective indicated (9)
    3. The Denial of Any Sinful Deeds (10)
        a. The view advanced (10a)
        b. The condemnation stated (10b)
- C. The Provision for Maintaining Fellowship (2:1-2)
    1. The Design for His Readers (1a)
    2. The Possibility of Committing Sin (1b)
    3. The Provision in Jesus Christ (1c-2)
        a. The personal Advocate with the Father (1c)
        b. The perfect propitiation for all sins (2)

D. The Signs of Fellowship Maintained (2:3-17)
  1. The Sign of Obedience (3-5a)
    a. The assurance from obedience (3)
    b. The verdict from the absence of obedience (4)
    c. The result of personal obedience (5a)
  2. The Sign of Imitation (5b-6)
    a. The assurance of the believer (5b)
    b. The resultant obligation of the believer (6)
  3. The Sign of Love (7-11)
    a. The characterization of the commandment (7-8)
      1) The commandment of love as old (7)
      2) The commandment of love as new (8)
    b. The application of the commandment (9-11)
      1) The profession without love (9)
      2) The individual who loves (10)
      3) The individual who hates (11)
  4. The Sign of Separation (12-17)
    a. The assurance concerning the readers (12-14)
      1) The first triad of assurances (12-13b)
        a) The readers as "little children" (12)
        b) The readers under a dual division (13ab)
      2) The second triad of assurances (13c-14)
        a) The readers addressed as "children" (13c)
        b) The readers under a twofold grouping (14)
    b. The appeal for separation from the world (15-17)
      1) The statement of the prohibition (15a)
      2) The reasons for the prohibition (15b-17)
        a) The personal condition revealed by love of the world (15b)
        b) The character of the things in the world (16)
        c) The contrasted ends (17)
II. Assurance from the Conflicts of Faith (2:18–4:6)
  A. The Conflict Between Truth and Falsehood (2:18-28)
    1. The Crisis Facing the Believers (18-19)
      a. The characterization of the time (18)
        1) The assertion concerning the time (18a)
        2) The sign of "many antichrists" (18b)
      b. The nature of the current crisis (19)
    2. The Resources of the Believers (20-21)
      a. The anointing from the Holy One (20a)
      b. The knowledge of the truth (20b-21)
        1) The assertion of their knowledge (20b)
        2) The reason for writing this to them (21)

3. The Confrontation with the Antichrists (22-25)
   a. The mark of false and true believers (22-23)
      1) The mark of the liar (22-23a)
      2) The confession of the true believer (23b)
   b. The appeal to the true believers (24-25)
      1) The statement of the appeal (24a)
      2) The results of letting the message abide (24b-25)
4. The Resources of Believers in the Face of Danger (26-28)
   a. The danger from the deceivers (26)
   b. The equipment through the anointing (27)
   c. The motivation from the hope of Christ's return (28)
B. The Conflict Between the Children of God and the Children of the Devil (2:29–3:12)
  1. The Marks of the Children of God (2:29–3:3)
    a. The practice of righteousness as the mark of the new birth (2:29)
    b. The dynamic reality of the new life (3:1-2)
      1) The amazing gift of God's love (1a)
      2) The world's failure to understand believers (1b)
      3) The implications of God's love-gift (2)
    c. The impact of Christian hope upon present living (3)
  2. The Revelation Inherent in the Practice of Sin (3:4-8a)
    a. The indication of the nature of sin (4-5)
      1) The nature of sin as lawlessness (4)
      2) The incompatibility of sin with Christ's mission (5)
    b. The distinction between the two classes of humanity (6-8a)
      1) The practice of the two classes (6)
      2) The moral character of the two classes (7-8a)
         a) The pastoral warning against deceivers (7a)
         b) The moral criterion for each class (7b-8a)
  3. The Deliverance from the Practice of Sin (8b-9)
    a. The divine provision in Christ's mission (8b)
    b. The human deliverance through the new birth (9)
  4. The Sign of the Children of God and the Children of the Devil (10-12)
    a. The criteria for the two classes of humanity (10-11)
      1) The children of the Devil (10b)
      2) The children of God (11)
    b. The negative illustration in the story of Cain (12)
C. The Conflict between Love and Hatred (3:13-24)
  1. The Revelation from the Practice of Love and Hatred (13-15)
    a. The reaction to the world's hatred of believers (13)

      b. The practice of love as the revelation of character (7b-8)
          1) The character of the one loving (7b)
          2) The character of the one not loving (8)
   2. The Manifestation of Redeeming Love (9-10)
      a. The manifestation of love in the incarnation (9)
      b. The manifestation of love in the atonement (10)
   3. The Practice of Brother-love (11-12)
      a. The obligation of mutual Christian love (11)
      b. The significance of our mutual love (12)
          1) The nature of God as unseen (12a)
          2) The relation between mutual love and God's love in us (12b)
   4. The Confirmation of Redeeming Love (13-16a)
      a. The confirmation through the gift of the Spirit (13)
      b. The confirmation through the apostolic testimony (14)
      c. The confirmation through mutual fellowship with God (15-16a)
          1) The condition for mutual fellowship with God (15)
          2) The experience of God's love by believers (16a)
B. The Results of Redeeming Love (4:16b–5:5)
   1. The Results in Our Own Lives (4:16b-18)
      a. The experience of reciprocal love (16b)
      b. The confidence of perfected love (17)
      c. The operation of perfect love (18)
   2. The Results in Our Relations to Others (4:19-21)
      a. The divine origin of Christian love (19)
      b. The consequent duty of brother-love (20-21)
          1) The exposure of a false profession of love (20)
          2) The command to love God and the brother (21)
   3. The Results in Our Relation to God (5:1-5)
      a. The relationship between saving faith and Christian love (1)
          1) The nature of saving faith (1a)
          2) The result of saving faith (1b)
      b. The revelation of love through obedience to God (2-3)
          1) The two directions of true love (2)
          2) The true nature of our love and obedience (3)
      c. The revelation of overcoming faith (4-5)
          1) The new birth as the principle of victory (4)
          2) The faith of the victorious individual (5)
IV. Assurance Through the Witness of the Spirit (5:6-12)
  A. The Historical Witnesses to Jesus Christ (6-9)
     1. The Historical Facts Connected with Christ's Coming (6)

3

Prologue: The Reality of the Incarnation

1:1 That which was from the beginning, which we have heard, which we have seen with our eyes, which we have looked upon, and our hands have handled, of the Word of life;
2 (For the life was manifested, and we have seen *it,* and bear witness, and shew unto you that eternal life, which was with the Father, and was manifested unto us;)
3 That which we have seen and heard declare we unto you, that ye also may have fellowship with us: and truly our fellowship *is* with the Father, and with his Son Jesus Christ.
4 And these things write we unto you, that your joy may be full.

Eliminating all opening epistolary formalities, John at once plunges into a weighty theological prologue which verifies the heart of the Christian gospel, namely, that eternal life has been made manifest in the incarnate Son of God. This Prologue elaborates on the reality of the incarnation in the apostolic experience, a reality that is crucial to the faith and life of the Christian believer. The tone of this opening paragraph is not polemical. The cardinal truth set forth is the cornerstone of the Christian faith; as such it is also the touchstone with which to test and expose false doctrine.

This paragraph is unusually involved and intense, unlike John's usual style. Structurally it consists of two sentences of very unequal length.[1] The

---

[1]So the KJV, used as the English version in this study of the Johannine Epistles. This reading accepts that the last half of verse 3 is rightly taken as a part of the first sentence. Our English versions vary as to the number of sentences they make of the Prologue. The RV (1881) and the ASV (1901) print it as one long complicated sentence. The NASB (1971) and the RSV (1946) present it as *two* sentences. The TEV (1966) and the Jerusalem Bible (1969) make it *four* sentences; the NIV (1978) and the NEB (2nd ed. 1979) punctuate it as *five* separate sentences. Unique is *The Everyday Bible, New Century Version* (Fort Worth, Texas: Worthy Publishing, 1987), which prints this Prologue as no less than thirteen independent sentences.

first three verses constitute one involved sentence which, phrase by phrase, alluringly adds to the total picture John has in mind. Verse 4 is a second sentence which adds the writer's aim in declaring this message. In the words of Blaney, this Prologue "gives the impression that the author was so 'full of his subject,' so overwhelmed by the truth he sought to express, that his thoughts became crowded and his expression complicated."[2] Exegetes have often commented on the difficulty of this Prologue. Brown remarks, "The initial four verses of 1 John have a good claim to being the most complicated Greek in the Johannine corpus, a passage 'more remarkable for energy than for lucidity,' as Loisy has acidly observed (*Evangile-Epires* 531)."[3] And Houlden describes it "as formally at least, bordering on incoherence."[4] Admittedly the precise import of John's opening expressions are not readily apparent, but certainly John "begins in a manner calculated to capture the reader's attention."[5]

In this opening paragraph John declares the reality of the apostolic encounter with the incarnate Word of Life (v. 1), parenthetically presents the historical manifestation of eternal life (v. 2), and sets forth the crucial personal issues of this reality for faith and experience (vv. 3-4).

A. The Apostolic Encounter with the Word of Life (v. 1)

The four opening clauses, each beginning with "which" (*ho,* a neuter relative pronoun) and used without a connecting particle, are parallel in scope and declare the reality of the incarnation. All four phrases are the direct objects of the verb "declare" *(apangellomen),* which is not actually expressed until verse 3.[6] The use of the neuter "which" does not establish that John has in view an abstract message; rather, he was thinking about the comprehensive reality of the historical manifestation of eternal life in the incarnate Christ.[7]

---

[2]Harvey J.S. Blaney, "The First Epistle of John," in *Beacon Bible Commentary* (Kansas City, Mo.: Beacon Hill Press, 1969), 10:349.

[3]Raymond E. Brown, *The Epistles of John,* The Anchor Bible (Garden City, N.Y.: Doubleday & Co., 1982), p. 152.

[4]J. L. Houlden, *A Commentary on the Johannine Epistles,* Harper's New Testament Commentaries (New York: Harper & Row, 1973), p. 45.

[5]Donald W. Burdick, *The Letters of John the Apostle, An In-Depth Commentary* (Chicago: Moody Press, 1985), p. 95.

[6]A few modern English versions, such as the NIV and the NASB, anticipate the verb by inserting it in verse 1.

[7]"The neuter is sometimes used with reference to persons if it is not the individuals but a general quality that is to be emphasized." F. Blass and A. DeBrunner, *A Greek Grammar of the New Testament and Other Early Christian Literature,* trans. and rev. Robert W. Funk (Chicago: University of Chicago Press, 1961), p. 76.

The first clause relates to the fact of the incarnation itself; the remaining three declare the apostolic experience with the incarnate Christ.

Scholars have understood the initial clause, "That which was from the beginning" *(ho ēn ap' archēs)*, in various ways. Ebrard aptly remarks, "These words, considered in themselves, may say all that it is possible to say; and yet, when they are isolated, they declare fundamentally nothing,"[8] Clearly their intended significance must be determined in the light of what follows.

Some, such as Bultmann, hold that these words "apparently mean nothing other than what Jn 1:1 expresses in the form *en archēēn ho logos* (In the beginning was the word)."[9] Plummer accepts this connection with a recognized difference: In John 1:1 "the point is that the Word existed before the creation; here that the Word existed before the Incarnation."[10] But in view of the following parallel clauses, any view that the reference is to the preincarnate Christ is not obvious; the following three clauses clearly refer to the actual incarnation. In this Prologue the focus of John's interest is not creation but the incarnation.

The force of this opening clause is dependent upon the intended meaning of "was from the beginning" *(ēn ap' archēs)* in the light of the context. The verbal form "was" *(ēn,* denoting continuing being) does not in itself indicate that preincarnate existence is in view in this opening clause. The intended force of this continuing existence depends on the meaning of "from the beginning" *(ap' archēs)*. The existence in view here is presented as having its starting point *"from* the beginning," not as already being in existence *"in* the beginning" (John 1:1). One must determine the meaning of the expression "the beginning" by the context. The noun "beginning" *(archēs)* occurs eight times in 1 John (1:1; 2:7, 13, 14, 24 twice; 3:8, 11), always preceded by the preposition "from" *(ap')* as marking the beginning of a period of time. In keeping with the following clauses in verse 1, it seems best to understand "the beginning" in view here to denote the unique events, described in Luke 1-2, which culminated in the actual incarnation. The message of the Prologue, proclaiming the appearing of eternal life in visible form, "must seem incredible until we start where he starts–at Bethlehem."[11]

The noun "beginning," used without a definite article, here does not so much point to a specific event, which went largely unnoticed by the world,

---

[8]John H. A. Ebrard, *Biblical Commentary on the Epistles of St. John,* trans. W. B. Pope (Edinburgh: T. & T. Clark, 1860), p. 46.

[9]Rudolf Bultmann, *The Johannine Epistles,* Hermeneia–A Critical and Historical Commentary on the Bible (Philadelphia: Fortress Press, 1973), pp. 7-8.

[10]Alfred Plummer, *The Epistles of S. John,* Cambridge Bible for Schools and Colleges (1883; reprint ed., London: Cambridge University Press, 1938), p. 72.

[11]R.E.O. White, *Open Letter to Evangelicals* (Grand Rapids: Eerdmans, 1964), p. 27.

but rather serves to characterize that èvent as a new beginning in God's manner of speaking to mankind (Heb. 1:1-2). John's expression "was from the beginning" marks the continuing reality of the incarnation since the birth of the virgin Mary's babe in Bethlehem. "The assumption of human nature by the Son of God is the most stupendous fact in the history of providence."[12] Thus viewed in context, this opening clause is parallel to the opening assertion in John 1:14, "The Word was made flesh, and dwelt among us," whereas the remaining three "which" clauses are parallel to the added words in John 1:14, "(and we beheld his glory, the glory as of the only begotten of the Father)." During the first thirty years of His earthly life the fact of the incarnation was an abiding reality, the same as that openly displayed during His public ministry.

The remaining three clauses of verse 1 depict varied aspects of the apostolic experience with the incarnate Christ. They declare that the fact of the incarnation is firmly grounded in historical reality. There are three verbs in the first-person plural and two first-person plural pronouns. Critical scholars have advanced varied explanations of this "we" to avoid a claim of explicit apostolic authorship for the epistle;[13] yet the natural meaning is that the author thus includes himself among those who experienced these personal encounters with the incarnate Christ. Thus John is speaking as the representative of the apostles, all of whom bore united witness to the reality of the incarnation. The verbs employed summarize their experiences with Jesus during the years of His ministry and imply a growing intimacy with Him.

The words, "which we have heard" *(ho akēkoamen),* declare that they have received a revelation made in terms which human beings can understand. The message to which the apostles bore witness was presented by a historical person. The verb "have heard" involves all the utterances and activities of the speaker conveying His message to them. The reports they first heard about Him led to their hearing Him personally and repeatedly during their years of intimate association with Him. What they heard had a transforming impact on them, leaving them unshakably assured as to the true identity of their teacher. Their relationship as His personal hearers has been terminated, but the perfect tense, "have heard," implies that the revelation received, the message He communicated, still rings in John's ears. The expression embodies the training which John and his fellow apostles received from Jesus.[14]

---

[12]James Morgan, *The Epistles of John* (1865; reprint ed., Minneapolis: Klock & Klock Christian Publishers, 1982), p. 4.

[13]See Brown, pp. 158-61, for a discussion of the different views of the meaning of John's "we."

[14]Simon J. Kistemaker, *Exposition of the Epistle of James and the Epistles of John,* New Testament Commentary (Grand Rapids: Baker, 1986), p. 234.

The clause "which we have seen with our eyes" *(ho heōrakamen tois ophthalmois hēmōn)* declares their visual encounter with the incarnate Christ. The verb "have seen" implies intellectual apprehension of the significance of what they beheld. The added words "with our eyes" underline that what they observed was no phantom, nor merely an inward or spiritual vision. Westcott remarks, "The addition *with our eyes,* like *our hands* below, emphasizes the idea of direct personal outward experience in a matter marvelous in itself."[15] The perfect-tense verb "have seen" *(heōrakamen)* implies that what they had seen still lingered before the mind's eye. In this and the following clause John focuses attention on the revealer Himself.

The further clause "which we have looked upon, and our hands have handled" *(ho etheasametha kai hai cheires hēmōn epsēlaphēsan)* adds further evidence from sight and touch for the reality of the incarnation. "Have looked upon" *(etheasametha)* is no mere repetition. The verb now used denotes an intelligent looking-upon which interprets the significance of that which is beheld. This verb is used "in the New Testament apparently always in a literal, physical sense of 'careful and deliberate vision which interprets . . . its object.' "[16] The Twelve "scrutinized Him so thoroughly that they had no doubt concerning His physical reality."[17] The aorist tense now used presents this beholding as a completed historical reality. It is the term used in John 1:14, "we beheld his glory."

The second aorist-tense verb, "and our hands have handled" *(epsēlaphēsan)*, brings in the sense of touch as the culminating evidence for the reality of the incarnation. The aorist tense again summarily states the historic fact, while "our hands" again underlines the personally experienced reality of His bodily presence. Their physical contact with the body of Jesus was no mere accidental brushing against His body but a purposeful touching of His body to verify its physical reality. This verb was used by Jesus, after His resurrection, to challenge the disciples to prove the reality of His bodily presence. Some, such as Plummer, hold that this verb here "seems to be a direct reference to the test demanded by S. Thomas (John xx. 27) and offered to the other disciples (Luke xxiv. 39)."[18] Thus Lias remarks, "No one could have been a witness of the scene between our Lord and St. Thomas without having the whole event indelibly impressed upon his mind. So here we have a strik-

---

[15]Brooke Foss Westcott, *The Epistles of St. John, The Greek Text with Notes,* 3rd ed. (1892; reprint ed., Grand Rapids: Eerdmans 1950), p. 6.

[16]G. Abbott-Smith, *A Manual Greek Lexicon of the New Testament,* 3rd ed. (Edinburgh: T. & T. Clark, 1937), p. 203.

[17]Burdick, p. 99.

[18]Plummer, p. 73.

ing reference to that scene.''[19] If that scene is explicitly in view here, then this is the only clear reference to the resurrection of Christ in this epistle. Then the fact of the incarnation is also extended to the risen Christ as an abiding reality. But, as Burdick well notes, "In the context of 1 John 1:1, the apostle is not trying to prove the reality of the resurrection. His point here is that Jesus was most surely incarnate in a 'flesh-and-bones' body.''[20]

No governing verb follows these four object clauses. Instead John continues with a prepositional phrase standing in apposition with all that has preceded: "of the Word of life" *(peri tou logou tēs zōēs)*. "Of" *(peri,* "around") summarily depicts all that has preceded as gathering around "the Word of the life" as the unifying theme. The use of the definite article with both nouns, literally, "the Word of the life," makes both terms specific. For John neither term was a purely abstract, impersonal concept. Both terms denoted vital realities with which John was familiar.

Some interpreters, such as Dodd,[21] Houlden,[22] and Westcott,[23] hold that "the Word" *(ho logos)* is impersonal, "the word, or message" conveyed by the gospel. Thus Westcott insists that this term here refers to "the whole *Gospel,* of which He is the centre and sum, and not to Himself personally.''[24] It is held that the four preceding neuter clauses support this nonpersonal meaning. But one may understand these neuter designations as referring to *what* John declares concerning the incarnate Word of life. Brooke accepts the impersonal meaning and holds that the expression "the word of life" means "the whole message which reveals, or which gives life.''[25] In favor of the message motif Brown notes "the fact that, when the author finishes the Prologue and moves on to the body of his work, he does so in terms of 'the gospel *[angelia]* . . . that we declare to you,' '' thus equating "the word" with the gospel.[26]

But it is more probable that for John the meaning of "the Word" here is essentially personal, gathering up the truth of the four preceding clauses depicting the fact of the incarnation. John's thought centers on the historical

---

[19]John James Lias, *An Exposition of the First Epistle of John* (1887; reprint ed., Minneapolis: Klock & Klock Christian Publishers, 1982), p. 15.

[20]Burdick, p. 99.

[21]C. H. Dodd, *The Johannine Epistles,* Moffatt New Testament Commentary (New York: Harper & Row, 1946), pp. 3-6.

[22]Houlden, pp. 50-52.

[23]Westcott, pp. 6-7.

[24]*Ibid.,* p. 7.

[25]A. E. Brooke, *A Critical and Exegetical Commentary on the Johannine Epistles,* International Critical Commentary (New York: Charles Scribner's Sons, 1912), p. 5.

[26]Brown, p. 165.

reality of the incarnation in Jesus Christ; not only does the message of the gospel center around Him, but also He is Himself eternal life incarnate. Thus Plummer notes that in 5:9-10 of the epistle John uses the preposition "of" *(peri)* "of testimony concerning *persons* (cf. also John 1:15, 22, 30, 48; 2:25; 5:31, 32, 36, 37, 46; etc.)" and concludes that "the preposition is strongly in favour of 'Word,' i.e. the personal Logos, rather than 'word,' i.e. doctrine."[27] This would agree with the view that "the Word" *(ho logos)* here, as in the Prologue of the Fourth Gospel, has a personal connotation. Although John has just used four neuter clauses, Marshall notes that what is said supports the personal meaning here. He remarks,

> It is a strange message which is visible, and the qualification "with our eyes" leaves no doubt that literal seeing is meant. The point is hammered home by the further statement that the writer has gazed upon it and touched it with his hands.[28]

Burdick further supports this personal meaning by noting that "the parenthetical explanation in verse 2 demands the personal interpretation."[29] The use of the capital for "the Word" in several of our versions[30] suggests this personal meaning. The genitive "of life" in the expression "the Word of life" *(tou logou tēs zōēs)* may be understood as appositional, "the Word which is the life," or as an ablative of source, "the Word which gives life." The definite article, "the life," implies that the reference is to the life that is life indeed (cf. John 17:3).

The ambiguity in John's expression, which Smalley suggests possibly "is an intentional ambivalence at this point,"[31] makes it possible that John intends to include both meanings. If the thought of the *message* is prominent in the first part of the verse, the personal meaning is clearly expressed before the completion of the second verse. The ambiguity that the interpreters find in John's statements is inherent in the nature of John's subject, the abiding reality of the incarnation. As Marshall remarks, "Jesus is both the preacher of God's message and the message itself. Paul could say, 'We preach Christ' (1 Cor. 1:23; cf. 2 Cor. 4:5), showing that the message and the person are ultimately identical."[32]

---

[27]Plummer, p. 73. Italics in original.

[28]I. Howard Marshall, *The Epistles of John*, New International Commentary on the New Testament (Grand Rapids: Eerdmans, 1978), p. 101.

[29]Burdick, p. 100.

[30]It is printed with a capital letter, "the Word," in KJV, NASB, RV (1881), NIV, and Rotherham, but it is printed "the word" in RSV, NEB, and New American Bible.

[31]Stephen S. Smalley, *1, 2, 3 John*, Word Biblical Commentary (Waco, Texas: Word Books, 1984), p. 6.

[32]Marshall, p. 102.

B. The Historical Manifestation of the Eternal Life (v. 2)

Structurally verse 2 forms a parenthesis in John's long and involved opening statement. Its double affirmation–the declared appearance of the incarnate life and the eternal nature of the life revealed–conveys the heart of the epistle. The conjunction "for" (*kai,* better "and") indicates that something further must be added concerning "the Word of life," developing the nature of "the life" that has appeared.

The initial assertion, "for the life was manifested" *(kai hē zōē ephane-rōthē),* declares the appearing of the incarnate life here on earth as a historical reality. For John "the life" was no abstract principle but a real person. The aorist verb "was manifested," a common term in this epistle as well as the Fourth Gospel,[33] comprehends the entire process whereby this life became visible and tangible; the passive implies the divine initiative behind the disclosure. Vine notes that in Scriptural usage the verb denotes more than mere appearance, "to be manifested is to be revealed in one's true character."[34] In 2:28 this same verb is used of Christ's Second Coming.

Another "and" connects this historical manifestation with the personal experience and testimony of the apostles: "and we have seen *it,* and bear witness, and shew unto you that eternal life." The perfect verb "we have seen" *(heōrakamen)* comprehends the visible ministry of Jesus as observed by the apostles. It again declares that this incarnate life was the object of an intelligible, abiding sense perception on their part. They perceived His true identity as the divine revelation of "the life."

Yet another "and" connects their past experiences with the incarnate life and their present double activity: "and bear witness and shew unto you that eternal life." Two verbs, "bear witness" *(martupoumen)* and "shew" *(apanggellomen,* "proclaim"), both in the present tense, declare their continuing present activity. Both verbs relate to the same activity under different aspects. As Haupt notes, in the first verb "the emphasis lies on the communication of *truth,*" while in the second "the emphasis lies on the *communication* of truth."[35] For an effective expansion of the Christian faith both aspects are needed. The verb "bear witness," another favorite term with John,[36] looks back to the experiences declared in the four verbs in verse 1;

---

[33] It occurs nine times in 1 John, nine times in the Gospel, and twice in Revelation.

[34] W. E. Vine, *An Expository Dictionary of New Testament Words with Their Precise Meanings for English Readers* (London: Oliphants, 1939), 1:65.

[35] Erich Haupt, *The First Epistle of St. John. A Contribution to Biblical Theology,* trans. W. B. Pope (Edinburgh: T. & T. Clark, 1893), p. 17. Italics in original.

[36] The verb *martureō* occurs thirty-three times in the Fourth Gospel; six times in 1 John; four times in 3 John; four times in Revelation. The noun *marturia* ("witness") occurs fourteen times in the Gospel; six times in 1 John; once in 3 John; and nine times in Revelation.

and those amazing experiences qualified them to bear an authentic witness concerning the incarnation. Unshakably convinced of the authenticity of their message, and having been commissioned by the risen Christ to make that message known to the ends of the world (Matt. 28:18-20), they now actively "shew" or "proclaim" that message "unto you" *(humin)*, the readers of this epistle. The writing of this letter is only a part of their standing assignment to spread abroad the truth of the incarnation. "We," as the subject of both of these verbs, expresses John's deep sense of solidarity with the apostolic testimony. "More than one man's personal memories lay behind the apostolic testimony."[37]

The theme of their authoritative proclamation was "that eternal life" *(tēn zōēn tēn aiōnion,* literally, "the life, the eternal [life]"). The repeated article with the adjective "eternal" underlines the distinctive quality of this life. The adjective "eternal," which occurs seventeen times in John's Gospel and six times in this epistle, is the only adjective which John applies to the word "life" in these books.[38] It is a life that is characterized as coming from another "age," or sphere. Lias remarks that the adjective "eternal" *(aiōnios)* denotes "not so much the endlessness of life as its stability, its fixedness, its vastness from every point of view, that of endurance and every other, its unchangeableness as contrasted with the shifting conditions of everything in time."[39] This adjective, like the cognate noun *aiōn* ("age"), may at times be applied to a long but limited period of time, but its predominant usage in the New Testament denotes eternal, or unending, duration. As Hogg and Vine note,

> It is used of persons and things which are in their nature endless, as, e.g., of God, Rom. 16:26, of His power, I Tim. 6. 16, and of His glory, I Pet. 5.10; of the Holy Spirit, Heb. 9. 14; of the redemption effected by Christ, 9. 12, and of the consequent salvation of men, 5. 9, as well as of His future rule, 2 Pet. 1. 11, which is elsewhere declared to be without end, Luke 1. 33; of the life received by those who believe in Christ, John 3:16, concerning which He said "they shall never perish," 10. 28, and of the resurrection body, 2 Cor. 5. 1.[40]

Not merely unending continuance but the very nature of God characterizes this life. The added identification "which was with the Father" *(hētis ēn pros ton patera)* explicitly declares its eternal, pre-existent quality. The

---

[37]White, p. 29.

[38]In Revelation 14:6 it is applied to the noun *gospel,* "an eternal gospel."

[39]Lias, p. 19.

[40]C. F. Hogg and W. E. Vine, *The Epistles to the Thessalonians, with Notes Exegetical and Expository* (1914; reprint ed., Grand Rapids: Kregel, 1959), pp. 232-33.

word rendered "which" *(hētis)* is a compound relative pronoun that carries the idea of characteristic quality as well as identity, "which was such as." Brooke suggests that "it introduces the designation of a class to which the antecedent belongs."[41] The fact that the author characterizes this "eternal life" as the kind of life that "was with the Father" *(ēn pros ton patera)* marks it as personal. The verb "was" denotes the past continuous existence of this life (cf. John 1:1), whereas the prepositional phrase "with the Father" indicates the distinct personality of the life. The preposition "with" *(pros)* depicts a "face-to-face" relationship with the Father. As Plummer notes, "Had the Apostle written 'which was *in* God,' we might have thought that he meant a mere attribute of God."[42] The preposition John uses portrays the identity of this life as distinct from the Father, yet in active communion and fellowship with the Father. It portrays "the closest sort of face-to-face fellowship, existing in the eternal mystery of the Godhead."[43] In John 1:1 this relationship is assigned to "the Word" *(ho logos)* but here to "the eternal life," the preincarnate Christ as Himself the very embodiment of eternal life. In 1 John 2:1 the author uses the same expression to describe the relation of the risen and ascended Christ to the Father as our "advocate." The term "Father" is the favorite Johannine expression for God; it occurs twelve times in this epistle alone.[44] This Father-Son relationship is basic to John's high Christology.

This personal, pre-existent life "was manifested unto us" *(ephanerōthē hēmin)* in the incarnate Christ. The repetition of the verb "was manifested" at the end of the verse indicates John's intent to underline this fact as a unique historical reality. But now the added "unto us" returns the thought to the personal encounter of the apostles with this incarnate Life.

C. The Personal Issues of the Apostolic Proclamation (vv. 3-4)

In verses 3-4 John advances to the crucial significance of the incarnation for himself and his readers. He makes a summary restatement of the content of the proclamation (v. 3a), indicates the apostolic aim in making the proclamation (v. 3b), and announces the goal of his letter (v. 4).

---

[41]Brooke, p. 7.

[42]Plummer, p. 75.

[43]David Jackman, *The Message of John's Letters,* The Bible Speaks Today (Downers Grove, Ill.: Inter-Varsity Press, 1988), p. 20.

[44]The Greek term *patēr* "father" occurs 138 times in the Fourth Gospel, and 122 times it denotes God the "Father." Of its 14 occurrences in 1 John, 12 refer to God. Its 4 occurrences in 2 John all refer to God, likewise its 5 occurrences in Revelation.

1. The Summary of the Apostolic Proclamation (v. 3a)

Structurally, verse 3 resumes the sentence begun in verse 1. But because of the parenthesis in verse 2, he repeats two verbs from verse 1, "that which we have seen and heard," in reverse order and united under the relative pronoun *ho*, "that which." With these two verbs John recalls the objective character of the apostolic message being proclaimed. The repetition of these verbs from verse 1 clearly ties the object clauses of that verse to the main verb, "we declare." Whether the reverse order of the verbs used here is simply due to a desire for literary variation or has some subtle theological implication is uncertain. Brooke conjectures that the order here "may perhaps throw more emphasis on the earthly life of the Incarnate Logos, in which what was seen naturally takes precedence of what was heard."[45] Kistemaker well remarks, "By reiterating the same verbs, John seems to warn the readers against false doctrines that deny the human nature, physical appearing, and bodily resurrection of Jesus."[46]

The observed reality of the incarnation and the instruction received from the incarnate one "declare we unto you" *(apanggelomen kai*[47] *humin)*. Schniewind suggests that this compound verb, which occurs only in verses 2-3 in this epistle, has something of an official tone "to signify the activity of envoys."[48] It involves the picture of passing on to others what has been authoritatively imparted to them. The sense of privilege and duty prompted their proclamation. Orr observes, "The habitual sense of the present tense may be understood here: *we make it our business to proclaim.*"[49] The reading *kai,* "also," does not occur in the Textus Receptus, but various modern scholars accept it as authentic. (See note 47.) If "also" is accepted as part of the original, it may mean that others besides John were proclaiming the message to the readers; more probably John means that he is giving this message to them as well as to others.

---

[45]Brooke, p. 7.

[46]Kistemaker, p. 237.

[47]The *kai,* "also," "is missing in the Vulgate, important Coptic Witnesses, a minor Syriac version, and in the Byzantine tradition; but its omission by scribes is explicable as an imitation of 2c, whereas its addition by scribes would be hard to explain" (Brown, p. 70). For the textual evidence see Nestle-Aland, *Novum Testamentum Graece,* 26th ed. (Stuttgart: Deutsche Biblestiftung, 1979). It is accepted as part of the text in B.F. Westcott and F.J.A. Hort, *The New Testament in the Original Greek,* 2nd ed. (1881; reprint ed., New York: Macmillan Co., 1935); Kurt Aland et al., ed. *The Greek New Testament,* 3rd ed. (New York: United Bible Societies, 1975); Nestle-Aland; and R.V.G. Tasker, *The Greek New Testament, Being the Text Translated in the New English Bible 1961* (Oxford; Cambridge: University Press, 1964).

[48]Julius Schniewind, *"apanngellō,"* in *Theological Dictionary of the New Testament,* ed. Gerhard Kittel (Grand Rapids: Eerdmans, 1964), 1:64-65.

[49]R. W. Orr, "The Letters of John," in *A New Testament Commentary* (Grand Rapids: Zondervan, 1969), p. 609.

2. The Aim of the Apostolic Proclamation (v. 3b)

John's proclamation to the readers aims at a clearly intended result: "that ye also may have fellowship with us" *(hina kai humeis koinōnian echēte meth' hēmōn)*. The words "ye also" *(kai humeis,* "also you") suggest that although the readers did not have the same personal experiences with the incarnate Christ that the apostles had, yet by personally accepting the reality of Christ proclaimed they can share a common spiritual fellowship. The present-tense verb "may have" *(echēte)* indicates that by their adherence to the message proclaimed they can continue to enjoy the full fruit of the revelation. John is anxious that they will not allow the false teachers to mar or disrupt their mutual fellowship by perverting the apostolic message.

The word "fellowship" *(koinōnian)* "is a richly significant theological term"[50] which occurs only in this first chapter (vv. 3, 6, 7) in the Johannine writings. Based on the Greek adjective meaning "common" *(koinos),* it denotes a joint ownership or an active sharing of that which one has in common with others. The nature of that which is mutually shared molds the nature of the group. Here, as in Acts 2:42, the bond of fellowship which unites the group is their common faith in Christ as set forth in the apostolic message. Any other ground for entering into the fellowship of the Body of Christ than the true gospel does not result in genuine Christian fellowship. In Romans 15:26 and 2 Corinthians 8:4 Paul speaks of a fellowship with fellow believers in a voluntary sharing of material means with those in need. By its nature the new life in Christ motivates and directs the expression of fellowship in its various aspects. As Smalley notes, "The writer uses the phrase *koinōnian echein,* 'to have fellowship,' not the verb *koinōnein* ('to fellowship,' see 2 John 11); and this expresses not only the *fact,* but also the conscious *enjoyment.*"[51] The use of the preposition *meth'* ("with"), rather than *sun,* seems to suggest more prominently the personal relationship in this fellowship. The present subjunctive "may have" *(echēte)* indicates John's desire to promote a continuing experience of true Christian fellowship "with us." This fellowship is not limited to those of a common culture or racial background but is solely grounded in a mutual adherence to the apostolic gospel. As Findlay observes,

> The Apostle is writing to Greeks, to men far removed from him in native sympathy and instinct; but he has long since forgotten all that, and the difference between Jew and Greek never appears to cross his mind in writing this letter. The only difference he knows is between those who "are of God" and those who "are of the world."[52]

---

[50]Smalley, p. 12.

[51]*Ibid.,* p. 12. Italics in original.

[52]George C. Findlay, *Fellowship in the Life Eternal, An Exposition of the Epistles of St John* (1909; reprint ed., Grand Rapids: Eerdmans, 1955), p. 89.

In seeking to preserve and enhance this horizontal fellowship between true believers, John calls attention to the vertical aspect of Christian fellowship: "and truly our fellowship *is* with the Father, and with his Son Jesus Christ" *(kai hē koinōnia de hē hēmetera meta tou patros kai meta tou huiou autou Iēsou Christou).* By his use of two conjunctions rendered "and truly" *(kai . . . de),* John underlines that more needs to be said about Christian fellowship. The former conjunction seems to mark the connection, while the latter *(de)* stresses that something more but different needs to be said. The words "and truly our fellowship" *(kai hē koinōnia de hē hēmetera,* literally, "and the fellowship, moreover, the ours") emphasize this vital Godward aspect of Christian fellowship. The expression "the ours" *(hē hēmetera)* is a strong one; it is not the usual genitive of the personal pronoun but rather the first-person plural of the possessive pronoun and denotes an actual mutual possession. One can understand this plural as restricted to the apostles and original witness-bearers, but clearly John chooses this form to include his readers in this further aspect of their fellowship. No verb is used in the Greek but our versions generally insert the indicative "is" *(estin),* rather than a subjunctive as in the previous clause, as marking a positive assertion. For true believers this Godward fellowship is a fact, although a call to guard and deepen it may always be in order. This vertical fellowship is vital for true Christian fellowship horizontally. Those who reject Christian fellowship with John and those he represents show thereby a fatal defect in their professed fellowship with God.

The true grandeur of this vertical fellowship lies in the fact that it is "with the Father, and with his Son Jesus Christ" *(meta tou patros kai meta tou huiou autou Iēsou Christou).* The use of the preposition and the definite article with both marks the distinctness and equality of the Father and the Son; the Father and the Son are one in Godhood. The preposition *meta* marks the believer's personal association with the Father and the Son as the amazing privilege of this fellowship. Dammers remarks that the thought is that of "communion with God, not absorption in Him; a vital distinction to make in Hindu and Buddist lands today as it was in John's Hellenistic world."[53]

John had learned the designations "the Father" and "his Son" from the lips of Jesus Himself. The full designation "his Son Jesus Christ" is solemn and weighty. Here for the first time in the epistle, John gives the historical identity of the one whose incarnation he has been talking about. "His Son" explicitly declares the divine nature of the person historically known as "Jesus Christ." The name "Jesus" *(Iēsous)* is a Greek transliteration of the Hebrew name "Joshua," which means "Saviour" (Matt. 1:21), and is the

---

[53] A. H. Dammers, *God Is Light, God Is Love, A Running Commentary on the First Letter of John* (New York: Association Press, 1963), p. 19.

name of His humanity. The name "Christ" *(Christos)* is a Greek translation of the Aramaic or Hebrew word for "Messiah," meaning "anointed." (In John 1:41 and 4:25 the Greek transliteration of the Hebrew, *messias,* is used). On the early pages of the New Testament the designation "the Christ" (Matt. 2:4; John 1:20, 25, 41; 4:25) is a title of office. The term thus marks Jesus as the personal fulfillment of the messianic office, and the early Christian Church never quite lost sight of this fact. But eventually the designation *Christos,* used with the name Jesus, came to be employed as a personal name, Jesus Christ, the man Jesus who was also Christ. John's designation here explicitly identifies God's Son with the man Jesus Christ. "This identification," Burdick notes, "leaves no room for any kind of Gnostic distinction between the divine Son and the human Jesus."[54] John repudiates both Cerinthian and Docetic heresy.

While clearly marking the distinctness and equality in nature between the Father and the Son, John draws them together as the true object of our Godward fellowship. Candlish well observes,

> In some views and for some ends it may be quite warrantable, and even necessary, to distinguish the fellowship which you have with the Father from that which you have with his Son Jesus Christ. As Christ is the way, the true and living way, to the Father, so fellowship with Him as such must evidently be preparatory to fellowship with the Father. But it is not thus that Christ is here represented. He is not put before the Father as the way to the Father, fellowship with whom is the means, leading to fellowship with the Father as the end. He is associated with the Father. Together, in their mutual relation to one another and their mutual mind or heart to one another, they constitute the one object of this fellowship.[55]

Although the finite human mind can never fully comprehend the nature of our God, who has revealed Himself to us in His Son Jesus Christ, it is yet our high privilege, through the way which He has provided, to have fellowship with Him. What such a fellowship demands, and the tests to determine the validity of human claims to such fellowship, will be developed subsequently.

3. The Goal of the Apostolic Letter (v. 4)

With his connective "and" *(kai)* John adds a further truth: "And these things write we unto you, that your joy may be full" *(kai tauta graphomen hēmeis hina hē chara hēmōn ē peplērōmenē).* The fact that other versions offer renderings different from the familiar King James text calls attention to the fact of textual problems in this verse. The manuscripts reveal variant

---

[54]Burdick, p. 106.

[55]Robert S. Candlish, *The First Epistle of John* (1871; reprint ed., Grand Rapids: Zondervan, n.d.), pp. 7-8.

readings for the personal pronouns in both parts of the verse. In the first clause the manuscripts vary between "write we unto you" *(graphomen humin),* the dative of the recipients, and *"we* write" *(graphomen hēmeis),* the emphatic first-person plural. The former, the reading of the Textus Receptus, is the majority reading and is strongly supported by later manuscripts, but the emphatic first person plural *(hēmeis)* has good and early support.[56] Generally modern textual editors accept the emphatic "we" *(hēmeis)* as original "because of the quality of its support, . . . and because copyists were more likely to alter *graphomen hēmeis* to the expected *graphomen humin* . . . than vice versa."[57] Brown believes that the dative "is probably a scribal improvement to harmonize 4a with 3b (where there is a 'to you') and to alleviate the awkwardness of the unusual placing of the 'we.'"[58] The probability is that the emphatic *hēmeis* was the original reading. The second variant will be treated in connection with the latter part of the verse.

In the opening phrase, "these things we write," the intended scope of "these things" *(tauta)* is open to two views. Various scholars such as Plummer,[59] Smalley,[60] and Westcott[61] accept that "these things" looks forward to the whole epistle, which, Brooke suggests, is "already present in the writer's mind."[62] Plummer assumes that this demonstrative pronoun looks forward to "the whole Epistle, of which he here states the purpose, just as in John xx. 31 he states the purpose of the Gospel."[63] But it would be much more natural to compare the statement of purpose in 5:13 with the stated purpose of the Gospel in 20:31. In support of this view Brooke notes that in John's use of the demonstrative expression "the reference forward would seem to be his prevailing custom."[64] Stott counters with this observation: "But it is not always so (e.g. ii. 22, iv. 6, v. 20, and especially ii. 26 and v. 13, where the similar phrase *these things I have written* occurs and in each case refers to the previous paragraph)."[65] Burdick concludes that the

---

[56]For the manuscript evidences see Nestle-Aland, *Novum Testamentum Graece,* 26th ed.

[57]Bruce M. Metzger, *A Textual Commentary on the Greek New Testament* (London: United Bible Societies, 1971), p. 709.

[58]Brown, p. 172.

[59]Plummer, p. 76.

[60]Smalley, p. 14.

[61]Westcott, p. 13.

[62]Brooke, p. 9.

[63]Plummer, p. 76.

[64]Brooke, p. 9.

[65]J.R.W. Stott, *The Epistles of John,* Tyndale New Testament Commentaries (Grand Rapids: Eerdmans, 1964), p. 65.

term here "seems more naturally to refer to the items John has been discussing in verses 1-3."[66] Lenski accepts this backward look: " 'We are writing these things' expounds 'we are testifying and declaring to you'; for the readers of John much of this testimony of the apostles is in the form of writing."[67] Thus Lenski accepts that John with his emphatic "we are writing" unites himself with the other apostolic witnesses who have added writing to their oral witness to proclaim "these things" concerning the incarnate Christ to others. He continues: "It was the calling of the Twelve 'to disciple all nations,' and that included also the nations of all future ages. . . . They are discipling the nations now by these writings. We who now believe their testimony and their writings are in *their* fellowship."[68] Thus understood, John with his emphatic "we are writing" unites himself with the other apostolic witnesses as he composes this letter to portray and defend the reality of the incarnation. The writing of this letter is in keeping with his apostolic commission.

The statement of purpose, "that your joy may be full" *(hina hē chara hēmōn ē peplērōmenē)* involves the second textual variant in this verse. The manuscripts are fairly evenly divided between "our" (hēmōn) or "your" *(humōn)* joy. Here both readings make good sense. "Your joy," the reading of the Textus Receptus, gives the normally expected sense and agrees with John's expressed concern for his readers. If "your" was the original reading, it is difficult to see why the scribes would make the change. Remembering John 16:24, "that your joy may be full," they would be prone to change the unexpected first-person plural to the second person. The reading "our joy," intrinsically more difficult, seems to be the original reading. This reading can be understood as a delicate personal touch to refer to the writer himself, being "similar to one the same author made in 3 John 4: 'I have no greater joy than to hear that my children are walking in the truth.' "[69] Then the writer expresses his own joy in the success of the apostolic message in the lives of the readers. More probably the scope of this "our" is as wide as the "we" in the preceding clause. Then the reference is to John and those with him as the proponents of the apostolic message. So understood, this is the joy of the Christian teachers whose hearts rejoice when they observe that the message is effective in the lives of their hearers.

---

[66]Burdick, p. 106.

[67]R.C.H. Lenski, *The Interpretation of the Epistles of St. Peter, St. John and St. Jude* (Columbus, Ohio: Wartburg Press, 1945), p. 380.

[68]*Ibid.,* p. 380. Italics in original.

[69]Zane C. Hodges, "1 John," in *The Bible Knowledge Commentary, New Testament* (Wheaton, Ill.: Victor Books, 1983), p. 884.

One may also understand the words "our joy" in an inclusive sense to include both writers and readers. Thus the New English Bible renders "the joy of us all." This inclusive meaning seems natural in view of the possessive plural pronoun "our fellowship" in verse 3. It is an instance of pastor and people rejoicing together in the fellowship of the gospel.

Under either view the joy arises out of the fellowship which is produced by the knowledge of the person and message of the incarnate Christ. It is one of the necessary fruits of the Spirit (Gal. 5:22), evidence of the new life in Christ. Such joy is present whenever true Christian fellowship is experienced. But, as Barker notes, "joy can never be perfectly known or fully complete because the fellowship itself, though real, is imperfectly realized."[70] Smalley suggests that John's expression, "may be made complete" *(ē peplēeōmenē),* a perfect passive subjunctive periphrastic construction, implies an eschatological dimension in his desire.[71] The perfect passive points to a joy continuing as fully complete, while the subjunctive suggests a future fulfillment beyond this present life. "The present joy in the fellowship is a token of the ultimate expression of joy, which depends on the final revelation of the Son."[72] Yet John's concerns in writing relate to the immediate situation and are intensely practical.

---

[70]Glen W. Barker, "1 John," in *The Expositor's Bible Commentary* (Grand Rapids: Zondervan, 1981), 12:308.

[71]Smalley, pp. 14-15.

[72]Barker, p. 308.

The Body of the Epistle:

The Grounds for Christian Assurance
(1:5–5:12)

The Prologue (1:1-4) lays a solid foundation for the message of the epistle. Over against this weighty Prologue at the beginning stands the important Epilogue at its close (5:13-21). They delineate the body of the epistle (1:5–5:12).

In the Prologue John announces his aim to foster full-orbed Christian fellowship, with the resulting increase of joy, in the experience of his readers. As he proceeds with the presentation of his message it soon becomes clear that other concerns were involved. In 2:1 he states that his purpose is to deter any sin in the lives of the readers, thus indicating that true Christian faith and conduct are interrelated. Then in 2:26 John indicates that what he has written is related to the efforts of the false teachers who are seeking to lead them astray. This fact is basic to his portrayal of the Christian life as characterized by its conflicts with its enemies. For true victory believers need to appropriate all the resources available to them.

In the Epilogue John states that his purpose in writing has been to provide his readers with the assurance of salvation (5:13). Thus at the end John specifically declares his overarching purpose in writing the epistle. As we view the contents of the entire epistle in the light of this concluding statement of purpose, it is evident that it provides essential guidance toward a progressive interpretation of its cyclical contents.

In presenting his message, John's method is not that of syllogistic logic. His thought moves in cycles rather than in a straightforward linear manner. In seeking to ground his readers in the assurance of their salvation, John discusses various broad areas that provide valid grounds for assurance. Having announced the theme of fellowship (1:3), John promotes in 1:5–2:17 true fellowship through a treatment of the various aspects of Christian fellowship. His discussion of the signs that establish the fact of true fellowship leads to a discussion of the varied aspects of the conflict which true faith inevitably encounters (2:18–4:6). Having developed the assurance to be drawn from these two fundamental aspects of the Christian life, John gives attention to two further matters important for Christian assurance. In 4:7–5:5 he elaborates on the vital importance of Christian love for true assurance, and in 5:6-12 he points out the need for the witness of the Spirit in confirming the assurance of the believer.

In the Epilogue John summarily states his basic purpose in writing (5:13), elaborates on the resulting confidence of believers before God (5:14-17), and concludes with three ringing certainties of the Christian life (5:18-20). A cryptic warning against idols (5:21) concludes the epistle.

4

Assurance Through the Test of Fellowship (1:5–2:17)

The opening phrases of verse 5 mark the close connection of this section with the Prologue. The reality of Christian fellowship, announced in verse 3, is now developed as the first test to establish Christian assurance. John begins with a declaration of the nature of God as the valid basis for fellowship (1:5), sets forth false views of sin as hindrances to fellowship along with the needed corrective (1:6-10), declares the divine provision for maintaining fellowship with God (2:1-2), and points out a series of signs which show that fellowship is being maintained (2:3-17).

A. The Basis for Christian Fellowship (1:5)

1:5 This then is the message which we have heard of him, and declare unto you, that God is light, and in him is no darkness at all.

Without a break John moves into his discussion of the first test of assurance. His expression, "This then[1] is the message" *(Kai estin hautē heē anggelia)*, points forward to the double statement in the last part of the verse, introduced by "that" *(hoti)*. "This is" *(estin hautē)*, a construction common in the Johannine epistles (3:11, 23; 5:3, 11, 14; 2 John 6), places the emphasis on the continuing existence of the message or person being indicated. The term rendered "message" *(anggelia)*, which occurs only here and in 3:11 in the New Testament, simply denotes the sum and substance of the message received and being transmitted to others. Since the word "gospel" *(euanggelion,* "good news") does not occur in the Fourth Gospel or the Johannine

---

[1] The KJV rendering of *kai,* "and," as "then" indicates the continuity in the thought. This connective *kai* is omitted in RSV, NEB, and NIV.

epistles,[2] Brown suggests that *anggelion* "may well be its technical Johannine equivalent."[3] Clearly the message in view is not one of momentary significance but has continuing value and importance for its recipients.

This message is important because of its source, "the message which we have heard of him" *(hē anggelia hēn akēkoamen ap' autou).* The perfect-tense verb "have heard" (cf. vv. 1, 3) again underlines the abiding impact of the specific message heard "of him" *(ap' autou,* "from him"). In indicating the source of this message John simply uses a personal pronoun *(autou)* rather than the name. Although John's use of this pronoun is not always precise, grammatically it naturally refers back to "his Son Jesus Christ" (v. 3), the last named personal antecedent. Since this message, which was heard by the apostles, concerns the nature of God Himself, it is obvious that they heard the message from Jesus directly. It is a message about God and ultimately from Him; yet it was delivered to men through the incarnate Son of God (cf. John 1:18). Its source makes clear that this message was "a revelation and not a discovery."[4] Neither was it a mere fortuitous philosophical deduction.

The further statement, "and declare unto you" *(kai ananggellomen humin),* implies the apostolic commission to make that message known to others. The verb, "declare" here used in a slightly different form than that rendered "declare" in verse 3, the difference being only in the preposition used in the compound form. The former term *(apangellomen),* if the implied distinction between the prepositions is pressed, suggests the act of publishing or diffusing the knowledge of the message by a qualified spokesman, whereas the term here *(ananggellomen)* basically implies telling the message again or rehearsing it for the benefit of others. But in practical usage the two forms were used quite interchangeably. As the representative of the apostolic recipients of the message, John declares his desire and effort to pass the message on to his readers.

Characteristically, John states the content of this message both positively and negatively: "that God is light, and in him is no darkness at all." The statement "God is light" is one of three fundamental assertions concerning the nature of God from the pen of John, namely, "God is a Spirit" (John 4:24); "God is light" (1 John 1:5) and "God is love" (1 John 4:8, 16). Other Biblical writers tell us about the attributes and activities of God; John alone with these profound assertions tells us what God is. "All three," as

---

[2]It occurs in Revelation 14:6 in the expression "an everlasting gospel."

[3]Raymond E. Brown, *The Epistles of John,* The Anchor Bible (Garden City, N.Y.: Doubleday & Co., 1982), p. 193.

[4]Quoted in A. E. Brooke, *The Johannine Epistles,* International Critical Commentary (New York: Charles Scribner's Sons, 1912), p. 11.

Barker observes, "stress the immateriality of God and the 'Goodness' of God–viz., God in his essence."[5]

The assertion "God is light" *(ho theos phōs estin)* stresses His nature. The articular noun "God" is the subject; "light," without an article, is the predicate nominative; the two terms cannot be interchanged. The phrase states not merely that God "has light" or gives light, but that He Himself *is* light. Although He created light (Gen. 1:3), He Himself is uncreated light. Plummer remarks that "no figure borrowed from the material world could give the idea of perfection so clearly and fully as *light*."[6] This figure was used of God in the Old Testament as well as in oriental pagan religions. Wilder comments that this is "a well-known formula . . . to which all readers would agree."[7] Yet only in Christianity were the full implications of the figure unfolded. The nature of God as light became visible in Jesus, His incarnate Son, who said, "I am the light of the world" (John 8:12). There is no indication in the Gospels that Jesus ever explicitly declared that "God is light"; yet in view of the incompleteness of the records (John 20:30), John may have recalled Him making such an assertion. Probably John used this double assertion concerning the nature of God because he knew that this message "sums up the teaching of the Master and the general impression left by his doctrine."[8]

As in this world there can be no life apart from light, so in the spiritual realm God as light is the true source of all life. In the Prologue of his Gospel, John links light and life together (John 1:4); the incarnate Christ, Himself the embodiment of eternal life, was sent to be "the light" of men, who by nature are in darkness (John 8:12). It is the very nature of this spiritual light "to communicate itself and to prevade everything from which it is not of set purpose shut out."[9]

The assertion that "God is light" is probably as near an approach to a definition of the nature of God that human intelligence can comprehend; it is meaningful to the simplest mind, yet unfathomable to the most profound thinker. In this epistle John uses it in connection with the thought of man's fellowship with God. Whatever other thoughts this designation may involve,

---

[5]Glenn W. Barker, "1 John," in *The Expositor's Bible Commentary* (Grand Rapids: Zondervan, 1981), 12:309.

[6]Alfred Plummer, *The Epistles of S. John,* Cambridge Bible for Schools and Colleges (1883; reprint ed., London: Cambridge University Press, 1938), p. 79. Italics in original.

[7]Amos N. Wilder and Paul W. Hoon, "The First, Second, and Third Epistles of John," in *The Interpreter's Bible* (New York: Abingdon Press, 1957), 12:222.

[8]Bonsirven, quoted in Donald W. Burdick, *The Letters of John the Apostle* (Chicago; Ill.: Moody Press, 1985), p. 118.

[9]Plummer, p. 79.

it clearly involves the intellectual and the moral, *enlightenment* and *holiness*. God's nature determines the conditions of fellowship with Him. His nature as light has an inescapable bearing on the faith and the conduct of the believer.

The added negative assertion, "and in him is no darkness at all" (*kai skotia en autō ouk estin oudemia,* very literally, "and darkness in Him not is, not one bit"), stresses the absoluteness of His nature as light. In His being there is not a single trace of darkness. For John "darkness" is not merely the absence of light; it has a moral quality (John 3:19-21), standing in direct antithesis to all that has the character of light. For the pagan masses in John's day, familiar with the Greek and Roman mythologies, that was a startling assertion. As Findlay notes,

> They had gods that could cheat and lie, gods licentious and unchaste, gods spiteful and malignant towards men, quarrelsome and abusive toward each other. They had been accustomed to think of the Godhead as a mixed nature, like their own, only on a larger scale–good and evil, kind and cruel, pure and wanton, made of darkness and light.[10]

Whenever men create their own gods, they create them in their own moral image (cf. Rom. 1:21-23). To be sure, some of their pagan philosophers rejected such gross conceptions of the gods and conceived the divine nature to be above human desire and infirmity; yet their philosophical speculations were likewise powerless to redeem mankind from its inborn love for darkness and sin. Gnostic philosophies attempted either to mix the two realms of light and darkness or to maintain that they had been enlightened so that the realm of darkness no longer impinged upon them. In view of the nature and demands of fellowship with God as light, neither suggestion is possible. As Himself pure and unalloyed, God cannot condone or have fellowship with anything that is contrary to His nature.

This is the first instance in this epistle where John marks the existence of two separate and distinct spheres of existence. Light and darkness represent two antithetical realms that cannot be mixed. They do not overlap, and there is no neutral zone between them. This antithesis is basic to the various other antitheses that John will delineate in the epistle.

---

[10]George G. Findlay, *Fellowship in the Life Eternal, An Exposition of the Epistles of St John* (1909; reprint ed., Grand Rapids: Eerdmans, 1955), p. 96.

5

Assurance Through the Test of Fellowship (Part 2)

B. The Hindrances to Christian Fellowship (1:6-10)

1:6 If we say that we have fellowship with him, and walk in darkness, we lie, and do not the truth:
7 But if we walk in the light, as he is in the light, we have fellowship one with another, and the blood of Jesus Christ his Son cleanseth us from all sin.
8 If we say that we have no sin, we deceive ourselves, and the truth is not in us.
9 If we confess our sins, he is faithful and just to forgive us *our* sins, and to cleanse us from all unrighteousness.
10 If we say that we have not sinned, we make him a liar, and his word is not in us.

In view of the fact of God's nature as light (1:5), John proceeds to deal with three hindrances to fellowship with God, treated in an ascending order of seriousness. These hindrances are three false views concerning the reality of sin, which by its nature belongs to the realm of darkness. In verses 6-7 John cites a denial of the seriousness of sin and indicates the corrective, and in verses 8-9 he cites a denial of human sinfulness and states the corrective. In verse 10 he mentions the denial of having committed any sinful deeds.

1. The Denial of the Sinfulness of Sin (vv. 6-7)
The first hindrances to fellowship with God that John deals with is a failure to recognize the sinfulness of sin. John indicates the view advanced (v. 6a), expresses his condemnation (v. 6b), and sets forth the corrective (v. 7).

a. The view advanced (v. 6a). The hindrance to fellowship lies in the obvious inconsistency between the profession and the practice: "If we say that we have fellowship with Him, and walk in darkness." This statement is hypothetical;[1] while not actually stating that the view is being expressed, it assumes the probability that the claim is being made.

The opening formula, "if we say" *(ean eipōmen),* used to introduce each of these three false views, indicates that this is not merely an unexpressed mental concept but implies an open assertion. No doubt the false teachers posing as professed Christians actually advanced these hypothetical claims. With his use of "we" John delicately includes himself and his readers as well as the false teachers with their vaunted claims, because all believers need to be alert to the danger of entertaining false views about sin. The aorist subjunctive, "if we should say," implies the possibility of giving expression to such a view.

The content of the profession is "that we have fellowship with him" *(hoti koinōnian echomen met' autou,* more literally, "that fellowship we are having with Him"). The stress is on the claim that fellowship is being continually experienced with God. It is a profession to be "united with God by a living bond of common sympathy, interest, purpose, and love."[2] Over against this high claim stands the contradictory course of conduct, "and walk in darkness" *(kai en tō skotei peripatōmen,* "and in the darkness may be walking").[3] The articular designation "in the darkness," placed emphatically forward, marks the actual sphere of conduct as antithetical to the nature of God. Westcott remarks, "The compatibility of indifference to moral action with the possession of true faith has been maintained by enthusiasts in all times of religious excitement."[4] It is a claim to inner enlightenment which is not manifested in outward conduct. But, in the words of Plummer, "Light can be shut out, but it cannot be shut in."[5] "Walk" is a common New Testament figure of speech to denote moral conduct; the present tense denotes the habitual course of action. The compound verb[6] denotes the whole round of activity in daily life, including thought and deed.

---

[1]"The Third class: Undetermined, but with Prospect of Determination. This condition *states* the condition as a matter of doubt, but with some expectation of realization." A. T. Robertson and W. Hersey David, *A New Short Grammar of the Greek Testament* (New York: Harper & Brothers, 1937), p. 353.

[2]J. M. Gibbon, *Eternal Life, Notes of Expository Sermons on the Epistles of S. John* (London: Richard D. Dickinson, 1890), p. 11.

[3]The NASB and NIV add "yet" to mark the contradiction; the NEB renders, "while we walk in the darkness." Similarly RSV.

[4]Brooke Foss Westcott, *The Epistles of St. John, The Greek Testament with Notes,* 3rd ed. (1892; reprint ed., Grand Rapids: Eerdmans, 1950), p. 19.

[5]Alfred Plummer, *The Epistles of S. John,* Cambridge Bible for Schools and Colleges (1883; reprint ed., London: Cambridge University Press, 1938), p. 70.

[6]The verb *peripateō* is a compound of the preposition *peri,* "around, about," and *pateō,* "to be walking."

b. The condemnation stated (v. 6b). John unhesitatingly pronounces his twofold verdict on this contradiction: "we lie, and do not the truth." John's positive evaluation is "we lie" *(pseudometha), suggesting that the claim is a known falsehood. It is not an innocent mistake but the assertion of a conscious, deliberate lie. Whenever there is a clear conflict between an individual's "talk" and his "walk," it is always his walk and not his talk that reveals what he really is.

The negative evaluation is we "do not the truth" *(ou poioumen tēn alētheian,* more literally, "not we are doing the truth"). The present-tense verb declares a persistent failure to give expression to the truth in daily life. This is the first occurrence of the words "the truth" in this epistle; it appears twenty times in the Johannine epistles, generally with the definite article, "the truth," and "denotes the revelation of God's nature and salvific purpose in Jesus his Son."[7] This revelation is now embodied in the gospel. The expression "to do the truth" indicates that the human response to God's revealed truth cannot be merely intellectual but must be morally and volitionally expressed in conduct. The personal possession of "the truth" of God "relates to action, and conduct and feeling, as well as to word and thought."[8] Personal fellowship with God demands that His truth be incorporated in daily conduct and character. As Kysar remarks, "It is the overriding purpose of 1 John to stress the necessity of a morality which issues from the saved relationship with God."[9]

c. The corrective presented (v. 7). With "but" *(de)* John sets out the contrasting truth which provides the corrective to this false position. He presents the nature of this corrective (v. 7a) and adds the twofold result (v. 7b).

1) *The corrective conduct* (v. 7a). "But if we walk in the light, as he is in the light" sets forth the conduct that will correct the false view of sin just condemned. The conditional statement implies that the believer must personally accept this corrective if it is to be operative in his own life. Although it is assumed that the believer makes a profession of fellowship with God, the corrective lies not in a mere orthodox profession but in a consistent daily walk in the light. When one consistently walks in the light, those around will readily recognize that fact and no vaunted public claim need be advanced.

The standard and pattern of this walk in the light is not left to us to determine but is established by the divine nature, "as he is in the light" *(hō*

---

[7]Stephen S. Smalley, *1, 2, 3 John,* Word Biblical Commentary (Waco, Texas: Word Books, 1984), p. 23.

[8]A. E. Brooke, *The Johannine Epistles,* International Critical Commentary (New York: Charles Scribner's Sons, 1912), p. 14.

[9]Robert Kysar, *I, II, III John,* Augsburg Commentary on the New Testament (Minneapolis: Augsburg, 1986), p. 38.

autos estin en tō phōti, literally, "as he himself is in the light"). The emphatic pronoun *(autos)* marks the basic contrast between God and the individual human being who seeks fellowship with Him. As Himself "light" (v. 5), He is ever "in the light," "dwelling in light unapproachable" (I Tim. 6:16 ASV) to the unsaved. The expression "in the light" does not denote His nature but rather depicts the environment around Him that His nature creates; light is, as it were, His home. It is there that we have fellowship with Him. "We then must make our spiritual atmosphere similar to His, that our thoughts and conduct may reflect Him."[10]

2) *The twofold result* (v. 7b). Our walk in the light has a horizontal result: "we have fellowship one with another" *(koinōnian echomen met' allēlōn).* The term "fellowship" is a reminder that this is a relationship based on something held in common. Although some understand the phrase "one with another" to denote the resultant fellowship between God and man,[11] it is more natural to understand the reciprocal pronoun as indicating fellow believers. The pronoun *(allēlōn)* occurs seven times in 1 and 2 John,[12] and in each of the other places it clearly expresses a human relationship. Thus "instead of contenting himself with an exact antithesis, he carries the thought a step further."[13] The resultant fellowship with fellow believers is the visible sign of the correlative fellowship with God. He who consistently has trouble maintaining fellowship with others walking in the light should examine his own claim of fellowship with God.

The believer's habitual walk in the light also involves a vertical result: "and the blood of Jesus Christ[14] his son cleanseth us from all sin." The order is significant: the walk in the light, resulting in fellowship with fellow believers, also enables God to show us our continual need for personal cleansing. "And" *(kai)* points to a connection between the horizontal and the vertical result. Our walk in the light does not produce the cleansing but only makes us continually conscious of our deep need for cleansing.

The cleansing agent is "the blood of Jesus Christ his Son" *(to haima Iēsou tou huiou autou).* The one whose blood has this cleansing power is none other than "Jesus His Son." The name "Jesus" declares His humanity

---

[10]Plummer, p. 81.

[11]So Zane C. Hodges, "1 John," in *The Bible Knowledge Commentary, New Testament* (Wheaton, Ill.: Victor Books, 1983), p. 885; J. Dwight Pentecost, *The Joy of Fellowship* (Grand Rapids: Zondervan, 1977), p. 24.

[12]1:7, 3:11, 23; 4:7, 11, 12; 2 John 5.

[13]Brooke, p. 15.

[14]The reading "Jesus Christ" (KJV) follows the Textus Receptus. On the basis of the manuscript evidence most modern editors omit "Christ" here. For the textual evidence see Nestle-Aland, *Novum Testamentum Graece,* 26th ed. (Stuttgart: Deutche Biblestiftung, 1979).

as a real man here on earth, while "His Son" asserts His deity as the incarnate Son of God. This reference to His dual nature is a clear repudiation of the false views of Gnosticism. Cerinthus taught that it was a mere man whose blood was shed, while Docetic Gnosticism maintained that He only appeared to be a human being and had no real blood to shed.[15] It is His unique nature as God incarnate that gave His blood this cleansing power. But it is the blood of the cross, voluntarily shed in atonement for human sin, that has this cleansing power.

His sacrificial blood is fully competent to "cleanse us from all sin." The present-tense verb "cleanseth" *(katharizei)* delineates the repeated experience of cleansing as we continue to walk in the light. The cleansing in view here is not our initial "cleansing" or "washing" in regeneration (John 13:10; 1 Cor. 6:11) but rather the repeated cleansing from the defilement incurred in daily life. "If our fellowship with God must wait until we are no longer sinners, then John himself was still outside of the fellowship according to his own confession (v. 8)."[16] This cleansing process has well been called progressive sanctification as distinct from the believer's positional sanctification imparted at regeneration (1 Cor. 1:30; 6:11; 2 Thess. 2:13). As Plummer notes, "One who lives in the light knows his own frailty and is continually availing himself of the purifying power of Christ's sacrificial death."[17]

Although this is the first occurrence of the word "sin," the concept clearly has been present in John's mind since his reference to "darkness" in verse 5. The noun "sin" *(hamartia)*, which Vine calls "the most comprehensive term for moral obliquity,"[18] literally means "a missing of the mark," a falling short of the divine standard; but the New Testament usage of the term makes it clear that sin is not merely a regrettable inadequacy but in reality is a deliberate rebellion against and departure from the requirements of God. Its nature brings it under the judgment of God. But through Christ's atonement the believer can now appropriate cleansing "from all sin" *(apo pasēs hamartias)*. This cleansing from "all" sin may be understood in two ways. It may denote the thoroughness of the cleansing from any sin, leaving no tell-tale smudge as a witness against us. More probably the cleansing is viewed as comprehensive, sin in all its varied forms and manifestations. No sin, however heinous, is beyond the cleansing power of Christ's blood.

---

[15]See our Introduction, pp. 21-22.

[16]R.C.H. Lenski, *The Interpretation of the Epistles of St. Peter, St. John and St. Jude* (Columbus, Ohio: Wartburg Press, 1945), p. 390.

[17]Plummer, p. 82.

[18]W. E. Vine, *An Expository Dictionary of New Testament Words with Their Precise Meanings for English Readers* (London: Oliphants, 1939), 4:432.

2. The Denial of Human Sinfulness (vv. 8-9)

A second hindrance to fellowship with God is the failure to acknowledge human sinfulness. John makes a hypothetical statement of the denial (v. 8a), expresses his condemnation of the claim (v. 8b), and points out the corrective to this false view (v. 9).

a. The view advanced (v. 8a). Again John apparently makes the hypothetically stated view, "If we say that we have no sin," in view of the claims of the false teachers; the view involves a direct attack upon the Christian view of sin. The singular word "sin" may denote a specific act of sin and the resultant guilt. In John 9:41 the expression is rendered "you would have no guilt" (RSV); it is the view of Law[19] that John here also refers to the guilt of sin. John is referring then to the subtlety of the Gnostics that an act of sin was a matter of the flesh and did not defile their spirit; hence they were free from any guilt from the act. But in view of verse 10 it seems more probable that the singular "sin" conveys a denial of inner sinfulness. So understood it may express the claim of the Gnostics–when told that they were walking in the darkness (v. 6)–that they had advanced to a stage beyond human sinfulness.

The expression "have no sin" is peculiar to John (cf. John 9:41; 15:22, 24; 19:11). As distinguished from the verb "to sin," it points to the inner sinful nature as distinguished from the act of sin. Such a denial of sinfulness may be a forthright rejection of the Biblical teaching concerning the fall of mankind. This denial implies that human nature is inherently good and requires only personal growth and development. Near the beginning of the present century a certain professor in a liberal theological school maintained that human nature was inherently good and what orthodox Christians characterized as a man's "sinful nature" was simply the survival of his past animal ancestry which man had not yet outgrown. Such a view of human sinfulness and its manifestations relegates sin to the limbo of mistakes, frailties, or pardonable errors due to human limitation, all insignificant and negligible in the sight of God!

Certain "eradicationists," believers who confess that they once had a sinful nature but that this ugly root has now–through a deeper experience–been completely eradicated, have also at times advanced such a claim to sinlessness. Years ago this writer noticed an advocate of this view who quoted this verse as follows: "If we say that we have [had] no sin, we deceive ourselves." It is freely admitted that they once had a sinful nature, but no more! As Barker notes, "Whatever the shape of the argument, and regardless of whether it is an affirmation from the ancient world or a modern restatement,

---

[19]Robert Law, *The Tests of Life* (Edinburgh: T. & T. Clark, 1909), p. 130.

it remains true that whenever the principle of sin is denied as an ongoing reality, there follows a denial of responsibility for individual actions."[20]

b. The condemnation stated (v. 8b). Again John expresses his verdict on this claim both positively and negatively. Positively, the result of such a claim is "we deceive ourselves" (*heautous planōmen*, "ourselves we are deceiving" or "leading astray"). The reflexive pronoun as the object of the verb, placed emphatically forward, stresses that the resultant deception is our own doing; we have no one but ourselves to blame. The verb denotes a leading astray from the right path and implies a serious departure from the truth. It is not a simple mistake but an action that will have serious consequences unless we are willing to lead ourselves back to the right way. In Matthew 24:5 Jesus uses the term of the coming false teachers who "shall deceive many," and in Revelation John frequently uses the verb of what Satan, the arch-deceiver, is persistently endeavoring to do (Rev. 12:9; 13:14; 20:3, 8, 10). Moody remarks, "One of the sickening things about self-deception is that it leads to the sophisticated assumption that others are as blind to our sins as we are, but this is never so."[21] Such a self-deceived claim seldom deceives other people and never deceives God.

"And" introduces the negative result–"and the truth is not in us"–and implies a close connection. Such self-deception is made possible by our deliberate refusal to accept the revealed truth concerning our true nature. "When the principle of sin is denied, truth as an inner principle of life cannot exist."[22] "The truth" (*hē alētheia*), as a specific body of truth, does not exclude the possession of natural truths related to this world but denotes the revealed truth of the gospel which meets the true needs of man's nature. He who excludes the divine light thereby opens himself to the darkness of sin. As Lenski observes, "When, 'the truth' is not in us, we are not by any means empty but are full of fictions, fables, myths, self-made fancies, notions that are *not so*."[23]

c. The corrective indicated (v. 9). John uses no connective particle to link this verse with the preceding. His explicit requirement, "if we confess our sins," implies that the preceding denial of human sinfulness needs to be abandoned, because confession of our sinful deeds acknowledges our sinful nature as the source of those acts. The hypothetical form again challenges the readers to be willing to make this confession. "If we confess our sins" (*ean homologōmen tas harmartias hēmōn*) delineates the needed course of

---

[20]Glen W. Barker, "1 John," in *The Expositor's Bible Commentary* (Grand Rapids: Zondervan, 1981), 12:309.

[21]Dale Moody, *The Letters Of John* (Waco, Texas: Word Books, 1970), p. 28.

[22]Barker, p. 312.

[23]Lenski, pp. 391-92. Italics in original.

action. To "confess" *(homologeō)* basically means to "say the same thing"; it is the willingness publicly to acknowledge and to admit our sins and to call them what God calls them. Such a confession is more than a general acknowledgement that we all are sinners by nature; such a confession costs little and does not meet the need. We must honestly confront and frankly confess the sins we are guilty of without defending ourselves or excusing our sinful deeds. The plural "sins" demands that the specific sins be named and confessed. It is a humbling experience and guarantee of our sincerity. The present tense underlines that such confession is to be our standing practice whenever sins do occur.

This is the only instance in the New Testament where the verb "to confess" *(homologeō)* refers to the confession of sins. It is generally used in connection with a confession of Christ or of truth about Him. The usage of the verb implies that some form of public confession, rather than a private confession by the individual to God, is involved. John does not indicate to whom the confession is to be made. Our confession of any sin to God is always involved, and at times our confession need be made only to God. But as a member of the Christian brotherhood, the confession of any act of sin should be as wide as the knowledge of the sin. At times there may also be need for restitution.

God's favorable response to our confession is assured by His nature, because "he is faithful and just" *(pistos estin kai dikaios)*. The first adjective, "faithful," "describes God's reliability, consistency, dependability. God can be trusted to do what has been promised."[24] The second adjective, "just" or "righteous," declares that when God forgives the sin of the penitent believer He acts in full accord with His righteous and holy nature. We might have expected John to say that God is "merciful" in forgiving our sins; although true, that would have been less assuring to our troubled hearts. Conscious of our persistent failures, we might come to fear that God would say, "Your sinning no longer deserves my merciful forgiveness." But the declaration that He is righteous reminds us that in forgiving our sins God acts in full moral consistency with His character in view of the cross. "Since Christ has fully atoned for sin, God is bound by His righteousness to forgive all who repent and confess their sins."[25] (See Rom. 3:25-26.)

God's response to our confession of our sin is twofold: "to forgive us *our* sins, and to cleanse us from all unrighteousness" *(hina aphē hēmin tas hamartias kai katharisē hēmas apo pasēs adikias)*. The *hina* introducing the clause looks back to the preceding two adjectives and usually indicates purpose or result; it may be rendered "that." Thus Smalley notes, "The

---

[24]Kysar, p. 40.

[25]Donald W. Burdick, *The Letters of John the Apostle* (Chicago: Moody Press, 1985), p. 127.

faithfulness and righteousness of God are such 'that' he *will* forgive/purify (purpose), and *does* so (result).''[26] Plummer accepts the original force of purpose here and remarks, ''It is God's decree and aim that His faithfulness and righteousness should appear in His forgiving us and cleansing us.''[27] But Brooke concludes that Johannine usage of *hina* indicates that its usual telic force has given way to the definitive and may be translated as an infinitive.[28] Our English versions commonly render ''to forgive . . . cleanse.''

The words ''to forgive us *our* sins'' indicate God's response to the guilt of our sins. As a failure to conform to God's law, our sins make us guilty and subject to punishment. But when we confess them to Him He acts to ''forgive'' *(aphē)*, as a definite act ''to remove,'' more literally ''to send away,'' those sins so that they no longer stand between us and God. They are ''sent away as a cloud is dissolved, never to appear again.''[29] And we should not allow Satan to bring up those sins again and use them to disrupt our peace with God.

The added phrase ''and to cleanse us from all unrighteousness'' declares that our sins not only make us guilty but also make us unclean. The aorist verb ''cleanse'' *(katharisē)* declares that upon our confession God specifically acts to cleanse us from the pollution of our sins. Sin produces a defilement which only God can remove. He acts to remove ''all unrighteousness'' *(pasēs adikias),* underlining that the cleansing is total, not partial. ''All unrighteousness'' is similar to ''all sin'' in verse 7, but the noun ''unrighteousness'' here describes our sin as a failure to measure up to the standard of right as set forth by the Word of God. This total cleansing restores us to fellowship with God. The ''blood of Jesus Christ his Son'' (v. 7) is the cleansing agent, not our confession; but the confession of our sins makes possible the application of the divine cleansing. Stott offers the reminder, ''There are many warnings in Scripture about the danger of concealing our sins, and many promises of blessing if we confess them.''[30]

3. The Denial of Any Sinful Deeds (v. 10)

A third false claim which makes fellowship with God impossible is that we have not committed acts of sin. Again John indicates the claim (10a) and pronounces his verdict (10b).

---

[26]Smalley, p. 32. Italics in original.

[27]Plummer, p. 84.

[28]Brooke, p. 19.

[29]Lenski, p. 394.

[30]J.R.W. Stott, *The Epistles of John,* Tyndale New Testament Commentaries (Grand Rapids: Eerdmans, 1964), p. 78.

a. The view advanced (v. 10a). "If we say that we have not sinned" *(ean eipōmen hoti ouch hēmartēkamen)* is a blatant refusal to acknowledge any sinful deeds in our conduct. The perfect tense, "have not sinned," asserts a past condition of sinlessness which continues up to the present moment. The scope of this denial has been differently understood. If John is understood to present the claim of the false teachers who profess to be Christians, then, with Bennett, we may understand their claim to mean "since conversion." He insists that "this interpretation is required by verse 8 and the general context."[31] Brown agrees that "such a limitation would make sense in the context, for the four preceding verses all concern the behavior of Christians and how they walk after they have seen the light."[32] But the statement itself does not express any time limitations for the claim. As Burdick points out,

> The perfect-tense verb refers to the past and with the negative it includes all of past time up to the last minute. It claims that one is now in the state of never having committed sin. It is therefore a denial that one has ever sinned.[33]

This is obviously the climax of the false claims being presented. Kistemaker boldly stamps it as "the blatant attitude of the unrepentant, unregenerate infidel."[34]

b. The condemnation stated (v. 10b). John announces his double verdict on such a defiant claim. Positively, by making such a claim "we make him a liar" *(pseustēn poioumen auton)*. It is one thing to reveal that we ourselves are liars; it is a far more serious thing to make a liar out of God. Such a claim is a direct attack upon the character of God and impugns His whole program of human redemption. As Lias notes, "All the doctrines of the Christian faith, the Incarnation, the Sacrifice upon the cross, the descent and sanctifying influences of the Holy Spirit, are not merely unnecessary, but false, save upon the supposition of man's sin."[35] The noun "liar," emphatic by position, not merely charges God with telling lies but also declares that in character He is a liar, false in His very nature. It reduces God to the level of the Devil (cf. John 8:44).

---

[31]W. H. Bennett, *The General Epistles, James, Peter, John, and Jude,* The Century Bible (London: Blackwood, Le Bas & Co., n.d.), p. 293.

[32]Raymond E. Brown, *The Epistles of John,* The Anchor Bible (Garden City, N.Y.: Doubleday & Co., 1982), p. 212.

[33]Burdick, p. 128.

[34]Simon J. Kistemaker, *Exposition of the Epistle of James and the Epistles of John,* New Testament Commentary (Grand Rapids: Baker, 1986), p. 247.

[35]John James Lias, *An Exposition of the First Epistle of John* (1887; reprinted ed., Minneapolis: Klock & Klock Christian Publishers, 1982), p. 49.

Such a claim also reveals a negative reality concerning the one making it, "and his word is not in us" *(kai ho logos autou ouk estin en hēmin)*. The reference is not to the personified *Logos* (John 1:1) but to the aggregate message from God. That divine message, personally communicated and embodied in the Christian gospel, has found no lodging in his life and being. Unlike in verses 7 and 9, John now offers no corrective. The only hope for this individual is to utterly repudiate the claim and to accept the message presented in 2:1-2.

6

Assurance Through the Test of Fellowship (Part 3)

C. The Provision for Maintaining Fellowship (2:1-2)

2:1 My little children, these things write I unto you, that ye sin not. And if any man sin, we have an advocate with the Father, Jesus Christ the righteous:
2 And he is the propitiation for our sins: and not for ours only, but also for *the sins of* the whole world.

Having shown that sin hinders fellowship with God, John appropriately points out the divine provision for maintaining fellowship. These two verses set forth the heart of the Christian gospel; the provision in Christ Jesus enables sinful men to be forgiven and to have fellowship with a holy God. John states his design for his readers in writing these things (v. 1a), recognizes the fact that believers may sin (v. 1b), and sets forth the adequate provision in Christ (vv. 1c-2).

1. The Design for His Readers (v. 1a)

The Apostle's deep pastoral concern for his readers now prompts him to address them directly, "My little children" *(Teknia mou)*. The diminutive "little children" does not imply immaturity on the part of the readers but is rather an expression of endearment on John's part. The term occurs seven times in 1 John; aside from Galatians 4:19, where the reading is uncertain, it occurs elsewhere in the New Testament only in John 13:33. John heard this expression of tender affection from the lips of Jesus, and now, in his old age, it is a favorite term with him. His fatherly heart goes out to his spiritual children as he seeks to aid them and to warn them against sin and the false teachers.

He tells them expressly his design in writing to them: "these things write I unto you, that ye sin not." In 1:4 John uses the plural "we write" to associate himself with the other apostolic witnesses. In the remainder of the epistle John uses the singular to indicate his personal relationship with his readers. Brooke remarks that "these things" *(tauta)* "must refer to the contents of the whole Epistle, already present to the mind of the writer."[1] But as Brown notes, "the purpose clause that follows ('to keep you from sin') is too narrow a goal for the whole Epistle."[2] It is generally accepted that "these things" looks back to what has preceded. He is aware that his rejection of the false views concerning sin might be misinterpreted as a discouragement to personal holiness. If sin is a characteristic of believers and forgiveness is freely available, his readers might be prone to conclude, "Shall we continue in sin, that grace may abound?" (Rom. 6:1). His design in writing was the very opposite, "that ye sin not" *(hina mē hamartēte).* His words do not suggest that his readers are living in sin; the aorist tense indicates that his purpose is to support their resolve not to condone even a single act of sin. What he has just said should make them realize that "sin is so heinous in the sight of God that it may not be indulged in even once."[3] John had no sympathy with the claims of the professional perfectionists; he also refused to concede that any act of sin is consistent with a life of fellowship with God, in whom there is no darkness at all.

2. The Possibility of Committing Sin (v. 1b)

Having set forth as the goal of the Christian life to live above any act of sin, John concedes the ever-present possibility: "and if any man sin" *(kai ean tis harmartē).* The conjunction "and" implies that John also wants to make his readers aware of this sad fact. He was fully aware of the fact of human frailty and the seductive power of sin and Satan. Because the conjunction joins two antithetical clauses, the rendering "but"[4] seems preferable here. The aorist tense again implies an act of sin into which the believer may be carried contrary to the true tenor of his life. Such a fall into sin does not destroy his membership in the family of God, but it disrupts fellowship between the Father and His child. God's holiness demands that it be dealt with. The indefinite "any man" *(tis,* "anyone") makes this an individual matter; the possibility of sinning is not limited to any class or status among believers.

---

[1] A. E. Brooke, *The Johannine Epistles,* International Critical Commentary (New York: Charles Scribner's Sons, 1912), p. 23.

[2] Raymond E. Brown, *The Epistles of John,* The Anchor Bible (Garden City, N.Y.: Doubleday & Co., 1982), p. 215.

[3] Raymond E. Gingrich, *An Outline and Analysis of the First Epistle of John* (Grand Rapids: Zondervan, 1943), p. 55.

[4] The conjunction *(kai)* is here rendered "but" in NEB, RSV, New American Bible, and Jerusalem Bible.

3. The Provision in Jesus Christ (vv. 1c-2)

Whenever the believer may fall into some sin, he is not left to his own poor efforts to effect restoration. The divine provision for restoration and continued fellowship centers in the person and work of Jesus Christ. The believer can appeal to his Advocate in the presence of the Father (v. 1c) and lay claim to His propitiatory sacrifice for sins (v. 2).

a. The personal Advocate with the Father (v. 1c). The divine provision for forgiveness and restoration centers in a unique person: "we have an advocate with the Father, Jesus Christ the righteous." In writing "we have" *(echomen)*, rather than the expected "he has," John makes clear his own need for this Advocate. The present tense plainly affirms that believers actually possess and experience the means of restoration to fellowship in our "advocate with the Father" *(paraklēton echomen pros ton patera)*. The term rendered "advocate" *(paraklēton)*, often transliterated into English as "Paraclete," is a compound noun meaning "one who is *summoned to the side of* another" to aid the one who calls for his services. The nature of the service desired depends upon the individual's need and may take various forms. In the New Testament the term occurs only here and in the Fourth Gospel. The term occurs four times on the lips of Jesus in His Upper Room Discourse (14:16, 26; 15:26, 16:7), always of the Holy Spirit and always rendered "Comforter" in the King James Version.[5] Only here is the term used directly of Jesus Himself; in John 14:16 Jesus implies His own identity as Paraclete by referring to the Holy Spirit as "another Comforter" *(allon paraklēton)*. In the Gospel the Holy Spirit is presented as sent to take the place of Christ in the lives of His disciples, to represent Him and to plead His cause. As the Holy Spirit presents the cause of Christ in our hearts and before the world, here on earth, so Jesus Christ as our heavenly Paraclete presents our cause before the Father.

Whenever a believer falls into sin, we are assured that we have an Advocate "with the Father" *(pros ton patera)*, indicating an intimate personal relationship between Him and the Father. In 1:2b John uses this expression to denote Christ's preincarnational relationship with the Father; here it portrays His postresurrectional relationship with the Father in glory. The fact that we have such an Advocate with the Father assures the effectiveness of His work on our behalf. John explicitly identifies Him as "Jesus Christ the righteous" *(Iēsoun Christon diakon)*. The three terms, as Burdick points out, indicate three characteristics of our Advocate:

---

[5]In its four occurrences in the Fourth Gospel *The Amplified Bible* (Grand Rapids: Zondervan, 1965) amplifies the meaning of the term *paraklētos* as follows: "Comforter (Counselor, Helper, Intercessor, Advocate, Strengthener, Standby)."

The name *Iēsoun* speaks of His humanity by which He is identified with us and thus can function as our representative. *Christon* in 1 John refers not so much to His Messiahship in the Hebrew sense as to His deity, by virtue of which He is in face-to-face fellowship with the Father. *Dikaion* appears in the predicate position and literally means "Jesus Christ being righteous."[6]

The adjective "righteous," without the article, points, not to His identity, but to His character as "a righteous one," conforming to the divine standard in character and deed. As such He never resorts to anything crooked or unworthy to get His client "off the hook" with the Judge. In 1:9 John also uses this adjective to characterize the Father. Whenever we may sin, Christ represents us before the Father as a guilty member of His family.

Christ's work on our behalf as our Advocate may be understood as involving a judicial setting, acting in our behalf as "a defense attorney who takes up the case of his client before a tribunal."[7] Because we have sinned, He counters the charges made against us by Satan, "the accuser of our brethren" (Rev. 12:10). Or the scene may be viewed in the light of the Mosaic ritual, "especially to the intercession of the high priest with the blood of the bullock and the goat on the Day of Atonement."[8] If John's readers had a Gentile background, the former picture would more readily come to their mind since they would be acquainted with the legal usage in connection with the term "advocate." It pictures Him as "one who speaks to the Father in our defense" (NIV). But as Findlay notes, "the case is not that of love pleading with justice–so the Gospel has often been distorted; *justice pleads with love* for our release!"[9]

b. The perfect propitiation for all sins (v. 2). The opening "and" *(kai)* in verse 2 marks the connection between Christ's present activity as our Advocate and His propitiatory self-sacrifice as its basis: "and he is the propitiation for our sins" *(kai autos hilasmos estin peri tōn hamartiōn hēmōn)*. The emphatic personal pronoun "Himself" *(autos)*, not expressed in the King James rendering, underlines the identity of the Advocate with "the propitiation for our sins." Since John has just described Jesus Christ as our personal Advocate, one might have expected him to speak of Him as the "propitiator" *(hilastēr)*. Then His work would have been equated with that of the high priest on the Day of Atonement when he sprinkled sacrificial

---

[6]Donald W. Burdick, *The Letters of John the Apostle* (Chicago: Moody Press, 1985), p. 131.

[7]Zane C. Hodges, "1 John," in *The Bible Knowledge Commentary, New Testament* (Wheaton, Ill,: Victor Books, 1983), p. 887.

[8]Alfred Plummer, *The Epistles of S. John,* Cambridge Bible for Schools and Colleges (1883; reprint ed., London: Cambridge University Press, 1938), p. 87.

[9]George G. Findlay, *Fellowship in the Life Eternal, An Exposition of the Epistles of St John* (1909; reprint ed., Grand Rapids: Eerdmans, 1955), p. 11. Italics in original.

blood on the mercy seat to cover the sins of the people so that God could again deal with them in mercy. But that would have been to miss the heart of the Christian gospel. Unlike the Old Testament high priests, Jesus Christ is Himself the propitiation for human sin. John's statement declares that Jesus is the sacrificial victim as well as the officiating high priest. The present tense, "is" *(estin),* declares that His sacrifice possesses a continuing quality; He was, and is, and will continue to be, the atoning sacrifice for our sins.

In turning to present the basis for Christ's effective advocacy on our behalf, the thought passes from the heavenly court to that of the heavenly temple. The noun rendered "propitiation" *(hilasmos),* found elsewhere in the New Testament only in 1 John 4:10, is a sacrificial term and denotes the means whereby sins are covered or remitted and the offense removed. In pagan usage this noun and the cognate verb *(hilaskesthai)* were used of an offering made to their capricious gods to propitiate their wrath and so regain their favor. But Scripture presents God Himself as taking the initiative in sending His Son as the propitiation for our sins (4:10). The cause of the estrangement between God and man lay in man, not God. God did not cease to love mankind when the fall occurred, but man's initial act of rebellion against the command and authority of God resulted in an inevitable estrangement between a holy God and sinful humanity. In His holiness and sovereignty, God could not simply ignore man's sin and receive sinful human beings into fellowship with Himself, as though no estrangement had taken place. His nature as light without any admixture of darkness (1:5) demanded that sin must be punished and removed. Human sinfulness as a fact of life produced an estrangement that God in His holiness could not ignore; but His love prompted Him to provide the remedy. When He sent the incarnate Christ to earth and on the cross made "Him who knew no sin *to be* sin on our behalf" (2 Cor. 5:21 NASB), God achieved the true and lasting solution to the sin problem. Christ's death as "the propitiation for our sins" paid the penalty for human sins and enables God to "be just and the justifier of the one who has faith in Jesus" (Rom. 3:26 NASB). Christ's death as the "propitiation for our sins" involves an element of propitiation as well as expiation. In paying the full penalty for human sin through His death, Christ enabled God to assume a new attitude in dealing with sinful human beings because judgment upon sin had been carried out. His death also effected expiation for sin because the just penalty had been paid in behalf of the sinner, who can now be forgiven and restored as the work of Christ's death on his behalf is appropriated by faith. For the instructed Christian, the work of Christ on the cross is not merely accepted doctrine; he maintains his fellowship with God through his continual appropriation of the reality thereof.

The added words "and not for ours only, but also for *the sins of* the whole world" point out the true scope of Christ's atoning sacrifice. "The propitiation is as wide as the sin.''[10] The negative words ''and not for ours only'' *(ou peri tōn hēmeterōn)* acknowledge that, as believers, we find His sacrifice efficacious for our own sins, but we can never assume that its scope is so limited. The adversative ''but,'' ''but also for *the sins of* the whole world'' *(alla kai peri holou tou kosmou),* marks the contrasted scope between *our* sins and those of *the whole world,* the people of this world, all guilty of sins. The thrice repeated preposition *peri* (''for'') indicates that the intended scope of Christ's atoning work gathered around, or was concerned with, not merely our sins as believers but also those of the whole world. The expression offers no valid basis for universalism, but it declares that ''no one is, by Divine pre-determination, excluded from the scope of God's mercy; the efficacy of the propitiation, however, is made actual for those who believe.''[11] It reminds believers that they are not the exclusive objects of God's redemptive concern. ''The world'' *(tou kosmou),* another favorite term with John, here denotes the world of mankind in its alienation from God, lost in sin. But Christ's atoning work has made it possible for any one in the world to be saved, but each sinner must personally accept Christ as his Redeemer (cf. 1 Tim. 4:10.) ''Men may–yea, and do–reject the propitiation when they reject the Propitiator–the Lord Jesus Christ.''[12]

---

[10]John Albert Bengel, *New Testament Word Studies,* trans. Charlton T. Lewis and Marvin R. Vincent (1864; reprint ed., Grand Rapids: Kregel, 1971), 2:786.

[11]W. E. Vine, *An Expository Dictionary of New Testament Words with Their Precise Meanings for English Readers* (London: Oliphants, 1939), 4:32.

[12]Gingrich, p. 60.

7

Assurance Through the Test of Fellowship (Part 4)

D. The Signs of Fellowship Maintained (2:3-17)

2:3 And hereby we do know that we know him, if we keep his commandments.

4 He that saith, I know him, and keepeth not his commandments, is a liar, and the truth is not in him.

5 But whoso keepeth his word, in him verily is the love of God perfected: hereby know we that we are in him.

6 He that saith he abideth in him ought himself also so to walk, even as he walked.

7 Brethren, I write no new commandment unto you, but an old commandment which ye had from the beginning. The old commandment is the word which ye have heard from the beginning.

8 Again, a new commandment I write unto you, which thing is true in him and in you: because the darkness is past, and the true light now shineth.

9 He that saith he is in the light, and hateth his brother, is in darkness even until now.

10 He that loveth his brother abideth in the light, and there is none occasion of stumbling in him.

11 But he that hateth his brother is in darkness, and walketh in darkness, and knoweth not whither he goeth, because that darkness hath blinded his eyes.

12 I write unto you, little children, because your sins are forgiven you for his name's sake.

13 I write unto you, fathers, because ye have known him *that* is from the beginning. I write unto you, young men, because ye have overcome the wicked one. I write unto you, little children, because ye have known the Father.

14 I have written unto you, fathers, because ye have known him *that is* from the beginning. I have written unto you, young men, because ye are

strong, and the word of God abideth in you, and ye have overcome the wicked one.

15 Love not the world, neither the things *that are* in the world. If any man love the world, the love of the Father is not in him.

16 For all that *is* in the world, the lust of the flesh and the lust of the eyes, and the pride of life, is not of the Father, but is of the world.

17 And the world passeth away, and the lust thereof: but he that doeth the will of God abideth for ever.

The fact that God is light without any trace of darkness in His nature (1:5) is fundamental to any true understanding of the nature of the Christian life. In view of God's nature, in 1:6-10 John presents three denials that hinder true fellowship with God, and in 2:1-2 he declares the divine provision for maintaining fellowship.

In 2:3-17 John points out four signs that assure that fellowship with God is being maintained. In verses 3-6 he sets forth two closely related signs: the sign of obedience (vv. 3-5a) and the sign of imitation (vv. 5b-6). He presents two further signs in greater detail: the sign of love (vv. 7-11) and the sign of separation from the world (vv. 12-17)–the positive and negative manifestations of the same relationship.

1. The Sign of Obedience (vv. 3-5a)

The opening "and" of verse 3 links these verses with verses 1-2; it introduces the signs that indicate that the divine provision for maintaining fellowship operates in daily life. Verse 3 states the assurance derived from the practice of obedience; verse 4 states the conclusion that must be drawn from the absence of obedience; verse 5a concludes the discussion with a declaration concerning the assured result of obedience.

a. The assurance from obedience (v. 3). In saying "hereby we do know that we know him" *(en toutō ginōskomen hoti egnōkamen auton)* John equates "knowing" God with the fact of having fellowship with Him. He first states the contents of this assuring Christian knowledge and then indicates its ethical basis. The opening words "and hereby" *(en toutō)* look forward and receive appositional unfolding in the following "if" clause. The very formulation of the sentence implies John's conviction that one can never divorce true spiritual knowledge of God from obedience to His revealed will.

Here we have the first of twenty-five occurrences of the verb "to know" *(ginōskō)* in 1 John. It denotes a personal knowledge gained through observation, experience, and instruction.[1] Here the double use of the verb, "we do know that we know Him" *(ginōskomen hoti egnōkamen auton),* denotes assured knowledge; the present tense followed by the perfect tense declares that we have the continuing realization that we have entered into an abiding knowledge of Him. The pronoun "him" makes clear that the knowledge in view is not an abstract conception but is essentially the knowledge of a person. It is not certain whether "him" refers to God the Father or to Jesus Christ, and scholarly views differ.[2] Burdick concludes from the context that "John must be referring to knowing *Christ* and obeying His commands,"[3] but Brown insists that "the problem that the author is dealing with is how to know the God who is light, not how to know Christ."[4] In reality the believer knows both, since the Father has revealed Himself through His Son. It seems clear that John's emphasis upon the Christian's certain knowledge of God is meant to assure his readers of the true nature of their knowledge of God in contrast to the Gnostic claims to a mystic knowledge of God which had enlightened them apart from any moral demands upon their daily conduct.

The "if" clause, "if we keep his commandments" *(ean tas entolas autou tērōmen),* declares the ground for our assurance. The conditional statement again recalls that this may not be true of some who loudly claim to have an abiding knowledge of God. The conditional formulation challenges each one to examine himself to discover whether he fulfills the condition. The plural "his commandments" points to the various commands, or specific precepts, wherein God has made known His will. The present-tense verb "keep" *(tērōmen)* depicts the keeping of God's commandments as the characteristic practice of the individual. The verb denotes a watchful and sympathetic concern to obey that which has been commanded. The one who has been brought into a saving relationship with God finds within himself a growing love for and desire to obey His commands. As Plummer points out, "There is only one way of proving to ourselves that we know

---

[1] John also uses the kindred verb *oida* "to know" sixteen times in this epistle. In Classical Greek *oida* denoted "knowledge grasped directly or intuitively by the mind, whereas *ginōskō* referred to knowledge gained mediately by experience or instruction." Donald W. Burdick, *The Letters of John the Apostle* (Chicago: Moody Press, 1985), p. 127. While John thought of Christian knowledge as essentially experiential, rather than merely intuitive, occasionally the two verbs seem to be used interchangeably without any sharp distinction. Brown notes that "the theme of knowing God or Christ (under various titles) occurs in 1 John 11 times, always with *ginōskein* (2:3, 4, 13; 3:1, 6; 4:6, 7, 8; 5:20)." Raymond E. Brown, *The Epistles of John,* The Anchor Bible (Garden City, N.Y.: Doubleday & Co., 1982), p. 250.

[2] See the list of scholars on both sides of the problem in Brown, p. 249.

[3] Burdick, p. 134. Italics in original.

[4] Brown, p. 249.

God, and that is by loving obedience to His will."[5] Such a keeping of God's command is not legalism but a voluntary internalization of His commands as a pattern for practical conduct.

b. The verdict from the absence of obedience (v. 4). The author now drives home the importance of such obedience by the negative restatement: "He that saith, I know him, and keepeth not his commandments, is a liar, and the truth is not in him." The hypothetical "if" construction is now replaced by the articular participle *(ho legōn).* The "if" construction places the emphasis upon the hypothetical claim being advanced; this construction centers the attention on the individual advancing the indicated claim. The claim he advances is given in his very words, "I know him" *(hoti[6] egnōka auton,* "I have come to know him"), portraying him as claiming an abiding personal acquaintance with God. But a second participle governed by the preceding article presents a further portrayal of this individual, "and keepeth not his commandments" *(kai tas entolas autou mē tērōrn,* more literally, "and his commandments is not keeping"). The order clearly indicates his persistent failure to keep God's commands. The two present-tense participles under one article *(ho legōn . . . mē tēron)* mark the sharp contradiction between his profession and his daily life; his conduct invalidates his claim. For John the knowledge of God can never be merely mental or speculative; it must be practical and pervade all of life.

John's evaluation of the individual is twofold. Positively, such a person "is a liar" *(pseustēs estin,* "a liar he is"), making a claim which deep within he knows is false; his character is bad. Negatively, "the truth is not in him" *(en toutō hē alētheia ouk estin,* "in this one the truth not is"). The demonstrative "this one" *(toutō)* points back to the individual just described, "the one who dares to make such a claim while his life is marked by disobedience.'"[7] "The truth," setting forth the abiding connection between true faith and conduct, has not gained a hold in his inner being. (Cf. 1:10.)

c. The result of personal obedience (v. 5a). With "but" *(de)* John sets forth the opposite picture. He "swings to the opposite pole, but as always with each swing he adds a little more to what he is saying":[8] "but whoso keepeth his word, in him verily is the love of God perfected." The construction now employed, "whoso keepeth His word" *(hos d' an tērē autou ton logon,* very literally, "but he who if he may be keeping His word"), is

---

[5]Alfred A. Plummer, *The Epistle of S. John,* Cambridge Bible for Schools and Colleges (1883; reprint ed., London: Cambridge University Press, 1938), p. 90.

[6]The *hoti* here is recitative, the equivalent of our quotation marks.

[7]Burdick, p. 136.

[8]David Jackman, *The Message of John's Letters,* The Bible Speaks Today (Downers Grove, Ill.: Inter-Varsity Press, 1988), p. 49.

impersonal and general; it includes all genuine believers. Such an individual is characterized by his practice, "keepeth his word." The position of the pronoun "his" *(autou)* before the articular noun "the word" marks the word being kept as "his." The singular "his word" seems to be wider than "His commandments" in denoting the sum total of God's revealed will, but Brown holds that the term here simply "means God's ethical demands, i.e., His commandments."[9] Clearly John's varied terms, "his commandments" (vv. 3-4), "the truth" (v. 4), and "his word" are closely related expressions. The individual in view is marked by his plain, everyday obedience to God's known will.

The sure conclusion concerning such a one is "in him verily is the love of God perfected" *(alēthōs en toutō hē agapē tou theou teteleiōtai)*. The adverb "verily" *(alēthōs)*, placed emphatically forward, describes his condition as corresponding to "truth," to reality. Smalley suggests that John possibly uses the adverb "at this point to distinguish sharply a false claim to the knowledge of God (such as he discovered in v. 4) from its positive counterpart."[10] The designation "in him" *(en toutō,* literally, "in this one") looks back to the kind of individual who "keepeth his word." In such an individual it is true that "the love of God" is "perfected" *(hē agapē tou theou teteleiōtai)*. The noun "the love" is the first of eighteen occurrences of this term in this epistle and designates an important concept for John. The expression "the love of God" is open to several different interpretations, depending upon how the genitive "of God" *(tou theou)* is understood. (1) One widely held view accepts the genitive as *objective,* "man's love for God."[11] The RSV reflects this view by rendering the phrase "in him truly love for God is perfected." In support of this view Plummer insists that "this is the common usage in the Epistle (ii. 15, iii. 17, iv. 12, v. 3)," and asserts that only in 4:9 is this not the meaning, where the context makes clear that the genitive is subjective.[12] It is also true that one can most easily think of human love for God as being perfectible. (2) A second view is that the genitive is *subjective,* denoting God's love for human beings. The NIV represents this view in its rendering, "God's love is truly made complete in him." In support of this view Kistemaker points to the immediate context: "Compare the parallel in verses 4 and 5–'[God's] truth is not in him' (v. 4) and 'God's love is in him.' Both truth and love originate in God but not in

[9]Brown, p. 254.

[10]Stephen S. Smalley, *1, 2, 3 John,* World Biblical Commentary (Waco, Texas: Word Books, 1984), p. 48.

[11]See Brown for a list of scholars holding to different views, pp. 256-57.

[12]Plummer, p. 91.

man.''[13] This is the only possible meaning in 4:9 and may well be the meaning here. (3) A third view is that the genitive is qualitative, denoting that the love has a divine quality. This seems to be the intended meaning in the NEB rendering, ''The divine love has indeed come to its perfection.'' All three views make some sense here, but we agree that the second is the most probable. Lenski remarks, ''Only in 5:3 does the context require the sense our love for God; in all the other passages (notably 4:12) God's love for us is clearly referred to.''[14] This view is fully consistent with the meaning of the verb ''has been perfected'' (ASV) *(teteleiōtai)*, the perfect passive presenting God's love as having been brought to its goal objectively. The verb basically means ''to bring to an end, to bring to its goal.'' The passive voice indicates that the believer's characteristic obedience to God's will has brought God's love to its initial goal for him. The perfect tense does not imply a resultant static relationship but rather that God's love, having attained its intended purpose within the believer, continually vitalizes the experience of fellowship in his life.

2. The Sign of Imitation (vv. 5b-6)

The last statement in verse 5, ''hereby know we that we are in him,'' may be taken with what precedes or follows. Views are divided.[15] If these words relate to what precedes, John concludes his discussion of the sign of obedience, and verse 6 is in effect a restatement of that sign. If taken with verse 6 the words introduce a second but closely related sign offering assurance that fellowship is being maintained. The punctuation in the KJV connects these words with what precedes; our modern versions (RV, ASV, NIV, NEB, RSV, Jerusalem Bible) generally connect them with what follows. In favor of the forward look of ''hereby'' *(en toutō,* ''in this thing'') is its parallel usage in verse 3. Viewed as a second sign, John now points to an objective standard by which the believer may measure his own conduct. In verse 5b John states the assurance of the believer and in verse 6 sets forth the resultant obligation.

a. The assurance of the believer (v. 5b). The words ''hereby know we that we are in him'' *(en toutō ginōskomen hoti en autō esmen)* give a new expression to the believer's assurance. The expressed assurance now is not that ''we have come to know Him'' (v. 3 NASB) but that ''we are in him'' *(en autō esmen).* To be ''in him'' expresses the reality of an intimate union

---

[13]Simon J. Kistemaker, *Exposition of the Epistle of James and the Epistles of John,* New Testament Commentary (Grand Rapids: Baker, 1986), p. 257.

[14]R.C.H. Lenski, *The Interpretation of the Epistles of St. Peter, St. John and St. Jude* (Columbus, Ohio: Wartburg Press, 1945), p. 408.

[15]See Brown, p. 258, for a list of scholars in support of either view.

with Him; He is the sphere of being that shapes the life and conduct of the one united to Him. The phrase declares one of the central realities of the Christian life. As Vine notes, "The condition of being 'in Him' is not a matter of absorption into Deity, as Pantheism teaches, but of spiritual relationship and unity of life, which involves the removal of the alienation of man in his unregenerate state before God, and the enjoyment of fellowship with God and oneness with Him in His will and purpose."[16] It is not certain whether John's reference to being "in Him" refers to Jesus Christ or to the Father. Stott accepts the former meaning and compares the expression to Paul's characteristic description of the Christian as being "in Christ."[17] But others, such as Marshall[18] and Brown,[19] understand John to mean the Father. Bennett, indeed, suggests that the phrase was "perhaps used with intentional ambiguity, so that it may be understood either of God or Christ."[20] Since the believer's relationship with God is mediated through the incarnate Son, John often does not stop to mark a sharp distinction. But in view of virtually the same expression in verse 6a, it seems best to take "Him" as referring to the Father.

b. The resultant obligation of the believer (v. 6). The words "he that saith he abideth in Him" *(ho legōn en autō menein)* picture the individual believer giving expression to his spiritual relationship with God. The verb "abide" *(menō)*, a characteristic Johannine term occurring twenty-four times in this epistle, points to the fundamental relationship of the Christian life. The present tense, "to abide" *(menein)*, points to the ongoing fellowship with God as the resultant experience of being "in Him." The verb presents the believer as abiding or dwelling "in Him" as the vital sphere of his life and being. It denotes "not a static condition but an active relation that endures."[21]

John notes that, in keeping with his open declaration, he "ought himself also so to walk, even as he walked" *(opheilei katōs ekeinos periepatēsen autos houtōs peripatein,* very literally, "he ought even as that one walked himself thusly to be walking"). The use of "ought" rather than "must" *(dei)* makes it clear that the compelling power for such conduct is not an external compulsion but an abiding inner consciousness that "he who de-

[16]W. E. Vine, *The Epistles of John, Light, Love, Life* (Grand Rapids: Zondervan, n.d.), p. 25.

[17]J.R.W. Stott, *The Epistles of John,* Tyndale New Testament Commentaries (Grand Rapids: Eerdmans, 1964), p. 91.

[18]I. Howard Marshall, *The Epistles of John,* New International Commentary on the New Testament (Grand Rapids: 1978), p. 127.

[19]Brown, p. 259.

[20]W. H. Bennett, *The General Epistles, James, Peter, John, and Jude,* The Century Bible (London: Blackwood, Le Bas & Co., n.d.), p. 295.

[21]Kistemaker, p. 258.

clares his position is morally bound to act up to the declaration which he has made."[22]

The pattern set before him is "even as that one walked" (literal trans.). The adverb "even as" *(kathōs)*, rather than "as" *(hōs)*, calls for an imitation not merely in broad outline but a close duplication of the way "he" *(ekeinos, more literally, "that one")* walked. John does not give the name of "that one," but the reference is clearly to the earthly life of Jesus. This is a favorite designation for Jesus used by John in this epistle (2:6; 3:3, 5, 7, 16; 4:17). "So paramount was the Lord in John's thought," Burdick remarks, "that He could be designated by the remote demonstrative pronoun and it would be perfectly clear whom the apostle had in mind."[23] The aorist tense, "he walked" *(periepatēsen)*, summarily presents, like a snapshot, the completed earthly life of Jesus as the pattern.

With this pattern of life before him, the believer is obligated "to walk, even as he walked" *(kai autos houtōs peripatein,* more literally, "also himself thusly to be walking"). The present infinitive *(peripatein)* marks the continuing active life of the believer as long as he is still here on earth. The adverb "even as" *(houtōs)* again points to the close conformity of the pattern before him. In thus appealing to the sign of imitating Jesus as being an assuring evidence of one's being a true believer, John apparently recalls the words of Jesus to His disciples, "I gave you an example that you also should do as I did to you" (John 13:15 NASB). This is one of several instances in the epistles in which the earthly life of Jesus is used as an appeal to believers to motivate moral Christian conduct (1 Cor. 11:1; Eph. 5:2; Phil. 2:5; 1 Pet. 1:21; 1 John 3:16). In thus insisting that the believer's union with Christ involves the obligation of a consistent moral conduct, John delivers a crucial blow against the Gnostics who tried to divorce their claimed spiritual enlightenment from their daily moral manner of life.

3. The Sign of Love (vv. 7-11)

In these verses John points to the practice of love as a third assuring sign that one is maintaining fellowship with God. He first characterizes this commandment of love (vv. 7-8) and then applies the commandment to two classes of individuals (vv. 9-11).

a. The characterization of the commandment (vv. 7-8). The paragraph begins with a term of direct address. The KJV here uses "brethren" *(adel-*

---

[22]Plummer, p. 91.

[23]Burdick, pp. 139-40.

phoi), but its use here presents a textual problem.[24] It is the reading of the Textus Receptus, but its manuscript support here is late. Elsewhere in this epistle it occurs as a term of address only in 3:13. The alternative reading, "beloved" *(agapētoi),* has strong textual support and textual editors accept it as the more probable reading here. This term is the first of six occurrences of this affectionate address in this epistle (2:7; 3:2, 21; 4:1, 7, 11). The term characterizes them as the beloved people of God but also asserts John's own love for them. In writing to them John is motivated by a deep, persistent love which desires the true welfare of his readers. As Smith remarks, "About to enjoin love, he begins by loving."[25]

1) *The commandment of love as old* (v. 7). In declaring "I write no new commandment unto you, but an old commandment," John does not stop to indicate the contents of this command. In contrast to "his commandments" in verses 3-4, the singular now implies that some specific command is in view. Although the obligation in verse 6 to imitate the example of Christ may be the command referred to, the context suggests that John is looking to the commandment of love elaborated in verses 9-11.

In characterizing the commandment in view John declares, negatively, "I write no new commandment unto you" *(ouk entolēn kainēn graphō humin,* "not a commandment new I am writing to you"). The position of the negative and the direct object before the verb stresses the negation. What he is writing to them is "not a new commandment," not something "new" *(kainēn)* in kind or quality. He emphatically denies that he is formulating some further obligation which was not inherent in the original apostolic proclamation. This negation is confirmed by the positive fact that he is referring to "an old commandment which ye had from the beginning" *(all' entolēn palaian hēn eichete ap' archēs).* It is "old" *(plaian)* in the sense of being of long duration, old as contrasted to recent. Further, it is a commandment "which ye had" *(hēn eichete)* as a continuing possession through the years, in fact, "from the beginning" *(ap' archēs).* One must always understand this expression in the light of the context. It cannot refer to the beginning of the human race in the sense that brother-love is an implanted human instinct. Neither can it refer to the beginning of the Old Testament law with its command, "thou shalt love thy neighbor as thyself" (Lev.

---

[24]The manuscript evidence is divided between "brethren" *(adelphoi)* and "beloved" *(agapētoi).* The latter reading is strongly supported by Aleph, A, B, C, P, Vg, and the Syrian Coptic, and Armenian versions. The former, the Textus Receptus, follows K, L, and most minuscules. Brown, p. 263, suggests that the reading "brethren" "is a scribal correction under the influence of lectionaries where 'brethren' was used to introduce pericopes from the NT writings attributed to apostles."

[25]David Smith, "The Epistles of St. John," in *The Expositor's Greek Testament* ([1897]; reprint ed., Grand Rapids: Eerdmans, n.d.), 5:175.

19:18). Conceivably John means the beginning of Christ's ministry when He gave His love-command to His disciples (John 13:35; 15:12). If this is the case, the reference would reach back some sixty years, within the lifetime of at least of some of John's readers. John's use of the imperfect tense *(eichete)* supports the view that he is thinking of the initiation of his readers into the experience of love when they first heard and accepted the gospel preached to them. John's reason for stressing that this is not a new commandment seems to be to heighten the contrast of his message with the "newer" teaching of the false teachers which placed knowledge above love.

The added words "the old commandment is the word which ye have heard" explicitly connects this old commandment with their past Christian experience. The wording now used, "the old commandment" *(hē entolē hē palaia,* "the commandment, the old one"), makes clear that the reference is to the commandment just referred to. It is identified with "the word" *(ho logos),* the apostolic message as first proclaimed to them, which embodies this commandment of love. The aorist-tense verb "ye have heard" *(ēkousate)* points back to the time they first heard this message. Their experience confirmed that the commandment in view is not something new and extraneous to their Christian faith.

The recurrence of the words "from the beginning" follows the reading of the Textus Receptus. The repeated phrase does not occur in the older texts, but the thought is latent in the added assertion that they heard this old commandment; since they "had" it from the beginning, it is obvious that they also "heard" it from the beginning. Textual evidence suggests that the phrase here is a scribal addition to bring out this latent thought.[26]

2) *The commandment of love as new* (v. 8). John's further statement, "Again, a new commandment I write unto you" *(palin entolēn kainēn graphō humin),* recognizes paradoxically that, looked at in another way, this commandment of love is indeed new. The opening adverb *(palin)* does not introduce a new subject but continues the matter of this love-command viewed from a different perspective. Unlike the novel views of the Gnostics, this commandment is not a recent innovation; yet it is qualitatively new as experienced in Christ. The double feature of this command as both old and new assures those who oppose any innovation in connection with their Christian faith and also satisfies those who yearn for something fresh and invigorating.

The words "which thing is true in Him and in you" *(ho estin alēthes en autō kai en humin)* verify this newness. The neuter pronoun "which thing" cannot relate directly to "commandment" *(entolē),* which is a feminine noun, but alludes rather to the newness or new quality of the law of

---

[26]For the textual evidence see Nestle-Aland, *Novum Testamentum Graece,* 26th ed. (Stuttgart: Deutsche Biblestiftung, 1979).

love. This newness "is true" *(estin alēthes)*, exists as a factual reality, "in him and in you" *(en autō kai en humin)*. In the incarnate Christ this new quality of love manifested itself in His life and teaching and supremely in His vicarious death. And through the indwelling Holy Spirit this newness is true also "in you," John's readers, true in their experience as being "in Christ." John's use of "in you" *(en humin)* rather than "in us" *(en hēmin)*[27] "commends the readers for conduct that is truly characterized by this new command to love one another."[28] But, as Plummer notes, John's repeated use of "in" *(en)* implies that "it is true in the case of Christ in a different sense from that in which it is true in the case of Christians."[29]

The explanatory comment, "because the darkness is past, and the true light now shineth," provides the evidence that this new commandment of love is already operative in the lives of true believers. Clearly John's words relate not to Christ but to believers "because there is no sense in which the darkness is passing away in Christ. Such a departure of darkness can only be true in redeemed men."[30] For John, as already made clear in 1:5, "the darkness" *(hē skotia)* and "the light" *(to phōs)* are not merely two impersonal realms; the two terms are figurative designations for the moral realm of spiritual darkness and light which stand in active conflict with each other and cannot rightly be intermingled. "The darkness" denotes the realm of moral evil under the domination of Satan and his hosts whereas "the light" denotes the realm of God and all that relates to Him. It is amid this darkness that the illuminating love of God is uniquely revealed.

In saying "because the darkness is past" *(hoti hē skotia paragetai)* John makes clear that the impact of the light upon the darkness is already being felt. The present tense *(paragetai)* more literally pictures the "passing away" of the darkness as already in progress.[31] The darkness is not yet totally gone, as the KJV rendering might suggest; nor is its passing away wholly a matter of the future, to be accomplished at Christ's return. God's redeeming love has already initiated the process of eliminating moral darkness, but the process will be fully consummated only when Christ the redeemer personally returns to earth to banish the darkness. The verb *(paragetai)* may be either middle or passive in form. Interpreters generally regard it as being in the passive voice, the form thus stressing the part that the light

---

[27]The reading "in us" *(en hēmin)* is found in a few manuscripts, expressing a scribal desire to enlarge the scope of the statement. For the textual evidence see Nestle-Aland, *Novum Testamentum Graece*, 26th ed.

[28]Kistemaker, p. 261.

[29]Plummer, p. 93.

[30]Burdick, p. 143.

[31]The KJV rendering, "is past," is inaccurate; it would imply the use of the perfect tense here.

plays in pushing back the darkness; the darkness must recede in the presence of the light. But Burdick holds that the verb is in the middle voice and "stresses the part the subject of the verb plays in the action of passing away. The darkness contains within itself the seeds of its own dissolution, and thus is of itself passing away."[32]

The passing away of the darkness is explained by the fact that "the true light now shineth" *(to phōs to alēthinon ēdē phainei)*. The repeated article with the adjective, "the light, the true," stresses the nature of the light. The adjective "true" *(alēthinon)* declares the genuine character of this light in contrast to the spurious "light" which the false teachers offer. Any professed "gospel" which distorts or counterfeits the true apostolic teaching only prolongs the operation of the darkness. The present-tense verb "now shineth" *(phainei)* pictures this light as continually dispensing illumination out of its own brightness. The adverb "now" *(ēdē)* implies that this light, which will ultimately banish all darkness from the earth, is now offering spiritual enlightenment to all who will accept Christ as the personal embodiment of that light. But it is possible now for any individual to refuse that light and deliberately remain in the realm of spiritual darkness.

b. The application of the commandment (vv. 9-11). In verses 9-11 John applies the test of this enlightening love to professed believers. His three present-tense articular participles present a triad of individuals, each marked by a characteristic activity. In keeping with the dual picture of darkness and light, these three individuals belong to two realms. The one individual who obeys the commandment of love is encased between two instances of individuals who fail to meet the test. But as Plummer notes, this triple formulation, characteristic of John, "is no weak tautology or barren see-saw. The emphasis grows and is marked by the increase in the predicates."[33]

1) *The profession without love* (v. 9). The individual pictured in this verse displays a conflict between his claim and his conduct. Two present-tense participles governed by one article depict an individual marked by two antithetical activities: "He that saith he is in the light, and hateth his brother" *(ho legōn en tō phōti einai kai ton adelphon autou misōn,* literally, "the one saying in the light to be and the brother of him hating"). He characteristically maintains that he "is in the light" and that the sphere of "the light" is the sphere of his life and being; he claims to have fellowship with the God who is light (1:5). "And" *(kai)* adds the contradictory practice: literally, "and the brother of him hating." The word order stresses the flagrant contradiction between his profession and his practice. "His brother," placed next to his claim to be in the light, is best understood as denoting a fellow Christian

---

[32]Burdick, p. 144.

[33]Plummer, p. 94.

with whom he should naturally have a close relationship. Brown rejects the astonishing claim of Bultmann that " 'brother' means . . . not especially the Christian comrade in faith, but one's fellowman, the 'neighbor',"[34] and notes that this is the first of sixteen occurrences in the Johannine Epistles "for spiritual relatives (presumably females as well as male)."[35] If he fails to show love within the family circle, one cannot expect him to show love in the broader relationships of life. This assertion does not imply that he is at liberty to hate the non-Christian; the non-Christian simply is not in view in John's stated test. The singular noun "brother" is generic, mentioned as a representative of the Christian brotherhood. Kysar asserts, "That the term is a masculine expression reflects only the predominance of the patriarchal culture of the first century world; its meaning embraces those of both sexes."[36] The present-tense participle "hating" *(misōn)* stands emphatically at the end of the dual description of this individual and reveals that hatred is his characteristic attitude; he is guilty not merely of an occasional flash of hatred but persistently displays a hateful attitude. Such an attitude of ill-will and active malice is no trifling matter; it can have no part in a genuine Christian relationship with other members of the Christian family circle.

The test reveals that such an individual "is in darkness even until now" *(en tē skotia estin heōs arti,* "in the darkness is until now"). His persistent practice nullifies his vaunted claim. He is still in the realm of "the darkness," having never experienced the transformation which conveys the true believer from the realm of darkness into the realm of "the light." (Cf. Col. 1:13.) "Until now" stresses his present condition but implies that he need not stay there. Kistemaker suggests that John's "until now" "tactfully leaves the door open so that [he] may repent and come to the light."[37]

2) *The individual who loves* (v. 10). The individual now portrayed, "He that loveth his brother" *(ho agapōn ton adelophon auton),* is the very opposite of the one in verse 9. There is no neutral ground between the two. No reference is made to his claim to love. It is assumed that he gives testimony to his faith as appropriate, but his practice speaks for itself without any loud profession. The present participle denotes that his love is no occasional, sporadic matter but a continual, habitual practice. This term for "love" *(agapaō)* denotes that it is "not so much a manifestation of the emotions as it is a manifestation of the will."[38] It is an intelligent and

---

[34]Brown, p. 270.

[35]*Ibid.,* p. 269.

[36]Robert Kysar, *I, II, III John,* Augsburg Commentary on the New Testament (Minneapolis: Augsburg, 1986), pp. 49f.

[37]Kistemaker, p. 263.

[38]J. Dwight Pentecost, *The Joy of Fellowship* (Grand Rapids, Zondervan, 1977), p. 43.

purposeful love that seeks to promote the highest good for the one loved, even at the expense of self. Such a love is not natural to unregenerate human nature but is the result of the love of God having been poured out in the believer's heart through the indwelling Holy Spirit (Rom. 5:5).

The individual's practice of such God-given love reveals two facts concerning him. Positively, it reveals that he "abideth in the light" *(en tō phōti menei),* that he lives in, is spiritually at home in, the sphere of "the light," the sphere associated with the presence and power of God. His practice reveals that he has joined the brotherhood of those who live in "the light." "And" *(kai)* adds a further negative reality concerning him, "and there is none occasion of stumbling in him"*(kai skadalon en autō ouk estin).* Interpreters understand the wording of this negative advantage in various ways. Since the pronoun *autō* may be either neuter or masculine, the statement may be rendered "and in it there is no cause for stumbling" (RSV), that is, the light in which he lives and moves offers nothing that causes stumbling. Smalley insists that the neuter "it" "fits the context, and is supported both by the content of v. 11 and by the parallel thought expressed in John 11:9 ('a man who walks by day will not stumble, for he sees by this world's light')."[39] This view makes good sense. Then John insists that "the light," unlike "the darkness," has no adverse or destructive impact upon the one living in it. But we agree with those who accept that the pronoun here is personal. In these verses John's attention centers on the individual rather than on the light.

The intended force of the noun rendered "occasion of stumbling" *(skandalon)* is not wholly clear. In classical Greek the term denoted the trigger stick that released a deadly trap, and the term was accordingly used of a deadly entrapment. Lenski insists that "when this word is used metaphorically it means bringing spiritual death."[40] But the usage of the term in the Septuagint indicates that it commonly came to be used to denote a stumbling block. This clearly seems to be the import of the term here, namely, something that causes stumbling or gives offense.

Views differ as to who is made to stumble. Does the individual cause others to stumble, or is the stumbling block in his own way? In favor of the former is the fact that in the New Testament the term usually denotes an offense to others (Matt. 16:23; 18:7; Rom. 14:13; 16:17; I Cor. 1:23; Gal. 5:11; Rev. 2:14). Thus Wilder comments, "Such a one is not the occasion of any offence to others as are the troublemakers who spread confusion in the church."[41] And Vine remarks, "Love is the best safeguard against the

---

[39]Smalley, p. 62.

[40]Lenski, p. 415.

[41]Amos N. Wilder and Paul W. Hoon, "The First, Second, and Third Epistles of John," in *The Interpreter's Bible* (New York: Abingdon Press, 1957), 12:234.

woes pronounced by our Lord upon those who cause others to stumble."[42]
But others point to the parallel with verse 11 as favoring the second view.
Plummer notes that there is nothing in verse 11 that "suggests the notion that
the brother-hater leads *others* astray: it is his own dark condition that is con-
templated." He further points to "the very close parallel in John xi. 9, 10,"
and cites Psalm 119:165, " 'Great peace have they which love Thy law: and
nothing shall offend them': i.e., there is no stumbling-block before them."[43]
The second view seems preferable here; yet Smalley remarks, "Perhaps, in
typically Johannine style, both meanings are involved in this passage."[44]

3) *The individual who hates* (v. 11). The third individual pictured is
again the opposite of the preceding. While parallel to verse 9, the emphasis
is now upon the blinding impact of hate. The individual is tersely identified:
"But he that hateth his brother" *(ho de misōn ton adelphon autou).* The
opening "but" *(de)* marks the antithesis to the individual portrayed in verse
10. The present-tense participle again depicts his characteristic attitude:
hatred is the outstanding mark of this individual. The brother who should
be dear to him is the object of his hatred.

No reference to his spiritual pretensions is made but three verbs portray
the impact of his life of hatred. The first two statements, "is in darkness,
and walketh in darkness" *(en tē skotia estin kai en tē skotia peripatei),*
declare his present sphere of existence spiritually and the daily round of his
activities. The article with "darkness" *(tē skotia,* "the darkness") makes
the reference specific, pointing to the spiritual realm which in 1:5 the author
first depicted as the opposite of the divine realm of "light." That darkness
marks this individual's separation from God and remains the one unaltered
and controlling reality of his life. As Lias remarks, "Whatever he does, or
wherever he goes, or whatever changes may take place in him in other
respects, he is in the darkness still."[45]

The third reality concerning this individual stems from the preceding
two: "and knoweth not whither he goeth" *(kai ouk oiden pou hupagei).*
"And" marks the inevitable sequence. Surrounded by darkness, he has no
true perception of the road he is traveling with its inevitable destiny. The
negative with the verb "knoweth" *(oiden,* a second perfect form with a
present meaning) declares that as he continues his walk in the darkness he
has no true perception of the nature of the road he is following and has no

---

[42]W. E. Vine, *An Expository Dictionary of New Testament Words with Their Precise Meanings for English Readers* (London: Oliphants, 1939), 3:129.

[43]Plummer, pp. 95-96.

[44]Smalley, p. 62.

[45]John James Lias, *An Exposition of the First Epistle of John* (1887; reprint ed., Minneapolis: Klock & Klock Christian Publishers, 1982), p. 98.

innate understanding of the end awaiting him. The verb "goeth" (*hupagei,* literally, "goes" or "leads under") implies that he is unaware of what he is moving toward and will be mastered by. Those who persist in the tactics of hatred inevitably end up under the domination of its blinding result.

He is unaware of the ultimate outcome of a life of hatred "because that darkness hath blinded his eye" *(hoti hē skotia etuphlōsen tous ophthalmous autou).* The aorist verb "blinded" *(etuphlōsen)* simply records the blinding impact of hatred in the human heart. "So hate destroys any windows for light from God."[46] John's statement is pictorial, depicting a spiritual result based on observed physical realities. Fish living in the perpetual darkness of the Echo River in the depths of Mammoth Cave in Kentucky have eye sockets but undeveloped eyes. The darkness has effectively blinded their eyes. Persistence in hatred and sin inevitably leads to moral and spiritual blindness.

4. The Sign of Separation (vv. 12-17)

The writer has presented three tests (2:3-11) that offer assurance to the readers that they are maintaining true fellowship with God. Verses 12-14 seem to disrupt that theme as John directly addresses his readers in two triads. In two sets of carefully structured statements he expresses his confidence that his readers are genuine believers who possess a saving knowledge of Jesus Christ. His hard-hitting statements in verse 9-11 were not directed against them; they were written to them, not about them. In expressing his assurance concerning the spiritual assets which the readers possess, John shows "that what is true of the orthodox Christian was *not* true of the false claimants around" them.[47] But, as Jackman suggests, "It is perhaps an opportunity for the readers to assess the practical application of these truths to their own lives."[48] John's expression of personal assurance concerning his readers (vv. 12-14) provides the basis for his appeal for separation from the world as a further ground for assurance (vv. 15-17).

a. The assurance concerning the readers (vv. 12-14). John expresses his assurance concerning his readers in two sets of triads. Each expression of affirmation consists of three elements: (1) the assertion "I write (or "wrote") to you," (2) a noun of direct address, and (3) an affirmation about them introduced by "because" *(hoti).* Careful structuring is obvious; yet these three verses constitute one of the most debated passages in 1 John. These difficulties will be considered as we proceed.

---

[46] Glenn W. Barker, "I John," in *The Expositor's Bible Commentary* (Grand Rapids: Zondervan, 1981), 12:317.

[47] Smalley, p. 67.

[48] Jackman, p. 55.

1) *The first triad of assurances* (vv. 12-13b). John's triple use of the present tense, "I write unto you," *(graphō humin)* clearly denotes the present letter now being composed, but the three designations for those being addressed have evoked much discussion. Clearly the terms employed are not mere physical age distinctions. Views differ as to how many groups are in view—one, two, or three. Some suggest that the three groups addressed are meant to indicate three levels of spiritual maturity. But this is questionable in view of John's inclusive usage of "little children" *(teknia)* elsewhere in the epistle, as well as the unusual order: "little children," "fathers," and "young men." Those who hold to three distinct groups tend to change John's order in their discussion, using either "little children," "young men," "fathers," or "fathers," "young men," "children."

A second view is that John first addresses all of his readers and then subdivides them into "fathers" and "young men." This view finds support in the fact that John elsewhere uses "little children" to denote all of his readers (2:1, 28; 3:18; 4:4; 5:21). This is also true of his use of the parallel term "children" *(paidia)* in 2:13c and 18. (The "little" in v. 18 in the KJV is doubtful.) Brown asserts, "It is almost impossible that suddenly here, and here alone, *teknia* and *paidia* could refer only to one group constituting one-third of the audience."[49] Further, the two other designations, "fathers" and "young men," are appropriate subdivisions of the whole group, for nowhere in the New Testament is either term used to address the whole Christian community. Brown notes that "this is the most popular view among modern scholars," and he appends an impressive list of names.[50]

A third view holds that all the readers are included each time, the designation being true of the experience ascribed to them.[51] Thus Dodd asserts, "All the privileges mentioned belong to all Christians, but emphasis and variety of expression are secured by distributing them into groups."[52] Plummer, while accepting the second view, remarks, "There is, however, something to be said for the view that *all* S. John's readers are addressed *in all three cases,* the Christian life of all having analogies with youth, manhood, and age; with the innocence of childhood, the strength of prime, and the experience of full maturity."[53] While recognizing the force of Plummer's

---

[49]Brown, p. 298.

[50]*Ibid.,* p. 298.

[51]So Marshall, p. 138; James Montgomery Boice, *The Epistles of John* (Grand Rapids: Zondervan, 1979), pp. 72-73; Zane C. Hodges, "1 John," in *The Bible Knowledge Commentary, New Testament* (Wheaton, Ill.: Victor Books, 1983), p. 890.

[52]C. H. Dodd, *The Johannine Epistles,* Moffatt New Testament Commentary (New York: Harper, 1946), p. 38.

[53]Plummer, p. 98. Italics in original.

remarks, we accept the second view as the most probable. It gives the most natural meaning to John's three terms.

a) *The readers as "little children"* (v. 12). John expresses his assurance concerning all his readers in his initial statement: "I write unto you, little children, because your sins are forgiven you for his name's sake." The diminutive term "little children" *(teknia),* like the cognate verb *(tiktō,* "to bring forth, to be born"), suggests the reality of the birth relationship.

As those who have been born into the spiritual family of God, John is assured of them "because your sins are forgiven you" *(hoti apheōntai humin hai hamartiai).* The particle *hoti,* used in each of John's statements, may be either declarative or causal. Some would here render it as declarative, "I am writing to you *that* your sins are forgiven you."[54] Then, this view holds, the writer feels a need to tell his "little children" *that* their sins are forgiven. "This," as Brown notes, "would imply a demoralized audience unsure of themselves and their status."[55] While grammatically possible, this rendering is improbable here. John is not directing these words to those who are wavering in their faith but to those who are loyal to the apostolic message. He is not telling them *what* he is writing but *why* he is writing to them. They stand close to him as "little children" *because* he is assured that "your sins are forgiven you" *(aphenōntai humin hai hamartiai).* The perfect-tense verb "are forgiven" denotes their past experience of sins forgiven, or sent away, resulting in their present state of being freed from the guilt of their sins. This experience, true of all genuine believers, was the basis of their fellowship with God and with one another. Without this assurance there can be no effective Christian life or God-honoring service.

The true basis for this assurance was the fact their sins had been forgiven "for his name's sake" *(dia to onoma autou,* "on account of the name of him"). "'God forgives sin not because of any merit in the sinner, but because of the infinite merit of the Saviour.'"[56] This is the first occurrence of the expression "the name" in the Johannine epistles. (See further 3:23; 5:13; 3 John 7.) Although not further identified, John's readers would at once understand the true import of this familiar Christian designation. As White observes, "His name is but shorthand for the whole character and work of Christ, the incarnate Son."[57] The forgiveness of sins is explicitly related to "the name" of Jesus since God's saving activity has been actualized in Him (Matt. 1:21; Acts 4:12;

---

[54]See Brown, pp. 300-301, for a list of scholars who support the declarative meaning.

[55]*Ibid.,* p. 301.

[56]George Williams, *The Student's Commentary on the Holy Scriptures, Analytical, Synoptical, and Synthetical,* 5th ed. (London: Oliphants, 1949), p. 1012.

[57]R.E.O. White, *Open Letter to Evangelicals, A Devotional and Homiletic Commentary on the First Epistle of John* (Grand Rapids: 1964), p. 60.

10:43; Rom. 10:13). The reference is a gentle reminder to his readers that they must steadfastly adhere to all that "His name" conveys and not be led astray from God's provision by the new theories of the false teachers.

b) *The readers under a dual division* (v. 13ab). John further expresses his assurance concerning his readers viewed as "fathers" and "young men." The two terms designate relative maturity. Jackman expresses a needed modern-day reminder: "In neither case should we allow the masculine terminology to obscure the application of what John says to the women and girls of the congregation as well."[58]

The first group, "I write unto you, fathers," addresses those among John's readers who are older in the faith and are characterized by spiritual maturity. "Fathers" *(pateres)* naturally implies some thought of authority and leadership as characteristic of those mature in their faith. Van Gorder suggests that the term implies that they were "believers in Christ who themselves had grown in grace and had begotten children in the gospel."[59] They had learned something of the seriousness of the responsibilities of the Christian life and the need to aid the less mature. One need not assume that John's designation denotes the official elders in their congregations.

John feels assured about them "because ye have known him *that is* from the beginning" *(hoti egnōkate ton ap' archēs)*. They are characterized by their mature knowledge of a person, not merely an inferential knowledge about Him. The perfect-tense verb "have known" denotes that they have come into a personal knowledge of Him in the past and now possess an abiding knowledge of Him. As Plummer remarks, "The word expresses the result of progressive experience, and is therefore very suitable to the knowledge possessed by the old."[60]

The person they know is characterized by His permanency, "from the beginning" *(ton ap' archēs)*. Taken by itself this designation might denote God the Father as the immutable I AM.[61] But Plummer notes that John "never speaks of the First Person of the Godhead under any designation but 'God' or 'the Father'."[62] The reference to "the Father" in verse 13c favors the view that John here means Jesus Christ, "him *that is* from the beginning." White points out that the designation "would have no particular significance here as a title for God, whereas the incarnation of the Logos, who was from the beginning, is the crux of the faith John writes to defend."[63]

---

[58]Jackman, p. 55.

[59]Paul R. Van Gorder, *Lessons from First John* (Grand Rapids: Radio Bible Class, 1978), p. 74.

[60]Plummer, p. 99.

[61]So Stott, p. 97; F. F. Bruce, *The Epistles of John* (Old Tappan, N.J.: Revell, 1970), p. 58.

[62]Plummer, p. 99.

[63]White, p. 59.

The expression echoes 1:1 and 2:7; it could refer to eternity past but more probably refers to the beginning of God's redemptive work in His Son (cf. 1:1, 3) or possibly to the beginning of the Christian Church (2:7). The second is the most natural here. It stresses the true nature of Jesus as revealed to His followers during His ministry. In writing to the "fathers" John draws assurance from his realization that their years of pondering on the gospel message and their personal experience with the incarnate Christ have stabilized them so that they will not be misled by the novel Christologies of the Gnostics.

The second group addressed, "young men" *(neaniskoi),* were believers who were younger in years and apparently not yet fully mature in their spiritual experiences. The term does not imply that they were spiritual "babes" *(nēpioi,* Rom. 2:20; I Cor. 3:1; Heb. 5:13). They are not distinguished for their immaturity but rather their personal strength and vigor. They are commended "because ye have overcome the wicked one" *(hoti nenikēkate ton ponēron).* The perfect-tense verb "have overcome" *(neni-kēkate)* does not mean that the battle is over for them but rather indicates that, having encountered the enemy and experienced victory, they now stand assured of the outcome. As Alford aptly remarks, "Whatever conflict remains for them afterwards, is with a baffled and conquered enemy."[64] That enemy John characterizes as "the wicked one" *(ton ponēron);* as one of the Biblical designations for the Devil, it depicts his nature as vicious, injurious, and destructive. It describes him as utterly bad. Hobbs suggests that "the evil one" here could be a reference to the Gnostics because they were "tools of the devil,"[65] but John here clearly intends the satanic foe himself. While the Devil admittedly uses men as his agents in the conflict with believers, the Devil, aided by his cohorts, is the believer's real and persistent enemy (cf. Eph. 6:10-12). Knowing that in Christ the Devil is a defeated foe (John 12:31; 14:30; 16:11), these young men have in faith courageously resisted the Devil and put him to flight (James 4:7; 1 Pet. 5:9). This position of victory over the Devil must be maintained daily with a firm faith in Christ and resolute striving against the Devil and his temptations.

2) *The second triad of assurances* (vv. 13c-14). This second triad of assuring statements clearly parallels the former triad,[66] but it is marked by

---

[64]Henry Alford, *The New Testament for English Readers* ([1865-1872]; reprint ed., Chicago: Moody Press, [1958]), p. 1707.

[65]Herschel H. Hobbs, *The Epistles of John* (Nashville: Thomas Nelson Publishers, 1983), p. 55.

[66]R. R. Williams, *The Letters of John and James,* Cambridge Commentary on the New English Bible (Cambridge: University Press, 1965), p. 26, even offers the conjecture that probably "only one set of three address-sentences was meant to stay in the letter. Possibly the second group of three sentences was meant as a better version of the first three, and the writer forgot to cross the first three out!"

two changes. Instead of the present tense, "I write" *(graphō)*, each of the three assertions now opens with the aorist tense *(egrapa)*.[67] The reason for this change is not obvious, and scholars have advanced varied suggestions. Candlish conjectures that as an old man John suddenly realizes that he might be gone when his readers receive the letter, and so changes to the aorist to urge his readers to receive this letter as his full and final testimony of them.[68] Another suggestion is that the present tense refers to the present epistle now being written whereas the aorist tense looks back to the Gospel of John.[69] A further suggestion is that John was interrupted after writing the first triad, and upon resuming his writing he picked up the train of thought with the use of the aorist verb.[70] Most of these suggestions are purely speculative. Various scholars suggest that the change is simply a stylistic variant.[71] Burdick plausibly remarks,

> The reason for repeating the triplet was to place particular emphasis on the author's confidence in the genuineness of his readers' salvation experience. And in order to avoid the monotony of the mere repetition, John used the epistolary aorist in the second triplet instead of the present tense.[72]

The epistolary aorist, a common Greek idiom, places the writer in thought at the time the readers receive his letter.

The second change in this triad is the use, in the first affirmation, of a different term of address; instead of the former *teknia*, "little children," John now uses *paidia*, which the KJV here likewise renders "little children." This diminutive form is likewise a term of endearment. As a term of address it occurs elsewhere in the New Testament only in 1 John 2:18 and John 21:5. Like *teknia* (v. 12), it again includes all the readers. The repeated use of "fathers" and "young men" again points to two groups among those addressed.

a) *The readers addressed as "children"* (v. 13c). As in the former triad, with this term *paidia*, "little ones," John again addresses all of his readers. The change may be due to the desire to relieve monotony, although there is

---

[67]Following the Textus Receptus, the KJV in verse 13c reads "I write," but has "I have written" in v. 14. For the textual evidence see Nestle-Aland, *Novum Testamentum Graece,* 26th ed. Perhaps the change was made to bring together the sequence *fathers, young men, little children* in v. 13. Perhaps this is the reason for the present verse division.

[68]Robert S. Candlish, *The First Epistle of John,* 2nd ed. (1869; reprint ed., Grand Rapids: Zondervan, n.d.), pp. 129-30.

[69]Alexander Ross, *The First Epistle of James and John,* New International Commentary on the New Testament (Grand Rapids: 1954), pp. 162-63.

[70]Robert Law, *The Tests of Life* (Edinburgh, T. & T. Clark, 1909), p. 309.

[71]Brown, pp. 296-97. See p. 297 for a list of scholars who accept the change as simply a stylistic variant.

[72]Burdick, p. 175.

some difference between the two terms. The former noun, from the verb "to bear" *(tiktō)*, views them as "little children" born into the family, while *paidia,* a diminutive noun based on *pais,* "boy, youth," implies their position as subordinate to the authority of those over them, hence, "little ones." In the words of Barker, "The use of *teknia* emphasizes more the relationship, the dependence or weakness of the infant, while *paidia* stresses the immaturity (subordination) of the child, the need to be under instruction or directions."[73] While confident of the spiritual stability of his readers, John thus seems to suggest that they can still profit from his instruction and guidance.

The assurance expressed in verse 12, "because your sins are forgiven you," John now rephrases to read, "because you have known the Father" *(hoti egnōkate ton patera),* thus expressing the result of the former reality. As Lenski notes, "Only those know the Father whose sins have been remitted for the sake of Christ's name."[74] The perfect-tense verb "know" *(egnōkate)* indicates an abiding, intimate knowledge of "the Father." The world has professed to know God under various guises,[75] but the readers know God personally as members of His family, living under His love and fatherly care. They came to know Him through their acceptance of Jesus Christ as the one who has revealed the Father (Luke 10:22). This knowledge of the Father is effected through the work of the indwelling Holy Spirit (Gal. 4:6).

b) *The readers under a twofold grouping* (v. 14). Again John uses the same grouping, "fathers" and "young men," that he used previously (v. 13). He leaves unaltered his statement of assurance concerning the "fathers": "because ye have known him *that is* from the beginning." "The repetition," Kistemaker suggests, "discloses the seriousness of the author's appeal; that is, the fathers cannot afford to relax the process of their spiritual growth."[76]

His statement of assurance concerning the "young men" is now enlarged into a triple statement. First is the recognition that "ye are strong"*(ischuroi este),* stressing the strength and vigor characteristic of youth. The adjective denotes power or ability and "places stress on the actual power that one possesses rather than on the mere principle of power."[77] The next two statements make clear that the strength in view is spiritual rather than merely physical. As young believers, not necessarily young in age, they are marked by "a freshness and virility and enthusiasm that proclaims them as the young men and women of the Kingdom."[78]

---

[73]Barker, 12:320.

[74]Lenski, p. 421.

[75]See White, p. 58, for an interesting list of various designations that have been advanced.

[76]Kistemaker, p. 268.

[77]Burdick, p. 176.

[78]Guy H. King, *The Fellowship, An Expositional Study of 1 John* (1954; reprint ed., Fort Washington, Pa.: Christian Literature Crusade, 1971), p. 44.

The use of "and" *(kai)* coordinates the three characteristics of these young believers. "And" connects their strength with the fact that "the word of God abideth in you" *(kai ho logos tou theou en humin menei)*. "The word of God" here does not refer to Christ but is rather the message of God as brought by Christ and now embodied in the inspired Scriptures. Strength is imparted as God's Word "abideth" *(menei)* in them, having been eagerly assimilated, and is now at home in their mind and will. It is readily available to strengthen, guide, and encourage them in their daily life. King justly remarks, "All big Christians have been Bible Christians; all who have been greatly blessed to others have been themselves steeped in it."[79]

Another "and" further coordinates: "and ye have overcome the wicked one" *(kai nenikēkate ton ponēron)*. The Word dwelling in them was the true source of their abiding victory over the Devil. Satan cannot resist the power of God's Word, as illustrated in the temptation of Jesus (Matt. 4:1-11; Luke 4:1-13). They were experiencing the reality of God's Word: "Resist the devil, and he will flee from you" (James 4:7).

b. The appeal for separation from the world (vv. 15-17). John abruptly states his prohibition against loving the world (v. 15a) and undergirds the prohibition with three sweeping realities (vv. 15b-17).

1) *The statement of the prohibition* (v. 15a). In verses 9-11 John insists that the Christian life must be characterized by love of the brethren; he now insists upon the complementary duty of separation from the world as the object of their love. As an appeal to the will, his negative command implies that love can be misdirected. His appeal again underlines that Christian faith and behavior are inextricably linked. His expressed assurances concerning their spiritual condition provide the basis for his appeal to maintain a proper attitude toward the world. It offers a danger no matter how far they have advanced in their spiritual maturity.

The prohibition is given a double statement: "Love not the world neither the things *that are* in the world." The first part is comprehensive: "Love not the world" *(Mē agapate ton kosmon)*. As a standard form for a prohibition, the negative *(mē)* with the present imperative usually denotes that an action which is in progress must be stopped.[80] Then John assumes that his readers are guilty of loving the world, at least to some extent, and he urges them to put a stop to the evil practice. More probably John expresses a categorical prohibition of the practice, "Don't be loving the world," without

---

[79]*Ibid.*, p. 45.

[80]F. Blass and A. deBrunner, *A Greek Grammar of the New Testament and Other Early Christian Literature,* trans. and rev. Robert W. Funk (Chicago: University of Chicago Press, 1961), p. 172.

asserting that his readers were actually doing it. It was a danger they must be constantly on guard against.

"The world" *(ton kosmon),* used six times in verses 15-17 alone, is a favorite term with John, having a variety of meanings. It is important to understand the force of this prohibition since it has been "used to denounce everything from buttons to beer."[81] The term "world" basically denotes order, arrangement (the opposite of chaos; cf. our English word "cosmetics"), hence an ordered system. The term is used to denote the earth (John 21:25) because of the order and system observed in our material world. It is also used to denote the human race, mankind in its various organizations and systems (John 3:16). But because of the fallen nature of the human race, the term predominantly has an ethical import, the human race in its alienation from and opposition to God. John here has in view the world of humanity steeped in sin and dominated by the evil one (1 John 5:19). As such, it is quite synonymous with "the darkness" in chapter 1. John is not calling for a monastic separation from the world but for an inner attitude of separation from the sinful world and its practices. As those loyal to God, John's readers are to be on guard against a permissive or kindly feeling towards the world's evil and are not to establish intimate relations of loyalty with it.

The added words "neither the things *that are* in the world" *(mēde ta en tō kosmō)* particularize, prohibiting such a love relationship with any particular aspect or feature of this evil world. These "things" are not necessarily material objects, which in themselves are nonmoral and can quite innocently be desired and possessed; but they become part of the prohibited world if they cause an attitude of alienation from God. They are those realities that are rooted in and characterized by the evil world.

2) *The reasons for the prohibition* (vv. 15b-17). John sets forth three reasons believers should not love the world: (1) because of the personal condition it reveals (v. 15b); (2) because of the character of the world (v. 16); and (3) because of the contrasted ends (v. 17).

a) *The personal condition revealed by love of the world* (v. 15b). Love for God and love for the world are by their nature antagonistic and cannot coexist in the same human heart. Here we have another aspect of that dualism between light and darkness that John set forth in 1:5.

The hypothetical picture "If any man love the world" *(ean tis agapa ton kosmon)* challenges the readers to consider the case of such an individual. The present-tense verb pictures anyone who persistently makes the world the object of his love. The conclusion negatively declares his inevitable spiritual condition—"the love of the Father is not in him" *(ouk estin hē*

---

[81]Quinton J. Everest, *Messages from 1 John* (South Bend, Ind.: Your Worship Hour, 1982), p. 64.

agapē tou patros en autō). The expression "the love of the Father," appearing only here in the New Testament, is capable of three meanings, as Burdick indicates: "It may refer to love that comes from the Father (ablative of source), it may refer to the Father's love for the person involved (subjective genitive), or it may speak of the person's love for the Father (objective genitive)."[82] As the opposite of the individual's love for the world, the last meaning seems clearly intended. Love for the Father and love for the world cannot mutually hold sway in the same human heart. John well remembered the reality declared by Jesus, "Ye cannot serve God and mammon" (Matt. 6:24). The tragic truth concerning such an individual is that love for God "is not in him," is not a motivating reality in his heart and life. He does not have that love for "the Father" which is the mark of those born into the family of God. But since our love for the Father is the result of His love for us (1 John 4:19), the subjective meaning, God's love for this individual, cannot be rigidly excluded. Smalley notes that "both ideas are probably present (cf. v. 5): love for the world inhibits a love for God which both answers his and derives from it."[83]

b) *The character of the things in the world* (v. 16). The opening "for" *(hoti)* points to the verification of his true condition from the nature of "all that *is* in the world" *(pan to en tō kosmō).* The neuter adjective *pan* may be rendered either "all" or "everything" and includes everything belonging to the class designated as being "in the world," belonging to the sphere of the world in its alienation from God. The following three phrases are a parenthetical unfolding of the character of these things: "For everything in the world–the cravings of the sinful man, the lust of his eyes and the boasting of what he has and does–come not from the Father but from the world" (NIV). The things enumerated as being "in the world" are not material objects but personal attitudes. As Jackman notes, "The 'worldly' characteristics of which the verse speaks are in fact reactions going on inside us, as we contemplate the environment outside."[84] John's three articular designations seem best understood as denoting the three basic spheres of worldliness. Although they do not offer exact parallels, these three realities are seen in the accounts of the temptation of Eve in the Garden (Gen. 3:6) and of Jesus in the wilderness (Luke 4:1-12).

"The lust of the flesh" *(hē epithumia tēs sarkos)* denotes the desire or craving which has its origin in the flesh. The noun rendered "lust" *(epithumia)* denotes a strong desire or craving, whether good or bad. The term is thrice used in the New Testament with a good meaning (Luke 22:15; Phil.

---

[82]Burdick, p. 178.

[83]Smalley, p. 83.

[84]Jackman, p. 61.

1:23; 1 Thess. 2:17), but predominantly it denotes an evil desire, properly rendered "lust." "Lust" is here collective, denoting the varied cravings of fallen human nature pursued in the interest of self in self-sufficient independence from God. The genitive "of the flesh" is not objective, "lust for the flesh," but subjective, the lust which has its seat in "the flesh," man's fallen nature with its disposition of hostility toward God. Plummer calls attention to the fact that John did not say "the lust of the body."[85] The cravings which God has placed in the human body in themselves are not sinful; they are God-given and essential for continuance of life here on earth. But they readily become sinful when used for illegitimate ends. The reference is to those temptations that arise from within.

Another aspect of "all that *is* in the world" John identifies as "the lust of the eyes" *(hē epithumia tōn ophthalmōn),* the cravings and lusts stimulated by what is seen. Now the reference is to those lusts which are aroused by what enters through the eye-gate. The reference is not merely to physical sight but includes intellectual visualization. One may understand the expression "the lust of the eyes," appearing only here in the New Testament, in two different ways. The reference may be to the craving to acquire the things seen. So understood, the expression "points to man's covetous and acquisitive nature."[86] Or, as Plummer notes, the lust may be "the desire of seeing unlawful sights for the sake of the sinful pleasure to be derived from the sight; idle and prurient curiosity."[87] The expression may well include both aspects. Some things an individual observes readily stimulate the craving to possess; other things he may desire to feast his eyes on without personally possessing. Under either view, "In a day of billboard advertising, movie and television screens, and eye-catching magazine spreads, this aspect of the world is predominant."[88]

A further aspect of "all that *is* in the world" is "the pride of life" *(hē alazoneia tou biou),* which the NASB suggestively renders "the boastful pride of life." While the two preceding aspects are inward, relating to what one wants, this is outward, relating to what one has or professes to have. The noun "the boastful pride" *(hē alazoneia),* which occurs only here and in James 4:16 in the New Testament, denotes "a state of pride or arrogance, but with the implication of complete lack of basis for such an attitude–'false arrogance, pretentious pride, boastful haughtiness.' "[89] It expresses the spirit

---

[85]Plummer, p. 103.

[86]Hodges, p. 891.

[87]Plummer, p. 103.

[88]Leo G. Cox, "First, Second, and Third John," in *The Wesleyan Bible Commentary* (Grand Rapids: Eerdmans, 1966), 6:334.

[89]Johannes P. Louw and Eugene A. Nida, ed., *Greek-English Lexicon of the New Testament Based on Semantic Domains* (New York: United Bible Societies, 1988), 1:765.

of the professional "braggart" *(alazōn),* one who extols his own virtues or possessions. The genitive "of life" *(tou biou)* is the same word rendered "this world's goods" in 3:17. The term occurs ten times in the New Testament and basically denotes "the means of life, livelihood." John's expression, "the boastful pride of life," appearing only here in the New Testament, portrays an attitude of boastfulness and a hollow self-exaltation based on material possessions or social prominence. It is the disposition to "show off" before others on the basis of worldly possessions or personal abilities and achievements. Thus as Plummer notes, "The first two may be the vices of a solitary; the third requires society. We can have sinful desires when we are alone, but we cannot be ostentatious without company."[90]

Having parenthetically set forth the nature of "all that *is* in the world," John concludes his sentence with a double assertion concerning the source of this moral depravity: "is not of the Father, but is of the world" *(ouk estin ek tou patros, alla ek tou kosmou estin).* The typical Johannine negative-positive statement of source *(ek,* "out of, from") again reminds the reader of the two fundamental antithetical realms of light and darkness. John's assertion that these things are "not from the Father" continues the thought of the spiritual family already underlined in his expression of confidence in the readers (vv. 12-13). Because these things do not derive their origin from *(ek)* the Father, and so are contrary to His nature and purposes, let the readers be warned against allowing such attitudes to establish their power over their lives.

c) *The contrasted ends* (v. 17). The opening "and" introduces a third reason that John's readers should not love the world. On the one hand is the transitory nature of the world: "And the world passeth away, and the lust thereof" *(kai ho kosmos paragetai kai hē epithumia autou).* The present tense, "is passing away," points out the on-going process of disintegration of that world which appears so attractive now. The reference is not to the material creation but to the system of evil under the domination of Satan. This transitoriness is likewise true of its "lust," those cravings, pleasures, and allurements of the world so appealing to the human heart. However strong their present appeal, the lusts of the world offer no lasting satisfaction and carry in themselves the seeds of their own deterioration. This process is now operative in the lives of individuals, but one day this world-system of evil will be swept off the scene in cataclysmic judgment at the return of Jesus Christ.

Over against the transitory nature of the world stands the abiding life of the true believer: "but he that doeth the will of God abideth for ever." As Culpepper notes, "Each element in the second half of the verse has a counterpart in the first half: the obedient versus the world, the will of God versus the

---

[90]Plummer, p. 104.

desire of the world, and 'abides for ever' versus 'passeth away.' "[91] Here is the true answer to the craving for permanence in the human heart. It is realized in "the one doing the will of God" *(ho de poiōn to thelēma tou theou)*. The present active participle characterizes him as actively engaged in doing God's will rather than pursuing the fleeting lusts of the world. Houlden remarks, "The 'mystical,' supernatural gift of God's love had certainly to be received (v. 15)–but the test of that was no mere spiritual 'feeling'; it was doing God's will, the keeping of his commands, in particular the command to love the brothers (v. 2f)."[92] John, like James, insists that saving faith must be functional in daily life.

It is this resolute obedience, imperfect though it may be, that brings the assurance of permanence amid the present scene of change and decay. It links the believer with the eternal, assuring him that he "abideth for ever" *(menei eis ton aiōnon,* literally, "into the age"), the coming eternal age of God's kingdom. Having been born again, he is already in the spiritual kingdom and no essential change in his spiritual life is ahead for him. There may be a break in the outer continuity of his life between death and resurrection, but his abiding spiritual union with Christ will remain unchanged.

---

[91]R. Alan Culpepper, *1 John, 2 John, 3 John,* Knox Preaching Guides (Atlanta: John Knox Press, 1985), p. 41.

[92]J. L. Houlden, *A Commentary on the Johannine Epistle,* Harper's New Testament Commentaries (New York: Harper & Row, Publishers, 1973), p. 75.

8

Assurance from the Conflicts of Faith
(2:18–4:6)

In the preceding portion of the epistle (1:5–2:17) John presents grounds for assurance through the test of fellowship. He notes that true fellowship is grounded in the nature of God (1:5), depicts hindrances to the experience of fellowship (1:6-10), presents the divine provision for maintaining fellowship (2:1-2), and sets forth four signs that fellowship is being maintained (2:3-17). In the long section beginning with 2:18, John offers further ground for assurance from the conflicts of faith (2:18–4:6). We can draw assurance concerning our Christian faith from the nature of the enemies it encounters. John insists that believers must understand the true nature of these enemies and recognize the dangers that they present; they must be defeated with the spiritual equipment that God has provided. These conflicts are portrayed under four aspects: (1) the conflict between truth and falsehood (2:18-28); (2) the conflict between the children of God and the children of the Devil (2:29–3:12); (3) the conflict between love and hatred (3:13-24); and (4) the conflict between the Spirit of God and the spirit of error (4:1-6).

A. The Conflict Between Truth and Falsehood (2:18-28)

2:18 Little children, it is the last time: and as ye have heard that antichrist shall come, even now are there many antichrists; whereby we know that it is the last time.

19 They went out from us, but they were not of us; for if they had been of us, they would *no doubt* have continued with us: but *they went out,* that they might be made manifest that they were not all of us.

20 But ye have an unction from the Holy One, and ye know all things.

21 I have not written unto you because ye know not the truth, but because ye know it, and that no lie is of the truth.

22 Who is a liar but he that denieth that Jesus is the Christ? He is antichrist, that denieth the Father and the Son.

23 Whosoever denieth the Son, the same hath not the Father: *[but] he that acknowledgeth the Son hath the Father also.*

24 Let that therefore abide in you, which ye have heard from the beginning. If that which ye have heard from the beginning shall remain in you, ye also shall continue in the Son, and in the Father.

25 And this is the promise that hc hath promised us, *even* eternal life.

26 These *things* have I written unto you concerning them that seduce you.

27 But the anointing which ye have received of him abideth in you, and ye need not that any man teach you: but as the same anointing teacheth you of all things, and is truth, and is no lie, and even as it hath taught you, ye shall abide in him.

28 And now, little children, abide in him; that, when he shall appear, we may have confidence, and not be ashamed before him at his coming.

The reality of the conflict between truth and falsehood is brought into sharp focus by the presence of the anti-Christian teachers. This conflict between divine truth and anti-Christian error assures the believer of the validity of his faith. John calls attention to the crisis facing believers (vv. 18-19), indicates the resources of true believers to deal with these heretical opponents (vv. 20-21), states the test to identify true and false believers (vv. 22-25), and instructs his readers in the face of the dangers (vv. 26-28).

1. The Crisis Facing the Believers (vv. 18-19)

In beginning his discussion of the conflicts of faith, John points to the reality of that conflict for his readers. He identifies the "end-time" character of the times (v. 18) and delineates the nature of the crisis confronting his readers (v. 19).

a. The characterization of the time (v. 18). John marks a new beginning by again addressing his readers as "Little children," or "Little ones" (*Paidia,* cf. 2:13). In support of the view that the term again includes all of John's readers, Plummer remarks, "It is difficult to see anything in this section specially suitable to children; indeed the very reverse is rather the case."[1] The term now used by John relates to the learning process and implies that in facing the present crisis his readers still need the guidance of the writer. John makes an assertion concerning the character of the time (v. 18a) and then points to the presence of the antichrists as confirmation (v. 18b).

1) *The assertion concerning the time* (v. 18a). John's assertion "it is the last time" (*eschatē hōpa estin,* literally, "last hour it is"), marks the crucial situation. The expression "the last hour" obviously is not intended as a

---

[1]Alfred Plummer, *The Epistles of S. John,* Cambridge Bible for Schools and Colleges (1883; reprint ed., London: Cambridge University Press, 1938), p. 105.

literal chronological assertion. Since the original does not have the definite article, two renderings–"the last hour" or "a last hour"–are possible. In support of the former rendering, commonly used in our various English versions, interpreters hold that "the idea is sufficiently definite without it, for there can be only one last hour."[2] Or one may view the expression as a technical term which does not need the definite article.[3] But Lenski believes that, since this exact expression occurs only here in the New Testament, it cannot be treated as a well-known concept which needs no article; he asserts that "the term is plainly qualitative."[4] Westcott likewise accepts the qualitative nature of the expression and defines it as "a period of critical change, 'a last hour,' but not definitely 'the last hour.' "[5]

The rendering "the last hour" is commonly understood to denote the time immediately preceding the return of Christ. Thus *The Living Bible Paraphrased* renders this phrase as "this world's last hour has come."[6] But this rendering is open to the charge that "John was wrong."[7] Marshall, however, while accepting the eschatological reference, notes that "John does not commit himself to any time-scale. Like the New Testament authors generally he does not delimit precisely the expected date of the parousia."[8]

Jesus told His disciples that the time of His return was unrevealed (Matt. 24:36) but instructed them to live in constant readiness for His return (Matt. 24:44; 25:12-13; Luke 12:40). He also told them that before His return, apostasy and the presence of false prophets would characterize the scene (Matt. 24:11-12; Mark 13:22-23). As John contemplates the appearing of "many antichrists" in his own day, he realizes that the characteristics of the end-time, as foretold by Jesus, are already present. Although John avoids any specific statement of time for the return of Christ, he believes it necessary to stress the urgency of the contemporary scene which clearly manifests eschatological characteristics. Clearly the characteristics of the end-time foretold by Jesus were already manifesting themselves before the close of the apostolic era.

---

[2]*Ibid.,* p. 105.

[3]H. E. Dana and Julius R. Mantey, *A Manual Grammar of the Greek New Testament* (1927; reprint ed., New York: The Macmillan Co., 1967), p. 149.

[4]R.C.H. Lenski, *The Interpretation of the Epistles of St. Peter, St. John and St. Jude* (Columbus, Ohio: Wartburg Press, 1945), p. 429.

[5]Brooke Foss Westcott, *The Epistles of St. John, The Greek Text with Notes,* 3rd ed. (1892; reprint ed., Grand Rapids: Eerdmans, 1950), p. 69.

[6]*The Living Bible Paraphrased* (Wheaton, Ill.: Tyndale House Publishers, 1971).

[7]William Barclay, *The Letters of John and Jude.* The Daily Study Bible (Philadelphia: Westminster Press, 1958), p. 71.

[8]I. Howard Marshall, *The Epistles of John.* New International Commentary on the New Testament (Grand Rapids: Eerdmans, 1978), p. 149.

The powers of the future eschatological kingdom actually entered the scenes of human history with the first advent of Christ (Heb. 6:5). The presence of the incarnate Messiah brought human history face to face with the reality of the eschatological kingdom. With the King's rejection, the kingdom in its eschatological character was not established; that event awaits His return in glory. But, according to J. H. Newman, that encounter with the eschatological future changed the direction of history. In speaking on "Waiting for Christ" he remarks:

> Up to Christ's coming in the flesh, the course of things ran straight toward that end, nearing it by every step; but now, under the Gospel, that course has (if I may so speak) altered its direction as regards His second coming, and runs, not towards the end, but along it, and on the brink of it; and is at all times near that great event, which, did it run towards it, it would at once run into. Christ, then is ever at our door.[9]

Marshall, after quoting and diagramming this comment, declares,

> This is a helpful analogy. It preserves the sense of urgency and imminence found in the New Testament on the basis of the principle that God is capable of extending the last hour (for the excellent reason in 2 Pet. 3:9) while retaining his own secret counsel on its duration.[10]

Thus understood, John's expression "the last hour" is qualitative yet carries an eschatological dimension. As Orr remarks, "John and his readers were living in *an eschatological hour,* electric with movements of the unseen principles which might burst into sight at any time."[11] And since John's day human history has repeatedly been strongly marked by the characteristics of "the last hour." And our own times strongly cry out the sense of impending destiny. Only God's longsuffering mercy holds back the manifestations of Christ's eschatological coming (2 Pet. 3:8-9).

2) *The sign of "many antichrists"* (v. 18b). With "and" *(kai)* John immediately adds the justifying evidence for his assertion: "and as ye have heard that antichrist shall come, even now are there many antichrists; whereby we know that it is the last time." The words "as ye have heard that antichrist shall come" *(kathōs ekousate hoti antichristos erchetai)* recall the prophetic teaching that John's readers had received. The aorist verb "heard" summarizes the fact that, as part of their instruction in the faith, they had been taught that "antichrist shall come" or "is coming." The present-tense

---

[9] J. H. Newman, "Waiting for Christ," in *Parochial and Plain Sermons* (London: Longman's, 1896), p. 241.

[10] Marshall, pp. 149-50.

[11] R. W. Orr, "The Letters of John," in *A New Testament Commentary* (Grand Rapids: Zondervan, 1969), p. 613. Italics in original.

verb "is coming" is a futuristic present; it "assumes the future coming of antichrist to be as certain as a present reality."[12] The singular noun "antichrist" points to a definite individual yet to come. John's readers are familiar with the apostolic teaching concerning the coming of a final, personal "Antichrist" (2 Thess. 2:3-4, 8-9), a teaching rooted in the ministry of Christ Himself (Matt. 24:11-15; Mark 13:14). The term "antichrist" *(antichristos)* occurs only in 1 and 2 John (1 John 2:18, 22; 4:3; 2 John 7), but the concept is important on the pages of Scripture (Dan. 7:11-14; Mark 13:14-23; 2 Thess. 2:3-12; Rev. 13:1-10; 19:19-20). In this compound term the prefix "anti" may mean either "against" or "instead of." The Biblical picture of the Antichrist suggests that both thoughts are involved in the designation. The term is quite synonymous with Paul's "man of sin . . . the son of perdition; who opposeth and exalteth himself above all that is called God, or that is worshipped" (2 Thess. 2:3-4). As Plummer remarks,

> The Antichrist is a *usurper,* who under false pretences assumes a position which does not belong to him, and who *opposes* the rightful owner. The idea of opposition is the predominant one.[13]

In writing "as . . . even now" *(kathōs . . . kai nun)* (v. 18b), John places the future coming of the personal Antichrist as a parallel reality to the existence of the "many antichrists" *(antichristoi polloi)* at the time of his writing. "Many" implies that they are a strong group. "Are there" is the perfect-tense verb "have risen" *(geognasin)*; it recognizes their historical arrival and their present impact upon the Church and the world. The verb, which literally means "have come into being," marks a contrast between these antichrists who have their origin during the course of history and the Christ who *was* from all eternity (John 1:1; 1 John 1:2).

The presence of these many antichrists assures John concerning the character of the time: "whereby we know that it is the last time." Their presence points to the coming of the Antichrist and shows that "the mystery of lawlessness is already at work" (2 Thess. 2:7 NASB), making clear the nature of the hour. While John believes it necessary to remind his readers of the spiritual significance of the situation, his use of the comprehensive "*we* know" *(ginōskomen)* implies that "the *actuality* is evident to every believer without exception."[14] John is well aware that these contemporary antichrists possess of the spirit of the coming personal Antichrist. But it is unwarranted to assume that John thereby "historicized" and "rationalized

---

[12]Donald W. Burdick, *The Letters of John the Apostle* (Chicago: Moody Press, 1985), p. 194.

[13]Plummer, p. 107. Italics in original.

[14]Stephen S. Smalley, *1, 2, 3 John,* Word Biblical Commentary (Waco, Texas: Word Books, 1984), p. 100. Italics in original.

the myth" of the personal end-time Antichrist.[15] John simply insists that these "many antichrists" point to the coming of the future Antichrist in that they already manifest the spirit of that final opponent of Christ. Their denial of the Christian doctrine of the incarnation is motivated by the spirit of the coming Antichrist. True believers in John's day needed the warning; the Church in our own day likewise needs the warning.

b. *The nature of the current crisis* (v. 19). John's statement "They went out from us, but they were not of us" expressly connects the appearing of these antichrists with recent events in the churches addressed. He omits all details since his readers already knew what had taken place. The aorist verb "they went out" *(exēlthan)* records a historical event which brought the heretical group into open existence as distinct from the orthodox majority. The active voice implies that they "went out" of their own accord; they were not excommunicated but voluntarily withdrew from further member- ship in the orthodox assemblies. Clark suggests that apparently "they were psychologically incapable of bearing up under strong orthodox teachings."[16] Clearly the orthodox majority repudiated their heretical views. Their with- drawal was not simply a matter of leaving one church to join another. Rather, their "departure, like Judas's going out from the community of disciples, pointed to betrayal, denial of faith, and separation from God's grace."[17] "From us" *(ex hēmōn),* placed emphatically at the beginning of the sentence, underlines John's self-identification with the orthodox majority. This "us" includes all true believers, whether of Jewish or Gentile background. Van Gorder notes that "this pronoun is used five times in verse 19, underscoring the wonderful fellowship that marked the early believers."[18] Those who withdrew obviously did not give up their profession to be Christians, but their action established a distinct group in opposition to the orthodox church. The two groups are emphatically marked by the repeated use of "they" and "us" (each five times) in this verse.

The departure of the heretics revealed their true nature, making clear that "they were not of us" *(all' ouk ēsan ex hēmōn).* The strong adversative "but" *(all')* marks the clear contrast. Their deliberate act of departure is set

---

[15]See Rudolf Bultmann, *The Johannine Epistles,* Hermeneia–A Critical and Historical Com- mentary on the Bible (Philadelphia: Fortress Press, 1973), p. 36, note 3; C. H. Dodd, *The Johannine Epistles,* Moffatt New Testament Commentaries (New York: Harper & Row, 1946), p. 49.

[16]Gordon H. Clark, *First John, A Commentary* (Phillipsburg, N.J.: Presbyterian and Reformed, n.d.), p. 75.

[17]Glen W. Barker, "1 John," in *The Expositor's Bible Commentary* (Grand Rapids: Zonder- van, 1981), 12:324.

[18]Paul R. Van Gorder, *In the Family, Lessons from First John* (Grand Rapids: Radio Bible Class, 1978), p. 88.

over against the continuing fact that they were "not of us." In the first phrase "out from us" *(ex hēmōn)* the preposition *ex* means "out from among us," whereas in the second phrase it denotes "of us" as not being a true part of our fellowship. Outwardly they had been members of the church but inwardly they never shared the inner spiritual life of the church. "Many a defaulter," King remarks, "has been spoken of as a backslider when, in reality, they never had been Christians at all."[19] The defection of the heretics had the effect of purifying the church and marking the clear distinction between truth and error.

With his "for" *(gar)* John adds the significance of their departure: "for if they had been of us, they would *no doubt* have continued with us." The "if" construction assumes a condition contrary to reality: "If they had been of us (but they weren't), they would have remained with us (but they didn't)." Their departure proved that they had a different spiritual origin; they belonged to another camp. It proved that they did not have the inner life of true believers. The test of experience had made clear the distinction between true and counterfeit Christians. Bruce observes, "Continuance is the test of reality."[20] "He who began a good work in you will perfect it until the day of Christ Jesus" (Phil. 1:6 NASB). Stott remarks, "This verse also gives biblical warrant for some distinction between the visible and the invisible Church."[21]

The added words "but *they went out,* that they might be made manifest that they were not all of us" declare a solemn but necessary purpose behind their departure. The adversative "but" *(all')* points to a strong contrast between their hypothetical continuance and their actual departure. The Greek construction *(all' hina)* is elliptical, implying the italicized words *"they went out."* The purpose clause *(hina,* "in order that") declares the purpose, not of the heretics, but of God, in their departure. God used their departure to lay bare the true nature of these heretics. It was decisive proof "that they were not all of us" *(hoti ouk eisin pantes ex hēmōn).*[22] Westcott points out that when the Greek verb stands between the negative *(ouk)* and "all" *(pantes),* as here, the negation is always universal rather than partial.[23] Their

---

[19]Guy H. King, *The Fellowship, An Expositional Study of 1 John* (1954; reprint ed., Fort Washington, Pa.: Christian Literature Crusade, 1976), p. 54.

[20]F. F. Bruce, *The Epistles of John* (Old Tappan, N.J.: Revell, 1970), p. 69.

[21]J.R.W. Stott, *The Epistles of John,* Tyndale New Testament Commentaries (Grand Rapids: Eerdmans, 1964), p. 106.

[22]The Greek is somewhat ambiguous and two renderings are possible: (1) "that not all in our company truly belong to us" (NEB), implying that not all formal members are truly saved; (2) "that none of them belonged to us" (NIV). The latter is the commonly accepted reading in our modern translations. The former is the reading of the KJV, but the New King James Version reads, "none of them were of us."

[23]Westcott, p. 72.

departure made clear that "none of them belonged to us" (NIV). Bruce suggests that John thus sought to assure "that his readers should not be shaken in their faith by the secession of their former associates."[24] In this verse John uses "of us" *(ex hēmōn)* four times and "with us" *(meth' hēmōn)* once to stress the unity of true believers with whom he associates himself. "Not those who deny the Christ are important, but the believers."[25]

2. The Resources of the Believers (vv. 20-21)

Faced with the peril created by the presence of the many antichrists, John reminds his readers of the resources they have to meet the crisis. They have an anointing from the Holy One (v. 20a) and the knowledge of the truth (vv. 20b-21).

a. The anointing from the Holy One (v. 20a). With his "But ye" *(kai humeis)* John again turns directly to his readers with assuring words. The use of the emphatic pronoun *(humeis)* lends support to the rendering "but" for the conjunction *(kai)*, usually rendered "and."[26] In spite of any special claims for themselves that the heretics have advanced, John assures his readers that they truly possess the needed spiritual equipment to resist these antichrists. Of primary importance is the fact that "you have an unction from the Holy One" *(chrisma echete apo tou hagiou)*. As the object of the verb, the noun "unction" or "anointing" stands emphatically forward. Based on the verb *chriō,* "to anoint," the noun does not denote the act of anointing but rather the result of the action. In the Septuagint the noun is used of the "anointing oil" (cf. Exod. 29:7; 30:25), and in Daniel 9:26 it is used metaphorically of "the Messiah." In the New Testament the term occurs only in 1 John (2:20, 27 twice). John does not stop to identify this "anointing," but it is generally accepted that the reference is to the Holy Spirit imparted to believers at regeneration. The figure of anointing is used of the Holy Spirit in connection with Jesus' ministry (Luke 4:18), and in 2 Corinthians 1:21-22 it is used of God's work in establishing the individual believer. John's statement here seems reminiscent of the promise of Jesus in the Fourth Gospel concerning the coming of the Spirit (John 14:17; 15:26; 16:13). The verb "ye have" *(echete)* asserts their continued possession of this anointing. It is the indwelling presence of the Holy Spirit that establishes believers in their faith and enables them to understand God's truth.

---

[24]Bruce, p. 70.

[25] Simon J. Kistemaker, *Exposition of the Epistle of James and the Epistles of John,* New Testament Commentary (Grand Rapids: Baker, 1986), p. 276.

[26]If the conjunction *kai* is rendered "and" or "also," the implication seems to be that these antichristian heretics made the vaunted claim that they had received a special "anointing" which distinguished them from the rest of the church members. Whatever the claims of the heretics, John assures his readers that they do indeed have "an anointing from the Holy One."

Dodd understands the metaphor differently; he holds that this anointing is the Word of God and characterizes it as "a prophylactic against the poison of false teaching."[27] He thinks that his view of the anointing frees the believer's knowledge of the truth from the danger of subjectivism.[28] But Burdick replies that Dodd's argument "that the work of the indwelling Holy Spirit is too subjective to be trustworthy loses its force in the light of Paul's declaration, 'The Spirit Himself bears witness with our spirit that we are the children of God' (Rom. 8:16)."[29] And Kistemaker notes that "Scripture never mentions the Word of God in relation to anointing."[30] We agree with those who hold that the "anointing" denotes the Holy Spirit, "since, according to verse 27, the anointing 'teaches.' This clearly suggests that the 'anointing' is conceived of as a Person."[31]

Marshall suggests that these two interpretations of the "anointing" should be combined.[32] We fully agree that the objective truth of the Word and the inner work of the Spirit must not be divorced in Christian experience; both are essential for balance in Christian life and faith. In verse 24 John urges that his readers adhere to the objective message which they have received. The Spirit is the agent who enables the believer to appropriate and apply the Word of God in daily experience.

John notes that this "anointing" is received "from the Holy One" *(apo tou hagiou),* thus stressing the sanctity of the Giver. The reference may be to God the Father, "the Holy One of Israel" (Isa. 1:4; 5:19, 24; etc.) or to the incarnate Son, "the Holy One of God" (Mark 1:24; John 6:69 NASB; Acts 2:27). Views differ as to the intended identity. Biblical references associate both the Father and Jesus Christ with the coming of the Holy Spirit (John 14:26; 15:26; Acts 2:33). The Holy Spirit is indeed "the Spirit of God" (Rom. 8:9) as well as "the Spirit of Jesus" (Acts 16:7 NASB). A study of the pronouns in verses 27-28 strongly suggests that the reference here is to Christ Himself. But as Smalley remarks, "John is possibly being deliberately ambivalent at this point."[33] Elsewhere John's pronouns often do not draw a sharp distinction between the Father and the Son, implying John's unquestioned acceptance of the full deity of the incarnate Son.

---

[27]Dodd, p. 63.

[28]*Ibid.,* pp. 63-64.

[29]Burdick, p. 197.

[30]Kistemaker, p. 279, note 55.

[31]Zane C. Hodges, "1 John," in *The Bible Knowledge Commentary, New Testament* (Wheaton, Ill.: Victor Books, 1983), p. 892.

[32]Marshall, p. 155.

[33]Smalley, p. 108.

b. The knowledge of the truth (vv. 20b-21). With his "and" (kai) John points to a second resource which his readers have in order to meet the current crisis. He asserts the fact that they all know (v. 20b) and then relates that fact to his writing to them (v. 21).

1) *The assertion of their knowledge* (v. 20b). A second resource which enables the readers to resist the antichrists is "and ye know all things" *(kai oidate pantes)*. The Greek manuscripts show two different readings, produced by the use of two different cases for "all." The reading of the King James Version, "and ye know all things," uses "all" *(panta)* as the direct object of the verb; this reading follows the Textus Receptus and is the reading of the majority of the later manuscripts. The reading, "and you all know," takes "all" *(pantes)* as the nominative in apposition to the subject of the verb; this is the reading of important early manuscripts.[34] The reading of the Textus Receptus certainly cannot be a sweeping assertion that John's readers "know all things." Those who support this reading reply that "all things" is limited by "the truth." But Lenski replies, "Even so, this says too much and says it unnecessarily. A Christian does not need to know everything in order to know who is an antichristian liar."[35] We accept the reading "you all know" as consistent with John's assurance that, as having God's anointing, they all know God's truth and so are not dependent upon the assertions of an elite few. They know the reality and reliability of God's truth through the teaching of the indwelling Spirit. The Greek verb "know" *(oidate)* suggests that the reference is not to studiously acquired knowledge but to an inner Spirit-imparted knowledge. The indwelling Holy Spirit enables them to perceive the difference between God's truth and the spurious claims of the Gnostics.

2) *The reason for writing this to them* (v. 21). In verse 21 John reiterates his assurance that his readers know and are adhering to "the truth" which they have received. "I have not written unto you because ye know not the truth, but because ye know it" assures them that he is not seeking to impart new truth but to support them in their adherence to the truth they already know as they face the false teachers with their new claims. With his epistolary aorist, "I have written" *(egrapsa),* John places himself at the time they would read what he had written. The reference may be to the whole epistle, but more probably he is thinking of what is being said in verses 18-20.

Negatively, he assures them that he has not written "because ye know not the truth" *(hoti ouk oidate tēn alētheian).* While the conjunction *hoti*

---

[34]For the textual evidence see Kurt Aland et al., ed. *The Greek New Testament,* 3rd ed. (New York: United Bible Societies, 1975); Bruce M. Metzger, *A Textual Commentary on the Greek New Testament* (London: United Bible Societies, 1971), p. 710.

[35]Lenski, p. 436.

can mean either "because" or "that," here it clearly indicates the reason for writing, not the content of what he writes. They can rest assured that he does not think he must now impart to them some new interpretation of "the truth" as revealed in the incarnate Christ. As adherents to the apostolic message, they already know God's truth as embodied in the divine Son and Saviour, Jesus Christ.

In typical Johannine fashion, he balances the negative with the positive assertion, "but because ye know it" *(all' hoti oidate autēn)*. This pastoral assurance is designed to confirm their rejection of the many antichrists with their spurious claims. As Barclay observes, "The greatest Christian defence is simply to remember what we know."[36]

The precise rendering of the added words, "and that no lie is of the truth" *(hoti pan pseudos ek tēs alētheias ouk estin)*, is less certain. Here *hoti* may have the meaning "that," with the following words understood as dependent upon the preceding "ye know": "and know that no lie is of the truth" (RSV).[37] Thus understood, John's positive reason is given a double statement; then these added words express his assurance concerning the knowledge of the readers as it relates to falsehood. But Plummer insists that if the conjunction means "because" in the first phrase, "it is the simplest and most natural to take the second and third in the same way."[38] Then these words express a further ground for John's own assurance concerning the readers. He is certain that truth and falsehood cannot mingle, that a lie can never be an inherent part of the truth. Since his readers know the truth they will not attempt to add a lie to their knowledge of God's truth.

3. The Confrontation with the Antichrists (vv. 22-25)

The presence of many antichrists demands that believers know the identifying marks of these antichrists (vv. 22-23). Having identified them, they must use their resources to resist them (vv. 24-25).

a. The mark of false and true believers (vv. 22-23). John emphatically declares the identity of the antichristian liar (vv. 22-23a) and simply states the basic criterion of the true believer (v. 23b).

1) *The mark of the liar* (vv. 22-23a). The rhetorical question, "Who is a liar but he that denieth that Jesus is the Christ?"–uttered without any connecting particle–is arresting in its abruptness.[39] Apparently John poses

---

[36]Barclay, p. 78.

[37]Similarly the KJV; Helen Barrett Montgomery, *The New Testament in Modern English* (Philadelphia: Judson Press, 1924); Gerrit Verkuyla, ed., *The Modern Language Bible, The New Berkeley Version* (Grand Rapids: Zondervan, 1969).

[38]Plummer, p. 112.

[39]The rendering "Who is the liar?" (NIV, NEB) sharpens the abruptness but does not accurately reproduce the form of the Greek sentence.

the question because of the claims of the heretics that they are the ones who possess a true understanding of spiritual realities. Only here does John use the definite article with the noun, "the liar."[40] His question, "Who is the liar?" *(tis estin ho pseustēs),* calls for the personal identification of such an individual whenever encountered. John thus passes from the abstract to the concrete in the daily experience of his readers. The conclusion of the sentence, "but he that denieth that Jesus is the Christ?" *(ei mē ho arnoumenos hoti Iēsous ouk estin ho christos;* literally, "if not the one denying, 'Jesus is not the Christ' "), indicates that anyone characterized by this crucial denial cannot escape justly being branded as "the liar." If he is not "the liar," then no one is. He is the liar *par excellence,* reflecting the attitude of the Devil himself (John 8:44, 55). He is marked by his characteristic denial, "he that denieth that Jesus is the Christ." The conjunction *hoti* is recitative and introduces the very words of his denial, "Jesus is not the Christ." He expresses no doubts concerning his position, nor is he hesitant openly to declare his rejection of the basic apostolic doctrine of the incarnation (John 1:14, 18; 1 John 1:1-3). It is not merely a Jewish rejection of Jesus of Nazareth as the personal Messiah, since John at once proceeds to identify Him as "the Son" (v. 22b). It is an attack upon the heart of the Christian message that God has made His ultimate self-revelation in the human Jesus as the incarnate Son of God (Heb. 1:1-3). As Morgan points out, "To receive or reject Jesus as the Christ has respect to all His offices, and consequently to all the blessings which we may obtain by embracing or refusing Him in them."[41]

The precise identity of these heretics has been much discussed, but it is generally accepted that some form of Gnosticism is involved. It was the basic philosophical dualism of Gnosticism that motivated this denial. Docetic Gnosticism held that the divine Christ-spirit was too holy to have been united with human nature. Cerinthian Gnosticism held that the aeon-Christ came upon the man Jesus at his baptism and empowered his ministry but left him before his crucifixion, and it was only a man who died on the cross. John gives no further indication as to the positive content of their teaching.

Whatever the precise identity of these heretics, John regards their denial as the height of heresy, constituting a direct attack upon the heart of the Christian message. Of such a heretic John declares, "He is antichrist" *(houtos estin ho antichristos).* "He" renders the demonstrative pronoun *houtos* ("this one") and, as it were, points out the individual and stamps

---

[40]The noun *pseustēs* ("liar") occurs in John 8:44, 55; 1 John 1:10; 2:4, 22; 4:20; 5:10.

[41]James Morgan, *The Epistle of John* (1865; reprint ed., Minneapolis: Klock & Klock Christian Publishers, 1982), p. 134.

him as "antichrist,"[42] not as the personal Antichrist but as the embodiment of his spirit. His denial is "seen not merely as erroneous thinking but as diabolically inspired."[43]

The appositional identification "that denieth the Father and the Son" *(ho arnoumenos ton patera kai ton huion)* establishes his antichristian spirit. The articular present participle *(ho arnoumenos,* "the one denying") again centers attention on the individual; the renewed reference to his active denial prominently marks this feature as his outstanding characteristic. His denial of Jesus as the Christ unavoidably involves a denial of "the Father and the Son." The heretical Christology of the Gnostics inevitably involved a denial of "the Father" who revealed Himself through "the Son," indicating that they had no personal relationship with "the Father" Himself. This absolute designation "the Son" occurs here for the first time in the epistle. In the first part of this verse "Jesus" was referred to as "the Christ"; now He is called "the Son." The two designations relate to the one person. As Westcott points out, "There is no passage in the mind of the Apostle from one personality to another, from the human to the divine, not yet from the conception of 'the man Christ Jesus' to that of 'the Word'; the thought of 'the Son' includes both these conceptions in their ideal fulness."[44]

In verse 23a John explicitly asserts the inescapable result of the denial: "Whosoever denieth the Son, the same hath not the Father" *(pas ho arnoumenos ton huion oude ton patera echei).* The expression "whosoever denieth" *(pas ho arnoumenos,* literally, "every one denying") underlines that this is a universal fact concerning all deniers of the Son. John does not accuse the heretics of directly denying the Father, but that is the sure result of their denial of His Son. They do not stand in any child-parent relationship with the Father. By their denial of His Son "they *ipso facto* excommunicate themselves from the great Christian family in which Christ is the Brother, and God is the Father, of all believers."[45]

2) *The confession of the true believer* (v. 23b). *"[But] he that acknowledgeth the Son hath the Father also."* The fact that the second half of verse 23 is in italics calls for some comment. The translators of the King James Version based their translation on the Textus Receptus. When they did not find this part of the verse in the Greek text before them they concluded that it was not a part of the original. But being aware of its contents from other sources, and recognizing its truth and value, they felt constrained to retain verse 23b as

---

[42]James Moffatt, *The New Testament, A New Translation,* rev. ed. (New York: Hodder & Stoughton, n.d.), suggestively renders "This is 'antichrists.' "

[43]Burdick, p. 201.

[44]Westcott, p. 76.

[45]Plummer, p. 113.

a valuable addition to the original by placing it in italics. The acceptance or rejection of the assertion in verse 23b as authentic must be based on the total manuscript evidence. The words are missing in the Greek Uncials K (9th cent.) and L (8th cent.) and most minuscule Greek manuscripts. But they are part of the Greek text in the Uncials Aleph (4th cent.), A (5th cent.), B (4th cent.), C (5th cent.), and P (9th cent.); various minuscule manuscripts; and in the Vulgate (4th-5th cent.), the Syriac (5th cent.), the Coptic (4th cent.), the Armenian (5th cent.), and Ethioptic (6th cent.) versions. The presence of the words in verse 23b in the early Uncials and various later minuscule Greek manuscripts, as well as in various early translations, strongly supports their authenticity. Their omission seems best accounted for from the fact that *ton patera echei* occurs twice and the probability that in copying the Greek text the scribe's eye skipped down from the first to the second occurrence of the expression, resulting in the accidental omission of the second assertion in verse 23. Textual scholars generally agree that this part of verse 23 is unquestionably an authentic part of the original.[46]

Over against the denial of the heretics as given in verse 23a stands the confession of the believers: "*[but] he that acknowledgeth the Son hath the Father also.*" The singular "he that acknowledgeth" (*ho homologōn,* literally, "the one confessing") marks this confession as an individual activity, not merely a rote group activity. In 1:9 the verb was used of the believer's confession of sin; here, as elsewhere in 1 John, the content of the confession is christological. It marks his open testimony to and acceptance of the revealed truth concerning "the Son" and brings the assurance that he "hath the Father also," indicating that he possesses a conscious communion with the Father; the Father unequivocally mediates His presence to the believer through His Son (John 14:6, 9).

b. The appeal to the true believers (vv. 24-25). The crucial importance of confessing the truth concerning "the Son" forms the basis for John's appeal to his readers to adhere to the truth that they had received. He states his appeal (v. 24a) and sets forth the results of abiding in the truth (vv. 24b-25).

1) *The statement of the appeal* (v. 24a). John's emphatic appeal to his readers is, "Let that therefore abide in you, which ye have heard from the be-

---

[46]Verse 23b is accepted as an authentic part of 1 John in the texts of B. F. Westcott and F.J.A. Hort, *The New Testament in the Original Greek,* 2nd ed. (1881; reprint ed., New York: Macmillan Co., 1935); Alexander Souter, *Novum Testamentum Graece,* 2nd ed. (1947; reprint ed., Oxford: Clarendon Press, 1962); Kurt Aland et al., ed. *The Greek New Testament,* 1st ed. (New York: American Bible Society, 1966); United Bible Societies, *Greek New Testament,* 3rd ed.; Nestle-Aland, *Novum Testamentum Graece,* 22nd ed. (New York: American Bible Society, 1956), Nestle-Aland, *Novum Testamentum Graece,* 26th ed. (Stuttgart: Deutsche Biblestiftung, 1979), and R.V.G. Tasker, *The Greek New Testament, Being the Text Translated in the New English Bible 1961* (Oxford; Cambridge: University Press, 1964). For the supporting textual evidence see Nestle-Aland, *Novum Testamentum Graece,* 26th ed.

ginning" (*humeis ho ēkousate ap' archēs en humin menetō,* more literally,
"Ye, that which ye heard from the beginning, in you let it be abiding"). The
emphatic personal pronoun (*humeis,*[47] "Ye, as for you") marks the shift of
attention from the heretics back to the readers. The use of "therefore" *(oun),*
omitted in many manuscripts, reminds the readers that the situation lays a resultant duty on them. "That" (*ho,* "that which") denotes the apostolic message, viewed as a coherent whole, to which they have adhered in contrast to
the new teachings advanced by the Gnostics. That true message they "have
heard from the beginning." Their acquaintance with that message goes back
to the time when they first heard and received it, but the aorist tense "have
heard" *(ēkousate)* summarily includes the entire period since then during
which they have been hearing that message proclaimed. John insists upon the
continuity of that message, and his appeal is that very message, "in you let it
be abiding" (literally), let it be at home and operative in their lives. The divinely revealed message is an active agent in the lives of those who receive it
and permit it to be operative within them. Its truths "exist as living realities,
independent of us, but they need to be permanently living in our minds and
wills."[48] The present imperative "let it be abiding" *(menetō)* calls on them
to let the message have its free course in their lives. This thought of "abiding" is important for John as is shown by the fact that he uses this verb three
times in this verse alone.[49] Strength and stability are assured by letting this
message be at home in them. It is the central characteristic of the mature believer. By contrast, "The continuous obsession for 'some new thing' is a
mark of the Athenian not the Christian (Act. xvii. 21)."[50]

2) *The results of letting the message abide* (vv. 24b-25). In setting forth
the results John deliberately restates the concept of abiding.[51] The conditional
statement "If that which ye have heard from the beginning shall remain in
you" *(ean en humin meinē ho ap' archēs ēkousate)* implies that believers
have a personal responsibility to assure that the condition is met. The aorist
verb "shall remain" *(meinē,* "may effectively abide") suggests the assured
result of their active cooperation.

The fulfilled condition in their lives assures that "ye also shall continue
in the Son, and in the Father" *(kai humeis en tō huiō kai en tō patri meneite).*

---

[47]The force of the emphatic pronoun is not adequately represented in the KJV, NIV, and RSV
renderings.

[48]David Jackman, *The Message of John's Letters,* The Bible Speaks Today (Downers Grove,
Ill.: Inter-Varsity Press, 1988), p. 75.

[49]The use of three different English words for the one Greek word in the KJV–"abide,"
"remain," and "continue"–blurs the emphasis gained by iteration.

[50]Stott, p. 113.

[51]In vv. 24-28 John mentions this concept of abiding no less than six times.

The "also" *(kai)* assures that as the divine message dwells in them they will "also" know the reality of abiding "in the Son, and in the Father." Smalley suggests that the plural pronouns "ye" carry, not merely an individual, but also a corporate and community reference: "As the gospel dwells in *the Church,* so the *Church* dwells in the Son and in the Father."[52] The Son is now named before the Father as "indicating that He is the key to any relationship with God (John 14:6)."[53] The force of the future "shall continue" *(meneite)* is progressive and expresses the continuing reality of fellowship with God.

The opening "and" *(kai)* of verse 25 introduces the supreme blessing of those who adhere to the Word of God: "And this is the promise that he hath promised us, *even* eternal life" *(kai hautē estin hē epanggelia hēn autos epēggeilato hēmin, tēn zōēn tēn aiōnion).* The feminine demonstrative pronoun "this" *(hautē)* most naturally looks forward to the expression "eternal life" as its appositional unfolding; the "this" is the predicate of the verb "is." Thus we may literally render the phrase as "the promise that He Himself promised to us is this: the life, the eternal." This supreme blessing of eternal life is God's promise to those who adhere to His Word. The noun "the promise" *(hē epanggelia)* occurs only here in John's writings,[54] but John emphasizes it by the relative clause "that He Himself promised to us." John stresses the nature of the promise by adding the cognate verb, "He promised," and the emphatic *autos,* "He Himself" (not represented in the KJV rendering), making the divine character of this promise unmistakable. In itself this emphatic pronoun is somewhat indefinite, but the added phrase "that he hath promised" *(epēnggeilato)* makes it clear that the reference is to the repeated promises of eternal life made by Jesus in the Fourth Gospel (3:14-15, 36; 4:14; 5:24; 6:40, 47; 10:28; 17:2-3).

The promised "eternal life" *(tēn zōēn tēn aiōnion)* is made emphatic by its position at the end of the sentence and the repeated article with the adjective, "the life, the eternal." As "eternal," this life will have its future eschatological unfolding in the ages of eternity for the glorified saints; but for the believer united to the living Christ, eternal life is already a present possession (John 3:16, 36; 5:24; 1 John 3:2, 14; 5:13-14). Our present "fellowship with God through an enduring faith in Jesus Christ is itself the essence of that life."[55] It is truly life in the highest sense of the term, both

---

[52]Smalley, p. 120. Italics in original.

[53]Burdick, p. 204.

[54]In 1 John 1:5 and 3:11 some scribes substituted "promise" *(epanggelia)* for the kindred noun "message" *(anggelia).*

[55]R. Alan Culpepper, *1 John, 2 John, 3 John,* Knox Preaching Guides (Atlanta, Georgia: John Knox Press, 1985), p. 51.

quantitatively and qualitatively new. In saying that this promise of eternal life was made "to us" *(hēmin)* John again unites himself with his readers in the possession of this supreme blessing.

4. The Resources of Believers in the Face of Danger (vv. 26-28)

Verses 26-28 are a summary, conveying renewed reminders to the readers in regard to the conflict between truth and falsehood. John reminds them of the danger from the deceivers (v. 26), recalls the equipment given them through the anointing they had received (v. 27), and points them to the hope of Christ's return as personal motivation for abiding in Him (v. 28).

a. The danger from the deceivers (v. 26). John again refers to the crisis facing his readers: "These *things* have I written unto you concerning them that seduce you." The words "These *things* have I written unto you" *(Tauta egrapsa humin)* do not refer to a previous letter; the aorist verb is epistolary, viewing this letter from the standpoint of the readers when they receive it. "These *things*" *(tauta)* could refer to the epistle as a whole but more probably refers to verses 18-25, since they contain the most explicit treatment thus far "concerning them that seduce you" *(perē tēn planōntōn humas)*. In verse 18 John calls them "antichrists," exposing their true character; now he characterizes them as "them that seduce you," which we may render as "them that are trying to seduce, or deceive, you." This rendering accepts the present-tense participle as conative, depicting their continuing efforts to "seduce" *(planaō)*, "lead astray, deceive." The KJV rendering, "them that seduce you," implies that they are actually deceiving the readers; but then clearly John would feel it necessary to seek to convince the readers of their error and try to restore them. Since John is not suggesting that his readers are being seduced or led astray, the present tense portrays the continuing efforts of the deceivers rather than their effectiveness. The articular present-tense participle pictures these deceivers as a definite group marked by their persistent efforts to deceive others. Although they have formally withdrawn from the Christian community (v. 19), these former members were still seeking to influence the faithful, intent on "deceiving" and leading them astray from the apostolic faith and fellowship. John does not underestimate the strength and subtlety of these heretics and wants his beloved readers to be continually on guard against the heretics' deceptive efforts. Jackman well remarks,

> The flourishing sects and cults of the late twentieth century have often gained impetus by deceiving and deluding uncertain Christians with their extravagant claims and clever theories. The remedy is not just 'truth' as an absolute, out there. It is also the experience of that Truth inwardly.[56]

---

[56]Jackman, p. 77.

b. The equipment through the anointing (v. 27). "But the anointing which ye have received of him abideth in you" *(kai humeis to krisma ho elabete ap' autou menei en humin)* assures the readers by pointing out the God-given equipment to face the danger. John marks a contrast by his emphatic "ye" *(humeis),* placed emphatically forward, setting them over against the deceivers. The contrast lies in "the anointing which ye have received." John's assertion in the latter part of the verse that "the same anointing teacheth you" makes clear that the anointing is a person, not merely an impersonal power. "Which ye have received" looks back to the beginning of their Christian life when by faith they accepted God's saving message (v. 24) and received the anointing "of him" *(ap' autou)* as His gift. Although again John does not explicitly identify "him," in view of verse 25, the reference seems to be to Christ Himself. That anointing now "abideth in you" *(menei en humin),* dwells in them as a continuing endowment, equipping them to stand firm against the deceivers. That equipment assures victory as they appropriate it in the experiences of daily life.

Again "and" *(kai)* adds the result, "and ye need not that any man teach you" *(kai ou chreian echete hina tis didaskē humas).* John obviously does not mean that they no longer need a teacher to instruct and guide them in gaining a fuller and firmer apprehension of the Christian faith and life. That is precisely what John is doing in this letter. Christian teachers are Christ's own gift to His Church (1 Cor. 12:28; Eph. 4:11; 2 Tim. 1:11). The apostle's words must be understood in the light of the context; he "is dealing not with the accumulation of the knowledge of the truth, but with the detection of the truth."[57] John here has in mind the teachings of the Gnostics who claimed to possess an enlightenment which rose higher than the revelation in Christ proclaimed by the apostles. Because the Holy Spirit indwells the true believer and enables him to discern heretical error, he has no need for some cult leader to initiate him into additional secret "knowledge" or professed spiritual insights.

Years ago Dr. H. A. Ironside related that one day while on the streets of Los Angeles he came across a street preacher vigorously preaching to a considerable audience around him. As he listened he soon recognized that the speaker was expounding the heretical views of a well-known cult. As he surveyed the audience he noticed a black man on the other side of the crowd attentively following the preaching. Occasionally the trace of a smile appeared on his face. Dr. Ironside felt sorry for the man being misled by the cult-preacher. When the preacher was finished Dr. Ironside made his way to the man he had watched, and, striking up a conversation, asked him, "And

---

[57]Roy L. Laurin, *First John, Life at Its Best* (1957; reprint ed., Grand Rapids: Kregel, 1987), p. 96.

what did you think of what the preacher said?'' His reply was, ''Well, he sure did tell us, didn't he?'' ''Yes, he surely did,'' Dr. Ironside agreed, ''but what did you think of what he preached?'' With a smile the man looked at him and replied, ''I sure couldn't answer him, but all the while he was preaching there was something inside me saying, 'It's a lie, it's a lie, it's a lie.' '' The Holy Spirit was teaching that Christian brother that he did not need a cult teacher to lead him into the truth of God. So John assures his readers that they do not need the Gnostic teachers to teach them ''new and deeper spiritual insights.''

John now grounds the preceding negative assertion in the positive unfolding of the function of the divine anointing in the believers' lives (v. 27c). The use of ''but'' *(all')* marks the contrasting reality in their experience: ''but as the same anointing teacheth you of all things, and is truth, and is no lie, and even as it hath taught you, ye shall abide in him.''

The Greek manuscripts show two different readings, ''the same anointing'' *(to auton chrisma)* and ''his anointing'' *(to autou chrisma)*. The latter reading establishes the personal nature of this ''anointing.''[58] This teaching function parallels the teaching ministry of the Holy Spirit as set forth by Jesus in John 14:26. The present tense marks this teaching as the continuing work of the Spirit, whereas the plural ''you'' *(humas)* indicates that all those indwelt by the Spirit receive this teaching. John maintains the competency of every born-again believer to discern the truth of God. As Kistemaker declares, ''Believers do not have to consult learned professors of theology before they can accept God's truth; in the sight of God, clergy and laity are the same; the Holy Spirit is the teacher of every believer, without distinction.''[59] Bruce appropriately remarks that ''the ministry of teaching must be exercised by men who themselves share the 'anointing' of which John speaks.''[60] The assertion that the anointing teaches believers ''all things'' *(peri pantōn)* does not mean that the Spirit teaches believers in all spheres of knowledge; ''there is no suggestion of omniscience here!''[61] Rather, the Spirit teaches believers about all the things concerning which they need His teaching so that they may distinguish truth from error in any teaching being advanced. On the other hand, John has no sympathy with a fanaticism which may profess no longer to have any need for Christian teachers.

---

[58]The reading in the KJV, ''the same anointing,'' follows the Textus Receptus reading *(to auto chrisma);* this is the reading of A, K, L, most minuscules, and the Coptic version. The reading ''His anointing'' *(to autou chrisma)* has strong early support, being the reading in Aleph, B, C, P, about twenty minuscules, the Vulgate, and several other versions and a number of the Church Fathers.

[59]Kistemaker, p. 286.

[60]Bruce, p. 76.

[61]Marshall, p. 163.

The typical positive-negative assertion, "and is truth, and is no lie" (*kai alēthese estin kai ouk estin pseudos,* "and true it is, and not it is a lie"), assures the readers that they do have the true equipment to resist the deceivers. One may understand this double assertion in two different ways. One may understand it as underlining the fact that their God-given anointing does indeed carry on such a teaching function. Then John, somewhat parenthetically, assures the readers that such a God-given teaching ministry is a reality in their lives as true believers. So understood, the teaching ministry of the Spirit in the life of His people is true and real; it is "no lie," as is the claim of the Gnostics to possess a higher, esoteric spiritual illumination. Or one may understand the double expression as depicting the nature of that which the God-given anointing teaches. Since the Holy Spirit is Himself "the Spirit of truth" (John 14:17; 15:26), the teaching He imparts is "true" and dependable, conforming to the truth, to reality; and as such it is "no lie" such as the heretical teachers espouse. Either view is possible; the latter seems more in keeping with the context.

The added words "and even as it hath taught you" *(kai kathōs edidaxen humas)* offer further assurance from their own experience of the Spirit's teaching ministry. The aorist-tense verb "it hath taught you" simply states the fact, whatever the length of their own experience with the Spirit's teaching ministry in their Christian lives. The third-person singular verb *(edidaxen)* may be rendered either "it taught" or "He taught." Our versions generally render the verb "it has taught" because the neuter noun "anointing" is understood as the subject in all of verse 27. If the verb is rendered "as He has taught" (NEB), indicating that Jesus is the subject, then we have a change of teachers in the verse; first "His anointing" (the Holy Spirit) is presented as continuing to teach them, and then "just as He has taught" is a reference to the past teaching of Jesus. In support of such a change of teachers in the verse, Burdick points to the double comparative, "as *(hōs)* His anointing teaches you" and "just as *(kathos)* it [He] has taught you."[62] But if in the second instance the reference is to the teaching of Jesus, it can be true of John's readers only in a secondary sense, since it is highly improbable that any of them shared in His personal teaching ministry. The former rendering seems more probable, as in keeping with the thrust of the verse as a whole. Then the change of tense in the verb declares that his readers are now being taught by the Holy Spirit, "even as" they were taught by the Spirit in their past experience.

The concluding clause of this long and grammatically difficult sentence, "ye shall abide in him" *(menete en autō),* presents textual and interpretative problems. The Greek manuscripts vary between their use of the present and the future tense for the verb. The use of the future tense in the King James

---

[62]Burdick, p. 207.

Version, "ye shall abide in him," follows the Textus Receptus.[63] But the present tense has strong manuscript support and textual scholars generally agree that the present tense should be accepted as the original. But there is no agreement as to whether the present-tense verb *(menete)* is indicative or imperative. If the mode of the verb is indicative, then this concluding clause summarizes John's assurance that his readers do adhere to the apostolic Christ. Kysar believes that the indicative "seems more in keeping with the comforting tone of the verse."[64] The indicative is in keeping with the declarative nature of verse 27 as a whole. But others hold that the verb here, as in verse 28, is imperative. "It is more reasonable," Burdick argues, "for the apostle to repeat the imperative in verse 28 than it would be for him to *declare* in verse 27 that the recipients are dwelling in Him and then in the very next sentence (v. 28) to *command* them to dwell in Him."[65] Smalley thinks that the imperative gives a theological balance to the whole verse: "John informs his readers both that Christ's *chrisma* dwells in *them,* and also that they are to abide in *him.*"[66] This switch to the imperative is another reminder that "Divine providence has its counterpart in human responsibility."[67]

c. The motivation from the hope of Christ's return (v. 28). The words "And now, little children" *(Kai nun, teknia)* apparently mark a concluding appeal from the realities in verses 26-27. Although the adverb "now" *(nun)* conveys the thought of a logical sequence, a temporal force also seems to be involved, i.e.,"as things now stand." Clearly John is appealing to his readers in view of the crisis created by the continued seductive efforts of the false teachers. The renewed use of the direct address "little children" (cf. 2:1) marks John's pastoral concern for his readers in view of the crisis they face. He now joins the urgency of the present with the strength to be drawn from the motivating power of the Christian hope for the future.

John's terse appeal is "abide in him" *(menete en autō).* The form of the verb could be indicative, but the following purpose clause marks it as imperative, and the pronoun *(autō)* most naturally refers to Christ since the remainder of the verse refers to "His coming." The present imperative calls for a continuing intimate fellowship with Christ as a standing duty. It is not a call to maintain a static relationship but rather to enjoy and deepen a vital

---

[63]The future is the reading of Uncials K and L (8th century or later) and most minuscules. The present is supported by important Uncials–Aleph, A, B, C, P. For the textual evidence see Nestle-Aland, *Novum Testamentum Graece,* 26th ed.

[64]Robert Kysar, *I, II, III John,* Augsburg Commentary on the New Testament (Minneapolis: Augsburg, 1986), p. 66.

[65]Burdick, p. 207. Italics in original.

[66]Smalley, p. 128.

[67]Kistemaker, p. 286.

personal fellowship with Christ. This is the last of six occurrences of the verb "abide" *(menō)* in verses 18-28.[68] Smalley notes that "of all the exhortations in 1 John, this is the only one which 'encourages an attitude directed immediately to Christ.' "[69]

The expressed motivation for such a continued abiding in Christ is eschatological in character: "that, when he shall appear, we may have confidence, and not be ashamed before him at his coming." John believed that our prophetic hope exerts a practical impact upon present Christian living.

The statement of our hope, "when he shall appear" *(ean phanerōthē,* more literally, "if he may appear"), does not express doubt concerning the fact of Christ's return but underlies the uncertainty as to the time. The King James reading "when" *(hotan)* follows the Textus Receptus which represents the reading of the majority of the later Greek manuscripts. But numerous earlier Greek Uncial and some minuscule manuscripts read "if" *(ean).*[70] The change from "if" *(ean)* to "when" *(hotan)* seems clearly to be a scribal effort to remove any uncertainty that "if" might create concerning the hope of Christ's return. If the original reading was *hotan,* it is difficult to see why the use of *ean* arose.

The early Church remembered that Jesus had told His disciples that the time of His return was unrevealed (Mark 13:32-33) and in view of that uncertainty had urged them to be ready (Matt. 24:44; 25:13; Luke 12:40). The aorist passive verb "shall appear," or "be revealed," points to Christ's being made visible when He returns to earth in open glory (Col. 3:4; 1 Pet. 5:4; 1 John 3:2). In 1:2 John uses this same verb to refer to the appearing of the incarnate Son in His earthly ministry, "was manifested unto us." He who appeared among men as the incarnate revelation of God to mankind will appear again in open glory. The return of the resurrected and glorified Christ is the hope of the Church. That return will vindicate the apostolic proclamation concerning His character and work and will terminate the danger from the powers of evil.

In keeping with his purpose to stimulate present abiding in Christ, John points to the impact upon believers when He does return. The benefit of present abiding for believers in that future day is stated both positively and negatively: "so that . . . we may have confidence and not shrink away from Him in shame at His coming" (NASB). With his change to "we" John includes himself with his readers. As Alford remarks, "This was not a matter in which Apostle and converts, teacher and hearer, were separate; but one

---

[68]This verb occurs twenty-four times in 1 John, three times in 2 John, and forty-one times in the Gospel of John.

[69]Smalley, p. 129.

[70]For the textual evidence see Nestle-Aland, *Novum Testamentum Graece,* 26th ed.

in which all had a share.''[71] The apostle associates himself with his readers in the blessings and demands of the gospel.

Present abiding in Christ will in that day assure that "we may have confidence" *(schōmen parrēsian)*. The aorist-tense verb "may have," rather than the present,[72] is more punctiliar in force, as pointing to the feeling of the believer in that day. The word "confidence" *(parrēsian),* the first of four occurrences of the term in this epistle, is a compound noun *(par* = "all" and *rhēsis* = "speech"); it here denotes that freedom and assurance or boldness which will enable the one now abiding in Christ to appear before Him confidently in that day and to speak with assurance and candor; he will be able to speak forth courageously rather than keep quiet out of fear. Hobbs suggests that the term expresses "the idea of intimate friends baring their hearts to each other.''[73] The hope of thus appearing before our Lord in that day should stimulate a close, obedient relationship with Him now. Here and in 4:17 this term is used of the believer's freedom and fearlessness before Christ at His return; in 3:21 and 5:14 it is used of the freedom that now belongs to the believer in prayer.

Negatively, present abiding in Christ is urged so as to avoid the embarrassment of some unresolved disobedience or sin in that day: "and not be ashamed before him at his coming" *(mē aischunthōmen ap' autou en tē parousia autou).* The verb rendered "be ashamed," appearing only here in the Johannine writings, is used only in the middle and passive voices in the New Testament. If middle, it basically means "be ashamed," if passive, "be put to shame." Brown states the difference as follows, "The passive reflects a legal situation where one is disgraced, while the middle has more the psychological aspect of the individual's feeling shame.''[74] The thought of people feeling shame and fear before the divine Judge at the final revelation is common to both the Old Testament (Isa. 24:21-23; Jer. 2:35-36; Hos. 10:8) and the New (Luke 23:30; Heb. 10:26-27; Rev. 6:15-17). Those who take the verb as passive understand John to mean that the shame comes from Him, that they will be openly put to shame by Christ. Thus Marshall remarks,

> For them the coming of Jesus will mean judgment and rejection. . . . Those who will be ashamed when he comes are the people who did not live in union with him on earth, those who were merely nominal in their allegiance

---

[71]Henry Alford, *The New Testament for English Readers* (1865-1872; reprint ed., Chicago: Moody Press, 1958), p. 1718.

[72]Although Codex Aleph and most of the later minuscules have the present tense, the aorist is better attested. See Nestle-Aland, *Novum Testamentum Graece,* 26th ed.

[73]Herschel H. Hobbs, *The Epistles of John* (Nashville: Thomas Nelson Publishers, 1983), p. 73.

[74]Raymond E. Brown, *The Epistles of John,* The Anchor Bible (Garden City, N.Y.: Doubleday & Co., 1982), p. 381.

to him, and their rejection at his coming will be the final confirmation of a life of spiritual separation from him.''[75]

But others hold that in this context the middle voice is more probable, as depicting the feeling of personal shame of those who have fluctuated in their devotion and service and have allowed things to come into their lives which they will then recognize as evoking Christ's disapproval. This is suggested in the rendering "shrink away from Him in shame" (NASB). "This intimates divine disapproval at the judgment seat of Christ, referred to in 4:17-19.''[76] Then the picture is not of an unsaved individual but of a born-again believer who has allowed sin in his life because of slackness in his relationship with Christ. In support of this view is the first-person, plural subject of the verb, as denoting John and his readers. Brown, in support of this view, thinks it preferable to take this verse as "chiastic parallelism where both lines say the same thing in different order:

so that (A) when he is revealed, (B) we may have confidence
and (B') not draw back in shame from him (A') at his coming.''[77]

Only here does John use the compound noun *parousia,* which means "coming" or "presence." Composed of *para* ("alongside of") and the substantival form of the verb *eimi* ("to be"), *parousia* literally means "a being alongside of," hence "presence." It is an important term in the New Testament for the return of Christ, one of three primary terms used to describe that prophetic event. The term *apokalupsis,* which means an "unveiling" or "revelation," pictures the future open disclosure of Him who is now veiled from human sight; the second term, *epiphaneia,* which means an "appearing," points to the visible nature of His return; the term used here pictures His personal coming with the result of His personal presence upon arrival. The thought here is not merely that of the personal coming of Christ but of His resultant presence and dealing with His own; implied is the Judgment Seat of Christ (Rom. 14:10; 1 Cor. 3:12-15; 2 Cor. 5:11). In view of that day, how important is a life of obedience now!

---

[75]Marshall, pp. 166-67.

[76]Hodges, p. 893.

[77]Brown, p. 381.

9

Assurance from the Conflicts of Faith (Part 2)

B. The Conflict Between the Children of God and the Children of the Devil (2:29–3:12)

2:29 If ye know that he is righteous, ye know that every one that doeth righteousness is born of him.

3:1 Behold, what manner of love the Father hath bestowed upon us, that we should be called the sons of God: therefore the world knoweth us not, because it knew him not.

2 Beloved, now are we the sons of God, and it doth not yet appear what we shall be: but we know that, when he shall appear, we shall be like him; for we shall see him as he is.

3 And every man that hath this hope in him purifieth himself, even as he is pure.

4 Whosoever committeth sin transgresseth also the law: for sin is the transgression of the law.

5 And ye know that he was manifested to take away our sins; and in him is no sin.

6 Whosoever abideth in him sinneth not: whosoever sinneth hath not seen him, neither known him.

7 Little children, let no man deceive you: he that doeth righteousness is righteous, even as he is righteous.

8 He that committeth sin is of the devil; for the devil sinneth from the beginning. For this purpose the Son of God was manifested, that he might destroy the works of the devil.

9 Whosoever is born of God doth not commit sin; for his seed remaineth in him: and he cannot sin, because he is born of God.

10 In this the children of God are manifest, and the children of the devil: whosoever doeth not righteousness is not of God, neither he that loveth not his brother.

11 For this is the message that ye heard from the beginning, that we should love one another.
12 Not as Cain, *who* was of that wicked one, and slew his brother. And wherefore slew he him? Because his own works were evil, and his brother's righteous.

The conflict between the proponents of antichristian falsehood and the adherents to God's revelation in His Son (2:18-28) is now portrayed as a conflict between the children of God and the children of the Devil. The two classes are rigidly distinct in origin and practice. True believers are children of God marked by the practice of righteousness, with love as the bond that holds the members of the family together. John delineates the marks of the children of God (2:29–3:3), depicts the realities inherent in the practice of sin (3:4-8a), declares the provision made for deliverance from the practice of sin (3:8b-9), and marks the distinction between the two classes (3:10-12).

1. The Marks of the Children of God (2:29–3:3)

The conflict between believers and the antichristian heretics prompts John to set forth the distinguishing marks of a true believer. He points out the practice of righteousness as the mark of the new birth (2:29), asserts the reality and the dynamic nature of the new life (3:1-2), and notes the practice of the believer's self-purification as prompted by the hope of the future (3:3).

a. The practice of righteousness as the mark of the new birth (2:29). The personal practice of righteousness reveals membership in God's family. John first appeals to the knowledge of the readers concerning the righteous nature of the head of the family. His use of the third-class conditional statement "if ye know that He is righteous" *(ean eidēte hoti dikaios estin)* does not imply that they were unaware of His righteous nature; rather, the condition is an appeal to them to confirm openly their personal perception of this reality. Their conscious affirmation of the fact "that He is righteous" will stabilize them in their conflict with unrighteousness.

The adjective "righteous" *(dikaios)* denotes that which is in full accord with what is right and just in character and conduct. The declaration "He is righteous" *(dikaios estin)* expresses a well-known axiom concerning the nature of God. As Lenski remarks, "Righteousness is one of his energetic attributes. He is righteous in all his ways: in his laws, his promises, his verdicts, or a single act of his."[1] Since the verb does not have an expressed subject, the reference may be to God the Father, as in 1:9, or to Jesus Christ, as in 2:1. Westcott holds that since Christ is the subject of verse 28 "it is

---

[1]R.C.H. Lenski, *The Interpretation of the Epistles of St. Peter, St. John and St. Jude* (Columbus, Ohio: Wartburg Press, 1945), p. 446.

therefore most natural to suppose that He is the subject of this verse also."[2] This conclusion is less certain if we accept verse 29 as introducing a new division. An obvious difficulty with this identification is the fact that the New Testament nowhere explicitly speaks of believers as "born of Christ." In this letter believers are referred to as "born of God" (3:9; 4:7; 5:1, 4), and in John 3:8 as "born of the Spirit," but nowhere as "born of Christ." In 3:1-2 (ASV) believers are expressly called "children of God," and "the Father" is named as bestowing the love-gift of sonship. Since the pronoun "him" in the last half of verse one seems clearly to refer to the Father, it seems best to accept a reference to the Father in the first part. But Bultmann holds that there is a sudden change in the meaning of the pronoun in this verse, from Jesus to God, and found in this supposed sudden shift support for his view that the phrase, "clumsily appended," demonstrates the composite authorship of 1 John.[3] But such a shift in the precise meaning of pronouns referring to God is quite possible in this epistle without Bultmann's proposed documentary dissection. Thus Marshall accepts that "He is righteous" refers to Christ but that "born of Him" refers to God the Father, and remarks, "It was probably so self-evident to him and his readers that spiritual birth was from the Father that he was not conscious of gliding from one antecedent for *autou* (Christ, 2:28, 29a) to another (God, 2:29b)."[4] However, such a shift of meaning in the pronominal designation within one sentence is not obvious. More probable seems the view that both pronouns refer to God the Father, but this uncertainty as to the intended identity of his pronouns is characteristic of John. Westcott remarks,

> The true solution of the difficulty seems to be that when St John thinks of God in relation to men he never thinks of Him apart from Christ (comp. c. v. 20). And again he never thinks of Christ in His human nature without adding the thought of His divine nature.[5]

John's concluding words, "ye know that every one that doeth righteousness is born of Him," underline that all members of God's family display the moral nature of their Father. The form of the verb "ye know" *(ginōskete)* may be indicative or imperative. Brown notes that "the imperative reading is favored by the Vulgate, early English versions," and by a number of

---

[2]Brooke Foss Westcott, *The Epistles of St. John, The Greek Text with Notes,* 3rd ed. (1892; reprint ed., Grand Rapids: Eerdmans, 1950), p. 83.

[3]Rudolf Bultmann, *The Johannine Epistles,* Hermeneia–A Critical and Historical Commentary of the Bible (Philadelphia: Fortress Press, 1973), p. 45.

[4]I. Howard Marshall, *The Epistles of John,* New International Commentary on the New Testament (Grand Rapids: 1978), p. 168, note 13.

[5]Westcott, p. 83.

commentators.[6] The Jerusalem Bible renders "you must recognize," and the TEV reads "you should know, then." Support for the imperative is found in John's use of the imperative in 2:28 and in 3:1. But Burdick replies that "nothing in the context demands a series of imperatives."[7] In addressing his Christian readers John can expect that they are acquainted with the fact that God's children can be identified by their righteous conduct. The presence of "also" *(kai)*[8] in many early Greek manuscripts indicates that the facts that God is righteous and that the conduct of the true believer is righteous belong together. This understanding enables a believer to feel assured that another whose life reflects the practice of righteousness is indeed a fellow believer.

The sure sign of the new birth is "every one that doeth righteousness." "Every one" *(pas ho)* asserts that this is true of every true believer without exception, and "that doeth righteousness" *(ho poiōn tēn dikaiosunēn,* literally, "the one doing the righteousness") declares the visible sign. The present active participle "denotes habit of life, the prevailing principle of one's life, not a single action, but a succession of acts which make up the life."[9] The article with "righteousness" ("the righteousness") may have a possessive force, "His righteousness" as revealing God's character, or more probably it points to the specific righteousness "that characterizes God the Father and is passed on to His children as a family characteristic."[10] Such a lifestyle of righteousness does not produce the new birth but is the visible evidence that the individual "is born of Him" *(ex autou gegennētai).* The perfect tense marks the past experience of the new birth and declares the continuing possession of this new life. The words "of him" *(ex autou)* mark the source of his new life; it is derived from God, not human nature. Laurin remarks,

> Many people exhibit deeds of morality who are not born of God. Such morality is the result of culture and comes from human kindness and it is the exception, not the rule. The characteristic of life apart from God is unrighteousness, although that unrighteousness may be sprinkled with moral

---

[6] Raymond E. Brown, *The Epistles of John,* The Anchor Bible (Garden City, N.Y.: Doubleday & Co., 1982), p. 382.

[7] Donald W. Burdick, *The Letters of John the Apostle, An In-Depth Commentary* (Chicago: Moody Press, 1985), p. 228.

[8] *Kai* does not occur in the Textus Receptus, although modern textual editors generally accept it as original. For the textual evidence see Nestle-Aland, *Novum Testamentum Graece,* 26th ed. (Stuttgart: Deutsche Biblestiftung, 1979).

[9] William G. Moorehead, *Catholic Epistles–James, I and II Peter, I, II, III John, and Jude,* Outline Studies in the New Testament (New York: Revell, 1908), p. 104.

[10] Burdick, p. 229.

deeds and may have the semblance of being right. Taken as a whole a godless world is an unrighteous world.[11]

This concept of the "new birth," here first introduced, is prominent in the rest of the epistle (3:9; 4:7; 5:1, 4, 18) and is a familiar New Testament truth. It is through this divinely imparted spiritual rebirth that believers enter into the family of God so that they truly are children of God. It implies a resultant relationship with God and carries ethical consequences. The reality of one's membership in the family of God is revealed to others through the practice of righteousness, imperfect though it may be. Other signs of the new birth in this epistle are love of the brethren (4:7) and faith that Jesus is the Christ (5:1).

b. The dynamic reality of the new life (3:1-2). Having become members of God's family through the new birth, believers find that their new life has deep present as well as future significance. John calls upon his readers to contemplate the amazing reality of present membership in God's family (v. 1a), reminds them that this explains the reaction of the world toward them (v. 1b), and stresses that this new life as God's children has present and future implications (v. 2).

1) *The amazing gift of God's love* (v. 1a). John's excitement is evident as he says to his readers, "Behold, what manner of love the Father hath bestowed upon us" *(idete potapēn agapēn dedōken hēmin ho patēr)*. The plural number of the aorist imperative, "Behold" or "See," calls upon the readers to take a heart-moving look at the amazing love which gave them membership in God's family. As Jackman remarks, "The force is that we need to take time to contemplate this love and allow its reality to sink down into the depths of our being."[12] Let them carefully note "what manner of love" *(potapēn agapēn)* the Father has bestowed on them. The adjective rendered "what manner" *(potapēn)* occurs only seven times in the New Testament[13] and implies a reaction of astonishment, and usually of admiration, upon viewing some person or thing. The expression conveys both a qualitative and quantitative force, "what glorious, measureless love!" This love, originating with God, ever seeks the true welfare of those being loved; it is amazing indeed when we remember the personal destitution of those He loves. God's is a love that works visible, transforming results in the lives of its recipients. The perfect-tense verb "hath bestowed" *(dedōken)* declares that this love is a permanent gift; it cannot be earned or purchased but is a gift that will not be withdrawn. Following his direct call to his readers, John's added expression

---

[11]Roy L. Laurin, *First John, Life at Its Best* (1957; reprint ed., Grand Rapids: Kregel, 1987), pp. 102-3.

[12]David Jackman, *The Message of John's Letters,* The Bible Speaks Today (Downers Grove, Ill.: Inter-Varsity Press, 1988), p. 81.

[13]It occurs in Matthew 8:27; Mark 13:1 (twice); Luke 1:29; 7:39; 2 Peter 3:11; 1 John 3:1.

"upon us" *(hēmin)* indicates that he explicitly includes himself among the recipients of this amazing love. To see the Father's love "aright is to sink down in adoration before it. It is beyond comprehension."[14] In the original the words "the Father" stand at the end of the statement, giving emphasis to the Fatherly character of the Giver and recall the intimate relationship He has established in making us His children.

The added clause "that we should be called the sons of God" *(hina tekna theou klēthōmen,* literally, "that children of God we should be called") is appositional, explaining wherein this amazing love is revealed. The use of *hina* with the subjunctive does not point to some future, as yet unrealized goal of God's love; rather, the force of the clause is factual, unfolding the nature of God's gift of love–"be called children of God." The aorist passive verb "be called" is effectual, indicating that God Himself acted to declare our status as members of His family. Used without the article, "children of God" calls attention to our character as members of the family, "God-children–a divine progeny."[15] The KJV rendering "sons" does not adequately render the force of the Greek term *tekna,* which denotes not the legal relationship of "sons" but rather the natural relationship of children as members of the family. Brown observes, *"Teknon* [child] is the technical Johannine term covering divine sonship/daughterhood, since *huious,* 'son,' is reserved for Jesus in relationship to God."[16]

The added comment "and *such* are we" (ASV), appearing in most of our English versions, does not appear in the King James Version, in that it follows the Textus Receptus, which does not contain these words. Scholars advance divergent evaluations as to authenticity of these words. Some hold that they are "probably a scribal addition,"[17] whereas others regard their absence in various manuscripts as due to "scribal oversight, perhaps occasioned by graphic similarity with the preceding word . . . or to deliberate editorial pruning of an awkward parenthetical clause."[18] On the basis of the

---

[14]Lenski, p. 449.

[15]H. E. Dana, *The Epistles and Apocalypse of John* (Kansas City, Kan.: Central Seminary Press, 1947), p. 49.

[16]Brown, p. 388.

[17]Zane C. Hodges, "1 John," in *The Bible Knowledge Commentary, New Testament* (Wheaton, Ill.: Victor Books, 1983), p. 893.

[18]Bruce M. Metzger, *A Textual Commentary on the Greek New Testament* (London: United Bible Societies, 1971), pp. 711-12.

textual evidence,[19] textual scholars generally accept them as authentic.[20] They certainly add to the force of the text.

These words, "and *such* are we" (*kai esmen,* "and we are"), emphatically declare that we are not merely God's children in name but in reality. They express a ringing note of assurance, encouraging and strengthening the readers. Lias notes that "the words 'children of God' were no mere *title,* but the expression of a *fact,* a fact which was to colour all their thoughts and actions, to banish superstitious fear, and to fill them with a thought of ever-present love, which should sustain them in all the trials and distresses of the world."[21]

2) *The world's failure to understand believers* (v. 1b). The amazing fact that we are now members of God's family explains the world's attitude toward believers: "therefore the world knoweth us not, because it knew him not." Interpreters are not agreed whether "therefore" (*dia touto,* "because of this") looks forward to the concluding clause "because it knew him not," or looks backward to the fact that we are now "children of God." Under the forward look the meaning is that the world does not recognize or understand believers because it never recognized Him; under the backward view John explains that the world does not recognize us because we are children of God. The backward view seems more natural. Lenski holds that "*dia touto* makes the previous statement the reason that the world does not know us, and *hoti* substantiates by pointing to something additional that the world does not know."[22] Because believers as members of God's family are radically different from the world, therefore "the world" (*ho kosmos),* the organized mass of lost humanity in its estrangement from God, "knoweth us not" (*ou ginōskei hēmas),* has no true understanding or appreciation of those who are born-again believers. "The mystery of regeneration is foolishness in its eyes; those who are children of God in Christ it considers deluded."[23] By its very nature the world, which "lieth in wickedness" (5:19), cannot truly understand or establish friendly relations with God's children.

God's children understand why the world does not understand them: "because it knew him not" (*hoti ouk egnō auton).* The aorist tense, "did not know" (*egnō),* records the historical fact of the world's failure to understand

---

[19]For the textual evidence see Zane C. Hodges and Arthur L. Farstad, *The Greek New Testament According to the Majority Text* (Nashville: Thomas Nelson Publishers, 1982); Kurt Aland et al., ed. *The Greek New Testament,* 3rd ed. (New York: United Bible Societies, 1975).

[20]For a full discussion of the textual problem see J. Harold Greenlee, *Introduction to New Testament Textual Criticism* (Grand Rapids: 1964), pp. 126-28.

[21]John James Lias, *An Exposition of the First Epistle of John* (1887; reprint ed., Minneapolis: Klock & Klock Christian Publishers, 1982), p. 199. Italics in original.

[22]Lenski, p. 450.

[23]*Ibid.*

divine reality. The precise failure in view is determined by the accepted identity of "him." If "him" is understood as a reference to God the Father, John summarily notes that "the world's whole course is one great act of non-recognition of God."[24] Repeatedly history has demonstrated that "the world through its wisdom knew not God" (1 Cor. 1:21 ASV). More probable is the view of Burdick that the aorist tense "points to a particular point in past time when the world did not know Him. It would be most natural to see here a reference to Christ's reception at His first coming."[25] The world failed to understand or receive God's supreme revelation of Himself in His Son (John 1:10-11; 15:18–16:4); it hated and rejected Him. John reminds his readers that this fact should help them to understand the world's reaction to His spiritual brothers and sisters. The fact of their rejection by "the world," which includes all unregenerated individuals, attests that they are indeed members of God's family. Therefore, as Barker notes,

> The author wants his readers to know that approval by the world is to be feared, not desired. To be hated by the world may be unpleasant, but ultimately it should reassure the members of the community of faith that they are loved by God, which is far more important than the world's hatred.[26]

3) *The implications of God's love-gift* (v. 2). Of vital significance for believers is the fact of God's transforming love. In enjoining his readers to contemplate God's love-gift, John gives personal expression to that love by addressing them as "Beloved" *(agapētoi)*. (Cf. 2:7). The recipients of God's love are also loved by the writer. He unites his readers with himself in contemplating God's saving love in relation to the present and the future: "Now are we the sons of God, and it doth not yet appear what we shall be." The renewed assertion "we are the sons of God" introduced by "now," the adverb of time *(nun tekna theou esmen,* literally, "now children of God we are"), marks the present amazing spiritual identity of John and his readers. With "and . . . not yet" *(kai oupō),* John contrasts the present with the future and links the two aspects in connection with our new life as God's children. This God-imparted life "is not static but dynamic. A son grows, develops, matures. His goal of growth is maturity in the likeness of Christ Himself."[27] While rejoicing in the present possession of eternal life,

---

[24] A. R. Fausset, "The First General Epistle of John," in Robert Jamieson, A. R. Fausset, and David Brown, *A Commentary, Critical and Explanatory, on the Old and New Testaments,* American ed. (Hartford, Conn.: S. S. Scranton Co, n.d.), vol. 2, *New Testament,* p. 531.

[25] Burdick, pp. 231-32.

[26] Glenn W. Barker, "1 John" in *The Expositor's Bible Commentary* (Grand Rapids: Zondervan, 1981), 12:330.

[27] Edward A. McDowell, "1-2-3 John," in *The Broadman Bible Commentary* (Nashville: Broadman Press, 1972), 12:207.

believers also look forward to the undisclosed future still ahead; they know that God's work in and with them is not yet complete. They are assured that the best is yet to come! What that future will bring "doth not yet appear"–has not yet received open, visible display. The fact that we are now children of God will not be changed, but "what we shall be" *(ti esometha)* is still veiled from our sight. As Lenski remarks, "A child of God is here and now, indeed, like a diamond that is crystal white within but is still uncut and shows no brilliant flashes from reflecting facets."[28] The use of the neuter pronoun "what" *(ti)* stresses the quality of that which God still has in store for His children. But the verb "appear" *(ephanerōthē),* a favorite word with John,[29] assures that what we shall be will yet be openly displayed.

While our destiny as God's children has not yet been openly revealed, John gives confident expression to its essence: "We know that, when he shall appear, we shall be like Him." "We know" *(oidamen),* a declaration of Christian faith, introduces a well-assured recognition grounded in the nature of the apostolic message. That anticipated display awaits a future undated event: "when he shall appear" *(ean phanerōthē,* literally, "if he may be manifested"). As in 2:28 the condition is again stated hypothetically; John has no doubt as to the certainty of Christ's return, but he was well aware that, from the standpoint of those cherishing this hope, its occurrence during their lifetime was uncertain. The condition expresses an attitude of expectancy, however. God in His wisdom left the date of Christ's return undisclosed so that each successive generation of believers may know the stimulating power of that blessed hope.

Since the subject of the verb "shall appear" *(phanerōthē)* is unexpressed, views differ as to whether to render "He," referring to Christ, or "it," as referring back to "what we shall be." The interpreters differ in their preferences,[30] but the rendering "He" is preferable. Since John is setting forth the believer's future complete Christ-likeness, it is more natural to accept that he associates that reality with the personal return of Christ rather than with the time when that disclosure is made.

---

[28]Lenski, p. 452.

[29]It occurs nine times in 1 John, nine times in the Fourth Gospel, and two times in the Book of Revelation.

[30]The rendering "it" is preferred by Henry Alford, *The New Testament for English Readers* ([1865-1872]; reprint ed., Chicago: Moody Press, [1985]), p. 1719; Alfred Plummer, *The Epistles of S. John,* Cambridge Bible for Schools and Colleges (1883; reprint ed., London: Cambridge University Press, 1938), p. 121; Lenski, pp. 451-52. The rendering "He" is preferred by Westcott, p. 98; Marshall, p. 172; Stephen S. Smalley, *1, 2, 3 John,* Word Biblical Commentary (Waco, Texas: Word Books, 1984), pp. 145-46; Simon J. Kistemaker, *Exposition of the Epistle of James and the Epistles of John,* New Testament Commentary (Grand Rapids: Baker, 1986), p. 295, note 5.

As members of God's family, our assurance is that when Christ returns "we shall be like Him" *(homoioi autō esometha)*. Some, such as Plummer, hold that "Him" *(autō)* denotes God the Father, since "the point is that children are found to be like their Fathers."[31] But since John refers to the personal return of Christ, it is more natural that the reference is to Christ Himself. This interpretation is in keeping with God's purpose that all of His children be "conformed to the image of His Son, that He might be the firstborn among many brethren" (Rom. 8:29). The indwelling Holy Spirit is already at work in the lives of believers, inwardly transforming them into the moral image of the Lord of glory (2 Cor. 3:18). When Christ returns, the believer's yearning for inner Christ-likeness will be fully realized. But our conformity to His image will also include our bodies, for the returning Saviour also will "transform the body of our humble state into conformity with the body of His glory" (Phil. 3:21 NASB). This glorious assurance must not be misinterpreted to mean that we shall become little gods. The adjective "like" *(homoioi)* "implies spiritual unity, but not complete identity."[32] As Burdick notes, "Believers can never be *equal* to Christ, since He is infinite and they are finite; but they can and will be *similar* to Him in holiness and in resurrection bodies."[33] As the incarnate Son of God, who died and rose again in a glorified body, He will ever be distinct as "the firstborn among many brethren" (Rom. 8:29). But the vast family of redeemed human beings, transformed into His image, supremely loving Him and universally imitating Him, will ever "be to the praise of His glory" (Eph. 1:12).

The explanatory addition "for we shall see him as He is" *(hoti opsometha auton kathōs estin)* may indicate either the reason for our assurance that we shall be like Christ or the cause of our being like Him. Under the former view "for" *(hoti,* or "because") is taken as introducing a dependent clause relating back to the main verb, "we know," giving the sense "we know that we shall be like Him, because we shall see Him." This rendering assumes that only those who shall be like Christ shall then be permitted to see Him as He really is. If the clause is connected with the immediately preceding words, "we shall be like him," then John explains that our future face-to-face encounter with the glorified Christ will complete our transformation into His likeness. Thus the amazing assertion that "we shall be like Him" receives the needed explanation. In the words of Bruce, "If progressive assimilation to the likeness of their Lord results from their present beholding of Him through a glass darkly, to behold Him face to face, to 'see

---

[31]Plummer, p. 122.

[32]Smalley, p. 146.

[33]Burdick, p. 234.

him even as he is,' will result in their being perfectly like Him.''[34] The comparative adverb ''as'' (*kathōs,* ''just as'') emphasizes that then our beholding of Christ will no longer be as ''through a glass, darkly,'' but we will truly be seeing our glorious Lord ''face to face'' (1 Cor. 13:12).

c. The impact of Christian hope upon present living (v. 3). With the connecting ''and'' *(kai),* John now states ''an all-important corollary of the Christian hope.''[35] The past experience of regeneration brings with it a living hope for the future, and this hope motivates present Christian living. ''And every man that hath this hope in him purifieth himself.'' As in 2:29, the comprehensive ''every man that hath this hope'' *(pas ho echōn tēn elpida tautēn)* again allows no exceptions for some elite group. The expression, ''every man that'' *(pas ho),* occurs six times in verses 3-10 (translated ''whosoever'' the other five times in the KJV) and suggests that John is refuting the claims of some who professed to be exceptions to the standards for ordinary Christians. John insists that the purifying impact of this eschatological hope is operative in the life of every true believer. The articular present-tense participle *(ho echōn)* pictures the individual as actively possessing and treasuring this hope as a sure possession. The designation ''this hope'' *(tēn elpida tautēn)* emphasized by the definite article and the demonstrative pronoun, summarizes verse 2. The word ''hope,'' which occurs only here in the Johannine literature,[36] concerns the unseen future, but it does not imply any uncertainty or mere probability. Christian hope is assured of future realization because it is grounded in the person of Christ and His sure word.

The familiar KJV rendering ''every man that hath this hope in him'' may be misunderstood as denoting a subjective hope which the believer holds in his own heart. Rather ''in him'' *(ep' autō,* ''upon him'') portrays the believer's hope as reaching out and resting ''upon Him'' as its sure and unchanging foundation. It is based upon and centers in our glorified Lord who has promised to come again. Our eschatological hope has objective validity and will certainly be fulfilled because Christ Himself is the guarantee of its fulfillment.

John insists that every individual who holds to this objective hope ''purifieth himself'' *(hagnizei heauton),* willingly and repeatedly exercises self-purification. In John 11:55, the only other occurrence of this verb in the Johannine writings, the reference is to ceremonial purification; here the term denotes inner moral purification. The present tense points to the repeated

---

[34]F. F. Bruce *The Epistles of John* (Old Tappan, N.J.: Revell, 1975), p.87.

[35]C. H. Dodd, *The Johannine Epistles,* Moffatt New Testament Commentary (New York: Harper & Row, 1946), p. 71.

[36]The noun ''hope'' occurs fifty-four times in the NT. The verb ''to hope'' *(elpizō)* occurs only in John 5:45, 2 John 12, and 3 John 14 in the Johannine writings (translated ''trust'' in KJV).

activity, and "himself" marks that the conscious need for purification centers in his own being. In 1:7 John states that it is the blood of Christ that cleanses us, whereas here he speaks of self-purification. Both are true and necessary. As the begrimed workman must personally apply the soap and water to be cleansed, so the believer appropriates the God-given means of cleansing from moral defilement that may have been incurred in daily life. Included in this self-purification is the believer's renunciation of objects, activities, and attitudes which he finds to be defiling.

Theology speaks of this repeated cleansing as "progressive sanctification" (cf. 2 Cor. 7:1). In 1 Peter 1:22 Peter uses this verb in the perfect tense, "seeing ye have purified your souls in your obedience to the truth" (ASV), to denote the cleansing that took place at regeneration (cf. John 13:10; 15:3; 17:19). That initial purification with its transforming result is the necessary antecedent to this personal self-cleansing in daily experience. The more intimate the believer's fellowship with God, who is "light" (1:5), the more conscious he becomes of his need to cleanse himself from all that is moral darkness (1:5-7). The more he contemplates this assured hope of being conformed to the image of Christ, the more eagerly will he strive for present personal purity (Phil. 3:13-14).

The added words "even as he is pure" *(kathōs ekeinos kagnos estin)* set before the believer the pattern for his self-purification. "Even as he" makes clear that "we are not to judge our lives by other peoples', but by Christ's, who is the standard or goal toward which we are to move."[37] "He" renders the demonstrative pronoun "that one" *(ekeinos),* which in this epistle seems always to refer to Christ (2:6; 3:3, 5, 7, 16; 4:17; 5:16), and sets Him apart from other individuals. As a man among men, Jesus was "pure" *(hagnos),* morally blameless, uncontaminated and sinless in character and conduct. John does not say "even as that one purified himself" but rather "is pure," thus asserting His unchanging nature. The incarnate and glorified Christ ever remains "pure" and "sinless." As such He is the perfect model, challenging believers constantly to purify themselves. Culpepper comments, "Those who hope for heavenly rewards but do not pursue righteousness have pipe dreams, not hope."[38]

2. The Revelation Inherent in the Practice of Sin (3:4-8a)

Having set forth that the practice of righteousness reveals the reality of the new birth (2:29), by contrast John next presents the revelation inherent in the practice of sin. Since the false teachers seem to have held that knowledge

---

[37]Herschel H. Hobbs, *The Epistles of John* (Nashville: Thomas Nelson Publishers, 1983), p. 81.

[38]R. Alan Culpepper, *1 John, 2 John, 3 John,* Knox Preaching Guides (Atlanta: John Knox Press, 1985), p. 59.

was all-important and that conduct did not really matter, John now declares the reality that sin and its practice are irreconcilable with the nature of Christianity. John has mentioned sin before (1:7, 8, 9; 2:1, 12), but now in verses 4-9 he mentions the concept of sin no fewer than ten times. John points out the true nature of sin (vv. 4-5) and that its practice establishes the distinctness between the two classes of humanity (vv. 6-8a).

a. The indication of the nature of sin (vv. 4-5). John shows that the nature of sin is lawlessness (v. 4) and that sin is contrary to the mission and character of Jesus Christ (v. 5).

1) *The nature of sin as lawlessness* (v. 4). The absence of any connecting particle sharpens the contrast between the practice of self-purification (v. 3) and the practice of sin (v. 4). Again John makes an assertion that allows for no exception: "Whosoever committeth sin transgresseth also the law" (*pas ho poiōn tēn hamartian kai tēn anomian poiei*, very literally, "every one doing the sin also the lawlessness is doing"). It portrays a class which is the opposite of those who practice righteousness (2:29). The present articular participle pictures the individual as actively engaged in "doing" sin. The reference is not to his being engaged in a definite act of sin but to his characteristic practice of sinning. Burdick notes that "the KJV translation, 'committeth,' is misleading in that it suggests a point of action rather than the continuing practice."[39] The use of the definite article with both "sin" ("the sin") and "lawlessness" ("the lawlessness") makes the two abstracts definite and indicates that John is thinking of two inclusive concepts rather than single occurrences.

John's assertion that the one who "practices sin also practices lawlessness" (NASB) enhances the seriousness of sin. In classical Greek the term "sin" *(hamartia)* denoted "failure, fault, sin," as suggesting the weakness of human nature in its failure to "hit the target." But in the New Testament this negative meaning is largely lost sight of, and sin is viewed as positive and active. As Stählin notes, "A complete transformation takes place when the NT uses *hamartia* to denote the determination of human nature in hostility to God."[40] Sin is a deliberate deviation from and infraction of the standard of right, a willful rebellion, arising from the deliberate choice of the sinner. "Sin is the greatest tragedy of the entire universe. It's actually rebellion against God."[41] Thus by its nature sin has the character of lawlessness.

The added statement, "for sin is the transgression of the law" (*kai hē hamartia estin hē anomia*, literally, "the sin is the lawlessness"), declares

---

[39]Burdick, p. 236.

[40]Gustav Stählin, *"hamartanō, hamartēma, hamartia,"* in *Theological Dictionary Of the New Testament,* ed. Gerhard Kittel (Grand Rapids: Eerdmans, 1964), 1:295.

[41]Quinton J. Everest, *Messages from 1 John* (South Bend, Ind.: Your Worship Hour, 1982), p. 90.

the essential nature of sin. Since both nouns have the definite article, the terms are interchangeable. Sin by its nature involves an element of lawlessness, and every form of lawlessness is sin. The term "lawlessness" *(anomia)* "does not mean a state of being without law, but the assertion of the individual will against and in defiance of the law of God, the refusal to live in accordance with the revealed standards of right and wrong."[42] It is thus the very opposite of righteousness, which is conformity to the standard or law of right. Thus John may intend his picture of the nature of sin to be a refutation of the heretics who maintained that their inner enlightenment lifted them above the demands of the moral law. Others suggest that, in view of the end-time motif in this epistle (2:18-19, 28; 3:3; 4:1, 17), this reference to "lawlessness" may identify the claims of the false teachers with the lawless spirit of the eschatological Antichrist (2 Thess. 2:3).[43]

2) *The incompatibility of sin with Christ's mission* (v. 5). The connective "and" *(kai)* points to a further fact revealing the seriousness of sin. "And ye know" *(kai oidate)* reminds his readers that this further fact concerning sin will be obvious to all those who have experienced the truth of the apostolic message concerning Christ's redemptive mission. The fact that "he was manifested to take away our sins" *(ekeinos ephanerōthē hina tas hamartias arē)* stamps the practice of sin as contrary to Christ's mission. The use of the demonstrative pronoun *ekeinos,* "that one," points back to the unique person who appeared on the scene of human history. John does not say He "was born" but "was manifested," was made visible to human eyes, implying His existence prior to His incarnate appearing. He appeared "to take away our sins," literally, "the sins" *(tas hamartias),* the multitudinous acts of human sin. The plural is in keeping with John's concern here with the actual practice of sin rather than the sinful inner nature which prompts the sinful deeds. Christ came to "take away" *(arē)* those sins. The verb may mean "to lift and bear" or "to take away." The latter is the meaning here and seems reminiscent of the testimony of John the Baptist, "Behold the Lamb of God, which taketh away the sin of the world" (John 1:29). The aorist tense *(arē)* indicates the effective removal of human sins as the goal of Christ's coming. Clearly this removal of sins is grounded in His expiatory sacrifice on the cross, although the stress here is on the effect of Christ's appearing on human conduct. The elimination of the practice of sin from the lives of Christ's followers now reveals the effectiveness of His mission; the total elimination of sin from the human scene awaits the eschatological future.

---

[42]R. J. Drummond and Leon Morris, "The Epistles of John," in *The New Bible Commentary* (Grand Rapids: Eerdmans, 1953), p. 1155.

[43]See Brown, pp. 399-400.

The reading "to take away our sins" follows the Textus Receptus *(tas hamartias hēmōn arē)*. The manuscript evidence for "our" is divided,[44] and it is not easy to decide whether it is authentic. If it is original, it strengthens John's insistence that the practice of sin is contrary to Christ's purpose for believers. For a professed believer to persist in the practice of sin reveals that he is still spiritually blind to the purpose and work of Christ or demonstrates that he willfully scorns and rejects the demands of Christ upon his daily conduct.

The added words "and in him is no sin" *(kai hamartia en autō ouk estin,* literally, "and sin in Him not exists") emphatically declare the sinlessness of the remover of sins. As such He is the perfect pattern of what the child of God should be.

b. The distinction between the two classes of humanity (vv. 6-8a). Viewed in the light of Christ's mission to remove sins, their distinctive moral conduct established the reality of two classes of humanity. The characteristic marks leave no room for a neutral third group. John states their contrasted moral conduct (v. 6) and then notes their distinctive character (vv. 7-8a).

1) *The practice of the two classes* (v. 6). The distinguishing practice of the two classes is tersely stated: "Whosoever abideth in him sinneth not; whosoever sinneth hath not seen him, neither known him." In both statements "whosoever" is literally "every one" *(pas ho),* the present active participle portraying the characteristic activity of the group, followed by a negative *(ouk)* with the verb to express a categorical denial: "everyone who . . . does not. . . ."

Everyone in the first group is characterized by his abiding relationship with Christ: "Whosoever abideth in him sinneth not" *(pas ho en autō menōn ouch hamartanei,* literally, "every one in Him abiding not is sinning"). The position of "in Him" *(en autō)* between the article and the present participle marks his ongoing relationship with Christ as an essential feature of his identity. He continually "abideth" in Christ as the true sphere of his life, dwelling in Him in whom there is no sin. This relationship of remaining "in him" implies obedience to Him (John 15:10) rather than following his own will. Of such a one John asserts that he "sinneth not" *(ouch hamartanei),* does not continue in willful, habitual sin. John has already indicated that the believer cannot claim never to commit an act of sin (1:8-9; 2:1). Sin may enter his experience as an exception which calls for immediate confession and cleansing; he is not at liberty to make occasional excursions into sin but should continually seek to avoid any lapse into sin. John's apparently contradictory statements concerning sin and the believer reflect that inner tension which Paul discusses in Romans 7.

---

[44]For the textual evidence see Nestle-Aland, *Novum Testamentum Graece,* 26th ed.; United Bible Societies, *The Greek New Testament,* 3rd ed.

Of the second group John asserts that "whosoever sinneth hath not seen him, neither known him." The construction again depicts a distinct class, all of its members characterized by the practice of sin as the ruling principle of their lives. The basic contrast between the two groups is sharply drawn; the first is marked by a continuing relationship with Christ, the second by the continuing practice of sin. There is also a strong contrast in the negative expressed concerning each group; the first group does not practice sin, but the second group "hath not seen him, neither known him" *(ouch heōraken auton oude egnōken auton)*. The two negations concerning the second group are not identical in meaning. The first verb, "hath seen" *(heōraken)*, here does not refer to a literal seeing of Jesus in the flesh, as in 1:2-3, but denotes a spiritual vision of Him through faith (cf. Eph. 1:18; Heb. 11:27); he has never arrived at a clear perception of the true nature of the incarnate Christ. The second verb "known" *(egnōken)* denies that he has entered into a personal relationship with Him so as to become familiar with the characteristics of the incarnate Christ.

2) *The moral character of the two classes* (vv. 7-8a). The moral identity of each group is established by its characteristic practice. John first expresses a pastoral warning (v. 7a) and then clearly evaluates the character of each group (vv. 7b-8a).

a) *The pastoral warning against deceivers* (v. 7a). The tender personal address to the readers, "little children" *(teknia;* see 2:1, 12), appeals to their consciousness that they are members of God's family. The warning "let no man deceive you" *(mēdeis planatō humas)* voices John's pastoral concern for the continued safety of his readers; he appeals to them to be constantly alert to the danger from the deceivers. Apparently the reference is to the false teachers who had left their assemblies (2:19) but were aggressively seeking to mislead those who had not withdrawn with them. While generally the negative *(mē)* with the present imperative calls for the cessation of an action already in progress, clearly John here does not imply that his readers are already being deceived. He calls for constant alertness against the deceptions of the false teachers. In 2:26 the warning was against doctrinal deception; here the reference is to deception concerning the moral demands of the gospel. John well knows that "the false teachers with their sophistry were capable not merely of condoning sin, but of making it seem virtuous."[45] To avoid deception let them discern the moral identity of the individual making his appeal to them.

b) *The moral criterion for each class* (vv. 7b-8a). The criterion for a true believer is, "he that doeth righteousness is righteous" *(ho poiōn tēn dikaosunēn dikaios estin)*. The present-tense participle makes clear that the test is

---

[45]Bruce, p. 91.

not the performance of an occasional righteous deed but rather the habitual practice of "righteousness," literally, "the righteousness" which is the product of the new birth (cf. 2:29). The practice of righteousness does not make the individual righteous but does reveal his inner nature. It is the test of Matthew 7:16–"Ye shall know them by their fruits." The test refutes any claim by the heretical teachers to be righteous because of their professed esoteric knowledge. John insists that the moral nature of an individual's conduct is the sure evidence that his inner life conforms to the righteousness of God.

The added words "even as He is righteous" *(kathōs ekeinos dikaios estin)* point out that the conduct of the true believer corresponds to the moral nature of the Christ to whom he is committed. "He" *(ekeinos)*, as elsewhere in this epistle, refers to Christ, not to the Father as Alford suggests.[46] The comparative "even as" *(kathōs)* does not mean that the believer is righteous to the same extent that Christ is, for the believer as a finite being still has a human nature that is fallible and prone to committing an act of sin (2:1). As one who is born again, his desire is to live a life morally consistent with the nature of the one who saved him.

The other group is also identified by its conduct (v. 8a): "He that committeth sin is of the devil" *(ho poiōn tēn hamartian ek tou diabolou estin)*. John centers attention on the individual, representative of his class, who is actively engaged in "doing the sin," the sin of rebellion and self-will which characterizes the realm of the Devil. Commenting on the present-tense participle *(poiōn)*, Trapp remarks that this sinner "makes a trade of it."[47] By his practice he reveals his diabolical nature. John does not say such a one is "born of the devil" (contrast 2:29) but "is of the devil." The "of" *(ek)* denotes source, not of his personal existence, but of the evil which dominates his life and practice (John 8:41-44). In the words of Augustine, "For the devil made no man, begat no man, created no man: but whoso imitates the devil, that person, as if begotten of him, becomes a child of the devil; by imitating him, not literally by being begotten of him."[48] By neglecting and rejecting the moral requirements of God's Word, the sinner reveals that his priorities are rooted in the realm of "the devil." This is the first of four occurrences of the name "Devil" in this epistle (3:8, 10); the name means "slanderer," one who knowingly and deliberately advances

---

[46]Alford, p. 1725.

[47]John Trapp, *Trapp's Commentary on the New Testament* (1865; reprint ed., Evansville, Ind.: The Sovereign Grace Book Club, 1958), p. 729.

[48]Augustine, Homily 4, sect. 10, in *Ten Homilies on the First Epistle of John,* trans. H. Browne, *Nicene and Post-Nicene Fathers of the Christian Church* (Reprint ed., Grand Rapids: Eerdmans, 1974), 1st series, 7:486.

false charges against God and His people. As the direct opponent of God, the Devil cannot be depersonalized as simply the power of evil. He works in and through those who yield themselves to his diabolical purposes.

The further comment "for the devil sinneth from the beginning" *(hoti ap' archēs ho diabolos hamartanei)* explains that the practice of sin is so diabolical because the Devil is its originator. The phrase "from the beginning" *(ap' archēs),* placed emphatically forward, does not mean from the beginning of his existence; that would make God responsible for this evil being or assert a Gnostic dualism. It rather points back to that primeval disaster when this august created being arose in self-willed rebellion against God and thus became the arch-opponent of God and His good purposes.[49] Ever since his fall the Devil "sinneth" *(hamartanei),* that is, has relentlessly persevered in his evil course of sin and rebellion.

3. The Deliverance from the Practice of Sin (vv. 8b-9)

The nature and results of sin make inevitable God's opposition to sin and the work of the Devil. John accordingly states the divine provision for deliverance from sin (v. 8b) and declares the reality of human deliverance from sin through the experience of the new birth (v. 9).

a. The divine provision in Christ's mission (v. 8b). Human deliverance from sin can be realized only through the work of the incarnate Son of God. God took the initiative in procuring human redemption: "For this purpose the Son of God was manifested, that He might destroy the works of the devil." The distinctive title "the Son of God," the first of seven occurrences in this epistle,[50] underlies the true identity of the one who "was manifested" to crush the power of sin and Satan. The aorist verb "was manifested" *(ephanerōthē)* indicates His visible appearing in incarnation; it points back to his pre-existence as the eternal Son of God. His identity marks the supernatural struggle involved in His coming "that he might destroy the works of the devil." His incarnate work provided the full counterpart to the "works of the devil."

The stated purpose, "that he might destroy the works of the devil" *(hina lusē ta erga tou diabolou),* presents Christ's redemptive mission as it relates to the Devil, the great spiritual antagonist of God and mankind. The plural "the works" points to the massive activities and achievements of the Devil in leading human beings into sin and rebellion against God. All these works have a certain coherence as being prompted by the personal hatred and

---

[49]For a survey of the Biblical picture of the Devil see D. E. Hiebert, "Satan," in *Zondervan Pictorial Encyclopedia of the Bible* (Grand Rapids: Zondervan, 1975), 5:282-86.

[50]Here; 4:15; 5:5, 10, 13 (twice), 20. Compare also John's frequent use of "son" or "His Son."

rebellion of the Devil himself. Prevailing human suffering and death are the results of Satan's work of leading mankind into sin.

The aorist verb "might destroy" *(lusē)* implies a decisive occurrence and seems most naturally to refer to Christ's victory over the Devil on the cross (John 12:31; Heb. 2:14). The verb does not mean "to annihilate" but variously means "to loose, break up, give release, render powerless or inoperative." On the cross, Christ in His victory over the Devil broke the chains of sin whereby the Devil had brought mankind under his domination (Heb. 2:14-15). Satan is now a defeated foe, but the individual can find release from his clutches only by personally appropriating Christ and His deliverance. This undoing of the Devil's works in breaking the power of sin, effectively initiated at Calvary, is now going forward through the Spirit-empowered preaching of the gospel and will be consummated at Christ's return and the incarceration of the Devil (Rev. 20:1-3).

b. The human deliverance through the new birth (v. 9). With his use of two finite verbs with a negative, John makes a double statement of the human experience of deliverance from sin as Christ's provision is appre-hended and appropriated by faith. Each statement is followed by an explan-atory clause. This verse, especially the second part, offers varied difficulties for the interpreter.

The first statement, "Whosoever is born of God doth not commit sin" *(pas ho gegennēmenos ek tou theou hamartian ou poiei,* literally, "every one having been born of God sin not is doing"), again expresses a universal assertion which allows no exceptions. The articular perfect passive participle *(ho gegennēmenos)* asserts the past fact of his new birth with the result that he is now a new-born being. The full phrase "born of God," declaring the action of God in his regeneration, occurs here for the first time (cf. 2:29, "born of Him") and is repeatedly used hereafter. Concerning every born-again individual, John asserts "sin not he is doing" (literal). The rendering "practice sin" (NASB) adequately gives the meaning. This is a restatement of verse 6 where his abiding in Christ explains his conduct; here the indicated empowerment is his new birth. The KJV rendering, "doth not commit sin," may readily be misunderstood to mean that he does not commit an act of sin.

John explains the born-again individual's termination of the practice of sin in adding "for his seed remaineth in him" *(hoti sperma autou en autō menei).* The indwelling of "His seed" motivates and empowers the believ-er's moral conduct. The metaphorical designation "His seed," appearing only here in the Johannine epistles, is variously understood. It may denote the Word of God, or the gospel message, as the regenerating agent that produces the new birth (cf. James 1:18, 21; 1 Pet. 1:23-25).[51] Others take

---

[51]Dodd, pp. 77-78; William Barclay, *The Letters of John and Jude,* Daily Study Bible (Philadelphia: Westminster Press, 1960), p. 94; Lenski, p. 463.

the term more generally as designating the divine principle of life, the new birth, which God implants in the believer.[52] Still others suggest that the reference is to the Holy Spirit as the life-giving agent.[53] Although the term "seed" *(sperma)* is not elsewhere directly used of the Holy Spirit, this view is in keeping with John 3:5-8 where Jesus associates the Holy Spirit with the new birth and the fact that "He is also the producer of Christian character in the believer (2 Cor. 3:18; Gal. 5:22-23)."[54] In response to these varied views, Smalley concludes that "the most satisfactory exegesis of this passage is one which brings together the two concepts of 'word' and 'Spirit.' "[55] Obviously the Word of God is the life-giving means which the Holy Spirit uses to implant and develop the new nature in the believers.

John's second statement concerning the born-again believer is "and he cannot sin, because he is born of God" *(kai ou dunatai hamartanein, hoti ek theou gegennētai)*. This statement is more sweeping than the former and has been the occasion of much discussion.[56] Some perceive the assertion "and he cannot sin" to be difficult or even inconsistent with John's teaching in 1:8–2:3, as well as the experience of the most saintly believer. John's categorical assertion here is grounded in the moral incongruity between the practice of sin and the nature of the divinely bestowed new birth. In seeking to understand the teaching here, one must keep in view the force of the present tenses, "doing sin" and "cannot sin," as suggesting the habitual practice of sin. John insists that the believer's inability to continue in the practice of sin is due to the fact that he has been born of God. The urge not to sin, implanted by the new birth, reflects the nature and purpose of God to eliminate sin, while the old nature within the believer (Rom. 7:13-25) continues as the inner urge to yield to the allurements of sin and Satan. It is this moral incompatibility between the believer's old and new nature that seems to be reflected in John's apparent inconsistency. The conflict proves the reality of the new birth. As Bruce observes,

> The new birth involves a radical change in human nature; for those who have not experienced it, sin is natural, whereas for those who have experienced it, sin is unnatural—so unnatural, indeed, that its practice constitutes a powerful refutation of any claim to possess the divine life. John's antitheses are clear-cut. While they are to be understood in the context of his letter and of the situation which it presupposes, any attempt to weaken them out

---

[52]Westcott, p. 107; Bruce, p. 92; Kistemaker, p. 303.

[53]A. E. Brooke, *A Critical and Exegetical Commentary on the Johannine Epistles,* International-al Critical Commentary (New York: Charles Scribners' Sons, 1912), p. 89; Burdick, p. 247.

[54]Burdick, p. 247.

[55]Smalley, p. 173.

[56]Brown, pp. 412-16, lists and evaluates seven different approaches to the difficulty.

of regard for human infirmity, or to make them less sharp and uncompromising than they are, is to misinterpret them.[57]

John's present-tense assertion "he cannot sin" (*ou dunatai hamartanein,* literally, "not he is able to go on sinning") does not declare a perfectionism which insists that the believer, as John here views him, can no longer commit an act of sin. Rather, as Barclay states, "He is demanding a life which is ever on the watch against sin, a life which ever fights the battle of goodness, a life which has never surrendered to sin, a life in which sin is not the permanent state, but only the temporary aberration, a life in which sin is not the normal accepted way, but the abnormal moment of defeat."[58]

4. The Sign of the Children of God and the Children of the Devil (vv. 10-12)

In verses 10-11 John restates the significance of personal conduct as the identifying sign of the two classes and adds that brother-love is an important aspect of this sign. In verse 12 he adds a negative reference to Cain as illustrating the distinctiveness of the two groups.

a. The criteria for the two classes of humanity (vv. 10-11). The words "in this the children of God are manifest, and the children of the devil" *(en toutō phanera estin ta tekna tou theou kai ta tekna tou diabolou)* point to a summary of the discussion concerning these two classes. "In this" *(en toutō,* or "herein") may refer either to what precedes or follows as pointing to the two distinct groups. The neuter plural adjective "manifest" *(phanera,* meaning "visible, plainly to be seen") stands emphatically forward to stress that the deeds of each group are readily identified. "A man's principles are invisible," Plummer notes, "but their results are visible."[59] This test reveals only two classes, "the children of God" and "the children of the devil." John knows of no intermediate class.

1) *The children of the Devil* (v. 10b). Having asserted that the marks distinguishing the two groups are "manifest," or "plainly to be seen," John now points out the significance of their absence: "whosoever doeth not righteousness is not of God" *(pas ho mē poiōn dikaiosumēn ouk estin ek tou theou).* The statement (*pas ho* with the negative) asserts that this negative reality is also all-inclusive and allows no exceptions. John assumes that the reality of the new birth, which produces righteous conduct, reveals its existence in daily action. The absence of righteous conduct demonstrates that the individual is not righteous in character. He is "not of God," does not have his spiritual origin in Him. As such, he is one of "the children of the devil" *(ta tekan tou diabolou,* v. 10a). The designation, "the children of the

---

[57]Bruce, p. 92.

[58]Barclay, pp. 96-97.

[59]Plummer, p. 128.

devil," occurs only here in the New Testament (but compare "child of the devil"–Acts 13:10, and "*your* father the devil"–John 8:44 as synonymous). The expression "the children of the wicked *one*" in Matthew 13:38 is a parallel designation.

The added negative test "neither he that loveth not his brother" *(kai ho mē agapōn ton adelphon autou)* makes clear that love of the brethren is an essential aspect of the practice of righteousness. Love is righteousness in relation to others: "For all the law is fulfilled in one word, even in this; Thou shalt love thy neighbor as thyself" (Gal. 5:14). Love is "an act of will. It is not feeling warm towards other people in a general way, but doing good to specific individuals."[60] "His brother " may denote a fellow human being, but apparently here John uses it in a narrower sense to mean a fellow member of the Christian community. His failure to love another member of the family of God was tangible evidence that he lacked the inner bond uniting the members of the family. He was motivated by a different spirit.

2) *The children of God* (v. 11). The opening "For" *(hoti)* introduces verification of the preceding negative assertion. The absence of love in the life of a professed child of God was inconsistent with the apostolic message proclaimed to them:"this is the message that ye heard from the beginning" *(hautē estin hē anggelia hēn ēkousate ap' archēs).* The demonstrative "this" *(hautē)* looks forward to the following "that" clause, "that we should love one another." This message came to them when they first heard the gospel; John is not seeking to impose a new stipulation upon them which they can safely ignore. The original apostolic message declared that believers should love one another, that the practice of mutual love was fundamental to the Christian faith. In saying "that we should love one another," John again unites himself with his readers in accepting this duty. The reciprocal pronoun "one another" *(allēlous)* marks the mutual operation of this love in social relations, each lovingly seeking the welfare of the other. In 1:7 John uses this pronoun of the mutual fellowship believers enjoy; the pronoun occurs five more times in this epistle, each time as the direct object of the verb "love," always in the present tense.[61] Such a love cannot be reserved only for select occasions or expressed only toward some members of the family!

b. *The negative illustration of the story of Cain* (v. 12). John cites the story of Cain as evidence that the absence of brother-love is a mark of a child of the Devil. This is the only reference to any Old Testament event in the Johannine epistles. John assumes that his readers are familiar with the details of the Biblical account. The opening words "not as Cain" *(ou kathōs Kain)* convey a negative analogy; John asks his readers to contrast themselves with

---

[60]Jackman, p. 96.
[61]1 John 3:11, 23; 4:7, 11, 12.

Cain. In 2:6, 3:3, 7; 4:17 John uses the comparative "as" *(kathōs)* positively to appeal to the authority of the life and character of Jesus.

Cain is identified as "of that wicked one" *(ek tou ponērou)*, another name for the Devil, one that marks his malignant and destructive nature (cf. 2:13b). Cain "drew his inspiration from the evil one, the devil, who is himself the archetypal murderer" (John 8:44).[62] This is a declaration of the character of Cain.

The added words "and slew his brother" *(kai esphaxen ton adelphon autou)* cite his conduct as establishing his evil character. The verb "slew" *(esphaxen)* occurs only here and in Revelation[63] in the New Testament and implies a violent death. In the Septuagint it was used of sacrificial animals, "to slaughter, butcher, cut the throat." The cognate noun *(sphagē)* occurs in Acts 8:32, Romans 8:36, and James 5:5 and is rendered "slaughter." The term thus points to the merciless, cold-blooded action of Cain.

John's unexpected and rhetorical question, "And wherefore slew he him?" *(kai charin tínos esphaxen auton;)*, serves to elicit the motive for his vicious deed. The unusual construction[64] strongly brings out the diabolical nature of the act and its agent.

John's own answer, "Because his own works were evil, and his brother's righteous *(hoti ta erga autou ponēra ēn, ta de tou adelphou autou dikaia)*, stresses the contrast between the deeds of the two brothers as manifestations of their character. The language reflects the reality of the two antithetical realms of being that John has already insisted on (cf. 1:5; etc.). The righteous deeds of Abel evoked Cain's jealousy, intensified a feeling of condemnation within him, and fed a vicious hatred that culminated in murder. As Stott remarks, "Jealousy–hatred–murder is a natural and terrible sequence."[65]

That ancient story conveyed a vital and needed lesson for John's readers who were subjected to the hatred of the antichrists who had gone out from the orthodox believers (2:18-19). It is still true that the believer's righteous character and conduct arouse the world's hatred. And, as in the case of Cain, that hatred is often expressed in vicious and violent action against believers.

---

[62]Marshall, p. 189.

[63]Revelation 5:6, 9, 12; 6:4, 9; 13:3, 8; 18:24.

[64]The use of *charin* as a preposition is rare in the NT, and only here does it stand before the word it governs. With the interrogative pronoun, *tínos,* the question literally is "on account of what?"

[65]J.R.W. Stott, *The Epistles of John,* Tyndale New Testament Commentaries (Grand Rapids: Eerdmans, 1964), p. 140.

10

Assurance from the Conflicts of Faith (Part 3)

C. The Conflict Between Love and Hatred (3:13-24)

3:13 Marvel not, my brethren, if the world hate you.

14 We know that we have passed from death unto life, because we love the brethren. He that loveth not *his* brother abideth in death.

15 Whosoever hateth his brother is a murderer: and ye know that no murderer hath eternal life abiding in him.

16 Hereby perceive we the love *of God,* because he laid down his life for us: and we ought to lay down *our* lives for the brethren.

17 But whoso hath this world's good, and seeth his brother have need, and shutteth up his bowels *of compassion* from him, how dwelleth the love of God in him?

18 My little children, let us not love in word, neither in tongue; but in deed and in truth.

19 And hereby we know that we are of the truth, and shall assure our hearts before him.

20 For if our heart condemn us, God is greater than our heart, and knoweth all things.

21 Beloved, if our heart condemn us not, *then* have we confidence toward God.

22 And whatsoever we ask, we receive of him, because we keep his commandments, and do those things that are pleasing in his sight.

23 And this is his commandment, That we should believe on the name of his Son Jesus Christ, and love one another, as he gave us commandment.

24 And he that keepeth his commandments dwelleth in him, and he in him. And hereby we know that he abideth in us, by the Spirit which he hath given us.

The conflict between truth and falsehood depicted in 2:18-28 was seen in 2:29–3:12 as a conflict between the children of God and the children of the Devil. The reference to the hatred of Cain in 3:12 introduces a further aspect of this conflict. In this further picture of the conflict of the Christian life, John clearly indicates that it is experientially a conflict between God-prompted love and Satan-inspired hatred.

John now sets forth that the practice of love and hatred establishes the moral identity of two distinct classes of human beings (vv. 13-15), portrays the objective manifestation of love and hatred (vv. 16-18), and presents varied aspects of the assurance which the practice of Christian love produces (vv. 19-24).

1. The Revelation from the Practice of Love and Hatred (vv. 13-15)

The antagonism between good and evil, as reflected in the story of Cain and Abel (3:12), has never ceased since that day. John reminds his readers that hatred is still the world's reaction toward the people of God (v. 13) and assures them that love of the brethren is the sign of the new birth (v. 14a) and that the practice of hatred is the sign of spiritual death (vv. 14b-15).

a. The reaction to the world's hatred of believers (v. 13). John urges his readers not to be surprised by the fact that the world hates them: "Marvel not, my brethren, if the world hate you." His use of the first-class conditional sentence makes clear that this is a recognized reality. By stating the conclusion before the condition, John places emphasis upon the admonition being given.

The prohibition "marvel not" *(mē thaumazete)* calls upon the readers not to yield to this natural reaction when they are the innocent object of unprovoked hatred. The verb denotes a personal reaction of wonder, surprise, and amazement when someone encounters hatred. The negative *(mē)* with the present imperative prohibits the continued response. John does not condemn the initial feeling of amazement when hatred assails them, but believers must not give way to such a feeling of surprise and self-pity. The prohibition is a direct echo of the teaching of Jesus in John 15:18-21. Compare also a similar message in Matthew 5:11-12 and in 1 Peter 4:13. When the world reveals its hatred toward the Christian, it is vitally important that the believer recognize that such hatred is the natural response of the sinful world toward righteousness. The hatred assures the believer of the moral identity of those hating him.

The added direct address, "my brethren" *(adelphoi),* occurs only here in the Johannine epistles,[1] although it is a common form of address in the New Testament epistles. With its use John consciously draws his readers together as fellow-members of the Christian community in contrast to an

---

[1]The word "brethren" *(adelphoi)* in 2:7 lacks sufficient manuscript support to be accepted as original. Cf. footnotes on 2:7.

antagonistic world. As their brother, John knows what it meant to be hated by the world. Perhaps the change from "little children" (3:7) to "brethren" was intended to remind the readers that their own position is spiritually comparable to that of Abel, the 'brother' of Cain. Although the use of "my" adds intimacy to the address, the strongest manuscript evidence indicates that the pronoun is not a part of the original.

The conditional statement "if the world hate you" *(ei misei humas ho kosmos)* presents this hatred, not as a future possibility, but as a present reality. Such a hatred is the characteristic attitude of the Christ-rejecting world toward His faithful followers. Stott remarks, "It is not just hatred, but hatred of Christian people, which reveals the world in its true colours, for in their persecution of the Church their antagonism to Christ is revealed."[2] Like Cain of old, the world in its alienation from and opposition to God cannot tolerate the presence of righteousness. In the words of Barker, "Whenever the community of faith acts so as to expose the greed, the avarice, the hatred, and the wickedness of the world, it must expect rejection; and if it should go so far as to interfere with its evil practices, as Jesus did in the temple, it may expect suffering and brutal death (cf. John 15:18-19, 25; 17:14)."[3] History confirms that the hatred of the world is most aggressive whenever the life and witness of the Church are vital and Spirit-empowered. Lias sadly remarks, "It is perhaps because our Christianity is often of a feeble and nerveless type, because we tamely acquiesce in wrong-doing, which long prescription seems to excuse, that we feel so little of it."[4]

b. The assurance of the new birth from love of the brethren (v. 14a). John's emphatic use of the personal pronoun, "We know" *(hēmeis oidamen),* marks the contrasts between the world, lost in sin and spiritually dead, and true believers, with their inner consciousness of their new life in Christ. *"We know what the world knows not."*[5] It is an appeal to the inner consciousness of the readers as to their true identity in facing a hostile world. The content of this knowledge is "that we have passed from death unto life" *(hoti meta-bebēkamen ek tou thanatou eis tēn zōēn).* They are assured that the promise of life in John 5:24 has been fulfilled in their own lives. The perfect tense,

---

[2]J.R.W. Stott, *The Epistles of John,* Tyndale New Testament Commentaries (Grand Rapids: Eerdmans, 1964), p. 141.

[3]Glen W. Barker, "1 John," in *The Expositor's Bible Commentary* (Grand Rapids: Zondervan, 1981), 12:335.

[4]John James Lias, *An Exposition of the First Epistle of John* (1887; reprint ed., Minneapolis: Klock & Klock Christian Publishers, 1982), p. 255.

[5] A. R. Fausset, "The First General Epistle of John," in Robert Jamieson, A. R. Fausset, and David Brown, *A Commentary, Critical and Explanatory, on the Old and New Testaments,* American ed. (Hartford, Conn.: S. S. Scranton, Co., n.d.), vol. 2, *New Testament,* p. 532. Italics in original.

"have passed," denotes a permanent transfer from one realm into another. Geographically, this verb was used of migrating from one country to another. Here it is used metaphorically to denote their spiritual transfer out of the realm of death into the realm of life. The definite article with both nouns, "out of the death into the life," highlights the distinctness of the two realms into which earth's inhabitants are divided. The designation "the death" here does not refer to physical death but rather to the spiritual state of mankind's separation from God, the alienation from God which is the result of the fall (Rom. 5:12). This state is the opposite, spiritually, of "the life." "As spiritual life is 'conscious existence in communion with God,' so spiritual death is 'conscious existence in separation from God.' "[6] There is no neutral ground between the two realms. This passing out of death into life is another way of designating what John 3:5 refers to as "entering into the kingdom of God." As Marshall remarks, "John never suggests that some people are by nature endowed with spiritual life; on the contrary, a process of spiritual birth is necessary."[7] For the believer, united to Christ by faith, possession of eternal life is already a present reality, not merely a state to be attained after physical death.

This assurance of possessing eternal life is grounded in Christian experience, "because we love the brethren" *(hoti agapōmen tous adelphous)*. The particle "because" *(hoti)* connects with "we know" and is causal in force; our love for "the brethren," fellow-members of God's born-again family, is the evidence of our new life, not the means of acquiring it. What we do reveals what we are. As Lenski notes, "Both the physical life and the spiritual life are not seen directly but are apparent only from their evidence, their activity."[8] The present tense, "we love," depicts the characteristic practice, not merely an occasional act of love. The verb denotes not natural affection stimulated by the loveliness of the one loved but a high ethical love which consistently seeks the true welfare of those loved. Fallen human nature is selfish and resists any claims on its time that conflicts with those of self; therefore, when an individual consistently places the welfare of others above his own, it is a sure sign that he has received a new nature. Implanted at regeneration, this love naturally manifests itself toward "the brethren"— all those who are members of God's family with us. Blaney indeed asserts, "Love for *the brethren* (14) is a better piece of evidence than love for the sinful world, because if one cannot love 'the children of God,' how could

[6]W. E. Vine, *An Expository Dictionary of New Testament Words with Their Precise Meanings for English Readers* (London: Oliphants, 1939), 1:276.

[7]I. Howard Marshall, *The Epistles of John,* New International Commentary on the New Testament (Grand Rapids: Eerdmans, 1978), p. 191.

[8]R.C.H. Lenski, *The Interpretation of the Epistles of St. Peter, St. John and St. Jude* (Columbus, Ohio: Wartburg Press, 1945), p. 469.

he be expected to love the 'children of the devil'?''[9] Although true Christian love will seek to do good to all people as there is opportunity, it will do so ''especially unto them who are of the household of faith'' (Gal. 6:10).

c. *The revelation from the practice of hatred* (vv. 14b-15). The practice of love is the determinative test for all who claim to be Christians. John applies this test both negatively and positively.

1) *The absence of love reveals spiritual death* (v. 14b). John tersely states the significance when such love is absent: ''He that loveth not *his* brother abideth in death'' (*ho mē agapōn menei en tō thanotō,* literally, ''the one not loving abides in the death''). The import of this negative assertion is arresting. As Morgan points outs,

> It charges as a crime the want of a grace and not merely the perpetration of evil. It is not the wrong that has been done, but that a good has not been rendered. It is sin under the form of a want of conformity to the law, not a transgression of it.[10]

This absence of love reveals his inner state, that he continues to abide in the realm of spiritual death. Whatever his claims to spiritual enlightenment, the absence of love proves that he still remains in the realm of death with its alienation from God. John does not say that he will die but rather that he still remains in his original state as spiritually dead (Eph. 2:1).

After the word ''love'' some Greek manuscripts add a direct object, ''the brother'' or ''his brother,'' but the shorter reading is to be preferred.[11] The shorter reading is attested by superior witnesses, and the scribes would more naturally add the object to complete the statement than to delete the object. Without a stated object, John's assertion is very strong and sweeping in its scope.

2) *The practice of hatred reveals a murderous personality* (v. 15). John supplements the preceding negative assertion with a sweeping positive assertion: ''Whosoever hateth his brother is a murderer'' *(pas ho misōn ton adelphon autou anthrōpoktonos estin).* John now equates the preceding negative, ''does not love,'' with active hatred. Love and hatred are mutually exclusive realms with no neutral ground between them. The fact that he actively hates his brother establishes his inner identity: he ''is a murderer.'' Love and hatred are moral opposites, but hatred and murder belong to the same moral realm.

---

[9]Harvey J.S. Blaney, ''The First Epistle of John,'' in *Beacon Bible Commentary* (Kansas City, Mo.: Beacon Hill Press, 1967), 10:381.

[10]James Morgan, *The Epistles of John* (1865; reprint ed., Minneapolis: Klock & Klock Christian Publishers, 1982), p. 244.

[11]For the textual evidence see Nestle-Aland, *Novum Testamentum Graece,* 26th ed. (Stuttgart: Deutsche Bibelstiftung, 1979).

The reference is not to someone who is caught in a surge of hatred toward someone but rather to one who as a continuing habit harbors hatred toward another. Hatred in its very nature is destructive; all hatred is potentially–and may in actual practice become–murderous. "Murder is in the heart before it is in the hand."[12] Murderous hatred always fills the emptiness left in the heart by the absence of love. Human law condemns a man for the overt act; God judges the evil inner desire. In God's eyes the hater–although he may refrain from actual killing because of his fear of the consequences–and the murderer are both guilty. John here does with the sixth commandment, "Thou shalt not kill" (Exod. 20:13), what Jesus in Matthew 5:27-28 did with the seventh commandment, "Thou shalt not commit adultery." The guilt of the sin lies in the inner motive, not merely the outward act.

The rare word "murderer" (*anthrōpoktonos,* literally, "man-killer") occurs in the New Testament only here and in John 8:44, where Jesus describes the Devil as "a murderer from the beginning." Satan revealed his murderous spirit in the beginning of human history by leading Eve and Adam into sin, into destructive rebellion against the Word of God. Hatred and murder belong to the realm dominated by Satan. He who has such a spirit cannot belong to the realm of light and love of which God is the center and motivating power.

Following his sweeping assertion concerning the murderer, John adds a confirmatory note expressing the Christian conviction of his readers: "and ye know that no murderer hath eternal life abiding in him." The verb "you know" *(eidate)* denotes knowledge that is generally accepted, axiomatic, or intuitive. It does not require searching inquiry or scientific demonstration to conclude "that no murderer hath eternal life abiding in him" (*hoti pas anthrōpoktonos ouk echei zōēn aiōnion en autō menousan,* literally, "that every murderer not is having life eternal in him abiding"). The inclusive "every murderer" allows no exceptions; it includes every individual whose governing spirit is murderous. The assertion does not refer to the ultimate fate of the murderer but relates to his present state. Nor does John mean that a murderer cannot repent, be forgiven, and receive eternal life. But the Christian conscience recognizes that no individual governed by a murderous spirit can have "eternal life abiding in him." The adjective "eternal" is qualitative, denoting a life that is related to the nature of God Himself; it is also quantitative as denoting unending duration, neither gained nor lost by physical death. The present participle "abiding" *(menousan),* emphatic by its position at the end of the sentence, marks the continuing indwelling of this God-given life in the individual. But human logic, as well as the Christian conscience, concludes that no one who holds on to a spirit of bitter hatred and hostility toward a fellow believer can at the same time have eternal life abiding in him.

---

[12]Herschel H. Hobbs, *The Epistles of John* (Nashville: Thomas Nelson Publishers, 1983), p. 90.

2. The Manifestation of Love and Hatred (vv. 16-18)

Having shown *what* the presence or absence of love in one's life reveals, John next points out *how* love and hatred are manifested. He stresses the supreme manifestation of love in the self-sacrifice of Christ (v. 16a), indicates the obligation of believers to practice love (vv. 16b-17), and issues a call to practice true love (v. 18).

a. The manifestation of love in Christ's self-sacrifice (v. 16a). The words "Hereby perceive we the love *of God*" (*en toutō egnōkamen tēn agapēn*, literally, "in this we have come to know the love") call attention to the true criterion of genuine love. "Hereby," or "in this," looks forward to Christ's self-sacrifice as the crucial manifestation of love. The perfect-tense verb "we perceive" *(egnōkamen)* indicates a knowledge that has been gained through diligent contemplation of the significance of that historical event. Having come to know this love through our past encounter with it, we now know the true nature of this love. In Christ's self-sacrifice we possess the supreme manifestation of "the love." (The KJV translators sought to identify this love by adding *"of God."*)[13] The kind of love John is talking about is not native to the human heart. As Smalley notes, "John's reference to love is deliberately couched in absolute terms. He is speaking in the most exalted way of *all* love, love in its essence; and he is showing how this may be identified."[14]

Christ's love is known by what He did: "because he laid down His life for us" *(hoti ekeinos huper hēmōn tēn psuchēn autou ethēken)*. As in 2:6 and 3:7, "he" is the demonstrative pronoun *(ekeinos,* "that one"), marking the distinctive identity of the one whose act of love is cited. He revealed His love by His voluntary and purposeful self-sacrifice when He "laid down His life for us." This expression occurs only here in 1 John, but it is characteristically Johannine (John 10:11, 15, 17, 18; 13:37, 38; 15:13). His love "is not mere sentiment or emotion, not simply words, but deeds."[15] The aorist active verb "laid down" *(ethēken)* denotes a deliberate and voluntary act, expressing a love that is willing to sacrifice self on behalf of others. He was not killed as a martyr but voluntarily gave Himself "for us" *(huper hēmōn),* acting in the interest of others. Although the preposition "for" *(huper)* may be used to present the message of Christ's substitutionary

---

[13]The KJV rendering, "the love *of God,*" is a correct interpretation, but the use of italics, *"of God,"* makes clear that "of God" lacks manuscript support. Raymond E. Brown, *The Epistles of John,* The Anchor Bible (Garden City, N.Y.: Doubleday & Co., 1982), comments "The absoluteness of the original reading ('love' without specifications) is more effective than scribal clarification" (p. 448.)

[14]Stephen S. Smalley, *1, 2, 3 John,* Word Biblical Commentary (Waco, Texas: Word Books, 1984), p. 192.

[15]David Jackman, *The Message of John's Letters,* The Bible Speaks Today (Downers Grove, Ill.: Inter-Varsity Press, 1988), p. 100.

atonement (cf. John 11:50; 1 Cor. 15:3; 2 Cor. 5:21; Gal. 3:13), that does not seem to be the intended message here; rather John is stressing one aspect of Christ's death, His being an example. Since one's own life is an individual's most precious possession, Christ's willingness to lay down that life on behalf of others constituted the greatest possible expression of love (John 15:13; Rom. 5:6-10). " 'Self-preservation' is the first law of physical life; but 'self-sacrifice' is the first law of spiritual life."[16] Such a love is the very opposite of hatred, which is destructive of the welfare of others.

b. *The duty of believers to practice love* (vv. 16b-17). With his use of "and" *(kai),* John at once relates the example of Christ's self-sacrificing love to the lives of believers. Our knowledge of our Saviour's love involves us in the obligation to practice love. John first states the supreme obligation of love (v. 16b) and then pictures the test of love in everyday affairs (v. 17).

1) *The supreme obligation of love* (v. 16b). The connecting "and" *(kai)* unites this obligation with the preceding picture. "Christian love is not born from within the character of the individual but originates in Christ's act."[17] In 2:6 John has already stated the obligation of believers to follow the example of Christ; now he indicates how sweeping that obligation is. The emphatic "we ought" *(hēmeis opheilomen),* which parallels "he" *(ekeinos)* just before, stresses that, like Him, "we ought to lay down *our* lives for the brethren"*(opheilomen huper tōn adelphōn tas psuchas theinai).* Instead of saying "must" *(dei),* which would have conveyed the thought of "logical necessity," John uses "ought" *(opheilomen)* which conveys an inner sense of "moral obligation."[18] The present tense marks this as a continuing obligation, indicating a continuing likeness to Christ. The aorist tense, "to lay down,"[19] denotes the supreme act of self-sacrifice to which Christian love, if necessary, should be willing to go, namely, the willingness to surrender our lives "for the brethren" *(huper tōn adelphōn).* Clearly John is not thinking of believers dying to atone for the sins of others. There were occasions in the life of the early Church, as there are certain tragic occasions in the present life of the Church, which may call for a literal obedience to this precept. Kistemaker remarks, "When the honor of God's name, the advancement of his church, and the need of his people demand that we love

---

[16]Warren W. Wiersbe, *Be Real* (Wheaton, Ill.: Victor Books, 1972), p. 127.

[17]Robert Kysar, *I, II, III John,* Augsburg Commentary on the New Testament (Minneapolis: Augsburg, 1986), p. 84.

[18]G. Abbott-Smith, *A Manual Greek Lexicon of the New Testament,* 3rd ed. (Edinburgh: T. & T. Clark, 1937), p. 99.

[19]The Textus Receptus has the present tense, *tithenai,* but the present tense lacks adequate manuscript support. For the manuscript evidence see Nestle-Aland, *Novum Testamentum Graece,* 26th ed. The present tense would imply a figurative usage of the verb "lay down."

our brothers, we ought to show our love at all cost–even to the point of risking and losing our lives.''[20] John is not seeking to stimulate a spirit of martyrdom in his readers, but he is stressing that this is the extent to which Christian love should be willing to go (John 15:12-13).

2) *The illustration of the lack of brother-love* (v. 17). The adversative ''But'' *(d')* marks a duty connected with, but different from, the ideal just presented. The duty now pictured is presented with down-to-earth practicality: ''whoso hath this world's good, and seeth his brother have need, and shutteth up his bowels *of compassion* from him, how dwelleth the love of God in him?'' The picture is hypothetical; ''whoso hath'' *(hos an echē,* literally, ''he who if he may be having'') introduces a conjectural but very probable scene which is unfolded with the use of three coordinated subjunctive verbs. The expression ''whoso'' (the relative pronoun *hos* without an expressed antecedent) is general and includes anyone who matches the picture.

This supposed individual is one who ''hath this world's good, and seeth his brother have need, and shutteth up his bowels *of compassion* from him.'' The first two verbs are in the present tense, graphically presenting the scene in progress. The first phrase describes his own condition; he ''hath this world's good'' *(echē ton bion tou kosmou),* possesses the material means which sustain life in this present world. In Luke 15:12 the words *ton bion* are translated ''his wealth'' (marg., ''his living'') in the NASB and ''his property'' in the NIV. The concept of luxury need not be entirely excluded from the expression ''this world's good,'' but clearly John does not mean to apply this test only to those who have wealth. The picture applies to anyone who possesses the material means to meet another's need.

''And'' continues the picture: ''and seeth his brother have need'' *(kai theōrē ton adelphon autou chreian echonta,* literally, ''and may be beholding his brother a need having''). The verb ''seeth'' is common in the Gospels and Acts but occurs only here and in Hebrews 7:4 in the New Testament Epistles. The present tense denotes, not a casual glance, but careful, contemplative observation of ''his brother'' ''as a spectacle on which he allows his eyes to rest.''[21] The term ''his brother'' denotes a member of the Christian community, whether male or female, who is described as ''a need having'' *(chreian echonta).* Whatever its nature, it is a need that material means can alleviate. The picture involves a deliberate contrast; both have something–the latter has a personal need and the former has the personal means to meet that need.

---

[20]Simon J. Kistemaker, *Exposition of the Epistle of James and the Epistles of John,* New Testament Commentary (Grand Rapids: Baker, 1986), p. 310.

[21]Brooke Foss Westcott, *The Epistles of St. John, The Greek Text with Notes,* 3rd ed. (1892; reprint ed., Grand Rapids: Eerdmans, 1950), p. 115.

The response to this observed need is tersely stated: "and shutteth up his bowels *of compassion* from him" *(kai kleisē ta splangchna autou ap' autou).* Now the verb "shutteth up" is in the aorist, depicting a specific response to what he observed. He has noted the other's need and is aware of the call for sympathetic action to meet that need; instead he restrains his initial sympathy and "shutteth up his bowels *of compassion.*" His self-centered interests lead him to shut out any consideration for the needs of the brother. The verb literally means to close or lock a door or gate; here it is used figuratively to depict his deliberate erection of a barrier between himself and the brother so that his sympathetic action cannot flow out to him. His response is the exact opposite of that of the Good Samaritan (Luke 10:33-34).

The neuter plural noun here rendered "his bowels" *(ta splangchna)* was used by the Greeks to denote the noble viscera—the heart, lungs, and liver—as the seat of the emotions. The traditional rendering "his bowels *of compassion*" is not very meaningful today. The usage is figurative for what we commonly call "the heart" as the seat of human affection and emotion. The rendering "his heart" adequately conveys the meaning, but Brown suggests that "the best rendering may be 'compassion.' "[22] In closing his heart "from him" *(ap' autou),* this individual deliberately and hardheartedly turns his back on the needy brother. James 2:15-16 pictures a similar heartlessness in putting off the destitute brother with empty words.

John's dramatic question "How dwelleth the love of God in him?" challenges his readers to express their own evaluation of this heartless response. The rhetorical question rejects the implied claim of the individual that "the love of God" *(hē agapē tou theou)* was abiding in him. Interpreters have understood the genitive "of God" *(tou theou)* in different ways. It may denote a love of which God is the source (subjective genitive);[23] or one may understand it as designating God as the object of the love, love for God (objective genitive);[24] it is also possible to take it as a descriptive genitive describing the quality of the love, a God-like love.[25] Westcott accepts an inclusive meaning, "the love of which God is at once the object and the author and the pattern."[26] Whatever the intended meaning here, in the operation of true Christian love

[22]Brown, p. 450.

[23]So Donald W. Burdick, *The Letters of John the Apostle* (Chicago: Moody Press, 1985), p. 270; Kistemaker, p. 311, note 38; Stott, p. 144.

[24]So Alfred Plummer, *The Epistles of S. John,* Cambridge Bible for Schools and Colleges (1883; reprint ed., London: Cambridge University Press, 1938), p. 133; Lenski, pp. 473-74; Gordon H. Clark, *First John, A Commentary* (Phillipsburg, N.J.: Presbyterian and Reformed, n.d.), p. 109.

[25]So Smalley, p. 197. Cf. NEB.

[26]Westcott, p. 115.

both the subjective and objective aspects of "the love of God" are involved (cf. 4:19-21). Jesus insists that the command to "love the Lord thy God" cannot be separated from the command to "love thy neighbor as thyself" (Matt. 22:35-40). He who professes to love God while refusing to express love toward his unfortunate brother through a compassionate sharing of his own means discredits his claim and subjects himself to the charge of hypocrisy.

c. *The exhortation to practice true love* (v. 18). In expressing his practical appeal, John again addresses his reader as "my little children" (*teknia,* cf. 2:28; 3:7).[27] He lovingly appeals to them as a spiritual father intent on encouraging the members of the family to give appropriate expression to the love implanted in their hearts when they were born into God's family (v. 14). In saying "let us" *(agapōmen),* John again includes himself in this standing obligation. The exhortation is expressed as a typical negative-positive contrast. The two terms in the negative statement seem intended to balance the two terms in the positive statement.

Negatively, John insists, "Let us not love in word, neither in tongue" *(mē agapōmen logō mēde tē glossē).* Both nouns are in the instrumental case, denoting agency. While Christian love must be a vital inner reality, by its nature love demands active expression. Negatively, John insists that true love cannot be restricted to mere verbalization. Strauss well remarks, "Kind and comforting words are not condemned in verse 18. We need to speak with soft and sympathetic words, but such words should be accompanied by helpful and heart-warming deeds."[28] "The tongue" (ASV) *(tē glossē)* is the only noun in this verse with the definite article, pointing out the well-known agency for the verbalization of love. Houlden suggests that this negative demand "may be a cut at 'heretics' of a speculative type, who . . . were notorious as word-spinners."[29] If the expression of love is limited to mere verbal expression, it is simply "mouth mercy,"[30] which is profitless and disappointing. (Cf. James 2:15-16.)

Positively, John insists that love must be expressed "in deed and in truth" *(en ergō kai alētheia).* Now the use of the preposition "in" *(en)* marks the sphere in which the active expression of love must operate.

---

[27]The KJV reading, "my little children," follows the Textus Receptus. For the textual evidence see Nestle-Aland, *Novum Testamentum Graece,* 26th ed. Brown comments, "The Byzantine tradition adds 'My,' a frequent scribal 'improvement' " (p. 451).

[28]Lehman, Strauss, *The Epistles of John* (1962; reprint ed., Neptune, N.J.: Loizeaux Brothers, 1984), p. 120.

[29]J. H. Houlden, *A Commentary on the Johannine Epistles,* Harper's New Testament Commentaries (New York: Harper & Row, 1973), p. 101.

[30]An expression used by John Trapp, *Trapp's Commentary on the New Testament* (1865; reprint ed., Evansville, Ind.: Sovereign Grace Book Club, 1958), p. 730.

Besides our verbal expressions, our love must express itself in the realm of "deed," in love-prompted, beneficent action. As Dodd remarks, "In rejecting a false legalism, and insisting upon the inwardness of true morality and religion, Christianity still demands that the spirit of charity should embody itself in definite outward action."[31] Christianity then is concerned about the nature and motivation of our deeds. The performance of our deed must be combined with "truth." "Truth" here possibly may mean no more than "in reality" as contrasted to mere appearance, for deeds may be hypocritical. But probably "truth" here carries its usual fuller Johannine meaning as being in accord with the divine truth in Christ (cf. John 4:24, "in spirit and in truth"). The truth of God which begets love in the believer must also govern and direct his outward expression of love.

3. The Assurance from the Practice of Love (vv. 19-24)

The practice of Christian love also has a beneficial impact on the one who loves. In these verses John sets forth different aspects of the assurance that will arise in the heart of the believer from his practice of love; it is the fruit of the Spirit. The practice of love will produce inner assurance of being in the truth (vv. 19-20), give confidence that prayer will be answered (vv. 21-22), and assure the believer of his intimate union with Christ (vv. 23-24).

a. The assurance of being of the truth (vv. 19-20). These verses are well called a *crux interpretum.* They present a number of textual, grammatical, and exegetical difficulties.[32] We shall consider them as we seek to understand John's message.

The textual evidence is divided as to the use of a connective "and" *(kai)* at the beginning of verse 19. It is part of the Textus Receptus and is used in the King James Version, but recent versions generally omit it (ASV, RSV, NASB, NEB, NIV). The evidence for and against its authenticity is about evenly divided; it seems preferable to accept it as original.[33] The use of "and" suggests that "hereby" *(en toutō,* "in this, herein") looks back to

---

[31]C. H. Dodd, *The Johannine Epistles,* Moffatt New Testament Commentary (New York: Harper & Row, 1946), p. 87.

[32]For an elaborate treatment of these difficulties see Brown, pp. 453-60. Brown, however, baldly asserts, "The epistolary author is singularly inept in constructing clear sentences, and in these verses he is at this worst" (p. 453).

[33]Zane C. Hodges and Arthur L. Farstad, *The Greek New Testament According to the Majority Text* (Nashville: Thomas Nelson Publishers, 1982), print *kai* as an authentic part of the text. Nestle-Aland, in their 22nd edition, omit *kai* in their text, giving the textual evidence in the footnote. (Nestle-Aland, *Novum Testamentum Graece,* 22nd ed. [New York: American Bible Society, 1956]). But in their 26th edition they place *kai* in square brackets in the text to indicate that the evidence for the reading is about evenly divided. So also Kurt Aland et al., ed. *The Greek New Testament,* 3rd ed. (New York: United Bible Societies, 1975) has *kai* in the text in square brackets.

verse 18, rather than to what follows. Manuscript evidence is also divided concerning the tense of the verb "know": the present tense, "we know," *(ginōskomen)* of the KJV follows the Textus Receptus, the Latin Vulgate, and the Syriac, whereas the major Greek codices have the future "we shall know" *(gnōsometha)*.[34] Textual evidence is also divided between the singular "our heart" and the plural "our hearts" in verse 19.[35]

Grammar and interpretation suggest that verses 19 and 20 should be kept together. A major difficulty in the interpretation of these two verses is the meaning of the first of the two occurrences of the Greek form *hoti* in verse 20. A second difficulty is the intended significance of the verb "shall assure" *(peisomen)*.

1) *The assurance as to our spiritual origin* (v. 19a). The assertion "hereby we know that we are of the truth" *(en toutō gnōsometha hoti ek tēs alētheias esmen,* more literally, "in this we shall know that out of the truth we are") presents the first aspect of the assurance that the practice of love produces. "In this" or "herein" most naturally refers back to verse 18, which sets forth a recognizable practice as concrete evidence of our spiritual origin. The use of the future tense in the verb "we shall know" *(gnōsometha)*, which is better attested than the present tense (KJV), should not be given an eschatological meaning, as in 3:2. In 3:19 John is referring to Christian assurance as a present experience. Here the future tense, as Westcott notes, "expresses the dependence of the knowledge upon the fulfilment of the specified condition."[36] The verb "know" points to an acquired knowledge based on our experience. The resultant knowledge is that we are "of the truth" *(ek tēs alētheias)*. The preposition rendered "of" *(ek,* "out of") clearly marks the source of our spiritual being, namely, "the truth." Used with the definite article, the noun retains its full theological significance as denoting the truth of God as revealed in Christ and His gospel. The phrase "out of the truth" occurs in the Johannine writings only in John 18:37, 1 John 2:21, and here. Stott remarks, "Truth can only characterize the behavior of those whose very character originates in the truth, so that it is by our loving others 'in truth,' that we know that we are 'of the truth.' "[37]

2) *The quieting of our conscience before God* (vv. 19b-20). "And" *(kai)* at once adds a further aspect of the assurance from love in action: "and shall assure our hearts before Him" *(kai emprosthen autou peisomen tēn kardian hēmōn)*. The adverb rendered "before" *(emprosthen* used as an improper preposition with the ablative) conveys the picture of the believer

---

[34]For the textual evidence see Nestle-Aland, *Novum Testamentum Graece,* 26th ed.

[35]See Nestle-Aland, *Novum Testamentum Graece,* 26th ed.

[36]Westcott, p. 116.

[37]Stott, p. 145.

standing "before Him," before God, without any necessary distinction between the Father and the glorified Son. The expression was at times used of the individual standing before the judge; although the judgment scene need not be pressed here, the expression does convey the believer's sense of accountability to the one before whom he appears. The future tense of the verb "shall assure" is parallel to the preceding "we shall know." A difficulty presented by this statement is the intended meaning of the verb rendered "shall assure" *(peisomen),* used only here in the Johannine writings. The usual meaning of this verb is "persuade," followed by an indication of the content of the persuasion. With this meaning the content of the persuasion may be the last part of verse 20, "that God is greater than our heart, and knoweth all things." But it is not obvious how the practice of love can be said to persuade us that God is superior to our heart. This verb can also mean "conciliate, pacify, set at rest," hence "assure."[38] This is its meaning in Matthew 28:14 and offers a more natural meaning here. It is in precisely this area of Christian love for others that the sensitive Christian heart often feels its own inadequacy and needs assurance. With his use of the first person plural, "we shall assure," John includes himself among those who have experienced such a need for assurance. Contrary to our practice, John uses the singular "heart" with the plural possessive pronoun nine times in his writings.[39] The use of the singular "heart"[40] here seems to suggest the oneness of God's people in the experience being described. In Greek usage the "heart" was thought of as the "center and source of the whole inner life, with its thinking, feeling, and volition."[41] Here the emphasis is on the conscience (cf. Acts 2:37; 7:54) as the center of man's moral nature. Although John never uses the Greek term *suneidēsis,* meaning "moral consciousness" or "conscience," it is generally agreed that he here implies it under the term "heart," for it is the conscience that assures and condemns us. John noted that Christians deal with their troubled conscience "before Him" *(emprosthen autou)* as the true judge of their inner character. Since this phrase is placed emphatically forward, Burdick observes that "John thereby emphasizes that the assurance is a justified assurance since it is experienced in the very presence of God."[42]

---

[38]William F. Arndt and F. Wilbur Gingrich, *A Greek-English Lexicon of the New Testament and Other Early Christian Literature* (Chicago: University of Chicago Press, 1957), p. 645.

[39]John 12:40; 14:1, 27; 16:6, 22; 1 John 3:19, 20 twice, 21.

[40]In v. 19 the KJV follows the Textus Receptus in using the plural "our hearts" *(tas kardias hēmōn),* but the plural has weak textual support and apparently represents a scribal change to express agreement with the plural pronoun "our." For the textual evidence see Nestle-Aland, *Novum Testamentum Graece,* 26th ed.

[41]Arndt and Gingrich, p. 404.

[42]Burdick, p. 272.

The use in the Greek of two *hoti* clauses in verse 20 offers a further problem for the interpretation of John's message.[43] As in the KJV, it is possible to begin a new sentence with verse 20 and take the first *hoti*, followed by *ean* ("if"), with the following verb and read "For if our heart condemn us, God is greater than our heart." But this reading omits the second *hoti* in this verse as redundant. A widely accepted solution is represented in the NASB rendering, "in whatever our heart condemns us" *(hoti ean kataginōskē hēmōn hē kardia)*. This reading takes these words as a continuation of verse 19 and takes *hoti* as *ho ti*, the neuter indefinite relative "whatever," with *ean* ("if" with the subjunctive verb), "whatever if" or "if whatever" as indicating the varied things that may cause our heart to condemn us. This gives a good meaning and preserves the force of the following *hoti*: "and shall assure our heart before him, in whatever our heart condemns us" (NASB). Although not totally free from difficulty, this seems to be the most probable solution.

John does not elaborate on the nature of the things that may cause our heart to condemn us, and it is not his purpose to catalogue such matters. But he knows well how readily an accusing conscience renders ineffective the testimony and service of such a believer. As Barker points out,

> Doubt, guilt, and failure are never far from any of us. Sometimes our misgivings are the result of our own actions or inactions. Sometimes it is the "accuser" who seizes our weaknesses and shortcomings and so elevates them that we wonder whether we can really be in the truth.[44]

Whatever the cause for our own heart's thus passing judgment upon us, the believer can take the matter before God for His judgment. Our conscience, troubled by the matter that it knows against us, can before God be quieted on the basis of the tests John here indicates. As Houlden notes, "First, there is the objective test of moral behavior–whether our love expresses itself in action. Second, there is the faith that God alone is the arbiter in this matter."[45]

In taking the charge of our conscience before God, our faith assures us because "God is greater than our heart, and knoweth all things" *(hoti meizōn estin ho theos tēs kardias hēmōn kai ginōskei panta)*. "For" *(hoti,* "that," better, "because") points to the ground for assurance. "It is not," as Jackman remarks, "that God minimizes or disregards our failures. In fact he knows them better than we do, for he sees and understands us even more deeply than we can ever know ourselves."[46] The conscience-smitten believer

---

[43]Burdick lists ten different possible ways of understanding vv. 19-20 (pp. 273-75).

[44]Barker, p. 337.

[45]Houlden, p. 101.

[46]Jackman, p. 104.

knows that his conscience, being imperfect and neither infallible or final, may be either too severe or too lenient in its verdict; God's verdict can be neither. As the moral sentinel which God has placed within each of us, our conscience cannot replace God in our lives.

The added words "and knoweth all things" seem to be a note of encouragement; it is better to have the all-knowing God as our judge than our own conscience. "It is the difference between conscience and Omniscience."[47] While He knows our failures and shortcomings, He also understands our true motives and desires, the innermost yearnings of our heart. His omniscience is also linked to His unchanging love and sympathy; He remembers His saving intentions and purposes for each of us. It is to that perfect knowledge that the conscience-stricken believer, like Peter in John 21:17, can appeal: "Lord, thou knowest all things; thou knowest that I love thee." The fact that He has implanted His love in our hearts assures us that He will not reject or disown us.

Some interpreters[48] understand this reference to God's greatness and knowledge not as a comfort but as a challenge to the believer. So understood, John is stressing the severity of God's judgment. Thus Alford remarks, "Our conscience is but the faint echo of His voice who knoweth all things; if it condemn us, how much more He?"[49] If it were evident that John was seeking to stimulate a consciousness of sin in his readers, this understanding of his words would be obvious. But such an interpretation is quite inappropriate in the present context. Smalley asserts, "John's chief purpose at this point is to reassure his readers that when believers are most aware of their shortcomings, in respect of God's standards, the love and mercy of the Father are present to heal their troubled conscience."[50] Clearly John's aim here is to heal the wounded conscience of the sensitive believer, not to widen the wound unnecessarily. But it is clear that whenever professed believers seek to stifle the demands of conscience by claiming to possess a superior enlightenment, his words do sound a needed warning.

b. The assurance of acceptance before God (vv. 21-22). The tender direct address "Beloved" *(Agapētoi)* expresses John's personal love for his readers who have known the struggles of an accusing conscience. Assuring them that

---

[47]Plummer, p. 136.

[48]John Calvin, *Commentaries on the Catholic Epistles,* trans. John Owen (1855; reprint ed., Grand Rapids: Eerdmans, 1948), pp. 222-23; Henry Alford, *The New Testament for English Readers* ([1865-1872]; reprint ed., Chicago: Moody Press, [1958]), pp. 1733-34; Kenneth Grayston, *The Johannine Epistles,* New Century Bible Commentary (Grand Rapids: Eerdmans, 1984), pp. 115-16.

[49]Alford, p. 1734.

[50]Smalley, p. 203.

this struggle can be resolved, he stresses the blessing of personal confidence before God (v. 21) and the further experience of answered prayer (v. 22).

1) *The blessing of confidence before God* (v. 21). Assurance of acceptance before God is based on the inner experience of a non-condemning conscience: "If our heart condemn us not, *then* have we confidence toward God." The conditional statement "if our heart condemn us not" *(ean hē kardia mē kataginōskē)*[51] leaves open the question of the present reality of that condition. Although the negative *(mē)* with the present subjunctive could mean "does not condemn us *as an ongoing condition*" because the heart has had no misgiving about our moral state, John seems clearly to mean that it "*ceases* to condemn us" because the charge of conscience against us has been resolved before God. Although every believer experiences occasions when his conscience for some reason condemns him, the present tense implies that such need not be the characteristic experience of the believer. Concerning such a life free from an accusing conscience Westcott remarks, "It does not imply a claim to sinlessness, nor yet an insensibility to the heinousness of sin, but the action of a living faith which retains a real sense of fellowship with God, and this carries with it confidence and peace."[52]

The resultant blessing is that "*then* have we confidence toward God" *(parrhēsian echomen pros ton theon)*. In 2:28 John speaks of "confidence" in connection with Christ's return. Here the noun, placed emphatically forward, speaks of the believer's free and uninhibited communion with God in daily life. The phrase "toward God" *(pros ton theon, "facing Godward")* depicts a confidence that is directed Godward, bringing us into an intimate face-to-face relationship with Him. (Cf. Heb. 4:16.)

2) *The blessing of answered prayer* (v. 22). John's "and" unites our fellowship with God and the answering of our prayers by God: "and whatsoever we ask, we receive of Him." As God's children who are conscious of our acceptance before our Heavenly Father, it is our privilege freely to ask of Him. The expression "whatsoever we ask" *(ho ean aitōmen,* literally, "that which if we may be asking") leaves entirely unrestricted both the content and the occasion for our request. The present tense denotes the varied requests being confidently raised to God.

Such praying is assured of God's answer: "we receive of Him" *(lambanomen ap' autou)*. The present tense, "receive," indicates the repeated an-

---

[51]The manuscripts vary as to the presence or absence of "our" with the noun "heart." The evidence for and against its authenticity is about evenly divided. There is also some textual confusion between "our" *(hēmōn)* and "your" *(humōn)*, due to the fact that the words were pronounced alike in later Greek. Manuscripts also differ as to whether a pronoun ("our" or "your") was repeated after the verb. For the variants see Bruce M. Metzger, *A Textual Commentary on the Greek New Testament* (London: United Bible Societies, 1971), pp. 713-14.

[52]Westcott, p. 118.

swers received, while "of Him" makes clear that these answers are not merely fortuitous circumstances but come from Him as His specific response. The fact that God responds to the prayers of His people is a common teaching of the Scriptures. This promise of an answer "of Him" must be kept in balance with the preceding picture of our "confidence before God" (v. 21).

John at once adds that this blessed experience of answered prayer is conditioned by our obedient and willing service. As Stott remarks, "Obedience is the indispensable condition, not the meritorious cause of answered prayer."[53] The indicated condition for answered prayer is "because we keep His commandments, and do those things that are pleasing in his sight" (v. 22b). The two verbs in this double statement, "we keep" *(tēroumen)* and "[we] do" *(poioumen)* are both in the present tense, denoting the characteristic conduct of those whose prayers are answered. Such conduct does not earn God's answer but provides "an objective, moral reason for the divine response; it does not simply depend upon the subjective ground of a worshiper's clear conscience."[54] God acts in keeping with His own nature when He beneficently responds to the prayers of those who obey Him and seek to please Him.

The statement "we keep His commandments" *(tas entolas autou tēroumen)* points to a conscious compliance with the varied explicit commands God has given, varied in their nature and scope. "His commandments," placed before the verb, denotes God's directives, rather than our own desires, as the primary consideration in directing the course of our lives.

Some view the further statement "and do those things that are pleasing in his sight" *(kai ta aresta enōpion autou poioumen)* as simply an equivalent restatement.[55] But in this epistle such restatements characteristically mark an advance in the thought. We accept that the two are not the same; the first calls for obedience to His commands, which may be carried out in a slavish spirit (cf. the older brother in Luke 15:28-30); the second implies a spontaneous activity motivated by love, freely undertaken because Christian love recognizes them as "those things that are pleasing in his sight." To illustrate: A farmer's wife and her ten-year-old daughter were just finishing their breakfast when a phone call urgently requested the mother to come to a neighbor's home a short distance away because of an emergency. Before leaving, the mother kindly asked her daughter to wash the dishes and tidy the kitchen while she was gone. Prompted by her love, the daughter gladly consented. She washed and carefully replaced the dishes, cleared off the kitchen stove, and swept the floor. Since her mother was still not back, she went into her brother's room and made the bed and cleaned the room. Then

---

[53]Stott, p. 149.
[54]Smalley, p. 205.
[55]See Brown, p. 462.

she took a broom and carefully swept the living room floor and the front porch because she knew it would please her mother. Her love prompted her to go beyond that which had been commanded. So the believer often faces situations in his own life which may not be covered by a specific commandment, but his love prompts him to act in ways he knows would be pleasing to the Lord. Thus Westcott notes that "the things that are pleasing" are "not simply 'things pleasing,' but definitely those which correspond with our position and duty."[56] The phrase "in his sight" (*enōpion autou,* "in His eyes") indicates that He is pleased as He observes us doing them.

   c. The assurance of union with Christ (vv. 23-24). Basic to the believer's assurance is the reality of his spiritual union with Christ. This assurance is grounded in the two-sided command to believers (v. 23), resulting in a two-sided fellowship which is given experiential confirmation through the indwelling Holy Spirit (v. 24).

   1) *The two-sided commandment to believers* (v. 23). John now gathers up the various commandments just referred to in one comprehensive commandment: "And this is his commandment" *(kai hautē estin hē entolē autou).* The singular "this" looks forward to the following "that" *(hina)* clause with two explanatory verbs expressing the content of the command: "That we should believe on the name of his Son Jesus Christ, and love one another." The two parallel verbs, "believe" *(pisteusōmen)* and "love" *(agapōmen),* together form one whole. As Lenski asserts, "You cannot believe without loving nor love without believing."[57] The Christian message calls for a vital union of faith and conduct. Thus Plummer suggests, "This verse is the answer to those who would argue from the preceding verses that all that is required of us is to *do* what is right; it does not much matter what we *believe.*"[58] This insistence upon a living union between faith and love is God's command, not a later apostolic stipulation.

   The command "that we should believe on the name of his Son Jesus Christ" *(hina pisteusōmen tō onomati tou huiou Iēsou Christou)* involves the first occurrence of the verb "believe" in the epistle.[59] The manuscript evidence is about evenly divided between the aorist *(pisteusōmen)* and the present tense *(pisteuōmen).*[60] It seems more probable that the present tense arose from a scribal desire to conform the tense of the two verbs or from

---

[56]Westcott, p. 119.

[57]Lenski, p. 479.

[58]Plummer, p. 137. Italics in original.

[59]The verb occurs 9 more times in the remainder of this epistle (4:1, 16; 5:1, 5, 10 thrice, 13 twice). The noun "faith" *(pistis)* occurs only in 5:4. The verb appears 98 times in the Gospel of John.

[60]For the evidence see Nestle-Aland, *Novum Testamentum Graece,* 26th ed.

the feeling that the aorist was unsuited to John's readers. The present tense would convey the command to "go on believing." The aorist tense may be understood as denoting "the initial resolution of the soul, which gave its direction to the whole future life."[61] Lenski insists that "the aorist is effective: definitely, effectively, once for all believe."[62] As such, the statement of the command carries with it John's appeal to his readers, confronted by the challenge of the heretics, once for all to settle the finality of their faith commitment. Smalley notes that for John true "believing" signifies more than "accepting as true" what is believed, for "confession is also vitally important."[63] In Romans 10:9-10 Paul insists that faith and confession are both part of a saving experience.

The content of the stated command is that we believe "*on the name of his Son Jesus Christ*" *(tō onomati tou huiou autou Iēsou Christou)*. The words have a creedal ring, being in fact a miniature confession of faith. John here uses no word for "on" or "in" but rather the dative of personal relationship, a personal committal to "the Name" as denoting the person and all that He is. His identity is explicitly stated: "his Son Jesus Christ." "His Son" stresses the true deity and the unique Sonship of this person. In His incarnate appearing He was identified as the historical person "Jesus Christ" (1:3). The name "Jesus" *(Iēsous)* is the Greek form of the Hebrew name Joshua, meaning "the Lord is salvation." It is the name of His humanity, given Him before His birth to declare His saving ministry (Matt. 1:21). "Christ" *(Christos)* is the Greek translation of the Hebrew term "Messiah" (transliterated *messias* in John 1:41 and 4:25) and declares His messianic identity. The double designation represents the earliest Christian confession of faith, "Jesus is the Christ" (Acts 2:36; 3:20; 5:42; cf. John 20:30-31). Christian faith accepts that He truly is all that this Name declares. Christian faith is highly christological. The doctrinal content of our faith is of crucial importance.

The other part of the command is "*and love one another*" *(kai agapōmen allēlous)*. The present tense calls for the practice of love in daily Christian living. The reciprocal pronoun insists that this love must be mutually expressed by members of the Christian community. Christian love is not a one-way street; it must flow in both directions. John has mentioned the need for mutual love before (2:10-11; 3:11, 14), but now for the first time he specifically unites faith and love. Both are essential as a test for a true Christian.

The added words "*as he gave us commandment*" *(kathōs edōken entolēn hēmin)* may seem redundant, but they add to the hortatory impact of the command. They may be connected with the command to love given just

---

[61]Lias, p. 282.

[62]Lenski, p. 282.

[63]Smalley, p. 207.

before[64] or with both parts of the double commandment.[65] The adverb "as" (*kathōs,* "even as") implies that Christian conduct must truly conform to the commandment given. Again "he" is not precisely identified, but in view of "his" in the preceding phrase "his Son Jesus Christ," it would seem to be God, although the disciples heard the commandment from Jesus. Kysar remarks, "This is still another instance of the way in which the author moves freely between God and Jesus in the use of the personal pronouns."[66]

2) *The reciprocal nature of Christian fellowship* (v. 24). "And" *(kai)* marks the connection with verse 23 when John adds, "And he that keepeth his commandments dwelleth in him and he in him." In practical life, obedience to the double command to believe and love resolves itself in obedience to a multitude of subordinate "commandments." The one thus characteristically keeping God's commandments experiences a reciprocal spiritual fellowship: "he dwelleth in him, and he in him" *(en autō menei kai autos en autō).* Such a mutual abiding marks the heart of a vital Christianity (John 15:1-5; Col. 1:27-28). The present-tense verb "dwelleth" marks the closest and most permanent union between the human and the divine. This is the first time that John mentions this mutual abiding in this epistle; he further develops it in 4:12-16. Again John's use of his personal pronouns does not clearly distinguish between God the Father and His Son, Jesus Christ. Generally he felt no need to press a rigid distinction since he always thought of the Father as working through the Son and the Son as revealing the Father. This spiritual union is portrayed in Christ's picture of the vine and the branches (John 15:1-10).

The second part of this reciprocal relationship, "and he in him," asserting the divine indwelling in the believers, elicits a further confirmatory statement: "And hereby we know that he abideth in us, by the Spirit which he hath given us." Standing first in the sentence, "hereby" *(en toutō)* may look either backward to what has preceded or forward to the concluding clause. Some, such as Westcott[67] and Burdick,[68] hold that the pronoun relates back to the keeping of the commandments as the objective evidence of the inner mystical union with God. But most interpreters agree with Smalley that "the more natural interpretation, confirmed by the parallel at 4:13, is to connect *en toutō* with what follows."[69] In other words, John insists that the ultimate source of our expe-

---

[64]So Plummer, p. 138; A. E. Brooke, *A Critical And Exegetical Commentary on the Johannine Epistles,* International Critical Commentary (New York: Charles Scribner's Sons, 1912), p. 105; Burdick, p. 280.

[65]So Lenski, pp. 481-82.

[66]Kysar, pp. 88-89.

[67]Westcott, p. 121.

[68]Burdick, p. 281.

[69]Smalley, p. 211.

rience of the divine indwelling in our lives is the Holy Spirit Himself. The certainty "that he abideth in us," which is the heart of true Christian assurance, is wrought in us "by the Spirit which he hath given us" *(ek tou pneumatos hou hēmin edōken)*. The Holy Spirit is the source from which the certainty of our relationship with God is drawn. The indwelling Spirit is God's gift to the believer. As Houlden remarks, "Whatever man has by way of relationship with God is never the result of his own effort or initiative, but the gift of God."[70] The aorist verb rendered "he hath given" *(edōken)* indicates a definite and memorable occasion when the Spirit was given. Dispensationally, the Spirit was given to the Church at Pentecost, marking the historical birthday of the Church, but individually the Spirit is given to each believer at the time of his regeneration. He brings assurance to the new-born believer by direct communication to the soul. "The Spirit Himself bears witness with our spirit that we are children of God" (Rom. 8:16 NASB). Also He produces effects in the life of the believer which can be ascribed only to Him.

This is the first explicit reference to the Holy Spirit in 1 John; indirect reference to the Spirit was made in 2:20, 27. John will refer to the Spirit six more times (4:2, 6, 13: 5:6 twice, 8). The adjective "Holy" is not used of the Spirit in the Johannine epistles[71] or Revelation, but the full designation "the Holy Spirit" occurs four times in the Fourth Gospel (1:33; 7:39 T.R.; 14:26; 20:22). This reference to the Spirit forms an effective transition to the discussion in 4:1-6.

---

[70]Houlden, p. 104.

[71]It does occur in 1 John 5:7 in the KJV in the famous interpolation in 5:7-8, but these words are not found in any Greek manuscript before the fourteenth century.

11

Assurance from the Conflicts of Faith (Part 4)

D. The Conflict Between the Spirit of Truth and the Spirit of Error (4:1-6)

4:1 Beloved, believe not every spirit, but try the spirits whether they are of God: because many false prophets are gone out into the world.

2 Hereby know ye the Spirit of God: Every spirit that confesseth that Jesus Christ is come in the flesh is of God:

3 And every spirit that confesseth not that Jesus Christ is come in the flesh is not of God: and this is that *spirit* of antichrist, whereof ye have heard that it should come; and even now already is it in the world.

4 Ye are of God, little children, and have overcome them: because greater is he that is in you, than he that is in the world.

5 They are of the world: therefore speak they of the world, and the world heareth them.

6 We are of God: he that knoweth God heareth us; he that is not of God heareth not us. Hereby know we the spirit of truth, and the spirit of error.

The first six verses of chapter 4 form a unit portraying the conflict between two spiritual realms, namely, "the spirit of truth, and the spirit of error" (v. 6b). These verses show no close connection with what follows and are best viewed as an elaboration of the reference to "the Spirit which he hath given us" in 3:24. The conflict now presented forms the final aspect of the conflicts that mark the Christian life which John has been depicting since 2:18. He has already dealt with the conflict between truth and falsehood (2:18-28), the conflict between the children of God and the children of the Devil (2:29–3:12), and the conflict between love and hatred (3:13-24). This section points to the supernatural character of this conflict as ultimately involving "the spirit of truth, and the spirit of error." It sets forth the crucial importance of the proclamation of a sound Christology for assurance and victory in the Christian community. Those who are truly of God must adhere to the apostolic message concerning Jesus Christ, whose person and work constitute the heart of the Christian gospel. Those who reject or mutilate that message thereby reveal their antichristian character.

John now urges his readers to test the spirits to determine their true identity (v. 1), gives them the criterion for testing the spirits (vv. 2-3), and sets forth the criterion for identifying the true character of the human speakers (vv. 4-6).

1. The Charge to Test the Spirits (v. 1)

In dealing with this crucial matter, John, as a wise and affectionate leader, again addresses his readers with the tender designation "beloved" (*agapē-toi;* cf. 2:7; 3:2, 21). It expresses his personal, loving concern for them as they face the subtle danger of the false spirits. He charges them to test the spirits to determine their nature (v. 1a) and indicates why such testing is necessary (v. 1b).

a. The command in regard to the spirits (v. 1a). John formulates his charge to the readers both negatively and positively. Negatively, his command is "believe not every spirit" (*mē panti pneumati pisteuete,* literally, "not every spirit believe ye"). John prohibits a gullibility prone to believe "every spirit" claiming to be from God. "The author has in mind," Kysar well notes, "not simply the anthropological spirits, but supernatural beings who inspire and lead humans."[1] The use of the dative *(panti pneumati)* with the verb warns against an attitude of personal acceptance and trust in the various spirits declaring their message through the human messengers. The force of the original order, placing "every spirit" between the negative *(mē)* and the present-tense verb, has been differently understood. Robertson holds that the negative is to be taken with the immediately following adjective "every."[2] This connection would negate an uncritical attitude which accepts every spirit, although permitting acceptance of those spirits which proved to be of God. Perhaps, as Kistemaker suggests, "the negative particle *mē* is separated from the verb for emphasis."[3] The circumstances confronting the readers make John's prohibition important. Generally the negative with the present imperative means "stop doing" what is prohibited. Thus Burdick

---

[1]Robert Kysar, *I, II, III John,* Augsburg Commentary on the New Testament (Minneapolis: Augsburg, 1986), p. 90.

[2]A. T. Robertson, *A Grammar of the Greek New Testament in the Light of Historical Research,* 5th ed. (New York: Richard R. Smith, 1914), p. 752.

[3]Simon J. Kistemaker, *Exposition of the Epistle of James and the Epistles of John,* New Testament Commentary (Grand Rapids: Baker, 1986), p. 324.

thinks that this prohibition "suggests that the readers had shown a tendency to give credence to the false teachers."[4] It is quite possible that some of the readers had been prone uncritically to accept the claims of these spirits speaking through the false teachers. But it seems unwarranted to assume that John was now censuring his readers by commanding them to stop the practice. More probably the present imperative with the negative states a standing prohibition without implying that the action was already in progress, i.e., "don't be yielding to the ever-present danger."[5] Let them be on guard against uncritically accepting the message of every spirit speaking through some human messenger. The reality of extraordinary and powerful spirits speaking through human beings as their mouth-piece, proclaiming varied and sundry messages, was well known in the pagan world of John's day.

The presence of such false prophets was long known to the people of Israel; it early manifested itself in the Christian Church (cf. 1 Cor. 12:1-3). It seems clear that John's prohibition was prompted by the presence of forceful spiritual powers making their appeals to the Christian churches, speaking through professed spokesmen for God. Whether any special signs and wonders accompanied their message is not indicated. At various periods in the history of the Church individuals have appeared claiming a supernatural endowment which exhibited itself in professed revelations, prophecies, miracles, and the like. Plummer remarks,

> About all such things there are two possibilities which must put us on our guard: (1) they may be unreal; either the delusions of fanatical enthusiasts, or the lies of deliberate impostors; (2) even if real, they need not be of God. Miraculous powers are no absolute guarantee of the possession of truth.[6]

It is a serious mistake simply to equate the presence of the extraordinary or supernatural with the divine. (Cf. Exod. 7:10-12, 22; 8:7, 18-19; Acts 8:9-11.) Spiritually sensitive believers have always felt the need for critical discernment of professed religious teachers and their pronouncements. And today, with the sweeping inroads of numberless cults and occultic forces, the need for spiritual discernment is urgent.

Positively, John adds that an active practice must accompany the prohibition: "but try the spirits whether they are of God." The use of the adversative "but" *(alla)* marks the contrast between an attitude of credulity and in-

---

[4]Donald W. Burdick, *The Letters of John the Apostle* (Chicago: Moody Press, 1985), pp. 291-92.

[5]F. Blass and A. Debrunner, *A Greek Grammar Of the New Testament and Other Early Christian Literature*, trans. and rev. Robert W. Funk (Chicago: University of Chicago Press, 1961), p. 172.

[6]Alfred Plummer, *The Epistles of S. John,* Cambridge Bible for Schools and Colleges (1883; reprint ed., London: Cambridge University Press, 1938), p. 141.

telligent discrimination. The present imperative verb "try" *(dokimazete)* marks the continuing or repeated practice, and the fact that it is second-person plural lays this duty upon all the readers. In 1 Thessalonians 5:21 Paul uses this same term in directing his readers to "examine everything *carefully;* hold fast to that which is good" (NASB). In 1 Corinthians 12:10 Paul mentions the "discerning of spirits" as a distinct gift, but clearly all believers must be alert to this necessity. Church history confirms that in all periods certain Christians have possessed outstanding ability to discriminate between true and false religious teachings. But as Clark remarks, "The fact that faithful pastors and orthodox professors are better able to evaluate does not excuse those in the pews from doing their own evaluating."[7] Neither the duty, nor the ability, to "try," or "test," the spirits is restricted to any ecclesiastical or educational groups. Palmer remarks that John calls upon his readers "to use their heads and to examine closely the theologies and doctrines of all their teachers. There are no benefits to ignorance or to sloppy thinking."[8]

The verb rendered "try" *(dokimazete),* which occurs only here in the Johannine writings, basically means "to put to the test, to examine," like coins being tested for genuineness or full weight. This verb, as Plummer notes, "commonly implies a good, if not a friendly object; to prove or test in the hope that what is tried will stand the test."[9] Another verb used in the New Testament *(peirazō),*[10] also has the general meaning of "putting to the test," but generally it implies a sinister purpose, a testing applied with the hope that the object will fail; hence it is generally rendered "to tempt." Trench notes that the verb John here uses *(dokimazō)* is never used of the work of Satan, "seeing that he never proves that he may approve, nor tests that he may accept."[11] As Stott remarks, in testing the spirits it is essential that believers maintain "the biblical balance, avoiding on the one hand the extreme superstition which believes everything and on the other the extreme suspicion which believes nothing."[12]

The specific point of the test is to determine the source whence the speakers receive their message, to see "whether they are of God" *(ei ek tou*

---

[7]Gordon H. Clark, *First John, A Commentary* (Phillipsburg, N.J.: Presbyterian and Reformed, n.d.), p. 123.

[8]Earl F. Palmer, *1, 2, 3 John, Revelation,* The Communicator's Commentary (Waco, Texas: Word Books, 1982), pp. 59-60.

[9]Plummer, p. 141.

[10]In the Johannine writings the verb *peirazō* occurs only in John 6:6, [8:6]; Rev. 2:2, 10; 3:10.

[11]Richard Chenevix Trench, *Synonyms of the New Testament* (1880; reprint ed., Grand Rapids: Eerdmans, 1947), p. 281.

[12]J.R.W. Stott, *The Epistle of John,* Tyndale New Testament Commentaries (Grand Rapids: Eerdmans, 1964), p. 153.

theou estin, "if out of God they are"). Barker notes that "the warning is not against those who feign the Spirit's presence but against genuine evil spirits inspiring the existence of false prophets."[13] Such testing implies the possession of an objective standard according to which the test is applied. John at once sets out such a standard in verses 2-3. Such a testing of the prophets has a clear precedent in the Old Testament. As Burdick points out,

> Moses gave the people criteria by which to test anyone who professed to be a prophet (Deut. 18:20-22), namely, (1) what he said must agree with what God had previously revealed, (2) he must speak in the name of the Lord, and (3) it must come to pass. See also Deuteronomy 13:1-5; Jeremiah 23:9-22; 28:9.[14]

The test John provides will effectively reveal whether the prophets are "of God," i.e., derive their inspiration and message from God. The test will inevitably establish the fundamental character of the prophet.

b. The fact necessitating the testing (v. 1b). John at once sets forth the historical situation which makes it necessary for believers aggressively to test the spirits: "because many false prophets are gone out into the world" *(hoti polloi pseudoprophētai exelēluthasin eis ton kosmon).* It is no mere future danger; "many false prophets" are already at work. The adjective "many" *(polloi)* makes clear that John's concern is not stirred by mere isolated instances of false prophets at work; they are numerous, exerting a strong impact on the contemporary scene. Jesus had explicitly foretold the coming of such false prophets (Matt. 7:15; 24:11, 15; Mark 13:21-23). Paul (Acts 20:28-30) and Peter (2 Pet. 2:1) had likewise foretold their coming. The use of the perfect tense "are gone out" *(exelēluthasin)* marks their presence as an abiding reality. Interpreters have understood the force of the preposition rendered "out" *(ex* or *ek* in the compound verb) in different ways. Generally its force is understood as an echo of the picture in 2:19 of the antichrists withdrawing from the Christian community. But in view of the use of two different prepositions, "out" *(ek)* and "into" *(eis),* Westcott suggests that "out" implies that these false teachers "are gone out on a mission of evil from their dark home," whereas "into" denotes their entry "into the world as the scene of their activity."[15] These evil spirits, speaking through the false prophets, are now making the world of mankind their lecture hall. Then John thinks of them as having arrived on the scene of

---

[13]Glen W. Barker, "1 John," in *The Expositor's Bible Commentary* (Grand Rapids: Zondervan, 1981), 12:340.

[14]Burdick, p. 293.

[15]Brooke Foss Westcott, *The Epistles of St. John, The Greek Text with Notes,* 3rd ed. (1892; reprint ed., Grand Rapids: Eerdmans, 1950), p. 140.

human history to carry out a mission from the evil one who sent them. So understood, John's expression reflects his terminology of the coming of Jesus in the Fourth Gospel (John 3:17, 31-34; 12:47, 49; especially 16:28). Thus John's terminology here may suggest that these false prophets are, in effect, a satanic parody on the mission of Christ. Even as Christ came out from the Father and came into the world to do the work of His Father, so these evil spirits have gone forth from their evil abode and come into the world to work through the false prophets in order to further the purposes of the evil one. The situation makes it imperative for true believers to "try the spirits whether they are of God" (v. 1).

The designation "false prophets" (literally, "pseudoprophets") may denote individuals falsely claiming to be prophets, but here the term clearly means individuals who proclaim a false message. The term "is applied to the rivals of the true prophets under the old dispensation (Luke vi. 26; 2 Pet. ii. 1); and to the rivals of the apostles under the new dispensation (Matt. vii. 15, xxiv. 11, 23, f.; Mk. xiii. 22; Acts xiii. 6)."[16] A prophet is not necessarily one who foretells the future but one who comes as bearing the message of God. These false prophets are not merely well-meaning teachers with an erroneous message; they are individuals who declare their message under the inspiration of evil spirits, the agents of Satan.

Various interpreters simply equate these "many false prophets" with the "many antichrists" in 2:18-19 who arose within the Christian community but separated themselves. Clearly the antichristian false teachers in 2:18 are included, but now the scene is broader. John's designation "many false prophets" also includes the various cults that claim to be Christian as well as numerous religious teachers not directly associated with Christianity who are aggressively propagating their fallacious systems. Today the sweeping inroads of occultic forces through the agency of mystical Oriental leaders with their fantastic teachings and dynamic appeal certainly constitute a ringing challenge to God's people to "try the spirits whether they are of God."[17]

2. The Criterion for Testing the Spirits (vv. 2-3)

John at once states the fundamental test in determining the true identity of the spirits. In verse 2 he states the test positively, indicating the assured

---

[16]*Ibid.*

[17]See Dave Hunt, *The Cult Explosion* (Irvine, Calf.: Harvest House Publishers, 1980); Dave Hunt and T. A. McMahon, *The Seduction of Christianity, Spiritual Discernment in the Last Days* (Eugene, Ore.: Harvest House Publishers, 1985); Ronald Enroth, *The Lure of the Cults and New Religions* (Downers Grove, Ill.: Inter-Varsity Christian Fellowship, 1987); Texe Marrs, *Dark Secrets of the New Age, Satan's Plan For a One World Religion* (Westchester, Ill.: Crossway Books, 1987).

presence of the Spirit of God; in verse 3 he states the test negatively, revealing the spirit of antichrist.

a. The evidence of the Spirit of God (v. 2). The words "Hereby know ye the Spirit of God" *(en toutō ginōskete to pneuma tou theou)* look forward to the test as formulated in the remainder of verse 2. In form the verb "know ye" *(ginōskete)* may be either imperative or indicative. The former view is seen in the KJV rendering, "Hereby know ye the Spirit of God." Those who take the form as imperative point to the corresponding imperatives in verse 1 ("believe not . . . but try").[18] But, as Brown remarks, John's phrase "seems to demand that a way of knowing be offered, not commanded."[19] The context suggests that John here is instructing, not commanding, his readers. Smalley notes, "John is appealing to his orthodox readers' knowledge and experience here, as so often in this letter (cf. 2:29; 4:6)."[20] The use of the plural, rather than the abstract singular "it is known," involves the readers directly in the application of the test. The resultant assurance concerning the identity of the spirit involves a mental deduction: carefully noting the content of the spirit's confession concerning Jesus Christ and then drawing the conclusion.

The decisive test is "Every spirit that confesseth that Jesus Christ is come in the flesh is of God" *(pan pneuma ho homologei Iēsoun Christon en sarki elēluthota ek tou theou estin,* very literally, "every spirit that confesses Jesus Christ in flesh having come out of God is"). "Every spirit" marks the comprehensiveness of this test; all are either approved or rejected on the basis of this test. The test centers on the confession made concerning the person of Jesus Christ. The verb "confesseth" *(homologei,* literally, "is saying the same thing") denotes not mere verbal acknowledgment but an open and forthright declaration of the message as one's own position. The present tense marks it as an ongoing acknowledgment, made whenever appropriate. Such a confession is crucial for a vital Christian faith (Rom. 10:9-10; 1 John 2:23; 4:15).

The determinative confession is "that Jesus Christ is come in the flesh" *(Iēsoun Christon en sarki elēluthota,* "Jesus Christ in flesh having come"). The insertion of "that," which is not in the original, makes it a confession of the doctrinal truth of the incarnation. The expression, which is in the accusative case as the direct object of the verb "confesseth," sets forth the

---

[18]Robert Law, *The Tests of Life, A Study of the First Epistle of St. John* (Edinburgh: T. & T. Clark, 1909), p. 396; Clark, p. 123.

[19]Raymond E. Brown, *The Epistles of John,* The Anchor Bible (Garden City, N.Y.: Doubleday & Co., 1982), p. 491.

[20]Stephen S. Smalley, *1, 2, 3 John,* Word Biblical Commentary (Waco, Texas: Word Books, 1984), p. 220.

person being confessed. Bultmann takes "Jesus" as the direct object and "Christ in flesh having come" as the predicate accusative.[21] The Moffatt translation represents this view—"every spirit which confesses Jesus as the Christ incarnate."[22] Then the point of the confession is that the human Jesus is the divine Christ (cf. 5:1). As such, the confession is a rejection of the Jewish claim that the human Jesus was not the promised Messiah. But this proposed separation of the double name in the accusative case is not certain. Kistemaker remarks,

> The combination Jesus Christ occurs eight times in John's epistles (1:3; 2:1; 3:23; 4:2; 5:6, 20; II John 3, 7). In two places John clearly separates the names by writing "Jesus is the Christ" (2:22; 5:1). Therefore when the names appear together they need to be translated as such.[23]

Keeping the two names together best represents John's insistence that in the historical person "Jesus Christ" we have the abiding union of the divine and the human, as indicated in the added words "is come in the flesh." The perfect tense marks this union as an abiding reality. The reality of the incarnation is the heart of Christianity. As Laurin remarks,

> Had there been no incarnation, Christ would have been an apotheosis, a man moving toward God. Christianity would have been only another approach toward God. Christ would have been only a godlike man. But there was an incarnation, *God moved toward man.* Because of that Christianity is in reality God's approach to man. Christ is in fact a manlike God. The incarnation is what makes Christianity distinctly unlike any other system.[24]

In saying that Jesus Christ came "in flesh" *(en sarki),* rather than "into flesh" *(eis sarka),* John repudiates Cerinthian Gnosticism. Cerinthus (c. A.D. 100), a late contemporary of John the Apostle at Ephesus, separated Jesus from Christ. He taught that the "Christ spirit" came upon the man Jesus, the son of Joseph and Mary, at his baptism and empowered his ministry but left him before his crucifixion; it was only the man Jesus who died and rose again. Cerinthus thus rejected the doctrine of the incarnation and consequently obliterated the Christian doctrine of the atonement.

When Jesus Christ came into the world to carry out His messianic mission, He came incarnate in a real human body as a real man. He did not

[21]Rudolph Bultmann, *The Johannine Epistles,* Hermenia–A Critical and Historical Commentary on the Bible (Philadelphia: Fortress Press, 1973), p. 62, note 6.

[22]James Moffatt, *The New Testament, A New Translation,* rev. ed. (New York: Hodder & Stoughton, n.d.).

[23]Kistemaker, p. 327.

[24]Roy L. Laurin, *First John, Life at Its Best* (1957; reprint ed., Grand Rapids: Kregel, 1987), p. 147. Italics in original.

just have the phantom appearance of a man, as Docetic Gnosticism maintained. This professed "high Christology" also vitiated the Christian truth of the incarnation. Thus John's stated test is the safeguard against various forms of doctrinal error concerning the person of Jesus Christ.

This permanent union of the divine and the human in the person of Jesus Christ qualifies Him to be the mediator between God and men (1 Tim. 2:5). He is the all-sufficient Saviour. The Apostolic teaching concerning the incarnate Christ "gathers within its total significance the other great doctrinal truths such as the Virgin Birth, the Crucifixion, and the Resurrection. The Incarnation is the essential creed of Christianity; on this doctrine all else which calls itself Christian stands or falls."[25] Every spirit that freely confesses the Apostolic message concerning the person of Jesus Christ thereby reveals that it is "of God," proceeding from the true God who has revealed Himself through His incarnate Son. John so intimately relates the spirit and the speaker whom the spirit inspires to proclaim this message that he presents the spirit as making the confession. The indwelling Holy Spirit gives and molds the message of His ministers (1 Cor. 12:8) and so provides the message of God (Rev. 2:7, 11).

b. The evidence of the spirit of antichrist (v. 3). The added "and" *(kai)* introduces the negative result that may flow from this testing of the spirits. For a complete picture concerning the spirits, this negative aspect is essential. Failure to recognize this negative fact would expose them to serious deception. John depicts the negative result of this testing as the spirit's failure to confess "Jesus" (v. 3a); this failure identifies the spirit as of antichrist (v. 3b) and confirms the fulfillment of prophecy (v. 3c).

1) The failure to confess Jesus (v. 3a). The negative aspect of the test is again stated inclusively: "every spirit that confesseth not that Jesus Christ is come in the flesh is not of God." In again saying "every spirit," John allows no intermediate position between the spirit that confesses Jesus Christ and the spirit that fails to confess Him. Here again we have the sharp antithesis between the two moral realms which John introduced in 1:5. Smalley appropriately points out, "John is not discussing the contrast between faith and unbelief; he is condemning those heretical beliefs, within and beyond his community, which amount to a determined and antichristian rebellion against God (v. 3b)."[26]

This statement of the negative result of the test is beset with textual variants. This negative statement of the result of the test in the King James Version follows the Textus Receptus. It is a full restatement, negatively, of

---

[25]Harvey J.S. Blaney, "The First Epistle of John," in *Beacon Bible Commentary* (Kansas City, Mo.: Beacon Hill Press, 1967), 10:388.

[26]Smalley, p. 223.

the positive result given in verse 2. But the total manuscript evidence suggests that it represents a scribal expansion based on the previous verse. The manuscript evidence presents no less than five variants.[27] "The variety of the supplements," Metzger notes, "is a further indication that they are secondary modifications of the original text."[28] Instead of this full restatement, modern textual critics generally accept that the original reading was "every spirit that confesseth not Jesus" (*ton Iēsoun*, "the Jesus") as set forth in the preceding verse, the human Jesus as the incarnate Son of God. It is possible to talk glowingly about the man Jesus yet refuse to accept the apostolic teaching that the historical Jesus of Nazareth was indeed God incarnate. Marshall well remarks, "If a person claims to believe in Jesus, it is proper to ask, 'Is your Jesus the real Jesus?' "[29] John rightly refuses to condone such half-truths concerning Jesus Christ. "Half-truths are always more dangerous than clearly discernible falsehoods, particularly when it comes to Christology and its implications for the Christian life."[30]

More important for the interpretation is the reading in various manuscripts of the Old Latin, the Vulgate, and some of the Latin Church Fathers which assumes that the original Greek verb was *luei,* "looses, destroys, annuls," rather than *mē homologei,* "not confesses." It would declare that the denier dissolves the union between "Jesus" and "Christ." A number of scholars have accepted this Latin reading as representing the original,[31] and Brown offers good arguments in its favor.[32] But the textual evidence is overwhelmingly against it as authentic.[33] It is the reading of no Greek manuscript and is found only in the margin of minuscule 1739, dating from the tenth century. The Latin variant apparently arose from the second century polemic against Gnostics, who made a sharp distinction between the earthly Jesus and the heavenly Christ. It seems that these variants arose as scribal efforts to explain the shorter and more difficult reading "the Jesus" *(ton Iēsoun).*

---

[27]For these varied readings and the manuscript support for each see Kurt Aland et al., ed. *The Greek New Testament,* 3rd ed. (New York: United Bible Societies, 1975). On a scale of A to D, the editors rate the reading *ton Iēsoun* as B.

[28]Bruce M. Metzger, *A Textual Commentary on the Greek New Testament* (London: United Bible Societies, 1971), p. 714.

[29]I. Howard Marshall, *The Epistles of John,* New International Commentary on the New Testament (Grand Rapids: Eerdmans, 1978), p. 207.

[30]R. Alan Culpepper, *1 John, 2 John, 3 John,* Knox Preaching Guides (Atlanta: John Knox Press, 1985), p. 81.

[31]See Marshall, pp. 207-9, note 11; Brown, 495-96, for a list of authors for either reading.

[32]Brown, pp. 494-95.

[33]See United Bible Societies, *The Greek New Testament,* 3rd ed. The editors rate the reading *mē homologei* as B.

Further, John's use of the negative *mē,* rather than the more usual *ou,* with the indicative verb "confess" has also evoked comment. Blass and DeBrunner, who accept *luei* as the original reading, simply stamp the negative as "a spurious reading."[34] David Smith suggests that the negative *"mē* makes the statement hypothetical: 'every spirit, if such there be, which does not confess.' "[35] But clearly John had no question as to the reality of such evil spirits. Robertson remarks that "there is a certain aloofness about *mē* here."[36] More probable is the view of Law who asserts that the use of *mē* expresses "the subjective conviction of the writer that there are no exceptions to the statement he is making."[37]

John's negative statement "every spirit that confesseth not that Jesus" is broader in scope than the positive "every spirit that denies Jesus" would have been. An open denial of "Jesus," as just set forth, at once establishes such a spirit as "not of God," not coming from nor proclaiming God's truth. But John's negative statement also includes any spirit that seeks to hide its true identity by endeavoring to avoid any discussion of the decisive issue. John knows that what such a spirit refrains from saying about "Jesus" in speaking of His person was also significant. In this epistle John never speaks about Jesus without adding some term to show that He is more than a mere man.

2) *The spirit of antichrist* (v. 3b). The failure of any spirit to confess the full truth concerning "Jesus" establishes its positive identity: "and this is that *spirit* of antichrist" *(kai touto estin to tou antichristou).* "And" *(kai)* adds the positive identification of the spirit that does not confess the true "Jesus." Since the word "spirit" is not actually expressed, some take the neuter demonstrative pronoun "this" *(touto)* to refer back to the spirit's failure to confess the true nature of Jesus. But it is more natural to take the demonstrative as closely united with the neuter article *(to),* with the word "spirit" rightly supplied from the context. John indicates that "that spirit," by its refusal to bear witness to "the Jesus," reveals its identity as "of antichrist." Westcott suggests that the omission of the Word "spirit" *(pneuma)* "gives greater breadth to the thought, so that the words include the many spirits, the many forces, which reveal the action of antichrist."[38] Over against the work of the Holy Spirit, inspiring the message of the true prophets of God, are the many evil spirits carrying on the deadly assault against the truth as revealed in Jesus Christ. Marshall well remarks, "John is in no doubt that denial

---

[34]Blass and DeBrunner, p. 221.

[35]David Smith, "The Epistles of John," in *The Expositor's Greek Testament* ([1897]; reprint ed., Grand Rapids: Eerdmans, n.d.), 5:189.

[36]Robertson, p. 1169.

[37]Law, p. 396.

[38]Westcott, p. 143.

of the apostolic confession about Jesus Christ is not merely intellectual error, still less 'advanced theology'; it represents the very spirit of rebellion against God and can only be condemned.''[39] These spirits already manifest the great rebellion against God which will find full expression in the eschatological Antichrist; in character and function they belong to the same realm.

3) *The fulfilment of prophecy* (v. 3c). John at once reminds his readers that the operation of such evil spirits should not surprise them since it is in accord with the prophetic warning they have received. The presence of these spirits was a matter "whereof ye have heard that it should come" *(ho akēkoate hoti erchetai)*. In 2:18 John reminded them that they had been warned that the Antichrist was coming; here he reminds them that they knew that the spirit of the antichrist also was coming. The perfect tense, "ye have heard," indicates that these realities were part of the regular Christian teaching concerning the future. The verb "should come" *(erchetai)* is frequently used of the historical coming of Jesus Christ; even so the coming of the spirit of antichrist, operating through these many antichrists, is also an historical reality.

The added words "and even now already is it in the world" *(kai nun en tō kosmō estin ēdē)* are a firm declaration that the spirit of antichrist is active on the scene of history. The term "the world" recalls that this evil spirit operates in this present world as estranged from and antagonistic to God and His truth. The use of "now" *(nun)* at the beginning of the statement underlines the active presence of this evil power as he writes (cf. 2 Thess. 2:7–"the mystery of lawlessness is already at work" NASB). This fact was obvious from the insidious and often violent attacks taking place against God's truth and His people. The added "already" *(ēdē)*, placed emphatically at the end, suggests, as Westcott notes, that "the prophecy had found fulfillment before the Church had looked for it."[40] It also implies that a fuller and more vicious manifestation of this spirit of rebellion against Christ awaits the coming of the eschatological Antichrist (Rev. 13; 2 Thess. 2:7-12). At the head of this rebellion is Satan himself.

3. The Criterion for Testing the Human Speakers (vv. 4-6)

Having set forth the criterion for testing the spirits (vv. 2-3), in these verses John states the criterion for testing those through whom the spirits speak. In verses 4-5 he states the criterion establishing the moral origin of these individuals. In verse 6a he points out the audience reaction to the speakers as a further indication of their nature. The last half of verse 6 summarizes the discussion.

---

[39]Marshall, p. 208.
[40]Westcott, p. 143.

a. The criterion for establishing their origin (vv. 4-5). In verse 4 John reminds his readers of the identity of the true people of God; in verse 5 he points out the identity of the false prophets.

1) *The sign of those who are of God* (v. 4). With genuine pastoral concern John assures his readers, "Ye are of God, little children, and have overcome them" *(humeis ek tou theou este, teknia, kai nenikēkate autous)*. The opening "Ye" *(humeis)* is emphatic, contrasting his beloved readers with the deluded world. As Wilder remarks, "The distinction between the two kinds of spirits is carried over now into one between two kinds of men, those *of God* and those *of the world.*"[41] As true believers, they "are of God" *(ek tou theou)*, have their spiritual origin in God and carry on His warfare against the evil of this sinful world. They have a personal relationship with God which the false teachers lack.

The affectionate address "little children" *(teknia;* cf. 2:1) recalls the fact of their new life and acknowledges them as members of the family of God. John has no fear that they will be deceived by the false teachers, but his fatherly heart prompts him to remind them of their true identity. Confronted by the increasing forces of alluring evil, his readers, like believers today, ought never to forget their divine heritage.

The added assertion " and have overcome them" *(kai nenikēkate autous)* gives evidence of their true identity. The masculine plural pronoun "them" marks the transition from the antichristian spirits to the false teachers who are their mouthpieces. They have tested these false teachers, identified the true nature of their teaching, and have rejected them. Gratefully John records that his beloved readers "have overcome" *(nenikēkate)* these false prophets. The perfect tense, "have overcome," implies a definite time when they faced these speakers with their alluring message, but, having tested their teaching, they have effectively rejected the messengers with their message, resulting in a state of being victorious over them. Their victory over these agents of Satan is grounded in the victory over the prince of this world which Christ won on Calvary (John 12:31-32; 14:30; 16:11). As Günther remarks, "The battle has thus been decided, even if it is not yet over. By faith Christians participate in this victory and are thus placed in a position to overcome the world for themselves."[42] But to maintain their victory, believers need to continue to adhere to and to obey the truth of God as taught by the apostles (Eph. 6:10-18).

---

[41]Amos N. Wilder and Paul W. Hoon, "The First, Second, and Third Epistles of John" in *The Interpreter's Bible* (New York: Abingdon Press, 1957), 12:276. Italics in original.

[42]W. Günther, *"nikaō,"* in *The New International Dictionary of New Testament Theology,* ed. Colin Brown (Grand Rapids: Zondervan, 1975), 1:651.

In adding "because greater is he that is in you, than he that is in the world," John reminds his readers of the true secret of their victory. While their understanding of and firm adherence to the apostolic truth was involved, the victory was produced by the divine indwelling, "he that is in you" *(estin ho en humin)*. The reference clearly is to one of the persons of the Godhead, but, characteristically, John does not explicitly identify the indwelling Enabler. Generally interpreters prefer simply to say "God."[43] Westcott suggests that the reference was to "God in Christ,"[44] whereas Smalley holds that the reference "combines an allusion to God as Father, Son *and* Spirit" and in support appeals to "the trinitarian character of John's theology in this section."[45] Still others understand it as a reference to the indwelling Holy Spirit.[46] This view has in its favor the explicit statement concerning the Holy Spirit in 3:24. Burdick further notes,

> In verses 2 and 3 John has been contrasting the Spirit of God with the spirit of antichrist, and he again refers to these two spirits in verse 6. In 2:27 the anointing (Holy Spirit) is said to dwell in believers.[47]

Brown likewise supports this view when he remarks, " 'He who is in you' echoes the description of the Paraclete/Spirit of Truth in John 14:16-17, where Jesus says that this Spirit is to 'be with you' and 'be in you' " *(einai en)*.[48] This view is fully in accord with the New Testament teaching concerning the indwelling and work of the Holy Spirit in believers (Rom. 5:5; 2 Cor. 1:22, 3:18; Gal. 4:6; Eph. 3:16-19; Titus 3:5-6).

John stresses, not the identity, but the superior greatness of this divine Enabler: "greater is he that is in you, than he that is in the world" *(meizōn estin ho en humin ē ho en tō kosmō)*. The masculine articles make clear that the contrast is between two personal powers, while the comparative adjective "greater" stresses the superior authority and power of the one who is in believers than the one who is in the world. This opponent is the Devil, "the prince of this world" (John 12:31), whose work the Son of God came to destroy

---

[43]So Henry Alford, *The New Testament for English Readers* ([1865-1872]; reprint ed., Chicago: Moody Press [1958]), p. 1737; Bultmann, p. 63; R.C.H. Lenski, *The Interpretation of the Epistles of St. Peter, St. John and St. Jude* (Columbus, Ohio: Wartburg Press, 1945), p. 490; Marshall, p. 208; David Smith, p. 190.

[44]Westcott, p. 144.

[45]Smalley, p. 227.

[46]So Barker, 12:341; F. F. Bruce, *The Epistles of John* (Old Tappan, N.J.: Revell, 1970), p. 106; Zane C. Hodges, "1 John," in *The Bible Knowledge Commentary, New Testament* (Wheaton, Ill.: Victor Books, 1983), p. 898; Kistemaker, p. 328; Warren W. Wiersbe, *Be Real* (Wheaton, Ill.: Victor Books, 1972), p. 135.

[47]Burdick, pp. 201-2.

[48]Brown, p. 498.

(1 John 3:8). Clearly John "does not subscribe to a dualist system in which the universe is the battlefield of two essentially equally powerful spiritual forces."[49] The Devil is already a defeated foe, and believers can enjoy personal victory over him through the power of the indwelling Holy Spirit.

Having assured his readers that this greater one is "in you," it might have been anticipated that John would refer to this personal evil opponent as being "in them," that is, in the antichristian false teachers. Instead John presents the Devil and his minions as being "in the world" *(en tō kosmō)*. The term "the world" here has a strong moral connotation, denoting the organized world of humanity in its hostility to God and His kingdom. This is the first of four references to this hostile realm in verse 4-5. John and his readers were well aware of the active hatred of the world.

2) *The sign of those who are of the world* (v. 5). "They are of the world" *(autoi ek tou kosmou eisin,* literally, "they, out of the world they are") marks the fundamental difference between the false teachers and true believers (v. 4). "Out of the world"(literal) indicates their spiritual derivation and their personal allegiance. In verse 3 John has identified the antichristian spirits negatively as being "not of God"; now their human agents are identified as being "of the world," indicating their essential orientation and character. In relation to the Church of God, they reflect the distinctly negative reaction of the Christ-rejecting world. The triple use of "the world" in verse 5 underlines their fundamental attitude and motivation. They belong to the godless world-system of which Satan is the prince (John 12:31; 14:30; 16:11).

John at once points out the evidence: "therefore speak they of the world, and the world heareth them." What they are is revealed by their message as well as by the followers they draw. The content of their message establishes that the false teachers are "of the world": "therefore speak they of the world" *(dia touto ek tou kosmou lalousin,* more literally, "because of this, out of the world they are speaking"). Because their being is rooted in the world, their message reveals what they are (John 3:31). They draw the substance of their teaching from the philosophy of the godless world, while the issues of eternity are left unmentioned or are perverted through their restatement of them. Thus they reveal that they have no connection with the divine fountain of revealed truth; because they have their origin in the world, therefore the things they speak belong to the world. In adjusting and formulating their message to conform to the spirit and interests of the world, they distort and deform the message of God. Therein lies their danger, for, as Bruce observes, "There is no form of 'worldliness' so inimical to Christianity as this kind of 're-statement.'"[50]

---

[49]J. L. Houlden, *A Commentary On the Johannine Epistles,* Harper's New Testament Commentaries (New York: Harper & Row, 1973), p. 110.

[50]Bruce, p. 106.

The additional comment "and the world heareth them" *(kai ho kosmos autōn akouei)* confirms their true identity by the fact that their message appeals to the world. The verb "hear" *(akouei,* "listen to") denotes a receptive hearing of the speaker's message. Their message arouses the interest of the world and stimulates its basic attitudes and desires. "The world of mankind in rebellion against God is attracted by the false prophets and their cults because fundamentally they have the same desires and inclinations."[51] John's statement implies that these false teachers were experiencing a good measure of success outside the apostolic circle of believers. His use of the genitive *(autōn),* rather than the accusative, in saying "the world hears *them*"[52] implies that it is the message of the false teachers, rather than the teachers themselves, that is so appealing to the world. It is a sad fact that heretics seem always to have a following; in one way or another their message makes its appeal to the desires and hopes of fallen humanity. Hobbs aptly remarks,

> Because the world goes to hear what it wants to hear anyway, it is no compliment to a preacher to say, "He speaks our language." It is condemnation when the world says, "He is one of us" or "He is my kind of preacher."[53]

This, of course, does not imply that a minister who draws large crowds is thereby shown to be a false teacher. It is a fact of history that, under the power of the Holy Spirit, large crowds are being drawn to hear the preaching of the gospel, and many of them are being brought to personal faith in Christ and drawn into the fellowship of His Church through a faithful preaching of the true gospel. Whenever there is a negative response to the faithful preaching of the gospel, the reaction may be due, Dodd remarks, "to a defect in the preacher's presentation of the message, or to his failure to understand sympathetically the people to whom he appeals."[54] In His parable of the sower in Matthew 13:3-15, Jesus makes it clear that the Word of God may be ineffective because of satanic activity as well as human sinfulness and personal laxity.

b. The criterion of the response to the speaker (v. 6a). The world's response to the false teachers leads John to point out a further test, namely, the character of the messenger is revealed by the kind of followers he draws.

---

[51]David Jackman, *The Message of John's Letters,* The Bible Speaks Today (Downers Grove, Ill.: Inter-Varsity Press, 1988), p. 115.

[52]"The Classical rule for *akouein* [to hear] is: the person whose words are heard stands in the genitive, the things about which (or whom) one hears in the accusative." Blass and DeBrunner, p. 95.

[53]Herschel H. Hobbs, *The Epistles of John* (Nashville: Thomas Nelson Publishers, 1983), p. 103.

[54]C. H. Dodd, *The Johannine Epistles,* Moffatt New Testament Commentary (New York: Harper & Row, 1946), p. 101.

The assertion "we are of God" *(hēmeis ek tou theou esmen)* marks the contrast between the false teachers of verse 5 and the apostolic messengers. Some[55] understand the intended scope of the emphatic "We" *(hēmeis)* to denote John and his readers, or the Christian community. Then this emphatic "we" is not really distinctive from the "ye" of verse 4. But more probably "we" here marks a contrast with the false teachers in verse 5. Then there is a double contrast in verses 4-6. The "ye" in verse 4 forms a contrast to the "they" of verse 5, a contrast between true believers and the false prophets. Here the "We" of verse 6a marks a second contrast, between the false prophets of verse 5 and John and his fellow apostles.[56] As Plummer notes, "The opposition here is not between true and false *Christians,* but between true and false *teachers.*"[57] John speaks as representing the apostolic company and the further faithful bearers of the apostolic message. His categorical assertion "we are of God" reflects the consciousness of certainty and authority manifested by Christ's chosen and commissioned messengers. In the words of Plummer,

> Here once more we have that magisterial tone of Apostolic authority which is so conspicuous in the Prologue (i. 1-4). It underlies the whole Epistle, as it does the whole of the Fourth Gospel. . . . It is the quiet confidence of conscious strength.[58]

In setting forth this criterion of audience reaction, John echoes the words of Jesus, "He who is of God hears the words of God; for this reason you do not hear *them,* because you are not of God" (John 8:47 NASB; cf. 10:4-5, 26-27). Both positively and negatively, the response to God's Word reveals the nature of the hearer.

Positively, "he that knoweth God heareth us" *(ho ginōskōn ton theon akouei hēmōn).* The present-tense articular participle pictures one who has a continuing and growing acquaintance with the true God. His relationship with God is "no mere intellectual knowing but a living apprehension with full effect on mind, heart, and life."[59] Such an individual "heareth us" *(akouei hēmōn),* that is, gives a receptive hearing to the message being

---

[55]So Bultmann, p. 64, note 15; Lenski, p. 491; Marshall, p. 209; Smalley, p. 229.

[56]So A. E. Brooke, *The Johannine Epistles,* International Critical Commentary (New York: Charles Scribner's Sons, 1912), pp. 115-16; Alford, p. 1738; Plummer, p. 145; Stott, pp. 157-58; Alexander Ross, *The Epistles of James and John,* New International Commentary on the New Testament (Grand Rapids: Eerdmans, 1954), pp. 198-99; R. W. Orr, "The Letters of John," in *A New Testament Commentary* (Grand Rapids: Zondervan, 1969), p. 617; James Montgomery Boice, *The Epistles of John* (Grand Rapids: Zondervan, 1979), p. 137.

[57]Plummer, p. 145. Italics in original.

[58]*Ibid.*

[59]Lenski, p. 491.

presented by God's messengers. He hears and heeds the divine message. The result is, as Westcott observes, "The hearer discerns the true message. The teacher discovers the true disciple. And this concurrence of experience brings fresh assurance and deeper knowledge."[60] The Holy Spirit in the heart of the speaker witnesses to the heart of the hearer and vitalizes the sense of their mutual fellowship in Christ.

A negative reaction to the apostolic message is also significant: "he that is not of God heareth not us." Any individual who refuses to accept the message being proclaimed thereby reveals that he "is not of God" *(ouk estin ek tou theou)*. Instead of saying that he "does not know God," John characterizes him as being "not of God," lacking the inner experience of being born of God. It is through the experience of the new birth that the individual comes to a living knowledge of God. Only one who has been born of God has ears that are habitually attentive to the Word of God. The Spirit-empowered preaching of the Word not only confirms the true nature of the speaker but also serves to lay bare the spiritual state of the hearer.

c. The summary concerning the testing of the spirits (v. 6b). John terminates the discussion with a summary comment: "Hereby know we the spirit of truth, and the spirit of error." "Hereby" *(ek toutou,* "out of this") looks back to the preceding discussion, but it is not clear whether "this" refers to the entire section (vv. 1-6), to the second part (vv. 4-6), or only to the first half of verse 6. Burdick holds that "this" "refers back to the positive and negative statement of the test in the first part of the verse–to the established fact that like listens to like."[61] Smalley accepts that the reference is "in the first place to the criterion mentioned in v. 6 itself (whether or not attention is paid to the apostolic proclamation)," but he agrees with those who hold that "an allusion to the earlier test (a proper acknowledgment of Jesus, vv. 2-3) is almost certainly in view as well."[62] This broader reference, including both tests which John mentioned, is essential for full certainty in testing the spirits. "Where there are conflicting voices within the church two tests may be applied: what are they saying, and who is listening to them."[63]

In this summary the plural "we know" *(ginōskomen)* is not restricted but ascribes to all true believers this ability to recognize or distinguish the true nature of the spirits. This ability was not limited to the apostolic messengers, nor is it restricted to the official leaders of the Church; but clearly some believers are more gifted to discern the spirits than others.

---

[60]Westcott, p. 145.

[61]Burdick, p. 304.

[62]Smalley, p. 230.

[63]Culpepper, p. 83.

Conditions then, as now, demanded that believers be alert to distinguish between "the spirit of truth, and the spirit of error" *(to pneuma tēs alētheias kai to peuma tēs planēs)*. These two spirits represent two distinct moral realms competing for control over the masses of humanity. Our translations generally parallel the two occurrences of the word "spirit" here, but the NIV and a few other versions[64] capitalize the first occurrence of the word to indicate that the reference is to the Holy Spirit, already referred to as "the spirit of God" in verse 2. The designation "the Spirit of truth" denotes the Holy Spirit in John 14:17; 15:26; 16:13. The genitive "of truth" seems best understood as descriptive, setting forth the nature of the Spirit Himself as the embodiment of "the truth" (cf. John 14:6) and as actively communicating and interpreting God's truth. Those who proclaim the truth of God do so under the inspiration of the Spirit of truth.

Opposing the work of the Spirit of truth is "the spirit of error" *(to pneuma tēs planēs)*, a phrase occurring only here in the New Testament. The genitive "of error" again is best viewed as descriptive of the relentless activities of the Devil and his cohorts. The noun rendered "error" *(planēs)* basically means "wandering, roaming" but is used figuratively to denote "error, delusion, deceit, deception."[65] It may be used with either an active or passive force. Actively it means "the leading astray, deceit," while passively it signifies "being led astray, error, delusion." The context clearly supports the active meaning here rather than the passive. The reference to the "false prophets" (literally, "pseudoprophets") in verse 1 clearly involves the concept of active deception; and in 2:26 John uses the cognate verb to warn his readers against "those who are trying to lead you astray" (NIV; cf. also 3:7). Satan here is not characterized as " the spirit of error" because he is the victim of error and deception; rather, he actively promotes error or deception and is deceptive by his very nature. Satan and his demonic forces are engaged in a relentless effort to lead believers into spiritual error and deception, working in and through their human agents. This warfare between "the Spirit of truth and the spirit of error," contending for control over the life and destiny of mankind, is indeed the climactic aspect of the conflicts of the Christian life.

---

[64]TEV, Richard Francis Weymouth, *The New Testament In Modern Speech*, revised by James Alexander Robertson (New York: Harper & Brothers, 1929); *The Everyday Bible, New Century Version* (Fort Worth, Texas: Worthy Publishing, 1987).

[65]William F. Arndt and F. Wilbur Gingrich, *A Greek-English Lexicon of the New Testament and Other Early Christian Literature* (Chicago: University of Chicago Press, 1957), p. 671.

12

Assurance from the Evidence of True Love (4:7–5:5)

In 1 John 4:7–5:5, the third major division of the epistle, John presents an elaborate development of the nature and results of Christian love. It is a fuller development of a theme that he has twice touched upon in the preceding treatment of the Christian life. In 1:5–2:17 John surveyed the Christian life under the theme of assurance through fellowship, and he noted in 2:7-11 that the practice of love is one of the signs of fellowship with God. In Part II John again made a survey of the Christian life under the theme of the conflicts which Christian faith encounters, and in noting those conflicts he indicated in 3:13-24 that the conflict between love and hatred is an assuring sign of a vital Christian life.

In Part III John turns to a fuller elaboration of the theme of true love as related to the nature of God Himself. In 4:7-16a John sets forth the nature of redeeming love, and in 4:16b–5:5 he points out the results of this love in the life of the believer. The presence and operation of this God-inspired love is a further ground of Christian assurance.

A. The Nature of Redeeming Love (4:7-16a)

4:7 Beloved, let us love one another: for love is of God; and every one that loveth is born of God, and knoweth God.

8 He that loveth not knoweth not God; for God is love.

9 In this was manifested the love of God toward us, because that God sent his only begotten Son into the world, that we might live through him.

10 Herein is love, not that we loved God, but that he loved us, and sent his Son *to be* the propitiation for our sins.

11 Beloved, if God so loved us, we ought also to love one another.

12 No man hath seen God at any time. If we love one another, God dwelleth in us, and his love is perfected in us.

13 Hereby know we that we dwell in him, and he in us, because he hath given us of his Spirit.

14 And we have seen and do testify that the Father sent the Son *to be* the Saviour of the world.

15 Whosoever shall confess that Jesus is the Son of God, God dwelleth in him, and he in God.

16 And we have known and believed the love that God hath to us.

In this portrayal of the nature of redeeming love, John notes that the presence of love is basic for Christian assurance (vv. 7-8), portrays the manifestation of true love in Christ Jesus (vv. 9-10), stresses the need for practical mutual love (vv. 11-12), and elaborates on the confirmation of redeeming love in Christian experience (vv. 13-16a).

1. The Assurance from the Practice of Love (vv. 7-8)

John prefaces his discussion of Christian love with the direct address "beloved" *(agapētoi),* expressive of his own love for his readers. Stott remarks, "The author practices what he preaches. In urging them to love each other, he first assures them of his own love for them."[1] Thus John skillfully reminds them that those being commanded to love others are themselves the recipients of love. John calls his readers to the practice of mutual love because of the source of true love (v. 7a), and he sets before them the significance—both positively and negatively—of such love (vv. 7b-8).

a. The practice of mutual love grounded in God's love (v. 7a). The appeal "let us love one another" *(agapōmen allēlous)* is a call for mutual love in which John includes himself. In form the verb may be either indicative, "we love,"[2] or hortative subjunctive, "let us love." Our versions and the commentators generally accept the latter view and understand it as a call for the mutual love within the Christian brotherhood. Such a love is natural to the redeemed soul; yet it is "very susceptible of culture, and may be much strengthened by the exercise of the duty."[3] John's purpose is to encourage and stimulate the practice of Christian love. The present tense calls for the continued or repeated expression of love, while the reciprocal pronoun "one another" insists that this love must be mutual, must flow freely in both directions. It is a call for a high, unselfish love which freely

---

[1] J.R.W. Stott, *The Epistles of John,* Tyndale New Testament Commentaries (Grand Rapids: Eerdmans, 1964), p. 160.

[2] Donald W. Burdick, *The Letters of John the Apostle* (Chicago: Moody Press, 1985), supports the indicative: "The main point being expressed in verses 7-16 is not an exhortation to love but a declaration that Christians do love because they have been born of God, who is love" (p. 317).

[3] James Morgan, *The Epistles of John* (1865; reprint ed., Minneapolis: Klock & Klock Christian Publishers, 1982), p. 306.

seeks the true welfare of the one loved. The presence of such love is known only from the gracious actions it prompts. It expresses itself most readily in the mutual relations between believers. Plummer notes, "The love of Christians to unbelievers is not expressly excluded, but it is not definitely before the Apostle's mind."[4] This unselfish love will prompt the believer to reach out with beneficent intention to the unsaved around him (Gal. 6:10), but this God-prompted love cannot find full mutual realization with unbelievers.

This exhortation is grounded in the fact that this love has a divine origin: "for love is of God" *(hoti hē agapē ek tou theou estin).* The use of the definite article with "love" *(hē agapē)* centers attention on the kind of love John is calling for, "the love" that has its source in God. In 3:11 John grounded the call for mutual love in the apostolic message they had received; here the exhortation to mutual love is grounded in the nature and being of God Himself. This love is not the natural love of the world for its own (John 15:19) nor the love of publicans for fellow-publicans (Matt. 5:46) but a self-sacrificing love rooted in God's own love as portrayed in verses 9-10. The preposition "of" *(ek,* "out of") denotes that this love "flows from Him, as the one spring, and in such a way that the connexion with the source remains unbroken."[5]

b. The practice of love as the revelation of character (vv. 7b-8). The connective "and" *(kai)* further undergirds the call to love with the fact that its practice is a sure revelation of spiritual identity. The resultant revelation is stated positively (v. 7b) and negatively (v. 8).

1) *The character of the one loving* (v. 7b). The positive statement "every one that loveth is born of God, and knoweth God" identifies the true believer. "Every one that loveth" *(pas ho agapōn)* includes every individual actively practicing the kind of love John is talking about. No object of love is expressed; it is an individual's practice of love, whether Godward or manward, that is the crucial test of his spiritual identity. The significance of such an active love is indicated in the double assertion about him: he "is born of God, and knoweth God" *(ek tou theou gegennētai kai ginōskei ton theon,* which Rotherham renders, "Of God hath been born, And is getting to understand God"). The original order draws the two verbs together, framed by the two references to God. The perfect passive verb "is born" *(gegennētai)* denotes the past definite experience of the new birth as wrought by God, with the result that he is now a member of God's family. "The divine begetting preceded the love: love is an activity of the implanted eternal life, and is

---

[4]Alfred Plummer, *The Epistles of S. John,* Cambridge Bible for Schools and Colleges (1883; reprint ed., London: Cambridge University Press, 1938), p. 146.

[5]Brooke Foss Westcott, *The Epistles of St. John, The Greek Text with Notes,* 3rd ed. (1892; reprint ed., Grand Rapids: Eerdmans, 1950), p. 147.

therefore a proof that the life is present."[6] The second assertion, "and knoweth God," records the sure result of the new birth. Now the use of the present tense verb *(ginōskei)* points to his daily experience as getting to know and understand God better and better. A living knowledge of God is not static but actively increasing.

2) *The character of the one not loving* (v. 8). In typical Johannine fashion, verse 8 presents the opposite picture: "He that loveth not knoweth not God." The negative with the present-tense participle *(ho mē agapōn)* pictures one who is unloving in attitude and practice. Again John's picture includes all those so characterized. The absence of love in the life of any individual proves that he "knoweth not God" *(ouk egnō ton theon);* he has never come to know God personally. The aorist tense apparently refers back to the time of his professed conversion. Not knowing this distinctive love reveals that he is still a stranger to God. The absence of this God-given love in his heart and life disqualifies such an individual as a trustworthy representative and interpreter of God because of the nature of God as love.

The explanatory assertion "for God is love" *(hoti ho theos agapē estin)* is another of the great Biblical statements concerning the nature of God. As Jackman points out, "John is not identifying a quality which God possesses; he is making a statement about the essence of God's being."[7] The statement stands parallel to two other crucial statements from the pen of John: "God is spirit" (John 4:24) and "God is light" (1 John 1:5). They set forth different aspects of the essential nature of God. In the words of Marshall, " 'God is spirit' describes his metaphysical nature, while 'God is light' and 'God is love' deal with his character, especially as he has revealed himself to men."[8] Although the reality that "God is love" seems most easily comprehended by the human mind, this assertion should not be set above the other two. All three are essential for an adequate presentation of the nature of God. "God's nature," Wilder notes, "is not exhausted by the quality of love, but love governs all its aspects and expressions."[9] Since love is a personal activity, the assertion "God is love" "stresses the personality of God to the fullest extent."[10]

---

[6]R. W. Orr, "The Letters of John," in *A New Testament Commentary* (Grand Rapids: Zondervan, 1969), p. 247.

[7]David Jackman, *The Message of John's Letters,* The Bible Speaks Today (Downers Grove, Ill.: Inter-Varsity Press, 1988), p. 118.

[8]I. Howard Marshall, *The Epistles of John,* New International Commentary on the New Testament (Grand Rapids: Eerdmans, 1978), p. 212.

[9]Amos N. Wilder and Paul W. Hoon, "The First, Second, and Third Epistles of John," in *The Interpreter's Bible* (New York: Abingdon Press, 1957), 12:280.

[10]Marshall, p. 213.

The two nouns in the statement "God is love" *(ho theos agapē estin)* are not interchangeable, because the definite article occurs with "God" but not with "love."[11] To make them reversible would offer a basis for pantheism. Although John has just said that "love is of God" (v. 7), one cannot say that "love is God," just as one cannot say that "light is God." Without the article, "love" is qualitative, depicting the nature of His being. The fact that God as a person "is love" does not invalidate the fact that He is also holy and righteous. All aspects of His nature belong together and unite in determining His action and response. In His attitude and actions He is totally consistent. "Because He is love, God works against whatever works against love."[12]

2. The Manifestation of Redeeming Love (vv. 9-10)

Fallen humanity would never have known such redeeming love apart from the fact that God took the initiative in revealing His love to mankind. Therefore, "all our definitions of what love is and how it behaves must be drawn from him if they are to accord with reality."[13] The true nature of God's love was manifested in the incarnation (v. 9) and in the atonement (v. 10).

a. The manifestation of love in the incarnation (v. 9). Having asserted that God is love, John at once sets forth how God revealed His love: "In this was manifested the love of God toward us, because that God sent his only begotten Son into the world." "In this" *(en toutō)* looks forward to and is interpreted by the following "that" clause. The rendering "by this" (NASB) interprets the preposition *(en)* as instrumental, namely, that God's love was revealed by means of the sending of His Son. The KJV rendering "in this" views the expression as locative, meaning that God's love was embodied in the sending of His Son. Then the incarnate coming of Christ was the unmistakable manifestation of divine love. The verb "was manifested" *(ephanerōthē),* a favorite term with John,[14] means "to make visible, make clear, come out into the open," and implies that, previous to the coming of Christ in incarnation, this love had not been displayed in such a personal, dynamic manner. In Him God's message of love reached its climax

---

[11]"The article with one and not with the other means that the articular noun is the subject. Thus *ho theos agapē estin* can only mean *God is love,* not *love is God. . . .* If the article occurs with both predicate and subject they are interchangeable." A. T. Robertson and W. Hersey Davis, *A New Short Grammar of the Greek Testament* (1931; reprint ed., New York: Harper & Brothers, 1935), p. 279.

[12]Herschel H. Hobbs, *The Epistles of John* (Nashville: Thomas Nelson Publishers, 1983), p. 109.

[13]Jackman, p. 119.

[14]The verb *phaneroō* occurs nine times in 1 John, nine times in the Fourth Gospel, and twice in Revelation. In all of Paul's epistles it appears twenty times, but only seven times in the rest of the New Testament.

(Heb. 1:1-2). The genitive "of God" here is clearly subjective, meaning God's own love, for God acted to manifest that love.

John's statement that this love was manifested "toward us" (*en hēmin,* literally, "in us") is differently understood. Some, such as Smith, understand it subjectively, " 'in our souls'–an inward experience."[15] But since John is referring to a historical event, such an inner subjective meaning seems unlikely. As relating to an objective event, the meaning may be "toward us" or "among us" as the sphere in which the manifestation took place. Because those who beheld this manifestation were not merely interested spectators, Lenski holds that "the phrase *en hēmin* means that the manifestation was 'in connection with us,' it involved us as the recipients of God's love."[16]

This manifestation consisted in the fact "because that God sent his only begotten Son into the world" (*hoti ton huion autou ton monogenē apestalken ho theous eis ton kosmon,* literally, "that His Son, the only begotten one, God has sent into the world"). The double conjunction "because that" in the KJV is an unusual rendering of *hoti;* "because" was apparently intended to call attention to the reason for our knowledge of God's love, and "that" to call attention to the event that gave us that knowledge. John's order places the object, "His only begotten Son," emphatically forward. The manifestation of His love was the sending of His Son personally. The repeated article with "His Son" and "the only begotten *one*" makes both designations prominent and distinct. The former marks His deity, the latter His uniqueness. "His Son" calls attention to the intimate Father-Son relationship between the sender and the one sent; in eternity past the Son was in an intimate face-to-face relationship with God (John 1:1). The second designation is climactic. As applied to Christ, the term is unique to John (John 1:14, 18; 3:16, 18; here). The Gospel of Luke uses the word of an only child (7:12; 8:42; 9:38), and Hebrews 11:17 uses it of Isaac as indicating his unique relation to Abraham as the only son of promise. Derived from *monos* ("only, single") and *genos* ("kind"), it denotes uniqueness rather than origin, "one of a kind."[17] The term denotes that "as the 'only' Son of God, He has no equal and is able fully to reveal the Father."[18] Marshall remarks

---

[15]David Smith, "The Epistle of St. John," in *The Expositor's Greek Testament* ([1897]; reprint ed., Grand Rapids: Eerdmans, n.d.), 5:191.

[16]R.C.H. Lenski, *The Interpretation of the Epistles of St. Peter, St. John and St. Jude* (Columbus, Ohio: Wartburg Press, 1945), p. 500.

[17]James Hope Moulton and George Milligan, *The Vocabulary of the Greek Testament* (1930; reprint ed., London: Hodder and Stoughton, 1952), notes that this Greek term "is literally 'one of a kind,' 'only,' 'unique' *(unicus),* not 'only begotten,' which would be *monogennētos (unigenitus)*" (pp. 416-17).

[18]*Ibid.,* p. 417.

that in the Septuagint the Hebrew word meaning "singly, only" is sometimes rendered into Greek as *agapētos* ("beloved") and sometimes as *monogenēs* and concludes that *"monogenēs* may contain the nuance 'beloved,' especially since an only child is particularly loved by his parents."[19] But Cremer notes that John's usage of *monogenēs* does not quite correspond to *agapētos* in the Synoptics but rather to Paul's "His own son" *(tou idiou huiou)* in Romans 8:32.[20] The familiar English rendering "only begotten Son" is based on Jerome's use of *unigenitus* in the Vulgate instead of the Old Latin translation *unicus* ("only"). The term implies the sacrificial nature of the Father's love in voluntarily sending His only Son. The perfect-tense verb "sent" *(apestalken,* "hath sent") points to the abiding impact of that crucial sending. As believers, we now enjoy the abiding blessings of the first advent. This compound verb, the first of three occurrences in this epistle,[21] literally means "to send forth" and embodies the thought of someone's being sent forth as the representative of another. The cognate noun *(apostolos),* commonly rendered "apostle," denotes one sent forth on a mission as the representative of another. In Hebrews 3:1 this noun is used of Jesus Himself as the commissioned representative of the Father. While the preposition *(apo,* "off, away from") in the compound verb implies His departure from the presence of the Father, the added phrase "into the world" *(eis ton kosmon)* states His destination. Here the term "the world" is used quite literally to denote the place where those live to whom He was sent (cf. John 3:17).

The stated purpose of this divine sending of the Son makes clear the redemptive nature of God's love: "that we might live through Him" *(hina zēsōmen di' autou).* The statement implies that those to whom the Son was sent were spiritually dead (Eph. 2:1, 5), but He came to give them life. Interpreters generally understand the aorist-tense verb "might live" as ingressive, "might come to live,"[22] but Lenski regards the aorist as "effective: actually live through him."[23] The aorist tense declares the purpose of Christ's mission as the actual bestowal of life with the resultant ongoing possession of eternal life. The added phrase "through him" declares that the Son Himself is the mediating agent of this bestowal of eternal life, imparted to them while

---

[19]Marshall, p. 214, note 8.

[20]Hermann Cremer, *Biblico-Theological Lexicon of New Testament Greek,* trans. William Urwick (1895; reprint ed., Edinburgh: T. & T. Clark, 1954), p. 150.

[21]1 John 4:9, 10, 14. In the Gospel of John it occurs seventeen times in relation to the sending of Jesus.

[22]F. F. Bruce, *The Epistles of John* (Old Tappan, N.J.: Revell, 1970), p. 108; Marshall, p. 214, note 9; Stephen S. Smalley, *1, 2, 3 John,* Word Biblical Commentary (Waco, Texas: Word Books, 1984), p. 242.

[23]Lenski, p. 502.

they are here on this earth. This God-given life is not merely future; through Christ it is received here in this life and will continue into the eternal future. "It includes the removal of the sentence of death, the return of spiritual life of the soul, and the final enjoyment of eternal life in heaven."[24]

b. The manifestation of love in the atonement (v. 10). The love that sent the Son that "we might live through him" is now related to the propitiatory self-sacrifice of the incarnate Son. The renewed statement "herein is love" (*en toutō estin hē agapē*, literally, "the love" as just depicted) again looks forward to the remainder of the verse; characteristically, John makes a negative and positive identification of this love.

John parenthetically inserts the negative, "not that we loved God" *(ouch hoti hēmeis egapēkamen ton theon)*, to contradict any misconception that God is naturally loved by fallen humanity. The emphatic "we" *(hēmeis)* here is inclusive in its scope to mark the contrast between sinful human beings and the loving God. Fallen humanity is not naturally in love with the God whom the Son came to reveal.[25] As such we did not and could not express the love John is here talking about.

Positively, John stresses two facts concerning God's love. "But" *(all')* marks the contrast to the negative reality just asserted. The first fact is "that he loved us" *(hoti autos ēgapēsen hēmas,* literally, "that He Himself loved us"). The emphatic "He Himself" *(autos)* continues the contrast between the preceding "we" *(hēmeis)* and God. He took the initiative in revealing His love. His love "was original and spontaneous, the source of all other love."[26] The aorist-tense verb "loved" refers to the historical, redemptive work of Christ, regarded as a distinctive landmark. The Christian gospel centers on that specific act of redeeming love.

The redemptive nature of God's love is made clear in the further fact that He "sent His Son *to be* the propitiation for our sins" *(apesteilen ton huion autou hilasmon peri tōn hamartiōn hēmōn)*. It is a summary statement of the redemptive mission of Christ in His first advent. A connection "and" *(kai)* links the fact of God's love with His loving act. The aorist "sent" *(apesteilen)* views the first advent as a mission which culminated in making "his Son *to be* the propitiation for our sins." Since no verbal form is used,

---

[24]Morgan, p. 319.

[25]There is some textual variation in the tense of the verb "we loved." Codex B and Psi and a few minuscules have the perfect *egapēkamen;* the majority of the manuscripts have the aorist *ēgapēsamen.* The aorist may be an attempt to conform the unusual perfect to the other aorist in this verse. For the textual evidence see Nestle-Aland, *Novum Testamentum Graece,* 26th ed. (Stuttgart: Deutsche Bibelstiftung, 1979).

[26]W. H. Bennett, *The General Epistles, James, Peter, John and Jude,* The Century Bible (London: Blackwood, Le Bas & Co., n.d.), p. 312.

the expression may be rendered "His Son *to be* the propitiation" or "His Son *as* the propitiation." John insists that the Son "Himself is the propitiation for our sins" (2:2 NASB). He was not sent merely to be "the propitiator for our sins," like the high priest under the Mosaic law, but He Himself became "the propitiation for our sins" by shedding His own blood for the remission of sin. He is *both* the propitiator and the propitiation for human sin. Christ's self-sacrifice for sin made full atonement for all sins, enabling God to pardon the sins of those who believe in Him and to restore them to acceptance and fellowship with Himself. In the words of Pentecost, "The death of Jesus Christ did not change the heart of God, as if One who hated us now loves us, rather it opened the floodgate so that the love of God for sinners could be poured out to them through Jesus Christ."[27] The words "our sins" bear witness to the consciousness of John and his readers concerning their personal need for such a propitiatory sacrifice.

3. The Practice of Brother-Love (vv. 11-12)

Having set forth the nature of redeeming love (vv. 9-10), John states the resultant obligation of believers to love one another (v. 11) and notes the significance of its practice (v. 12).

a. The obligation of mutual Christian love (v. 11). For the sixth and last time John addresses his readers as "beloved" *(agapētoi);* he thus reverts to the admonition with which he began this discussion of love (v. 7). No further direct address occurs until the very last verse of the epistle (5:21). The opening address as well as the formulation of the obligation mark this as a distinctly Christian obligation.

John's statement of this obligation is conditional, "If God so loved us, we ought also to love one another." The use of the first-class condition, "if God so loved us" *(ei houtōs ho theos ēgapēsen hēmas),* states the motivating reality as an accepted fact, a reality which lies at the heart of the Christian faith. The adverb "so" recalls the sacrificial love portrayed in verse 10 and "expresses both the manner, degree, and extent of God's love."[28] The use of the articular noun *ho theos* ("the God") stresses the majesty of the love shown by the God they have come to know personally. The verse echoes John 3:16, but now the use of the personal pronoun "us" marks the personal realization of this love on the part of John and his readers. God manifested this love for us "not because of our merit but because of our need."[29]

In view of God's unmerited love for us, "we ought also to love one another" *(kai hēmeis opheilomen allēlous agapan).* Brown notes that "the

---

[27]J. Dwight Pentecost, *The Joy of Fellowship* (Grand Rapids: Zondervan, 1977), p. 109.

[28]Hobbs, p. 111.

[29]*Ibid.*

initial *Kai* is strongly sequential'' and translates it ''in turn.''[30] The emphatic ''we'' marks the obligation resting upon us as believers, as the recipients of God's love. The verb ''we ought'' *(opheilomen)* denotes not the ''must'' of external compulsion but the inner constraint of conscious obligation. (Cf. 2:6; 3:16.) Jackman remarks,

> This is not just an extra ingredient that we might add to our discipleship if we feel especially moved to do so. We owe it to the loving Father not to slander his name any further by denying his love in our human relations. . . . If we have appreciated something of the infinite price paid for our redemption, then we shall see at once how vital it is that we do not continue to indulge ourselves in sin.[31]

God's love for us is the example as well as the stimulus for our practice of mutual love. The reality of our love for God will be tested, strengthened, and purified by our practice of mutual love as believers. In keeping with the teaching of Jesus (Matt. 22:37-40), John insists that love for God and love for our brother cannot be separated.

b. The significance of our mutual love (v. 12). John reminds his readers that God as the object of Christian love is unseen (v. 12a), but adds that the practice of mutual love confirms the operation of God's love in our lives (v. 12b).

1) *The nature of God as unseen* (v. 12a). John's assertion ''No man hath seen God at any time'' is unexpected. Houlden thinks that it ''has the air of being misplaced'' and suggests that it should stand before verse 20, but he admits that his conjecture has no manuscript support.[32] Marshall insists that its place here is deliberate and that John is refuting those who claimed to know and love God because of their mystical experiences.[33] The assumed logic is that since it is easier for us to love someone whom we can see and know directly than one whom we have never seen personally, how can they profess to know and love God whom they have never seen and yet hate the brother who is visibly present with them? For those who disparage the obligation to love the brethren, no vaunted mystical visions of God will ever enable them to attain to a vital relationship with God. John has already informed his readers that a direct vision of God awaits the time of the Parousia (3:2).

---

[30]Raymond E. Brown, *The Epistles of John,* The Anchor Bible (Garden City, N.Y.: Doubleday & Co., 1982), p. 520.

[31]Jackman, p. 122.

[32]J. L. Houlden, *A Commentary on the Johannine Epistles,* Harper's New Testament Commentaries (New York: Harper & Row, 1973), p. 114.

[33]Marshall, p. 216.

2) *The relation between mutual love and God's love in us* (v. 12b). John adds that our love for the brethren is closely related to our experience of God's love: "if we love one another, God dwelleth in us, and his love is perfected in us." The third-class condition, "if we love one another" *(ean agapōmen allēlous)*, leaves undetermined the actual fulfillment of the condition; John well knew that the indicated condition was not being carried out in the lives of some professed Christians. But the form challenges his readers to make sure that they do "love one another." Such mutual Christian love is evidence that "the unseen God, who was once revealed in His Son, is now revealed in His people if and when they love one another."[34]

The practice of mutual Christian love confirms that "God dwelleth in us" *(ho theos en hēmin menei)*. John asserts that whenever believers practice mutual love, God's love becomes visible in the lives of those in whom He abides. The love which He has implanted in the heart of the believer through the Holy Spirit (v. 13; Rom. 5:5) is thus visibly expressed and confirms the reality of God's indwelling presence.

The practice of mutual love further signifies that "His love is perfected in us" *(hē agapē autou teteleiōmene en hēmin estin)*. In 2:5 John pointed out that the believer's obedience to God's commands revealed that "in him verily is the love of God perfected." Here the evidence is the practice of mutual love. The genitive rendered "His love" *(hē agapē autou)* may be differently interpreted: (1) as an objective genitive, our love for God; (2) as a subjective genitive, God's love for us; or (3) as a qualitative genitive to describe this love's God-like quality. Some take this genitive as objective,[35] but this seems unlikely since the context speaks about God's love for us (vv. 10-11). The context suggests that the reference here is to God's love in us.[36] But it is possible that the second and third view combine in John's thought since the operation of God's love in the hearts of believers inspires and develops a love in them like His own. Whenever believers are motivated by the indwelling love of God to practice a consistent brother-love, then the love of God "is perfected" in them. The perfect passive verb "is perfected" *(teteleiōmenē . . . estin)* does not imply any previous imperfection in God's love but rather presents God's love as having been brought to its goal

---

[34]Stott, p. 164.

[35]So Henry Alford, *The New Testament for English Readers* ([1865-1872]; reprint ed., Chicago: Moody Press, [1958]), pp. 1741-42; Plummer, p. 150; Harvey J.S. Blaney, "The First Epistle of John," in *Beacon Bible Commentary* (Kansas City, Mo.: Beacon Hill Press, 1969), 10:391-92.

[36]So Lenski, p. 505; Rudolf Bultmann, *The Johannine Epistles,* Hermeneia–A Critical and Historical Commentary on the Bible (Philadelphia: Fortress Press, 1973), p. 68; Stott, p. 164; Simon J. Kistemaker, *Exposition of the Epistle of James and the Epistles of John,* New Testament Commentary (Grand Rapids: Baker, 1986), p. 335.

objectively in that life. (Cf. the same verb in 2:5.) Morgan suggests the following in illustration: "There is all the difference between its existence in the heart, and its expansion in the life, that may be observed between the root of the plant deposited in the soil and its rich and wide spred foliage, and its clusters of flowers or fruits."[37]

4. The Confirmation of Redeeming Love (vv. 13-16a)

In verses 13-16a John summarizes the grounds for assurance that believers have come to know personally the love of God. He mentions the divine gift of the Holy Spirit (v. 13), the apostolic testimony concerning God's saving work in Christ (v. 14), and the reality of the believer's fellowship with God (vv. 15-16a).

a. The confirmation through the gift of the Spirit (v. 13). The ringing words "Hereby know we that we dwell in him, and he in us" express the basic assurance of the Christian life. The words "hereby" *(en toutō)* here, as usually in 1 John, look forward to the following "because" *(hoti)* clause.[38] The present-tense verb "we know" *(ginōskomen)* indicates "the process of obtaining knowledge by experience, by observation, or by instruction."[39] This is an assuring and growing knowledge gained in the daily experiences of the believer. The content of this assuring knowledge is "that we dwell in him, and he in us" *(hoti en autō menomen kai autos en hēmin)*. The present-tense verb "dwell" portrays this reciprocal abiding as a close and intimate relationship–God dwelling in our lives and we in Him. John first mentions the reality of this mutual interrelationship in 3:24a. There this relationship is connected with the keeping of God's commandments; here it is connected with the duty of brother-love. In 3:24 and 4:15 this mutual indwelling is presented as the experience of the individual believer; but here the use of the plural pronouns, "we . . . us," presents this twofold relationship as the experience of the Christian community. Clearly it is a relationship that is true of every true believer. But it is the reality of God's abiding in us that vitalizes the relationship with fellow believers.

Our consciousness of this mutual relationship is not grounded in some professed esoteric insight into the nature of God, nor is it the result of any personal achievement on our part. Rather it is God's gift to us "because he hath given us of His Spirit" *(hoti ek tou pneumatos autou dedōken hēmin)*. The perfect-tense verb "hath given" points to the continuing indwelling of the Spirit imparted to us at regeneration. In 3:24 the use of the aorist tense

---

[37]Morgan, p. 332.

[38]Unlike most commentators, Kistemaker holds, "The words *by this* refer to the preceding context where John tells us that if we love one another, God lives in us" (p. 335).

[39]Burdick, p. 327.

asserts the historical fact that the Spirit was given to us; here His continuing presence is asserted. As Hobbs states, "The indwelling Spirit, therefore, is not an *extra* experience coming at a subsequent point in the Christian's life. At the outset, He serves as evidence that we are Christians–that God dwells in us and we in Him."[40]

Interpreters have understood the statement that God has given us "of his Spirit" *(ek tou pneumatos autou)* in two ways. Lenski holds that the preposition *(ek* with the ablative of source) means that God has given us *"from* His Spirit," namely, "when the Holy Spirit is given to us, he does not enter our hearts without gifts for us" but "has given us a number of gifts, all of which come 'from' the Spirit as the source."[41] Marshall suggests that John may have in mind the charismatic gifts which were the proof of the Spirit's indwelling.[42] But since John makes no mention of such gifts, it is better to accept with Burdick that "the statement refers simply to the presence of the Spirit. (See Rom 8:15-16.)"[43] The expression "of His Spirit" conveys a partative sense, that "Christians receive from God a share (only) in the Spirit who fills the whole church."[44] Only of the incarnate Son could it be said in the fullest sense that He received "the Spirit without measure" (John 3:34 NASB). But, as Jackman well notes, this understanding of the phrase does not imply that the Spirit is divisible into parts:

> This is the same mistake as thinking of the fullness of the Spirit as somehow getting more of the Spirit into us than we now have, as though we could receive him by installments. He is a person, one and indivisible; though we must also observe that the fact that he indwells one Christian does not mean that he cannot equally indwell all. So it is impossible for one to have 60% of the Spirit, but not at all impossible that he has less than all of us.[45]

b. The confirmation through the apostolic testimony (v. 14). With a connective "and" *(kai)* John adds that the objective criterion of the apostolic testimony is also needed: "And we have seen and do testify that the Father sent the Son *to be* the Saviour of the world." The words "we have seen and do testify" *(hēmeis tetheametha kai marturoumen)* stress the factual nature of this testimony. The force of the emphatic "we" *(hēmeis)* is differently understood. Some understand the scope of the "we" to be nondistinctive,

---

[40]Hobbs, p. 113. Italics in original.

[41]Lenski, p. 507.

[42]Marshall, p. 219.

[43]Burdick, p. 328.

[44]Smalley, p. 250.

[45]Jackman, p. 125.

as including both the author and his readers,[46] but it is more probable that this emphatic "we" basically refers to the apostolic witnesses.[47] The reality declared by the apostles is accepted by all true believers. In saying "we have seen and do testify," John affirms that the testimony of the original eyewitnesses was grounded in their personal experience; it was not a speculative philosophy. The verb "have seen" *(tetheametha)* denotes a close and careful observation, and the perfect tense indicates the abiding impact of what they had observed. In their association with the incarnate Son, they saw with their own eyes the outworking of His redemptive mission. What they beheld produced in them an abiding conviction concerning His true identity, and the conviction prompted them to "testify" *(marturoumen),* to continue to bear witness concerning Him. The Christian life rests upon the acknowledged reality of God's revelation of Himself in His Son and a personal acceptance, by faith, of the Son's unique person and ministry.

The heart of the apostolic witness was "that the Father sent the Son *to be* the Saviour of the world" *(hoti ho patēr apestalken ton huion sōtēra tou kosmou).* The acceptance of this message is the test of doctrinal orthodoxy. The assertion that "the Father sent the Son," although indicating the deity of both, continues the concept of a loving personal relationship which prompted the Son's redemptive activity. The perfect tense *(apestalken)* declares the abiding significance of the sending of the Son: "*to be* the Saviour of the world." The term "the Saviour" *(sōtēra),* used without a verbal form, is the predicate accusative, "sent *as Saviour*"; it describes what He is, not merely what He was sent to do. The salvation He wrought is inseparably connected with His person as the unique Son of God. "The world," as the object of His redemptive mission, "means sinful society, estranged from God and under the dominion of the evil one (cf. v. 19). Its urgent need was to be rescued from sin and Satan."[48] The scope of His saving work is comprehensive–all humanity, not merely the "enlightened Gnostics" or the chosen Jewish people. "There is no limit but the willingness of men to accept salvation by believing on the Saviour."[49]

In the New Testament the designation "the Saviour of the world" occurs only here and on the lips of the Samaritan believers in John 4:42. In classical

---

[46]Westcott, p. 153; John James Lias, *An Exposition of the First Epistle of John* (1887; reprint ed., Minneapolis: Klock & Klock Christian Publishers, 1982), pp. 324-25; Brown, pp. 522-23.

[47]So A. E. Brooke, *The Johannine Epistles,* International Critical Commentary (New York: Charles Scribner's Sons, 1912), p. 121; Stott, p. 166; Alexander Ross, *The Epistles of James and John,* New International Commentary on the New Testament (Grand Rapids: Eerdmans, 1954), p. 204; Lenski, p. 507; Kistemaker, p. 337.

[48]Stott, pp. 166-67.

[49]Plummer, p. 150.

Greek the term "saviour" was applied both to the gods and to men. In the Roman imperial cultus it was employed as one of the titles of the emperors, who often were some of the most immoral of men. In the New Testament the term is applied both to God the Father and to the Son.[50] The term is applied to the Father as the originator of the plan of salvation, who sent the Son into the world "that we might live through Him" (v. 9); the Son as the Saviour is the one who wrought our salvation through His atoning death and victorious resurrection. The term is not directly applied to the Holy Spirit, but the Father sent the Spirit to effect God's salvation in our hearts and lives (Gal. 4:4-6; Rom. 8:9-11). In verses 13-14 John accordingly mentions all three Persons of the Trinity in connection with his portrayal of redeeming love.

   c. *The confirmation through mutual fellowship with God* (vv. 15-16a). The reality of God's love is further confirmed through the experience of the individual believer. In verse 15 John indicates how believers enter into fellowship with God, and verse 16a restates the assurance of believers concerning God's love.

   1) *The condition for mutual fellowship with God* (v. 15). The conditional statement "Whosoever shall confess that Jesus is the Son of God, God dwelleth in him, and he in God" *(hos ean homologēsē hoti Iēsous estin ho huios tou theou, ho theos en autō menei kai autos en tō theō)* indicates how God's redemptive purpose in sending Jesus becomes operative in human lives. The scope of the third-class conditional statement "whosoever shall confess" *(hos ean homologēsē,* literally, "he who if he may confess") is restricted only by the individual's willingness to make the indicated confession. The aorist verb "confess" denotes a specific, and apparently public, confession born of an inner persuasion. It is a response to the apostolic testimony recorded in verse 14. The verb, which basically means "to say the same thing," denotes a personal acceptance of the reality being confessed. It is not merely a group's rote recital of a creedal confession. Brown observes, "The author is now talking about the (single) basic confession of faith that makes one a Christian."[51]

   The indicated confession, that "Jesus is the Son of God" *(Iēsous estin ho huios tou theou),* is an explicit acknowledgement of the abiding reality of the incarnation, that the man Jesus is indeed the Son of God incarnate. The definite article with the predicate, "the Son of God," stresses that Jesus

---

[50]Of the twenty-four occurrences of the word "Saviour," apparently eight refer to God the Father (cf. Luke 1:47; 1 Tim. 1:1; 2:3; 4:10; Titus 1:3; 2:10; 3:4; Jude 25) and sixteen to the Son (Luke 2:11; John 4:42; Acts 5:31; 13:23; Eph. 5:23; Phil. 3:20; 2 Tim. 1:10; Titus 1:4; 2:13; 3:6; 2 Pet. 1:1, 11; 2:20; 3:2, 18; 1 John 4:14).

[51]Brown, p. 524.

is not merely a son of God but the definite and distinctive Son of the God whom believers know and love. It is a confession which the false prophets whom John confronted refused to make. Because of the Gnostic philosophical presuppositions that spirit and matter were in opposition to each other, they regarded such a confession as impossible. But John insists that the confession is crucial; it is precisely those who accept and confess the reality of the incarnation that have true fellowship with God. "Any theory," Findlay remarks, "whether of the ancient Gnostic or the modern Unitarian type, which makes Christ's nature less than Divine, makes God's love less than perfect in the same proportion."[52]

The truth thus expressed as a confession of personal faith assures each believer that "God dwelleth in him, and he in God" *(ho theos en autō menei kai autos en tō theō)*. The present-tense verb "dwelleth" *(menei)* marks this twofold relationship as a present and progressive reality. In the two previous references to this mutual indwelling (3:24; 4:13), the believer's abiding in God is placed first; the reversal of the order here indicates that there is no set priority; the two aspects are mutually interrelated. As Westcott notes,

> The two clauses mark two aspects of the Christian's life. The believer has a new and invincible power for the fulfilment of his work on earth: "God is in him." And again he realizes that his life is not on earth, that he belongs essentially to another order: "he is in God." The divine fellowship is complete and effective in each direction.[53]

2) *The experience of God's love by believers* (v. 16a). The apostle now presents the amazing relationship with God just depicted as a living reality in the experience of true believers: "And we have known and believed the love that God hath to us." The opening "we" *(hēmeis)* is emphatic and includes John and all those who have made the confession just indicated (v. 15). God's love for us has evoked a response on our part: "we have known and believed" God's love. The two verbs "have known and believed" *(egnōkamen kai pepisteukamen)*, both in the perfect tense, indicate the resultant experience flowing from our initial faith and confession. Burdick notes that the order of the two verbs indicates that "a knowledge of basic facts must precede belief, for it is necessary to know what is to be believed. Faith must be intelligent or it is sheer gullibility."[54] Rightly so, but in John 6:69 these two verbs are used in the reverse order, thus indicating that in spiritual matters

---

[52]George G. Findlay, *Fellowship in the Life Eternal, An Exposition of the Epistles of St. John* (1909; reprint ed., Grand Rapids: Eerdmans, 1955), p. 346.

[53]Westcott, p. 155.

[54]Burdick, pp. 330-31.

knowledge and faith react on each other. Under either order "each completes the other. Sound faith is intelligent; sound knowledge is believing."[55]

The stated object of our growing knowledge and faith is "the love that God hath to us" *(tēn agapēn hēn echei ho theos en hēmin).* In verses 9-10 John set forth the historical manifestation of that love in Christ, but now the present tense, "hath to us" *(echei. . . en hēmin),* marks the continuing reality of that love in relation to His people. Interpreters have understood the words "to us" *(en hēmin)* in two different ways. The rendering "to us" may suggest that the love which God revealed in His incarnate Son, as seen and witnessed to by those around Christ, God intended for our salvation. But this phrase more literally means "in us"; it points to the operation of this love in our experience. God's love, poured into our hearts by the Holy Spirit (Rom. 5:5), is now at work manifesting its presence and power in our own lives. The manifestation of God's love in His incarnate Son is no longer visible here on earth, but God is now manifesting His love as it is being displayed in the lives of His people. Intelligent Christian faith recognizes and rejoices in the active operation of God's love in the redeemed community and in the interactions of its individual members.

---

[55]Plummer, p. 151.

13

Assurance from the Evidence of True Love (Part 2)

B. The Results of Redeeming Love (4:16b–5:5)

4:16b God is love; and he that dwelleth in love dwelleth in God, and God in him.

17 Herein is our love made perfect, that we may have boldness in the day of judgment: because as he is, so are we in this world.

18 There is no fear in love; but perfect love casteth out fear: because fear hath torment. He that feareth is not made perfect in love.

19 We loved him, because he first loved us.

20 If a man say, I love God, and hateth his brother, he is a liar: for he that loveth not his brother whom he hath seen, how can he love God whom he hath not seen?

21 And this commandment have we from him, That he who loveth God love his brother also.

5:1 Whosoever believeth that Jesus is the Christ is born of God: and every one that loveth him that begat loveth him also that is begotten of him.

2 By this we know that we love the children of God, when we love God, and keep his commandments.

3 For this is the love of God, that we keep his commandments: and his commandments are not grievous.

4 For whatsoever is born of God overcometh the world: and this is the victory that overcometh the world, *even* our faith.

5 Who is he that overcometh the world, but he that believeth that Jesus is the Son of God?

Having explored that nature of redeeming love, John next makes a sweeping survey of the results of redeeming love–looking inward, outward, and upward. He depicts the results of that love in our own lives (4:16b-18), in our relations to others (4:19-21), and in our relation to God (5:1-5).

1. The Results in Our Own Lives (4:16b-18)

Appropriately John begins with the results in the life of the one who practices Christian love. God's love abiding in the believer promotes the consciousness of reciprocal love (v. 16b), produces confidence in view of the future (v. 17), and casts out the feeling of fear (v. 18).

a. The experience of reciprocal love (v. 16b). The operation of love in our own lives is grounded in the fact that "God is love." This is the only New Testament declaration of the very essence of God that occurs twice (see 4:8). Although the restatement well summarizes the discussion in 4:7-16a, the following "and" *(kai)* connects this reality to the transforming results of love. Thus Kysar suggests that here "the author's intent is less to describe the nature of God than to epitomize the meaning of God's actions among humans."[1]

The fact that God is love is basic to the believer's daily life: "and he that dwelleth in love dwelleth in God, and God in him." The present-tense articular participle "he that dwelleth in love" *(ho menōn en tē agapē,* literally "the one abiding in the love"), characterizes the individual by his continual dwelling in the sphere of the divine love just described. Since God is love, to abide in love is to abide in God. He who lives in the sphere of love must necessarily be permeated with love, resulting in a mutual inter-relationship, he "in God, and God in him." The expression "dwelleth in love" occurs elsewhere only in John 15:9-10: "Abide in My love. If you keep My commandments, you will abide in My love; just as I have kept My Father's commandments, and abide in His love" (NASB). In verse 16b John uses the verb "dwelleth" *(menō)* three times, although the KJV leaves the third occurrence untranslated ("God in him dwelleth"). This triple use of the verb strengthens the fact of this continuing, transforming interrelation-ship. "To dwell in God is to have one's spiritual roots so deeply implanted in Him that His life flows through the total person and manifests itself in our life."[2] This is the last occurrence of the verb *menō,* a favorite with John,[3] in this epistle.

b. The confidence of perfected love (v. 17). The life of love also has an impact on the believer's future: "Herein is our love made perfect, that we

---

[1]Robert Kysar, *I, II, III John,* Augsburg Commentary on the New Testament (Minneapolis: Augsburg, 1986), p. 100.

[2]J. Dwight Pentecost, *The Joy of Fellowship* (Grand Rapids: Zondervan, 1977), p. 117.

[3]The verb *menō* occurs forty-one times in the Gospel of John, twenty-four times in 1 John, three times in 2 John, and once in Revelation.

may have boldness in the day of judgment: because as he is, so are we in this world.'' The intended reference in ''herein'' *(en toutō)* may be differently understood, as relating to the preceding statement or to one of the next two clauses. Thus John may be understood to say that love is perfected with us (1) by our abiding in Him and He in us (v. 16b); (2) by our being confident in the day of judgment (v. 17b); or (3) by our being just as He is (v. 17c). One can advance plausible arguments in favor of each of these views,[4] but the logic seems clearest if one takes ''herein'' as a reference to what has preceded and understands the following *hina* (''that'') clause as denoting the anticipated result. Then the meaning is that the double abiding spoken of in verse 16b brings love to its intended goal in our lives, with the result that we will have confidence in the future day of judgment. To take ''herein'' as looking forward to the following *hina* clause involves the awkward logic that ''*present* perfection of love [is] dependent on *future* confidence in the day of judgment, which is unnatural, if not impossible.''[5] To make ''herein'' look forward to the final ''because'' *(hoti)* clause of verse 17 is improbable because of the harsh and unnatural parenthesis thus produced by the intervening *(hina)* clause.

The statement ''Herein is our love made perfect'' (*En toutō teteleiōtai hē agapē meth' hēmōn,* literally, ''In this has been perfected the love with us''), as in 4:12, portrays the love in our lives as having been brought to its intended goal. The expression that love is perfected ''with us'' *(meth' hēmōn)* is unusual. It can mean ''in us'' or ''in our case,'' but the preposition with the genitive naturally means ''with us'' as ''our companion.''[6] God's love has reached its goal in our lives when we also love and communicate it to others. His love is the inspiration and abiding companion to our love.

The operation of this God-prompted love in our own lives, resulting in present communion with God, also has a future result, ''that we may have boldness in the day of judgment'' *(hina parrhēsian echōmen en tē hēmera tēs kriseōs).* In 2:28 John spoke of this confidence before Christ at His coming as gained through continual abiding in Christ; here its basis is the experience of abiding mutual love. This confidence will flow from an intimate relationship of love already established with the one who is our judge in that future day. Instead of fear, there will be an experience of ''boldness,'' or openness, toward Him because of solid evidence of a living personal

[4]See Raymond E. Brown, *The Epistles of John,* The Anchor Bible (Garden City, N.Y.: Doubleday & Co., 1982), pp. 526-27.

[5]Donald W. Burdick, *The Letters of John the Apostle* (Chicago: Moody Press, 1985), p. 333. Italics in original.

[6]R.C.H. Lenski, *The Interpretation of the Epistles of St. Peter, St. John and St. Jude* (Columbus, Ohio: Wartburg Press, 1945), p. 511.

relationship with Him. He who has lived his life under the inspiration and power of perfect love will in that day experience "boldness" freely to approach and commune with Christ the Judge.

While this is the only explicit reference in the Johannine Epistles to "the day of judgment" *(tē hēmera tēs kriseōs),* the truth of that future majestic day is clearly mentioned in 2:28. We fully agree with Brooke that the author of this epistle "has not eliminated from the sphere of his theological thought the idea of a final 'day' of judgment, when the processes which are already at work shall reach their final issue and manifestation."[7] Evangelical interpreters have understood the precise aspect of this eschatological "day" in different manners. Certainly the reference is not to a final judgment where the eternal destiny of the believer will be decided; John 5:24 assures the true believer that for him there is no such judgment. Some, such as Hodges,[8] take the judgment here to be the Judgment Seat of Christ when believers will appear before Him, not to determine their salvation, but for the evaluation of their lives for reward (2 Cor. 5:10; 1 Cor. 3:12-15). But others, such as Laurin, conclude that the reference here is not to the Judgment Seat of Christ, "for at that place there will be many things to adjust in the life and relation of all believers. It is rather that judicial judgment at the Great White Throne in respect to which I stand in the absolute perfection of Jesus Christ my Lord and Saviour. . . . We will be there, not to be judged before the Great White Throne, but to stand as a spectator."[9] We accept that the rapture and our appearing before Christ at the Judgment Seat are involved; in that solemn day the believer, because of the transforming love that has worked in his life, will have "confidence" that he will be received by Christ in spite of the imperfections in his life.

The added clause "because as he is, so are we in this world" *(hoti kathōs ekeinos estin kai hēmeis esmen en tō kosmō toutō)* indicates that our "boldness" in that day is grounded in present likeness to Christ. The demonstrative pronoun rendered "he" *(ekeinos,* "that one") here, as elsewhere in this epistle, denotes Christ. Both pronouns, "he" and "we," are emphatic, and the comparative "as" *(kathōs,* "even as") marks close resemblance, assuring us that our confidence is not presumption. Our love-produced likeness is the basis for the confidence that the Judge will deal with us as a friend. John's expression "as he is" *(kathōs ekeinos estin),* rather than "as he

---

[7]A. E. Brooke, *A Critical and Exegetical Commentary on the Johannine Epistles,* International Critical Commentary (New York: Charles Scribner's Sons, 1912), p. 124.

[8]Zane C. Hodges, "1 John," in *The Bible Knowledge Commentary, New Testament* (Wheaton, Ill.: Victor Books, 1983), p. 900.

[9]Roy L. Laurin, *First John, Life at Its Best* (1957; reprint ed. Grand Rapids: Kregel, 1987), pp. 159-60.

was,'' makes clear that John was not thinking of the man Jesus while He was here upon earth. The present tense, ''is,'' denotes His unchanging nature, ''as he is eternally—past, present, and future.''[10] Clearly the added phrase ''in this world'' *(en tō kosmō toutō)* relates only to the second member of the comparison. But the comparison indicates that what is true of Him in His unchanging character is already true of us while still ''in this world.'' Interpreters have expressed varied views as to wherein this likeness lies.[11] The context supports the view that it is a likeness in love. Love is the theme in this section (4:7–5:5), and in the next verse John explicitly singles out love as the antidote to ''fear'' in the believer's life. Clearly John believes in a God-given love which works redemptively in the lives of its recipients in this evil world and prepares them for the future.

c. *The operation of perfect love* (v. 18). The presentation of our love-relationship with God leads John to deal with the matter of ''fear'': ''There is no fear in love'' *(phobos ouk estin en tē agapē,* literally, ''fear not is in the love,'' the kind of love here under consideration). Fear and love are opposites in their nature and function. ''Fear, which is essentially self-centered, has no place in love, which in its perfection involves complete self-surrender.''[12] The word ''fear'' has two meanings: it may mean ''alarm, dread, fright,'' the self-regarding fear of the criminal or slave because of a sense of guilt (Rom. 13:3); or it can signify ''reverence'' or ''respect.'' The latter meaning is not in view here; God-inspired love is perfectly consistent with that reverential awe before God which keeps us from doing that which would displease and grieve Him. The feeling of ''fear'' or dread in view here is quite general, but the thought of fear in view of the judgment day (v. 17) seems involved.

The adversative ''but'' *(all',* ''on the contrary'') introduces the fact that fear and love are antithetical in action: ''but perfect love casteth out fear'' *(all' hē teleia agapē exō ballei ton phobon).* The adjective ''perfect,'' appearing only here in the Johannine writings, describes a love that has reached its end or intended goal; the expression carries the same meaning as the verb ''is perfected'' in verses 12 and 17 above. This love by its nature ''casteth out fear'' whenever it arises. John recognizes that fear is ever prone to assert itself in our experience. ''No believer's love has ever been so perfect as entirely to banish fear; but every believer experiences that as his love increases his fear diminishes.''[13] The present-tense verb ''casteth out'' *(exō*

---

[10]Burdick, p. 335.

[11]See Burdick for a summary of five different views, p. 335.

[12]Brooke, p. 124.

[13]Alfred Plummer, *The Epistles of S. John,* Cambridge Bible for Schools and Colleges (1883; reprint ed., London: Cambridge University Press, 1938), p. 152.

ballei) underlines that whenever fear seeks to grip the heart, perfect love acts to "cast out," throw outside, that fear. "Love must altogether banish fear from the enclosure in which her work is done."[14]

The action of love is due to the antithetical nature of fear: "because fear hath torment" *(hoti hē phobos kolasin echei,* more literally, "fear has punishment"). In the New Testament the noun "punishment" *(kolasin)* occurs only here and in Matthew 25:46, where Jesus speaks of "everlasting punishment," but it was common in secular Greek. Its root significance was that of "pruning, or checking the growth of trees,"[15] and so came to denote the process of correcting or punishing. In Hellenistic Greek it increasingly came to mean "punishment," as Matthew 25:46 indicates. The fear in view here clearly springs from a consciousness that punishment is deserved. Lenski understands this punishment as the future punishment "which all the wicked, 'the children of the devil' (3:10), must sooner or later suffer because of their unforgiven sins."[16] Then the reference is to the sense of fear that the prospect of future punishment evokes. But John's precise statement that "fear hath torment" implies that the punishment is not merely future but that fear involves present suffering because "fear anticipates and makes real the future punishment it contemplates."[17] Thus the expression may depict a conscious, continuing sense of "torment" or "torture." Such fear is destructive to inner peace and mars the consciousness of God's love. It is inconsistent with a full understanding of the nature of redemptive love which has removed our sins and established a living relationship with God in this life.

The impersonal principle "there is no fear in love" John restates in personal terms: "He that feareth is not made perfect in love" *(ho de phoboumenos ou teteleiōtai en tē agapē).* The conjunction *de,* omitted in the KJV, implies that a further note needs to be added concerning the believer whose life is harassed by fear. The present articular participle, "he that feareth" *(ho phoboumenos),* pictures an individual whose life is habitually beset with fear. In him "the love" *(tē agapē),* the God-prompted love John has in view, "is not made perfect," has not yet been enabled to attain its intended goal. The perfect passive verb "is made perfect" *(teteleiōtai)* indicates that in such an individual God's love has not been able to attain its goal of bring-

---

[14]Brooke, p. 125.

[15]Henry George Liddell and Robert Scott, *A Greek-English Lexicon,* 7th ed. (Oxford: Clarendon Press, 1890), p. 825.

[16]Lenski, p. 514.

[17]Stephen S. Smalley, *1, 2, 3 John,* Word Biblical Commentary (Waco, Texas: Word Books, 1984), pp. 260-61.

ing him into abiding communion with God. Such an individual "has no basis for assurance concerning his welfare when judgment day comes."[18]

2. The Results in Our Relations to Others (vv. 19-21)

In these verses John turns to the results of redeeming love in the lives of believers in relation to others. In verse 19 he asserts the origin of this love, and then he insists that this love involves the obligation to reach out in love to one's brother (vv. 20-21).

a. The divine origin of Christian love (v. 19). The amazing love of God in Christ is the true source of all the love that stirs the heart of the believer: "We love him, because he first loved us." One may take the words rendered "we love" *(hēmeis agapōmen)* as hortative, "Let us be loving," but the absence of any connecting particle and the use of the emphatic pronoun *(hēmeis)* support the indicative rendering.[19] Since the words "we love" naturally imply a recipient of our love, the KJV understandably reads "him" *(auton)* as the object of our love. Thus a number of manuscripts have "God" *(ton theon)* or "him" *(auton)* as the expressed object of our love.[20] The reading without an expressed object has good textual support and best explains the other readings. It is more probable that the object would be added than left out, especially if it were regarded as a hortative subjunctive. Without a stated object the love is left unrestricted in its scope. What follows makes it clear that this assertion of love cannot be limited to our love of God alone; true love has an outward as well as an upward relation.

The expression "we love" asserts our own conscious experience of this divinely inspired love. Candlish remarks,

> Hitherto, it has all turned on God's love; manifested by him; known and believed by us; communicated to us; present with us; and as present with us, made perfect; so perfect as to cast out fear. Now, it is our love that is asserted;—"We love."[21]

But as believers we can never forget how this love came into our lives.

The following words, "because he first loved us" *(hoti autos protōs ēgapēsen hēmas)*, explain the presence and operation of this love in our own lives. The subject "he" *(autos)* is emphatic; "he," and not "we," is the

---

[18]Burdick, p. 338.

[19]The Latin and Peshita Syrian versions, as well as some Greek manuscripts, accept the hortatory rendering and add a connective particle, *oun,* "therefore, then." See Nestle-Aland, *Novum Testamentum Graece,* 26th ed. (Stuttgart: Deutsche Biblestiftung, 1979).

[20]For the textual evidence for the variant readings see Kurt Aland et al., ed., *The Greek New Testament,* 3rd ed. (New York: United Bible Societies, 1975).

[21]Robert S. Candlish, *The First Epistle of John,* 2nd ed. (1869; reprint ed., Grand Rapids: Zondervan, n.d.), p. 422.

true source of love in our lives. The adverb "first" stresses the divine initiative in bringing this love into our lives. The aorist verb "he loved" *(ēpagēsen)* summarily looks back to the historic manifestation of God's love in the atoning death of the incarnate Son (4:9-10). He manifested His love in order to awaken love in us. In the words of Dora Greenwell,

> It was for me that Jesus died! for me, and a world of men
> Just as sinful and just as slow to give back His love again;
> He didn't wait till I came to Him, but He loved me at my worst;
> He needn't ever have died for me if I could have loved Him first.[22]

With his use of "he" John again makes no distinction between the Father and the Son; clearly the love of both is involved.

b. The consequent duty of brother-love (vv. 20-21). John insists that the love which His love evokes in us cannot be restricted to God alone; the nature of His love demands that we love those who are the fellow recipients of God's love. In verse 20 John exposes a false profession of love for God, and he adds in verse 21 that such brother-love is God's express command.

1) *The exposure of a false profession of love* (v. 20). John first of all pictures this false profession: "If a man say, I love God, and hateth his brother, he is a liar." The conditional statement presents the scene as hypothetical: "If someone says, 'I love God,' and hates his brother" *(ean tis eipē hoti agapō ton theon, kai ton adelphon autou misē)*. The aorist-tense "say" *(eipē)* records his explicit claim, marked by the recitative *hoti* as given in his very words, "I love God" *(hoti agapō ton theon);* he asserts his continuing love of God. The claim in itself is unobjectionable, but its truthfulness is contradicted by the fact that he "hateth his brother." The present tense marks his hatred of the brother as a continuing attitude, not merely a passing moment of hatred. The original language places "God" and "his brother" side by side, encompassed by the contradictory emotional responses of love and hatred, thus suggesting that these two cannot truly be the object of these opposite inner attitudes at the same time. Love and hatred are mutually exclusive; there is no neutral ground between them. The love in view here by its nature is constructive, seeking the welfare of the one loved; hatred by its nature is destructive, desiring the destruction of its object. The individual's failure to love his brother has a destructive impact on him. His "inward condition is easily measured by outward behaviour. . . . We always reveal what we are by what we do."[23]

---

[22]Dora Greenwell, *Selected Poems from the Writings of Dora Greenwell* (London: H. R. Allenson, 1906), p. 201.

[23]John Miller, *Notes on James, I and II Peter, I, II and III John, Jude* (Bradford, England: Needed Truth Publishing Office, n.d.), p. 90.

The contradiction elicits John's unhesitating verdict: "he is a liar" *(pseustēs estin,* "a liar he is"). "Just as hate is opposed to love (and God is love), so lying is opposed to truth (and Jesus is the truth)."[24] But John's use of the noun "a liar" declares that it is not merely a matter of making a false assertion; the noun insists upon his falseness of character. "He is either morally blind or a conscious hypocrite."[25] In reverting to this hypothetical form of statement (cf. 1:8-10), John's assertion is clearly directed against his opponents with their spurious claims.

The author now undergirds this supposed personal scene with a general principle: "for he that loveth not his brother whom he hath seen, how can he love God whom he hath not seen?" The opening "for" *(gar)* introduces the reason for John's stern verdict upon the preceding contradictory scene. The fact that he does not love "his brother" points to his personal relationship with a fellow member of his local congregation. The perfect-tense verb "hath seen" *(heōraken),* not "can see," points to their fixed relations from past visual contacts. By contrast he claims a relationship of love with God whom he has never seen. Stott remarks, "It is obviously easier to love and serve a visible man than an invisible God, and if we fail in the easier task, it is absurd to claim success in the harder."[26] It is a contrast not merely between the seen and the unseen, but between a man like ourselves and a God whose nature is very different from our own.

His failure to love on the lower and visible level involves an improbability, "how can he love God whom he hath not seen?" John's words are not a denial that a finite human being can love the invisible God, but he does declare that it is impossible for one to do so who harbors a continuing hatred for his brother. The inability is rooted in the moral contradiction of seeking to harbor love and hatred in the same heart.

The precise wording of the conclusion John draws from this portrait presents a textual problem. The KJV formulation of the conclusion as a rhetorical question, "how can he love God whom he hath not seen?" follows the reading in the Textus Receptus. But instead of the question "how can he love" *(pōs dunatai agapan),* various important manuscripts state that conclusion as a categorical denial, "he cannot love" *(ou dunatai agapan).* On a scale of A to D, the editors of the United Bible Societies, *The Greek New Testament,* 3rd ed., rate the latter reading as B.[27] Metzger suggests that the reading of the Textus Receptus arose as a scribal improvement based on

---

[24]Brown, p. 533.

[25]Plummer, p. 153.

[26]J.R.W. Stott, *The Epistles of John,* Tyndale New Testament Commentaries (Grand Rapids: Eerdmans, 1964), p. 171.

[27]United Bible Societies, *The Greek New Testament,* 3rd. ed., p. 822, note 4.

3:17 in order to heighten the rhetorical style.[28] The variant readings do not change the truth John insists on. As Lias remarks, "The meaning is clear, that love must be shown to those whom God loves, it must be displayed in the region of the immediate and visible, if it is love at all."[29]

2. *The command to love God and the brother* (v. 21). The connective "and" *(kai)* sets forth a further reason that there can be no deliberate division between our love for God and our love for our brother: "And this commandment have we from him, That he who loveth God love his brother also." Westcott notes, "That which is a spiritual necessity is also an express injunction."[30] The content of "this commandment" *(tautēn tēn entolēn)* is stated in the following "that" clause, but the added words "have we from him" again leave the precise identity of "him" uncertain. John's assertion that "we have" this commandment "from him" may mean that he is thinking of the summary of the Mosaic law quoted by Jesus: "Thou shalt love the Lord thy God. . . . Thou shalt love thy neighbor as thyself" (Matt. 22:37-39; Mark 12:30-31). But the substitution of "brother" for "neighbor" may suggest that John also has in mind the "new commandment" given by Jesus (John 13:34; 15:12). Clearly John feels no need to make a rigid determination of the source of this commandment. As Smalley notes,

> The love command stems ultimately "from" *(apo)* God himself, and it was eventually articulated by Jesus. Thus, even if the primary meaning of "him" is the *Father*, as the author of this command, the role of the *Son* in teaching the precept of love need not be excluded.[31]

The precise formulation of this love command, "That he who loveth God love his brother also" *(hina ho agapōn ton theon agapa kai ton adelphon autou)*, does not occur elsewhere. John's formulation of the command recalls what he has already stated in 2:3-11 and serves to underline the close union of the outward and the upward dimensions of Christian love. The two aspects cannot be separated. John thus refutes the claim of the heretics to love God while hating their brother. The present-tense verb "love" *(agapa)* indicates that this brother-love is a continuing obligation.

The opening "that" *(hina)* is generally taken as simply indicating the contents of the command. But Westcott holds that aim is also involved:

---

[28]Bruce M. Metzger, *A Textual Commentary on the Greek New Testament* (London: United Bible Societies, 1971), p. 715.

[29]John James Lias, *An Exposition of the First Epistle of John* (1887; reprint ed., Minneapolis: Klock & Klock Christian Publishers, 1982), p. 345.

[30]Brooke Foss Westcott, *The Epistles of St. John, The Greek Text with Notes,* 3rd ed. (1892; reprint ed., Grand Rapids: Eerdmans, 1950), p. 162.

[31]Smalley, p. 265. Italics in original.

"The final particle gives more than the simple contents of the commandment. It marks the injunction as directed to an aim; and implies that the effort to obtain it can never be relaxed."[32] This love is a quality of the new nature and therefore a normal part of the spiritual life. As an appeal to the human will, the Biblical commands to love make clear that this aspect of our spiritual life can be cultivated and increased. It is therefore possible that without proper spiritual cultivation this brother-love may receive inadequate expression. But this command also makes it clear that love for the brethren is not an optional aspect of Christian love which may safely be eliminated. God refuses to recognize such mutilated love as true love.

3. The Results in Our Relation to God (5:1-5)

The inward and the outward results of redeeming love are grounded in the divine love revealed in Christ Jesus. In the first five verses of chapter 5 John shows that the varied relationships of love are all related to God in the Christian life. He states the relationship between saving faith and the experience of love (v. 1), notes that love is revealed in our obedience to God's commandments (vv. 2-3), and portrays the power of saving faith in a life of victory over the world (vv. 4-5).

a. The relationship between saving faith and Christian love (v. 1). "Verse 1 joins the two great ingredients of New Testament Christianity, faith and love, together."[33] John first declares the nature of saving faith (v. 1a), and then he asserts the result of saving faith (v. 1b).

1) *The nature of saving faith* (v. 1a). John's assertion "Whosoever believeth that Jesus is the Christ is born of God" declares the content and result of saving faith. The designation "whosoever believeth" (*pas ho pisteuōn*, literally, "every one believing") is personal but includes every individual thus characterized. It includes every true believer. The present-tense participle depicts the individual's continuing, persistent faith. The verb, a favorite term with John,[34] means more than intellectual apprehension of the truth involved; it is not mere assent to a creed; it involves an active personal commitment to the truth believed. Smalley notes, "Such (orthodox) faith is virtually synonymous with the 'confession' or 'acknowledgment' demanded of the true be-

---

[32]Westcott, p. 162.

[33]David Jackman, *The Message of John's Letters*, The Bible Speaks Today (Downers Grove, Ill.: Inter-Varsity Press, 1988), pp. 133-34.

[34]The verb "believe" (*pisteuō*) in its varied forms occurs ninety-eight times in the Fourth Gospel. In 1 John it has already been used three times before (3:23; 4:1, 16) and occurs five times in 5:1-10. The noun "faith" (*pistis*) occurs only in 5:4 in John's epistles and does not occur in the Fourth Gospel.

liever according to 2:22-23; 4:2, 15."[35] Here the verb "believe" underlines the personal committal to the Him who is accepted by faith.

Saving faith intellectually accepts and actively commits itself to the fact "that Jesus is the Christ" *(hoti Iēsous estin ho Christos)*. The name "Jesus" involves an acknowledgment of His true humanity, a fact denied in Docetic Gnosticism whereas "the Christ" confesses Him as "the anointed one," the Messiah whose coming was announced in the Old Testament. The present tense, "is," declares that His incarnate identity is a continuing unchanging reality. As Plummer remarks,

> To believe that Jesus is the Christ is to believe that One who was known as a man fulfilled a known and Divine commission; that He who was born and crucified is the Anointed, the Messiah of Israel, the Saviour of the world. To believe this is to accept both the Old and the New Testaments; it is to believe that Jesus is what He claimed to be, One who is equal with the Father, and as such demands of every believer the absolute surrender of self to Him.[36]

It is the apostolic message that salvation is not merely for an elite few with their higher esoteric insights but is for all who will personally accept the message "that Jesus is the Christ."

Everyone who commits himself to this incarnate Saviour "is born of God" *(ek tou theou gegennētai,* literally, "out of God has been born"). The emphatic "out of God" stresses the source of the believer's birth; the perfect tense looks back to the time when God implanted the new life in the believer, and it depicts his continuing possession of that new life as a member of God's family. John's statement indicates that orthodox faith and regeneration are united. "Every one who believeth is born again, and every one who is born of God believes on Jesus."[37] But as Westcott observes, "Nothing is said of the relation between the human and the Divine—the faith of man, and 'the seed of God' (iii. 9)—in the first quickening of life."[38] Here the fact of the birth from God is connected with faith, but as Brown points out, "All the other I John statements (2:29; 3:9; 4:7; 5:18) relate the divine begetting to the Christian's behavior (acting justly, not sinning, and loving)—an indication that belief and behavior are two aspects of the same struggle in I John."[39]

---

[35]Smalley, p. 266.

[36]Plummer, p. 155.

[37]James Morgan, *The Epistles of John* (1865; reprint ed., Klock & Klock Christian Publishers, 1982), p. 387.

[38]Westcott, pp. 176-77.

[39]Brown, p. 535.

2) *The result of saving faith* (v. 1b). John's connective "and" *(kai)* closely joins this saving faith with a loving relationship to the Father and His children: "and every one that loveth him that begat loveth him also that is begotten of him" *(kai pas ho agapōn ton gennēsanta agapa ton gegennēmenon ex autou).* "As soon as we realize what has happened to us through the new birth," Jackman remarks, "our response is one of gratitude and love to God. He has now become our Father; we are members of a new family."[40] The repeated use of "every one that" *(pas ho)* again makes the designation personal but inclusive of all believers. The articular present-tense participle *(ho agapōn,* "the one loving") pictures the individual as marked by a continuing love for "him that begat" *(ton gennēsanta),* the one who by a definite action gave him spiritual birth. Since the Father is characterized as a God of love, the child born of Him is also marked by an attitude of love.

The believer's love for the Father naturally means that he "loveth him also that is begotten of him" *(agapa ton gegennēmenon ex autou).* Here again the form of the verb "loveth" *(agapa)* may be either the indicative or the hortative subjunctive, but the context favors the indicative: "he loves," not "let him love." The born-again believer, conscious that he has received new life from God, loves the one who gave him birth and also feels inspired to love the one in whom he sees that new life in operation. Thus, as Lias notes, "the Christian life harmoniously revolves in a perfect circle round God its centre."[41] John's use of the singular throughout this verse indicates that this God-prompted love operates on an individual basis; each member of the family of God is born not only to love but also to be loved. This love for other members of the family is the outward evidence that God has imparted new life. "This love," Hodges remarks, "does not spring from something loveable in the person himself, but from his paternity."[42] It does not necessarily express itself in warm emotional feelings toward the one loved, nor does it always run with the natural inclinations of our individual nature, but it does seek the true welfare of the one loved. True love reveals itself in its beneficent concern for the welfare of others.

b. The revelation of love through obedience to God (vv. 2-3). Having asserted that love is the basic nature of the new life, in these two verses John indicates how this love reveals itself. In verse 2 he indicates that this love operates in two directions, and in verse 3 that this love is revealed by its obedience to God's commandments.

---

[40]Jackman, p. 138.

[41]Lias, p. 356.

[42]Hodges, p. 901.

1) *The two directions of true love* (v. 2). In this verse John points out that love in the Christian life, by its very nature, flows in two directions: "By this we know that we love the children of God, when we love God, and keep his commandments." As in previous occurrences of the expression, views are divided as to whether "By this we know" *(en toutō ginōskomen)* refers to what precedes or to what follows.[43] The latter is the more natural view when taken as looking forward to the clause "when we love God." In 4:20-21 John insisted that true love for God also involves love of our brother. Here John stresses the converse reality: every instance of love and obedience to God is assurance that we love His children. "In short, love to God and love to the brethren confirm and prove each other. If either is found alone it is not genuine."[44] The temporal particle "when" *(hotan,* "whenever" with the subjunctive) points to the repeated occasions when we may be aware that we do indeed "love God, and keep his commandments" *(hotan ton theon agapōmen kai tas entolas autou poiōmen,* "whenever God we may be loving and His commandments may be doing"). The use of the subjunctive mode with the indefinite temporal particle indicates that the time of these experiences is indefinite; they do not occur according to a prearranged time schedule. John is well aware that these reassuring experiences may be precious to the sensitive believer whenever he experiences the reality of strained and irritating relations with the brethren. Whenever his soul may be harassed by unbrotherly relations, whenever he may feel like declaring before the brotherhood,

> To live above with saints in love,
>   That will indeed be glory;
> To live below with saints we know
>   Is quite another story;

whenever troubling questions seek to arise in his mind concerning his true status as a believer–then these varied experiences of true love for God can be of precious, reassuring significance to that believer.

The author gives the nature of this reassuring evidence in a double statement: "when we love God, and keep his commandments." The two actions of love and obedience are simultaneous. Our love for God expresses itself in our obedience to His commands. As Jackman observes,

> Because we love God, we truly want to please him, in our thoughts, words and actions. For us, it is no longer an external matter of moral duty in obeying a law, so much as pleasing a dearly loved Father, that lies at the

---

[43]See Brown, p. 536, for a list of scholars in support of both views.
[44]Plummer, p. 156.

heart of our Christian discipleship. And the glory of the new covenant is precisely the inner love for God which prompts obedience.[45]

Any inner emotional experience of love for God which ignores the moral demands of the laws of God cannot be accepted as true love for Him. Our love for God is shown and confirmed in each conscious effort to do His known will. The plural "his commandments" suggests that God has given various statements of His will for His people, relating to various aspects of Christian living. The present-tense verb, "keep" (*poiōmen,* literally, "do"), indicates the repeated occasions when we act deliberately to do God's will.[46] The verb *poiōmen* suggests a voluntary, love-prompted obedience. Elsewhere in this epistle John uses the verb "keep" (*tereō*) in connection with "the commandments" (2:3, 4; 3:22, 24; 5:3), suggesting the exercise of diligent care to maintain that which He enjoins.

2) *The true nature of our love and obedience* (v. 3). The opening "For" (*gar*) of verse 3 introduces an explanatory comment on the last clause of verse 2 and underlines the union between love and obedience: "For this is the love of God, that we keep his commandments." The emphatic expression "this is the love" (*hautē estin hē agapē*) looks forward to the following "that" clause, which gives the pithy definition that "the love of God" is obedience to God's commandments. The definite article with "the love of God" (*hē agapē tou theou*) "indicates that John has in mind the particular selfless love that has been under discussion throughout the epistle."[47] The genitive "of God" is clearly objective, denoting our love for God as revealed in the fact "that we keep his commandments" (*hina tas entolas autou tērōmen*[48]). Hobbs well remarks,

> While we cannot separate love and action, we do not love simply by *doing.* We *do* because we love. One might keep God's laws selfishly with a hope of reward, but this is no proper response to God's love. Christian love does not ask "must I" but "may I"; it does not count the cost, but weighs the privilege.[49]

The added words "and his commandments are not grievous" explain the place of these commandments in the experience of the obedient believer.

---

[45]Jackman, p. 140.

[46]The Greek manuscripts are divided on the verb used here. For the textual evidence see United Bible Societies, *The Greek New Testament,* 3rd ed. On a scale of A to D, the editors rate the reading *poiōmen* as C. It is probable that the unusual term here was changed by the scribes to harmonize with John's usage elsewhere, the verb *tereō,* in the epistle.

[47]Burdick, p. 345.

[48]The subjunctive mode of the verb is due to the *hina* construction.

[49]Herschel H. Hobbs, *The Epistles of John* (Nashville: Thomas Nelson Publishers, 1983), pp. 119-20.

The negative assertion that they are "not grievous" *(bareiai ouk eisin)* points out that the believer does not find them to be an intolerable burden which he seeks to avoid. "They are not like the 'burdens grievous to be borne' which the legal rigour of the Pharisees laid on men's consciences."[50] Love-prompted obedience finds that God's commandments are not a crushing burden which exhausts one's strength and destroys the sense of freedom in Christ. The believer finds that the new life in Christ implants in him a desire to do the will of God and finds that love makes obedience to His commands rewarding, for he realizes that God has given His laws for his own protection and true well-being. He finds in them guidance concerning "what the will of God is, that which is good and acceptable and perfect" (Rom. 12:2 NASB). For him "the statutes again become songs, and the commandments prove to be the stepping-stones to freedom."[51] As Dodd points out, John "does not mean that God's demands upon us are less exacting than we supposed, but that they are accompanied by the assurance of power to fulfil them."[52]

c. The revelation of overcoming faith (vv. 4-5). Although love is not directly mentioned in these verses, its presence is implied in the treatment of love-directed faith as the power of the believer's victory. In verse 4 John sets forth the new birth as the principle of victory in the Christian life, and in verse 5 he underlines the faith of the victorious individual.

1) *The new birth as the principle of victory* (v. 4). The fact that love does not find God's commandments burdensome is now explained as due to the faith-prompted victory which the new birth brings into the believer's life: "For whatsoever is born of God overcometh the world; and this is the victory that overcometh the world, *even* our faith." The use of the neuter, "for whatsoever is born of God" *(hoti pan to gegennēmenon ek tou theou),* stresses not "the victorious *person*" but rather "the victorious *power,*"[53] and the perfect-passive participle *(to gegennēmnon,* "that which has been begotten" or "born") presents this power as the abiding result of the new birth. The passive turns the attention from the believer himself to the God who wrought the new birth in him. This God-implanted new life is the true dynamic that "overcometh the world" *(nika ton kosmon).* The present-tense verb "overcometh" presents this victory as the characteristic experience of the believer, gained through continuing struggle against "the world." This familiar term "gathers up the sum of all the limited, transitory powers

---

[50]Plummer, p. 156.

[51]R.E.O. White, *Open Letter to Evangelicals, A Devotional and Homiletic Commentary on the First Epistle of John* (Grand Rapids: Eerdmans, 1964), p. 126.

[52]C. H. Dodd, *The Johannine Epistles.* Moffatt New Testament Commentary (New York: Harper & Row, 1946), p. 126.

[53]Plummer, p. 157. Italics in original.

opposed to God which make obedience difficult''[54] for the believer. The new birth enables the believer to recognize the evil nature of the world and "all that *is* in the world" (2:16) and to reject and defeat its various temptations and allurements. It is a warfare which no true believer can avoid; its scope and intensity may change, but the cause of God and His people is always involved. John's readers experienced this victory in their successful struggle against the heretics that had arisen in their midst (2:18-29).

John at once identifies this victorious power in the Christian life: "and this is the victory that overcometh the world, *even* our faith." The demonstrative pronoun "this" *(hautē)* looks forward to the appositional designation "our faith," placed emphatically at the end of the sentence. The new birth gives the believer the potential of victory, but the realization of actual victory depends on our active exercise of faith.

The noun "the victory" *(hē nikē)* occurs only here in the New Testament, but the term was common in contemporary Greek. The term here does not denote a concrete victory that has been achieved but is used figuratively to denote "the means for winning a victory" or "the power that grants victory."[55] Brown suggests the rendering "conquering power."[56] John further describes this victory as "the victory that overcometh the world" *(hē nikē hē nikēsasa ton kosmon,* "the victory, the one that overcame the world"). The use of the articular participle, "the one that overcame," rather than an adjective, strengthens the assertion of the active nature of this victory. The use of the aorist rather than a present active participle *(hē nikēsasa)* seems to denote some specific occasion when this victorious power was effectively displayed. Interpreters understand the intended identity of this occasion in various ways. Some see it as a reference to Christ's once-for-all victory over Satan (John 12:31-32; 14:30) and the world (John 16:33) through His work on the cross. Then the believer's victory is gained by his active appropriation of the victory that has already been won by Christ. Thus Marshall remarks, "To believe that Jesus has been victorious is to have the power that enables us also to win the battle, for we know that our foe is already defeated and therefore powerless."[57] But others insist that the victory in view here is not Christ's victory but rather the believer's victory, since John describes it as "our faith" *(hē pistis hēmōn).*[58] These interpreters understand the aorist

---

[54]Westcott, p. 179.

[55]William F. Arndt and F. Wilbur Gingrich, *A Greek-English Lexicon of the New Testament and Other Early Christian Literature* (Chicago: University of Chicago Press, 1957), p. 541.

[56]Brown, p. 570.

[57]I. Howard Marshall, *The Epistles of John,* New International Commentary on the New Testament (Grand Rapids: Eerdmans, 1978), p. 229.

[58]So Burdick, pp. 346-47; Kenneth Grayston, *The Johannine Epistles,* New Century Bible Commentary (Grand Rapids: Eerdmans, 1984), p. 134.

participle as timeless, that "the aorist expresses a fact that is always true."[59] If "our faith" is taken collectively of the body of believers, the victory in view may be that gained over the heretics, causing them to withdraw (2:18-19).[60] More probable seems the view that the reference is to the conversion of the individual believer. Then the aorist participle may be viewed as ingressive, "the aorist participle going back to the beginning of the victory."[61] Thus Lenski renders "and this is the victory, the one that became victorious over the world, our faith."[62] The plural pronoun "our" generalizes this experience with the accepted fact that the initial victory continues to be aggressively exercised. The believer's continuing exercise of victorious faith is portrayed in verse 5.

This passage does not mean that all who are born of God are necessarily victorious over sin and the evil one. The failure is on our side. Laurin points out:

> The new birth gives us the potentials of victory, but actual overcoming depends on faith. The new birth implants within us all the necessities for an overcoming life, but faith puts these things to work. It takes birth plus faith. It takes power plus personality. This means that both God and man must work together. God does not do it all for us nor can we do it all for ourselves.[63]

2) *The faith of the victorious individual* (v. 5). In verse 5 John's question turns the thought from the principle of victory to the victorious individual: "Who is he that overcometh the world, but he that believeth that Jesus is the Son of God?" The interrogative "who" *(tis)* asks for the personal identification of the one characterized as overcoming the world. The present tense, "the one who overcomes" *(ho nikōn),* makes clear that the conflict is not yet over but that the outcome is sure. His conflict is with the Christ-rejecting "world." This third use of the term in verses 4-5 makes prominent the moral nature of the enemy.

Instead of leaving the words "who is he that overcometh the world" as an independent question (as the NIV rendering has it), John continues with the suggested answer, "but he that believeth that Jesus is the Son of God?" *(ei mē ho pisteuōn hoti Iēsous estin ho huios tou theou,* more literally, "if not the one believing that Jesus is the Son of God?"). The implication is

---

[59]Simon J. Kistemaker, *Exposition of the Epistle of James and the Epistles of John,* New Testament Commentary (Grand Rapids: Baker, 1986), p. 351.

[60]Stott, p. 174. Kysar, p. 105, comments: "The world that is conquered is the unbelief represented in the separatists and their views."

[61]Lenski, p. 523.

[62]*Ibid.,* p. 522.

[63]Laurin, p. 166.

that if the one so described is not victorious over the world, then no one is. What distinguishes the true victor is the content of his faith: "he that believeth that Jesus is the Son of God" *(ho pisteuōn hoti Iēsous estin ho huios tou theou)*. For John not all faith is victorious. No one who denies the apostolic teaching that "Jesus is the Son of God" is truly victorious over "the world," which is characterized by its rejection of the Son of God (John 1:10-11). Involved is the basic fact of the incarnation, but Lias remarks that "it is not belief in the Incarnation, as a formula, but belief in One who has become incarnate."[64] This designation as "Son" was first introduced in the Prologue (1:3) and has recurred repeatedly (1:7; 2:22-24; 3:8, 23; 4:9-10, 14-15). In 5:5-13 there are eight references to "his Son," "the Son," or "the Son of God,"[65] and the designation occurs again in the summary statement in 5:20. To deny that "Jesus is the Son of God" is to destroy the whole gospel and effectively to nullify the apostolic message of salvation and the resultant victory in Him. Acceptance of this message gives the believer personal assurance and certain victory in his conflict with the forces of evil. True Christian faith is christological!

---

[64]Lias, p. 362.

[65]An apparent ninth occurrence in 5:5-13 of the KJV (the second in v. 13) is not supported by the best manuscripts.

14

Assurance Through the Witness of the Spirit (5:6-12)

In this last section of the body of the epistle, John stresses the witness of the Spirit as the final ground for Christian assurance. The unifying factor in this section is the concept of "witness," which, either as a noun or a verb, occurs no less than nine times in these verses. John opened the epistle with a passing reference to the apostolic witness concerning the manifestations of eternal life in the incarnate Son of God (1:2); in this final section he expands on that witness concerning the incarnate Son with the assurance that this is indeed the witness of God concerning His Son.

Our faith in the person of Jesus Christ is based on valid external and internal testimony. Beyond the human testimony is the fact that God bore historical testimony to the incarnate Son, and the indwelling Spirit confirms that testimony in the heart of the believer. The external witness is necessary to bring the human heart to faith in Christ; the internal witness of the Spirit confirms the believer in Christ.

In this section John points out the historical witnesses to Jesus Christ (vv. 6-9) and then underlines the Spirit's witness within as crucial to the possession of eternal life (vv. 10-12).

A. The Historical Witnesses to Jesus Christ (5:6-9)

5:6 This is he that came by water and blood, *even* Jesus Christ; not by water only, but by water and blood. And it is the Spirit that beareth witness, because the Spirit is truth.

7 For there are three that bear record in heaven, the Father, the Word, and the Holy Ghost: and these three are one.

8 And there are three that bear witness in earth, the spirit, and the water, and the blood: and these three agree in one.

9 If we receive the witness of men, the witness of God is greater: for this
is the witness of God which he hath testified of his Son.

In dealing with the historical appearing of Jesus Christ, John calls attention to two historical events connected with His coming (v. 6a), indicates
that the Spirit who bears witness is the truth (v. 6b), declares the perfect
agreement of the witnesses to Christ (vv. 7-8), and insists upon the trustworthiness of the divine witness (v. 9).

1. The Historical Facts Connected with Christ's Coming (v. 6a)

Concerning Him whom he had just identified as "Jesus . . . the Son of
God" (v. 5), John now asserts, "This is he that came by water and blood,
even Jesus Christ" (houtos estin ho elthōn di' hudatos kai haimatos, Iēsous
Christos). The opening demonstrative pronoun, "This" (houtos), refers back
to the designation in verse 5, and the appositional identification "Jesus
Christ" marks His historical identity as Jesus of Nazareth but associates
Him with His messianic office. The expression rendered "he that came"
(ho elthōn) suggests the varied Gospel references to the Messiah as "he that
cometh" (ho erchomenos; cf. Matt. 11:3; Luke 7:19-20; John 1:15, 27; 6:14;
11:27; 12:13); but the use of the aorist participle portrays His coming as a
past historical reality. The coming referred to here is not His birth in Bethlehem but rather His public appearing as the promised Messiah. This historical appearing, John insists, was "by water and blood," which somehow
served to reveal His messianic identity. This implies that "water and blood"
also point to known historical realities. The expression is obscure to the
modern reader, but obviously the intended significance was familiar to John's
readers; the expression apparently arose out of the theological controversy
with the heretical teachers (2:18-19). Scholars advance varied interpretations
concerning the meaning of "water and blood."

The oldest and most natural view understands "water" as a reference to
Christ's baptism, with the attendant witnesses to His identity, at the com-
mencement of His ministry (Matt. 3:13-17; Mark 1:9-11; John 1:31-34) and
"blood" to the consummation of His saving ministry on the cross. This
view is supported by the fact that "the context dictates that here *water* and
blood must validate the manner of Jesus' *coming.*"[1] The two terms serve to
sum up Christ's redemptive mission. As Plummer notes,

> Christ's Baptism, with the Divine proclamation of Him as the Son of God
> and the Divine outpouring of the Spirit upon Him, is not merely the opening

---

[1] R. Alan Culpepper, *1 John, 2 John, 3 John,* Knox Preaching Guides (Atlanta: John Knox
Press, 1985), p. 101. Italics in original.

but the explanation of the whole of His Ministry. The bloody death upon the Cross is not merely the close but the explanation of His Passion.[2]

A second view, adopted by Augustine (354-430)[3] and some other early interpreters, linked the "water and blood" with the "blood and water" that issued from His spear-pierced side upon His death (John 19:34-35). Although it has received some modern support,[4] this view seems scarcely tenable. The reverse order of the two terms is against it. The point of the two references is very different: here the terms are used to support the reality of the historical ministry of the incarnate Son of God; in John's account of the crucifixion, the mention of "blood and water" serves to establish the reality of His physical death. Nor does this view explain John's added words, "not with the water only, but with the water and the blood."

A third view, running back to the time of the Reformers, sees in the two terms a reference to Christian Baptism (water) and the Lord's Supper (blood). This view confronts the problem of the aorist tense of the participle rendered "that came" *(ho elthōn)* as denoting a specific past historical event, whereas Christian baptism and the Lord's Supper are recurring observances which relate to the ongoing life of the Christian Church. Further, the simple word "blood" would be a strange and unprecedented symbol for the Lord's Supper. Kysar aptly remarks, "That a reference to the sacraments is intended is reading too much into the symbolism."[5]

The view that "water and blood" are shorthand references to the inauguration and the consummation of the public ministry of the incarnate Christ is in accord with John's added assertion "not by water only, but by water and blood" *(ouk en tō hudati monon, all' en tō hudati kai en tō haimati,* literally, "not in the water only, but in the water and in the blood"). John insists that the realities denoted by "the water" and "the blood" cannot be separated in dealing with the coming and work of Jesus Christ. He clearly seems intent on countering the heretical view of the false teachers; in fact, his refusal to separate these two realities may well indicate a denial of two forms of incipient Gnosticism.[6] Docetic Gnosticism denied that Jesus Christ

---

[2]Alfred Plummer, *The Epistles of S. John,* Cambridge Bible for Schools and Colleges (1883; reprint ed., London: Cambridge University Press, 1938), p. 158.

[3]The dates are those given in J. D. Douglas, ed., *The New International Dictionary of the Christian Church* (Grand Rapids: Zondervan, 1974), p. 86.

[4]So W. Alexander, "The First Epistle General of John," in *The Speaker's Commentary, New Testament* (London: John Murray, 1881), 4:341-42, 348-50; F. W. Farrar, *The Early Days of Christianity* (New York: Cassell, n.d.), pp. 564-66.

[5]Robert Kysar, *I, II, III John,* Augsburg Commentary on the New Testament (Minneapolis: Augsburg, 1986), p. 107.

[6]See our Introduction to 1 John under "Polemical Purpose," pp. 20-22.

really had a human body and affirmed that He only appeared to be truly human; it was a blatant denial of the reality of the incarnation. Since these Gnostics held that He did not have a real body, they rejected the view that He experienced the physical agonies and death involved in crucifixion. But John in his account of the crucifixion insists upon the reality of His physical death (John 19:32-37). John's assertion also carries a rejection of the heretical view of Cerinthus, a later contemporary of the Apostle John at Ephesus. Cerinthus separated the man from the spiritual Christ. He regarded Jesus as a mere man, the son of Joseph and Mary; he taught that the divine Christ came upon the man Jesus at his baptism, empowered his ministry, but left him before his crucifixion. The man Jesus suffered death and rose again, but the divine Christ remained impassible. John's explicit assertion that Jesus Christ came "with the water and with the blood" (NASB) rejects all such attempts to sever the divine from the human in the nature of the incarnate Son of God.

John's change in the preposition in the two parts of verse 6 has evoked considerable discussion. He first speaks of Christ coming "by [*di'*] water and blood" and then as coming "not with [*en*] the water only, but with [*en*] the water and with [*en*] the blood" (NASB). The use of the definite article with both nouns clearly points back to the "water and blood" just mentioned as specific historical events, but the significance of the changed preposition is not so obvious. Brown remarks that "the majority of scholars see no significant difference in I John's variation between *dia* and *en*," and he lists ten names in support.[7] Burdick agrees that "John changes words for the sake of literary variety, but the meaning in both instances is the same."[8] But others think that the distinction between the two prepositions should receive recognition. Thus Kistemaker remarks that "the preposition *dia* conveys the meaning *by* or *through,* and the preposition *en* connotes 'accompanying circumstance.' "[9] Lenski states his view as follows:

> The mission on which God sent his Son and in which he came as "Savior of the world" (4:14) made him use these two means *(dia),* water and blood; when he came, it was not "in connection with" water alone (as the heretics claimed) but "in connection with the water and in connection with the blood." . . . The *dia* states what the connection indicated by *en* was: it was the connection of means.[10]

---

[7]Raymond E. Brown, *The Epistles of John,* The Anchor Bible (Garden City, N.Y.: Doubleday & Co., 1982), p. 574.

[8]Donald W. Burdick, *The Letters of John the Apostle* (Chicago: Moody Press, 1985), p. 368.

[9]Simon J. Kistemaker, *Exposition of the Epistle of James and Epistle of John,* New Testament Commentary (Grand Rapids: Baker, 1986), p. 355.

[10]R.C.H. Lenski, *The Interpretation of the Epistles of St. Peter, St. John and St. Jude* (Columbus, Ohio: Wartburg Press, 1945), pp. 525-26.

Plummer suggests that this use of "with" *(en),* "of the element or sphere in which a thing is done," may be due to the Septuagint rendering in Leviticus 16:3: "Thus Aaron shall enter into the holy place *in* a calf of the herd" *(en maschō ek boōn),* that is, "with a calf."[11] Whatever distinctions the author may have intended by the two prepositions, both refer to the same historical events. As Findlay remarks, "Thus the inauguration and consummation of our Lord's ministry were marked by the two supreme manifestations of His Messiahship; of both events this Apostle had been a near and deeply interested witness."[12]

2. The Witness of the Spirit (v. 6b)[13]

Beside the two historical events which bore witness to Jesus as the Messiah, John explicitly mentions the witness of the Holy Spirit:[14] "And it is the Spirit that beareth witness" *(kai to pneuma estin to marturoun,* literally, "and the Spirit is the one witnessing").[15] John now mentions the Spirit in connection with His activity as the witness-bearer. The present tense participle marks that "His testimony is given now and uninterruptedly."[16] Without His testimony the true significance of the "water and blood" remains unintelligible to the natural human heart. In verse 6a John uses the aorist tense to mark the actual coming of Jesus Christ to carry out His redemptive mission; here the present-tense participle stresses the continuing activity of the Spirit in interpreting and applying the true significance of Christ's mission to human hearts. The book of Acts is essentially a record of the witness of the Spirit through the Church and the Holy Scriptures. And He continues to bear witness "in the believer's heart and in the believing community; their experience of His power and guidance confirms the truth of the gospel to which they have committed themselves."[17]

---

[11]Plummer, *The Epistles of S. John,* p. 159.

[12]George G. Findlay, *Fellowship in the Life Eternal, An Exposition of the Epistles of St John* (New York: Hodder and Stoughton, n.d.), p. 383.

[13]When the RV (1881) dropped the spurious passage concerning the three heavenly witnesses, the verse numbering was moved back to give a more balanced verse division. This numbering was also used in the ASV, NASB, and RSV. The NEB, NIV, and the Jerusalem Bible more nearly adhere to the old KJV verse numbering.

[14]Henry Alford, *The New Testament for English Readers* ([1865-1872]; reprint ed., Chicago: Moody Press, [1985]), pp. 1749-50, mentions five different conjectures as to the meaning of "Spirit" here, all of which he rightly rejects as contrary to the context.

[15]The use of the neuter participle is in agreement with the grammatical gender of the Greek noun *pneuma.*

[16]Brooke Foss Westcott, *The Epistles of St. John, The Greek Text with Notes,* 3rd ed. (1892; reprint ed., Grand Rapids, Eerdmans, 1950), p. 183.

[17]F. F. Bruce, *The Epistle of St. John* (Old Tappan, N.J.: Revell, 1970), p. 119.

The added comment "because the Spirit is truth" (*hoti to pneuma estin hē alētheia,* literally, "is the truth") stresses the total reliability of this testimony. The opening *hoti* could be taken as declarative ("that"), as stating the content of the Spirit's testimony, but this would be inconsistent with the role of the Spirit to testify of Jesus (John 15:26) and not to speak on His own behalf (John 16:13). Further, such "self-attestation of the Spirit would have no relation to the context. It is the witnesses to Christ, to the identity of Jesus with the Son of God, that S. John is marshalling before us."[18] The validity of the Spirit's witness to Jesus is grounded in the very nature of the Spirit: "the Spirit is the truth." (Cf. John 14:17; 15:26; 16:13.) Not only is His witness "true" but He is also "the embodiment of the saving truth, which he thus also imparts by his testimony in order to save us."[19]

3. The Agreement of the Three Witnesses (vv. 7-8)

The statement in verse 7 (KJV) concerning the three heavenly witnesses, commonly known as the Johannine Comma, is an expansion of the Greek text upon the basis of the Latin and is devoid of any reliable textual support as a true part of the original.[20] Hodges and Farstad in the edition of *The Greek New Testament According To The Majority Text,* generally supportive of the Textus Receptus, rightly omit verse 7 entirely.[21] Erasmus did not find the words in any of the Greek texts upon which he based his first two editions of his Greek New Testament, but in the third edition, in a spirit of compromise, he reluctantly included them in his text. Accordingly they were contained in the Textus Receptus upon which the translators of the King James Version based their English rendering. Because verse 7 in the King James Version is not an authentic part of the Greek text, it is here not given any interpretative treatment. In verse 8 the words "in earth" are likewise a scribal addition to balance the reference to the three witnesses "in heaven" in verse 7.

Having already mentioned two impersonal witnesses, "water and blood" (v. 6a), as well as the personal witness of "the Spirit" (v. 6b), John next draws together these three witnesses: "and there are three that bear witness . . . the spirit, and the water, and the blood" (v. 8). The exact force of the connective conjunction *hoti,* "for" rather than "and" (KJV), is not obvious

---

[18]Plummer, p. 160.

[19]Lenski, p. 527.

[20]Concerning the expanded reading in the King James Version about the "three heavenly witnesses," commonly called the Johannine Comma, see our Introduction, "Famous Interpolation," pp. 26-27.

[21]Zane C. Hodges and Arthur L. Farstad, *The Greek New Testament According to the Majority Text* (Nashville: Thomas Nelson Publishers, 1982).

"since this clause does not offer another reason but a further specification."[22]
The rendering "for" indicates a rather loose usage of the conjunction to
specify the noteworthy fact that there are three witnesses.[23] Thus Smalley
and Brown[24] both render "indeed, there are three witnesses." The number
"three" stresses that the number of the witnesses assures that their testimony
is reliable and authentic (cf. Deut. 19:15). It is an important point in establishing an authentic testimony. Lenski remarks, "The law has ever required
and requires to this day that two or three testify (Deut. 17:6; 19:15; Matt.
18:16; II Cor. 13:1); God himself adheres to this principle, (Heb. 10:28, 29);
so does Jesus (Heb. 6:18; John 5:31-37)."[25] The present-tense participle
rendered "bear witness" *(hoti marturountes)* denotes the continuing activity
of these witnesses. In drawing these three witnesses together John names
them in a new order: "the Spirit, and the water, and the blood" *(to pneuma
kai to hudōr kai to haima)*. Although all three of these nouns are in the
neuter gender, the numeral "three" as well as the participle are in the
masculine gender, a fact which, according to Smith, constitutes "a testimony, the more striking because involuntary, to the personality of the
Spirit."[26] As Alford notes, "The Spirit is, of the three, the only living and
active witness, properly speaking: besides, the water and the blood are no
witnesses without Him, whereas He is independent of them, testifying both
in them and out of them."[27] In Jewish tradition personal testimony can be
given by inanimate objects when their history is known and understood. In
John 5:36 Jesus declares that His own works bear witness to Him; in Hebrews 11:4 the author asserts that the faith-prompted sacrifice of Abel still
speaks; in Genesis 31:48 a heap of stones put up by Jacob and Laban is
called "witness." (See also Josh. 22:10, 27; 24:27.) John here names the
Spirit first because His testimony animates the threefold witness.

Interpreters have understood the witness of "the water and the blood" in
verse 8 in two different ways. One view is that whereas in verse 6 they are historical, referring to Christ's baptism and crucifixion, in verse 8 they denote the

---

[22]Brown, p. 581.

[23]"For" is the rendering in the RV (1881), ASV, NEB, and NIV. It is omitted in the RSV
and TEV. The Jerusalem Bible renders "since the Spirit is the truth–so that there are three
witnesses."

[24]Stephen S. Smalley, *1, 2, 3 John*, Word Biblical Commentary (Waco, Texas: Word Books,
1984), p. 281; Brown, p. 581.

[25]Lenski, p. 528.

[26]David Smith, "The Epistles of St. John," in *The Expositor's Greek Testament* ([1897];
reprint ed., Grand Rapids: Eerdmans, n.d.), 5:195.

[27]Alford, p. 1750.

Christian sacraments of baptism and the Lord's Supper.[28] It is held that the present tense, "bear witness," cannot refer to the past life and death of Jesus but must refer to the repeated sacramental testimony of the Christian Church. But Burdick replies that such a proposed change of the meaning of "the water and the blood" here "is rather arbitrary since there is nothing in the context that indicates that John has changed the meaning of the two terms."[29] Nowhere in Scripture is the term "blood" used alone to designate the Lord's Supper. Further, "it is difficult to see in what sense baptism and the Lord's supper testify to the fact that Jesus is the incarnate Son of God."[30] We agree with those who hold that the two terms have the same meaning in both verses.[31] The present tense points to the fact that the water and the blood continue to bear witness concerning the incarnate Christ whenever the historical facts concerning His baptism and death are read or proclaimed.

When John adds "and these three agree in one" (*kai hoi treis eis to hen eisin,* quite literally, "and the three are [witnesses] unto the one thing"), he underlines the fact that these witnesses agree in proclaiming the same message concerning Jesus Christ, the Son of God. The agreement of these three witnesses is in striking contrast to the response of the false witnesses at the trial of Jesus who could not agree in establishing a valid charge against Christ (Matt. 26:59-61; Mark 14:55-59). But these three witnesses unite in bearing a consistent witness "to the reality of God's work in Christ by the Spirit, both in the believer and in the world; they declare jointly that through Jesus good is ultimately shown to be stronger than evil (cf. v. 5)."[32]

4. The Trustworthiness of the Divine Witness (v. 9)

In verse 9 John explicitly asserts that these varied witnesses are in reality God's witness concerning His Son and that therefore the witness is entirely trustworthy. John uses a conditional sentence to present the trustworthiness of God's witness: "If we receive the witness of men, the witness of God is greater." The conditional clause "if we receive the witness of men" implies no doubt and is an argument from the lesser to the greater. Thus the NIV turns the conditional expression into a statement of fact, "We accept man's testimony." Normally we accept human testimony; as reasonable individuals

---

[28]So Rudolf Bultmann, *The Johannine Epistles,* Hermeneia–A Critical and Historical Commentary on the Bible (Philadelphia: Fortress Press, 1973), pp. 80-81; C. H. Dodd, *The Johannine Epistles,* Moffatt New Testament Commentary (New York: Harper & Row, 1946), pp. 130-31.

[29]Burdick, p. 370.

[30]*Ibid.,* p. 371.

[31]Plummer, p. 161; Smalley, pp. 281-82; Kistemaker, p. 354.

[32]Smalley, p. 283.

we receive the words of others as trustworthy unless we have reasons to doubt the individual's honesty. If we receive the testimony of fallible human beings, then there is no valid reason for doubting God's testimony, because it is "greater" *(meizōn),* more reliable and trustworthy, more demanding of our acceptance. The term "greater" implies "both the greater trustworthiness of God's testimony because of its origin, and also its greater importance and value because of its content."[33] In neglecting or rejecting this testimony, the unbeliever is less reasonable with God than he is with fellow human beings.

In what follows John apparently indicates why the testimony of God is of greater trustworthiness. The words "for this is the witness of God which he hath testified of his Son" *(hoti hautē estin hē marturia tou theou, hoti memarturēken peri tou hoiou autou)* are beset with some uncertainty of interpretation. The first *hoti* seems to be explanatory and may be translated "for" or "because" (NIV). Then the words "for this is the witness of God" *(hoti hautē estin hē marturia tou theou,* or "because this is the witness of God") explain *why* God's testimony is of greater trustworthiness. The three-fold witness of verse 8 is really "the witness of God" because He is behind it all. It is God's testimony, not that of mere men.

The divine witness is "which he hath testified of his Son" *(hoti memarturēken peri huiou autou).* The force of this second *hoti* may be differently understood. It can be taken (1) as a relative *(ho ti,* "that which, whatever")* simply recording the fact that God has given His testimony concerning His Son; (2) as causal, "because he hath testified of his Son"; or (3) as declarative, the witness being "that he hath testified of his Son." The third view seems most probable. The threefold witness of verse 8 is trustworthy because it is God's witness "of" *(peri),* or better, "concerning His Son," having the Son as its center. This witness is great because it was given by God and is about His Son.

With his use of the perfect tense, "hath testified" *(memarturēken),* John declares that God has placed Himself permanently on record as bearing witness to His Son. This fact is a settled reality. He did so prophetically in the Old Testament, speaking through the various prophets concerning the Coming One. He did so explicitly on at least three occasions as recorded in the Gospels: at His baptism (Matt. 3:16-17; Mark 1:10-11); at His transfiguration (Matt. 17:5; Mark 9:7; Luke 9:35); and in the hearing of the multitude during Passion Week (John 12:27-29). He also did so nonverbally in the miracles at His crucifixion, as well as at the resurrection. According to Hebrews 1:1-2, the Son Himself was the embodiment of God's highest and final self-revelation to mankind.

---

[33]David Jackman, *The Message of John's Letters,* The Bible Speaks Today (Downers Grove, Ill.: Inter-Varsity Press, 1988), p. 151.

15

Assurance Through the Witness of the Spirit (Part 2)

B. The Efficacy of The Divine Witness (5:10-12)

5:10 He that believeth on the Son of God hath the witness in himself: he that believeth not God hath made him a liar; because he believeth not the record that God gave of his Son.

11 And this is the record, that God hath given to us eternal life, and this life is in his Son.

12 He that hath the Son hath life; *and* he that hath not the Son of God hath not life.

The historical witness to the Son of God is now shown to be effective in the life of the believer through the inner witness of the Spirit. The witness of the Spirit to the heart and conscience of the individual demands a human response to that witness. In verse 10 John sets forth the contrasted results of the human responses to the witness, and in verses 11-12 he underlines the crucial importance of the Son in the bestowal of eternal life.

1. The Responses to God's Witness (v. 10)

The objective witness which God has given concerning His Son demands a human response. As free moral agents, human beings respond either positively or negatively to that witness. The outcome of the response made is crucial. It divides men into two distinct categories.

a. The one believing God's witness (v. 10a). John first portrays the significance of a positive response: "He that believeth on the Son of God hath the witness in himself" *(ho pisteuōn eis ton huion tou theou echei tēn marturian en autō)*. The present-tense articular participle, "the one believing" *(ho pisteuōn)*, portrays the individual as exercising an active personal faith centered in the one to whom God bore witness. The verb "believeth," which occurs three times in this verse, embodies the essence of man's saving response to God's witness. It involves not merely an acceptance of the truthfulness of the message but also a personal trust in or committal to the one to whom witness is borne. The precise expression here used (*pisteuōn eis ton huion,* literally, "believing into the Son")[1] pictures his faith as moving toward and entering into union with the one who is the object of his faith. It is not the resultant human experience that saves him but rather his faith-wrought union with "the Son of God." Such a personal trust in and committal to the incarnate Son of God is central to a saving faith.

The resultant new birth assures that he "hath the witness in himself" *(echei tēn marturian en heautō).* The content of "the witness" that he now possesses is the reality witnessed to by "the Spirit, and the water, and the blood" (v. 8) and confirmed by God as His own witness (v. 9). With his new birth the believer realizes that the Spirit's witness is also internalized; he possesses it "in himself" *(en heautō).*[2] Following his regeneration there develops in the believer the growing inner conviction that the things that the Spirit has borne witness to are true and that they are true in his own life. He experiences the inner reality of Romans 8:16, "The Spirit Himself bears witness with our spirit that we are children of God" (NASB). (Cf. also Gal. 4:6.) The gospel message "which for others is external is for the believer experiential," becoming in him "an inner conviction of life and cleansing and redemption."[3] The realities which the Holy Spirit vitalizes in his own heart are grounded in and thoroughly consistent with the external testimony of God as now recorded in Scripture.

b. The one not believing God's witness (v. 10b). The picture of the unbeliever is again precisely drawn: "he that believeth not God hath made him a liar" *(ho mē pisteuōn tō theō pseustēn pepoiēken auton).* The present-tense articular participle again portrays the individual as the representative of this second group. The use of the negative *mē,* rather than the objective

---

[1]This is the first of three occurrences of *pisteuō* (believer) with *eis* in 1 John. It is a favorite description of saving faith in the Fourth Gospel where it occurs thirty-four times but only nine or ten times in the rest of the New Testament. W. F. Moulton and A. S. Geden, *A Concordance to the Greek Testament,* 3rd ed. (1926; reprint ed., Edinburgh: T. & T. Clark, 1950), pp. 805-8.

[2]The manuscripts are divided between *autō* ("in him") and the reflexive *heautō* ("in himself"). For the evidence see Nestle and Aland, *Novum Testamentum Graece.* In the 22nd ed. (New York: American Bible Society, 1956) they placed *autō* in the text, but in the 26th ed. (Stuttgart: Deutsche Bibelstiftung, 1979) they use *heautō.* The editors of *The Greek New Testament,* 3rd ed. (New York: United Bible Societies, 1975), rate the reflexive *heautō* as B on a scale of A to D. Whatever the original form, the meaning is clearly reflexive.

[3]Brooke Foss Westcott, *The Epistles of St. John, The Greek Text with Notes,* 3rd ed. (1892; reprint ed., Grand Rapids: Eerdmans, 1950), p. 186.

negative *ou*, "lays emphasis on the character rather than the fact of non-belief."[4] The wording is not an exact parallel to the first part. Instead of saying that this individual does not believe "in the Son of God," John writes that he does not believe "God" *(tō theō)*,[5] emphasizing the one whose testimony is being rejected. He does not merely fail to receive the Son but refuses to accept the Father's testimony concerning His Son.

John's categorical verdict "hath made Him a liar" *(pseustēn pepoiēken auton,* literally, "a liar he had made him") underlines that his rejection of God's witness is not an acceptable option. "He does not have the freedom to take or leave it without obligation, for God gives him this testimony with royal authority."[6] He obviously has no personal, trusting relationship with God. Indeed, his unbelief is an attack upon the very character of God; he attacks the truthfulness of God. Stott well remarks, "Unbelief is not a misfortune to be pitied; it is a sin to be deplored. Its sinfulness lies in the fact that it contradicts the word of the one true God and thus attributes falsehood to Him."[7]

John clearly underlines the evil nature of his unbelief: "because he believeth not the record that God gave of his Son" *(hoti ou pepisteuken eis tēn marturian hēn memarturēken ho theos peri tou huiou autou).* The negative *(ou)* denotes the actual fact of his rejection of God's witness, and the perfect tense *(pepisteuken,* "has not believed") marks the continuing result of his negative response to "the record" *(tēn marturian hēn memarturēken,* "the witness that he has witnessed") concerning His Son. His rejection of the Son inevitably involves an attack upon the character of the Father Himself.

2. The Resultant Relations to Eternal Life (vv. 11-12)

The opening "and" *(kai)* of verse 11 points to a further matter connected with the response made to God's witness. Involved is the matter of eternal life. In verse 11 John states what the witness of God involves whereas verse 12 states the contrasting results of these opposite reactions to the Son of God.

a. The witness to God's gift of life in His Son (v. 11). The response to God's witness is so crucial because of what His witness involves: "And this

---

[4]A. E. Brooke, *A Critical and Exegetical Commentary on the Johannine Epistles,* International Critical Commentary (New York: Charles Scribner's Sons, 1912), p. 139.

[5]This change from the first half of the verse resulted in the scribal production of textual variants, writing either "the Son" *(tō huiō)* or "the Son of God" *(tō huiō tou theou).* For the evidence see United Bible Societies, *The Greek New Testament,* 3rd ed. The editors rate *tō theō* as B.

[6]Simon J. Kistemaker, *Exposition of the Epistles of James and the Epistles of John,* New Testament Commentary (Grand Rapids: Baker, 1986), p. 357.

[7]J.R.W. Stott, *The Epistles of John,* Tyndale New Testament Commentaries (Grand Rapids: Eerdmans, 1964), p. 182.

is the record, that God hath given to us eternal life, and this life is in his Son." Eternal life for mankind is involved in that witness. In the phrase "this is the record" *(hautē estin hē marturia),* the demonstrative pronoun "this" stands emphatically first and looks forward to the following "that" as unfolding the content of the divine witness, namely, "that God hath given to us eternal life" *(hoti zōēn aiōnion edōken ho theos hēmin,* "that life eternal he gave, God, to us"). The forward position of the designation "eternal life" marks this life as the key concept involved in God's witness. Used without an article the term is qualitative: "it is the highest kind of spiritual and moral life, irrespective of time, which God enables the believer to share in relationship with Jesus."[8] Although this life continues on in the timeless ages of eternity, God has already imparted it to the believer as a present possession. The aorist verb "hath given" *(edōken)* stresses that God decisively made this gift available in the saving ministry of His incarnate Son, and, further, that it becomes a definite gift to the believer when it is appropriated by faith in His Son. Findlay appropriately remarks, "Our part is but to receive God's bounty pressed upon us in Christ; it is merely to consent to the strong purpose of His love, to allow Him (as St Paul puts it) to 'work in us to will and to work, on behalf of His good pleasure' (Phil. 2:13)."[9] With the plural pronoun "us" John again includes himself among those who by faith have actively appropriated this precious gift.

Plummer insists that the further words "and this life is in His Son" are "a new independent statement, coordinate with the first clause."[10] Then the words are John's own explanatory comment concerning God's gift to us. But it is more natural to take these words as still a part of the "witness" of God, declaring the further fact that this life is available only in union with the Son. "In relationship with him alone can it be obtained. He defines the sphere in which it is lived out and experienced."[11] This phrase explains why faith in Christ Jesus is so crucial. Boice remarks, "It is as impossible to have life without having Christ as it is impossible to have Christ without at the same time possessing eternal life."[12] The fact that this life is "in His Son" *(en tō huiō autou)* does not mean that this life is separate from God.

---

[8]Stephen S. Smalley, *1, 2, 3 John,* Word Biblical Commentary (Waco, Texas: Word Books, 1984), p. 287.

[9]George G. Findlay, *Fellowship in the Life Eternal, An Exposition of the Epistles of St John* (New York: Hodder and Stoughton, n.d.), p. 391.

[10]Alfred Plummer, *The Epistles of S. John,* Cambridge Bible for Schools and Colleges (1883; reprint ed., London: Cambridge University Press, 1938), p. 163.

[11]J. L. Houlden, *A Commentary on the Johannine Epistles,* Harper's New Testament Commentaries (New York: Harper & Row, Publishers, 1973), p. 132.

[12]James Montgomery Boice, *The Epistles of John* (Grand Rapids: Zondervan, 1979), p. 166.

"Believers united with Christ are in Him united with God. Comp. Rom. vi. 23; 2 Tim. i. 1."[13]

    b. The necessity of having the Son for eternal life (v. 12). John concludes the discussion with an affirmative/negative parallelism, stressing that human possession of eternal life is inseparably related to God's Son and is obtained only in union with Him.

    The positive reality is "he that hath the Son hath life" *(ho echōn ton huion echei tēn zōēn)*. The articular present-tense participle *(ho echōn)* pictures the individual as representative of his class. The possession of eternal life is experienced on the individual level. The present tenses mark the possession of this life as a present reality in the life of the believer. The possession of this life involves a reciprocal relationship: "we have life 'in' Jesus (v. 11); but, when this is appropriated, God through Christ lives 'in' the believer (cf. 3:24; also 2:24, 27, 28; 3:6, 9; 4:12, 13, 15, 16)."[14] The growth and the conscious development of this interrelationship strengthens the believer's assurance of possessing "life" *(tēn zōēn,* "the life"), the eternal life which quantitatively and qualitatively is life indeed.

    Over against this glorious reality, John solemnly places the opposite truth: "he that hath not the Son of God hath not life" *(ho mē echōn ton huion tou theou tē zōēn ouk echei)*. The use of the negative *mē* serves to generalize the portrait of this individual as representative of his class. Two small but significant changes in the statement may be noted. The full title "the Son of God" now spells out the true identity of the one whom the unbeliever is spurning. He is the very embodiment of "the life" that the unbeliever needs. In the preceding statement John places the articular designation "the life" after the verb; now "the life" is placed emphatically before the verb, making prominent the life which is beyond the grasp of the one who does not have the Son. Without Him he is spiritually dead. It is a sober message to realize that this sad assertion brings us to the close of the main body of the epistle. But, as Smalley notes, "a practical call to decision is also implicit. Life-giving faith is possible, and therefore it should be exercised and maintained!"[15]

---

[13]Westcott, p. 188.

[14]Smalley, p. 288.

[15]*Ibid.*, p. 289.

16

Epilogue: The Confidence and Certainties of Believers (5:13-21)

5:13 These things have I written unto you that believe on the name of the Son of God; that ye may know that ye have eternal life, and that ye may believe on the name of the Son of God.

14 And this is the confidence that we have in him, that, if we ask any thing according to his will, he heareth us:

15 And if we know that he hear us, whatsoever we ask, we know that we have the petitions that we desired of him.

16 If any man see his brother sin a sin *which is* not unto death, he shall ask, and he shall give him life for them that sin not unto death. There is a sin unto death: I do not say that he shall pray for it.

17 All unrighteousness is sin: and there is a sin not unto death.

18 We know that whosoever is born of God sinneth not; but he that is begotten of God keepeth himself, and that wicked one toucheth him not.

19 *And* we know that we are of God, and the whole world lieth in wickedness.

20 And we know that the Son of God is come, and hath given us an understanding, that we may know him that is true, and we are in him that is true, *even* in his Son Jesus Christ. This is the true God, and eternal life.

21 Little children, keep yourselves from idols. Amen.

The first four verses of 1 John form the Prologue to the epistle, setting forth the foundational realities of the Christian gospel; these concluding verses appropriately form an Epilogue to the epistle, restating and supplementing the ringing realities that have been set forth. In verse 13 John declares that his basic purpose in writing is to assure his readers that they have eternal life through faith in the Son of God. In verses 14-17 John enlarges upon the results of that assurance in relation to the believer's practice of prayer and intercession. In verses 18-20 he sums up the thrust of the apostolic message in three ringing certainties. He brings the epistle to an abrupt close in verse 21 with an urgent call to the readers to effectively keep themselves from idols.

A. The Purpose in Writing to Assure Believers of Eternal Life (v. 13)

Verse 13 seems clearly to introduce the conclusion to the epistle, as suggested by "its shift to the first person, its reference to the writing of the epistle, and its emphasis on knowing."[1] Viewed as a summary statement of 1 John, this verse has been characterized as "the text of the whole Epistle."[2] This statement of purpose at the close of the body of the epistle brings to mind the stated purpose of the Fourth Gospel: "that ye might believe that Jesus is the Christ, the Son of God; and that believing ye might have life through his name" (20:31). The stated aim of the Fourth Gospel is evangelistic, but the stated purpose here indicated that this epistle was written to confirm the faith of those "that believe on the name of the Son of God."

Verse 13 presents a textual problem. Following the initial clause, "These things I have written unto you," the King James Version, following the Textus Receptus, has a longer text: "These things have I written unto you that believe on the name of the Son of God; that ye may know that ye have eternal life, and that ye may believe on the name of the Son of God." This is the reading of three uncial manuscripts of the 8th and 9th centuries and most of the later minuscule manuscripts. Proponents of the longer reading suggest that the shorter text may have arisen through scribal elimination of the apparent redundancy. Hodges supports the longer reading with the following remarks: "It actually prepares the ground for the discussion about prayer which follows by inviting continued faith in God's Son on the part of those who already have received eternal life through Him."[3] But most modern textual editors[4] agree that it is more likely that the reading of the

---

[1] R. Alan Culpepper, *1 John, 2 John, 3 John*, Knox Preaching Guides (Atlanta: John Knox Press, 1985), p. 106.

[2] James Morgan, *The Epistle of John* (1865; reprint ed., Minneapolis: Klock & Klock Christian Publishers, 1982), p. 467.

[3] Zane C. Hodges, "1 John," in *The Bible Knowledge Commentary, New Testament* (Wheaton, Ill.: Victor Books, 1983), p. 902.

[4] Eberhard Nestle, *Hē Kainē Diathēkē* (London: British and Foreign Bible Society, 1904); Alexander Souter, *Novum Testamentum Graece*, 2nd ed. (1947; reprint ed., Oxford: Clarendon Press, 1962); Kurt Aland et al., ed. *The Greek New Testament*, 1st ed. (New York: American Bible Society, 1966); Kurt Aland et al., ed. *The Greek New Testament*, 3rd ed. (New York: United Bible Societies, 1975); Nestle-Aland, *Novum Testamentum Graece*, 26th ed. (Stuttgart: Deutsche Bibelstiftung, 1979); R.V.G. Tasker, *The Greek New Testament, Being the Text Translated in the New English Bible 1961* (Oxford; Cambridge: University Press, 1964).

earlier witnesses (Aleph B, Syriac) is the original, "especially since *hina pisteuēte* seems to have arisen as a scribal assimilation to the statement in Jn 20.31."[5] The Rotherham translation represents well the structure of the verse in its shorter form:

> These things have I written unto you–
>> In order that you may know that ye have Life Age-abiding–
>> Unto you who believe on the name of the Son of God.

Thus the opening clause refers to the things John has written, followed by a purpose clause indicating his aim and an appositional concluding clause explicitly depicting the spiritual identity of those addressed. Like the King James Version, the majority of our modern English versions reverse the second and third clauses.[6] In our study of the verse, we adhere to the original order.

In the opening clause, "These things have I written unto you" *(Tauta egrapsea humin),* the intended scope of "these things" has been differently understood. Some interpreters[7] hold that the reference is to 5:1-12 or to verses 11-12, based on the similarity in thought and language. Then verse 13 is viewed as emphatically applying these truths to the readers. But others hold that John's statement more naturally looks back to the epistle as a whole.[8] This connection is supported by the fact that this statement of purpose clearly sums up what John has been doing in this epistle. Plummer points to the close connection between the statement of purpose in 1:4 and 5:13 and remarks that "there is nothing there or here, as there is in ii. 26,

---

[5]Bruce M. Metzger, *A Textual Commentary on the Greek New Testament* (London: United Bible Societies, 1971), p. 718.

[6]So RSV, NASB, NIV, NEB, Jerusalem Bible, Goodspeed, Richard Francis Weymouth, *The New Testament in Modern Speech,* revised by James Alexander Robertson (New York: Harper & Brothers, 1929); Gerrit Verkuyla, ed., *The Modern Language Bible, The New Berkeley Version* (Grand Rapids: Zondervan, 1969).

[7]A. E. Brooke, *A Critical and Exegetical Commentary on the Johannine Epistles,* International Critical Commentary (New York: Charles Scribner's Sons, 1912), p. 142; Amos N. Wilder and Paul W. Hoon, "The First, Second, and Third Epistles of John," in *The Interpreter's Bible* (New York: Abingdon Press, 1957), 12:297; Hodges, p. 902.

[8]Alfred Plummer, *The Epistles of S. John,* Cambridge Bible for Schools and Colleges (1183; reprint ed., London: Cambridge University Press, 1938), p. 165; Brooke Foss Westcott, *The Epistle of St. John, The Greek Text with Notes,* 3rd ed. (1892; reprint ed., Grand Rapids: Eerdmans, 1950), p. 188; C. H. Dodd, *The Johannine Epistles,* Moffatt New Testament Commentary (New York: Harper & Row, 1946), p. 133; Rudolf Bultmann, *The Johannine Epistles,* Hermeneia–A Critical and Historical Commentary on the Bible (Philadelphia: Fortress Press, 1973), p. 83; J. H. Houlden, *A Commentary on the Johannine Epistle,* Harper's New Testament Commentaries (New York: Harper & Row, 1973), p. 137; Stephen S. Smalley, *1, 2, 3 John,* Word Biblical Commentary (Waco, Texas: Word Books, 1984), p. 289.

to limit 'these things' to what immediately precedes.''[9] As Burdick observes, ''In 1:4 John uses the present tense *graphomen,* 'we are writing,' to describe his task in its beginning, whereas in 5:13 he employs the aorist indicative (*egrapsa,* 'I have written') to look back on the task he has completed.''[10] This view is supported by the parallel to the statement of purpose in John 20:31, leading Brown to remark, ''One wonders could the author in 5:13 consciously have confined himself to just the preceding verses.''[11] It seems most natural to accept that here, as in John 20:30-31, the statement of purpose relates to all that has gone before, in each instance followed by supplementary material.

John's stated purpose in writing is ''that ye may know that ye have eternal life'' *(hina eidēte hoti zōēn echete aiōnion).* The verb ''know'' *(eidēte,* an old perfect subjunctive with a present meaning) denotes a ''knowledge that is characterized by assurance, something known with certainty.''[12] His aim is to strengthen and deepen the assurance they already have, thereby promoting ''the inward peace and firm confidence toward God which are essential to vigorous growth and sustained activity in the spiritual life.''[13] Such a purpose is still timely. Stott remarks,

> It is common today to decry any claim to assurance of salvation, to dismiss it as presumptuous, and to affirm that no certainty is possible on this side of death. But certainty and humility do not exclude one another. If God's revealed purpose is not only that we should hear, believe and live, but also that we should know, presumptuousness lies in doubting His word, not in trusting it.[14]

The assurance John has in view is not the result of wishful thinking but is firmly grounded in the varied evidences set forth in the epistle.

The content of this assured knowledge is ''that ye have eternal life'' *(hoti zōēn echete aiōnion,* literally, ''that life you are having eternal''). The position of the adjective ''eternal'' at the end of the clause emphasizes the nature of that life, ''life that is endless (as to time) and life that is God-

---

[9]Plummer, p. 165.

[10]Donald W. Burdick, *The Letters of John the Apostle* (Chicago: Moody Press, 1985), p. 385.

[11]Raymond E. Brown, *The Epistles of John,* The Anchor Bible (Garden City, N.Y.: Doubleday & Co. 1982), p. 608.

[12]Burdick, p. 386.

[13]George G. Findlay, *Fellowship in the Life Eternal, An Exposition of the Epistles of St John* (New York: Hodder and Stoughton, n.d.), p. 396.

[14]J.R.W. Stott, *The Epistles of John,* Tyndale New Testament Commentary (Grand Rapids: Eerdmans, 1964), p. 185.

breathed (as to quality).''[15] The present tense presents this assurance as a contemporary and ongoing conscious possession.

Those who have the assurance that they have eternal life are given expanded identification in the third clause in the Greek: ''that believe on the name of the Son of God'' (*tois pisteuousin eis to onoma tou huiou tou theou,* more literally, ''to those believing into the name of the Son of God''). They are a distinctive group characterized by their active faith ''on the name of the Son of God.'' The preposition ''on'' (*eis,* ''into'') pictures their faith as entering into a living union with ''the name of the Son of God.'' Here, as ''in the faith and thought of virtually every nation the name is inextricably bound up with the person,''[16] involving all that that person is and does. Thus, as in 5:10, John identifies a true believer as one who ''believeth on the Son of God,'' so here true believers are designated as believing ''on the name of the Son of God.'' Involved is all that John has insisted upon concerning the identity of the man Jesus with the Son of God. It marks the sharp antithesis between their faith and the heretical views of the false teachers. This is the ninth and last occurrence of the verb ''believe'' in this epistle, and again it presents a Christ-centered faith as fundamental to true Christianity.

B. The Confidence of Believers Before God (vv. 14-17)

In accepting verse 13 as a summary statement looking back to the epistle as a whole, questions naturally arise concerning the true character of the remainder of the epistle. Clearly the passage suggests the aspect of a post-script or appendix, analogous to the 21st chapter of the Gospel of John. Interpreters advance numerous conjectures as to its origin. Bultmann sees in verses 14-21 the work of a later redactor and repeatedly attributes the wording in this section to the assumed redactor.[17] Plummer remarks that some critics ''go so far as to conjecture that the same person added chap. xxi to the Gospel and the last nine verses to the Epistle after the Apostle's death.''[18] But historically there is no evidence for this conjecture since both Tertullian (c. 160/170–c. 215-20)[19] and Clement of Alexandria (c. 155–c. 220) quoted from these closing verses and ''both these writers in quoting mention S.

---

[15]Edward A. McDowell, ''1-2-3 John,'' in *The Broadman Bible Commentary* (Nashville: Broadman Press, 1972), 12:223.

[16]H. Bietenhard, ''Name, *Onoma,*'' in *The New International Dictionary of New Testament Theology,* ed. Colin Brown (Grand Rapids: Zondervan, 1976), 2:648.

[17]Bultmann repeatedly attributes the wording to ''the redactor'' in this section, pp. 85-91.

[18]Plummer, p. 164.

[19]The dates are those given in J. D. Douglas, ed., *The New International Dictionary of the Christian Church* (Grand Rapids: Zondervan, 1974).

John by name.''[20] Nor is it likely that a later redactor could compose an appendix so clearly reflecting the language and structure of John. Accepting these verses as an unquestioned part of the original epistle, we see no need to spend more time on these conjectures.

Having expressed his assurance concerning his beloved readers, John feels the need to add some further guidance based on their assurance. Lenski remarks, "The fact that John is thinking of the dangers that are besetting his readers becomes evident in what he adds."[21] As Findlay suggests, John has no desire simply to let his dear readers "rest in the quiet assurance of salvation, to luxuriate in the comfort of a settled faith and a clear sense of the Divine grace in Christ."[22] The connecting "and" in verse 14 indicates that he expects their assurance of a living relationship with God to express itself in active prayer and intercession. In verses 14-15 John deals with the believer's confidence before God in prayer, and in verses 16-17 he relates that confidence to the practice of intercession.

1. The Confidence of Answered Prayer (vv. 14-15)

John speaks of the condition for answered prayer (v. 14) and the assurance of answered prayer (v. 15).

a. The condition for answered prayer (v. 14). "And this is the confidence that we have in him" *(Kai hautē estin hē parrhēsia hēn echomen pros auton)* contains the fourth reference to the believer's "confidence" in this epistle. In 2:28 and 4:17 John uses the term in connection with the believer's confidence at Christ's return. In 3:21-22 and here it relates to the believer's present confidence as he stands before God in prayer. In each instance it is confidence Godward, grounded in our relationship with Him. As a compound noun, the word "confidence" *(parrhēsia, par* = "all" and *rhēsis* = "speech")* basically denotes that freedom of speech which enables us to express our thoughts and desires before God without hesitancy or fear of embarrassment. The relationship in view goes back to the fact of our "fellowship" with God with which John began the epistle (1:3) and then developed in Part I.

The demonstrative "this" *(hautē)* again looks forward to the following "that" clause, and "we have" *(echomen)* marks this confidence as the present possession of John and fellow believers. The preposition rendered "in" *(pros)*, "in him," basically means "near, facing,"[23] and with the

---

[20]Plummer, p. 164.

[21]R.C.H. Lenski, *The Interpretation of the Epistles of St. Peter, St. John and St. Jude* (Columbus, Ohio: Wartburg Press, 1945), p. 532.

[22]Findlay, p. 399.

[23]H. E. Dana and Julius R. Mantey, *A Manual Grammar of the Greek New Testament* (1927; reprint ed., New York: The Macmillan Co., 1967), p. 110.

accusative it pictures the believer in an intimate face-to-face relationship with God in prayer. The pronoun "him" *(auton)* may refer to "the Son of God" (v. 13) as the nearest antecedent, but more probably the reference is to God the Father, since Christian prayer is generally addressed to Him. This imprecision in the pronoun in relation to God is characteristically Johannine; he accepts both as truly one in nature and knows that prayer can freely be addressed to either.

The believer approaches God with the assurance "that, if we ask any thing according to his will, he heareth us." The indefinite "anything" *(ti)* leaves unrestricted the content of the request, indicating our "freedom to approach God in prayer anywhere and anytime."[24] Since John here uses the middle voice, "if we ask any thing" *(ean ti aitōmetha),* some, such as Westcott[25] and Lenski,[26] hold that the request being presented involves the personal interest of the one making it. Although a personal interest in the request being made is natural and desirable, others[27] insist that the classical distinction between the active and the middle can no longer be insisted on in the Koine Greek. Thus Arndt and Gingrich point to James 4:2-3 as an example of the interchangeable usage.[28] The verb in itself simply indicates a request being presented for something to be done, whether specifically concerning our own interests or not.

But the added phrase "according to His will" *(kata to thelēma autou)* marks an important limitation upon our assurance that a specific request will be granted. In 3:21-22 John speaks of confidence that our request would be answered "because we keep his commandments, and do those things that are pleasing in his sight." Here the condition is that our prayers are "according to his will." The two conditions set forth the human and the divine aspects for effective prayer. Any prayer that is assured of God's answer must be offered "according to" *(kata* with the accusative, "down along the line" or "in harmony with") God's will. "Answers to prayer do not depend on a right diagnosis or analysis of the problem by us as we pray," Jackman reminds us, "but on a childlike submission to the Father, knowing that he will give what is best *according to his will.* If he were to answer on any other basis, which of us would ever dare to pray again? We do not have that

---

[24]Simon J. Kistemaker, *Exposition of the Epistles of James and the Epistles of John,* New Testament Commentary (Grand Rapids: Baker, 1986), p. 360.

[25]Westcott, p. 190.

[26]Lenski, p. 533.

[27]Brooke, p. 144; Brown, p. 609; Smalley, p. 295.

[28]William F. Arndt and F. Wilbur Gingrich, *A Greek-English Lexicon of the New Testament and Other Early Christian Literature* (Chicago: University of Chicago Press, 1957), p. 25.

sort of wisdom."[29] Yet whenever we have a request concerning which we are not assured that it is in accord with His will, we can follow the example of Jesus in the Garden of Gethsemane when He prayed for the removal of "the cup" but added "nevertheless not what I will, but what thou wilt" (Mark 14:36; cf. also John 12:27-28). Prayer is not a device for imposing our will upon God, but rather the bending of our will to His in the desire that His good will may be done. "Prayer, according to God's will," G. Williams notes, "is an activity growing out of the consciousness of the sweet relationship of a child and a father. Such an intimacy involves harmoniousness of will and only asks for what accords with that will."[30]

When praying according to God's will, we are assured that "he heareth us" *(akouei hēmōn)*, not merely listens to our prayer but listens favorably. Culpepper remarks that this is "a bulwark against despair. Hope and confidence can always thrive when one knows that God listens to his children."[31] And in asking for what they know to be God's will, His saints have the glorious privilege of working together with God in furthering His sovereign purposes for themselves as well as the Church. Such praying "unites puny man to Almighty God in a miraculous partnership. . . . It is the most noble and most essential ministry God gives to His children."[32]

b. The assurance of the granted request (v. 15). Verse 15 restates and amplifies on the preceding verse. Thus the two verbs "ask/hears" are repeated but in reverse order to form a chiasmus: ("ask . . . heareth / hear . . . ask"), and "in him" reappears as "of him." John is intent on holding before his readers the exalted privilege of answered prayer.

The conditional statement "and if we know that He hear us, whatsoever we ask" implies no doubt; it is assumed *(ean* with the indicative)[33] that the stated condition in verse 14 is being met. There is the assurance that our confidence is justified. The use of the first-person plural "we" in both verses, Smalley suggests, "implies that John is thinking of those within his own community, and all orthodox members of the Christian Church."[34] Effective praying can be the experience of all true believers. The consistent use of the

---

[29]David Jackman, *The Message of John's Letters,* The Bible Speaks Today (Downers Grove, Ill.: Inter-Varsity Press, 1988), p. 161.

[30]George Williams, *The Student's Commentary on the Holy Scriptures, Analytical, Synoptical, and Synthetical,* 5th ed. (London: Oliphants, 1940), p. 1017.

[31]Culpepper, pp. 108-9.

[32]P. J. Johnstone, *Operation World, A Handbook for World Intercession* (Bromley, Kent, England: STL Publications, 1978), p. 15.

[33]The use of *ean* with the indicative occurs elsewhere in the New Testament only a few times. The usage is probably colloquial.

[34]Smalley, p. 295.

present-tense verbs seems to imply that such praying is the ongoing experience of the Christian community.

John now states the scope of our requests comprehensively: "whatsoever we ask" (*ho ean aithometha*, "in [or "as to"] that which if we may be asking"). It widens the possible scope of Christian praying to anything in God's will that will further the divine cause. Having submitted his will to God's will, the believer feels at liberty to make any request, however unusual, which he knows to be in God's will and purpose.

Assurance in asking results in assurance of God's answer: "we know that we have the petitions that we desired of him" (*oidamen hoti echomen ta aitēmata ha ētēkamen ap' autou*). The repeated use of "we know" echoes our personal assurance concerning "the petitions that we desired," the different things which formed the subject matter of our petitions. The present tense, "we have" (*echomen*), is not merely futuristic, "will have;" faith accepts them as ours. Their actual reception may not be immediately experienced, or their actual bestowal may be gradually realized in subsequent experience. The plural "the petitions" indicates that this is true of the varied petitions that we have asked "of Him" (*ap' autou*); the petitions were directed *to* Him with the expectation that the answers would flow *from* Him as their true source. Requests for things or events concerning the future must be viewed in relation to the future in view. There are requests for immediate spiritual needs in our own lives where we can by faith appropriate God's immediate response.

2. The Counsel in Respect to Intercession (vv. 16-17)

Without the use of any connective particle, John turns to the practice of intercession for others as an assumed aspect of Christian prayer. John notes an occasion which prompts the believer's intercession (v. 16a) and states the results of such intercession (v. 16b). He further notes that the nature of the sin in view may place a limitation on the practice of intercession (v. 16c). Verse 17 is a note of warning and also a word of encouragement for the intercessors.

a. The specific occasion prompting the intercession (v. 16a). The occasion is precisely presented: "If any man see his brother sin a sin *which is* not unto death." The opening "if" (*ean*) presents the scene as hypothetical, but the condition assumes that the situation depicted may actually occur. John realistically accepts the fact that a Christian may sin. The indefinite "if any man see" (*ean tis idē*, "if any one may see") opens the resultant intercessory function to any member of the church, regardless of his rank or status among the brethren. The call to him for his intercession comes whenever he may "see his brother sin a sin *which is* not unto death" (*idē ton adelphon autou hamartanonta hamartian mē pros thanaton*). The aorist verb "see" (*idē*, "may see" as a specific occurrence) makes clear that it is not merely a matter of personal suspicion but an observed fact. It is not a matter of becoming convinced of the purely inward sinful state of the one observed but of an actual sinful deed committed by "his brother," a known member of the Christian brotherhood. The unidentified believer has observed "his brother sin a sin" (*ton adelphon hamartanonta hamartian,* "the brother sinning a sin" or "sinning sin"). The expression "sinning a sin," occurring only here in the New Testament, marks the outward nature of the act and underlines its sinfulness. The present participle with the anarthrous noun "sin" may denote either that he was observed in the very act of committing a specific sin or that he was seen as he engaged in some sinful practice. Under either view the observing believer recognized the sinful nature of the event but understood that it was a sin *"which is* not unto death" (*mē pros thanaton,* "not facing death"). This striking expression occurs three times in verses 16-17, while its opposite, "a sin unto death," occurs once. John does not discuss the distinguishing mark of either.

The observed sin, characterized as "a sin *which is* not unto death," is recognized as not surely fatal. This is evident from the fact that the preposition used is not *eis,* ("into") but *pros* ("facing," or "moving in the direction of") death, but not as sin's ultimate outcome. Lias remarks that John was "accustomed to look forward to the ultimate result, not only of *actions* but of *conditions.*"[35] Sin as lawlessness (3:4) and unrighteousness (5:17) by its very nature moves in the direction of death (James 1:15), but that destiny is averted as the individual repents of the sin and is forgiven. John here envisions that fatal outcome being averted as the brother who had seen him sin engages in intercession for him.

b. The indicated result of the intercession (v. 16b). The response to the scene observed is stated: "he shall ask, and he shall give him life for them that sin not unto death" (*aitēsei, kai dōsei autō zōēn, tois hamartanousin mē pros thanaton*). Two future verbs depict the resultant action. The rendering of the first verb, "he shall ask," assumes that the future tense has the force of a gentle imperative, setting forth the way the believer should respond to the observed scene. But it is more probable that the verb has the force of a regular future, stating it as a matter of course that the one who observed "will ask" for his brother. As a true believer he will not be indifferent to what he has seen, nor say with Cain, "*Am* I my brother's keeper?" (Gen. 4:9; cf. 1 John 3:11-12). His love for his fellow believer will prompt him to engage in intercession for him. "For John," Barker observes, "it would be obvious that not to pray for a brother would be as

---

[35]John James Lias, *An Exposition of the First Epistle of John* (1887; reprint ed., Minneapolis: Klock & Klock Christian Publishers, 1982), p. 402.

much a betrayal of God's love as to withhold material aid from him if he hungered or thirsted (3:17)."[36]

The fact that neither of the two closely connected verbs, "he shall ask, and he shall give," has an expressed subject creates difficulty for the interpreter. Scholars advocate two views as to the intended subject of the second verb: either that *God* "shall give," or that the *intercessor* "shall give," assuming that the obvious subject of the first verb is also the subject here. Advocates of the latter view[37] hold that the construction indicates that the two closely related verbs have the same subject and insist that it "seems rather violent to give them different nominatives."[38] They insist that if John had intended the second verb to have a different subject than the first he would have thought it necessary to state the subject explicitly. It is pointed out that verses 14-17 are an unfolding of the believer's confidence expressed in verse 14. In support proponents of this view also appeal to James 5:20.

Proponents of the view that the subject of this second verb is God point to the contents of this epistle. "That God is the subject is supported by the Johannine view that God gives life (5:11) and the believer possesses it (5:12) rather than distributes it; cf. John 5:26; 10:28; 17:2."[39] Certainly the Scriptures teach that God is the only true source of spiritual life and that sinful mankind can receive eternal life only from Him. But the ambiguity in John's statement seems to suggest that God delights to perform His saving work on behalf of His sinning people in connection with the Spirit-prompted intercession of the saints. Such intercessory prayer does make a needed impact on the sad situation. In 2:1 John presents Christ as the sinning believer's Advocate with the Father, but Revelation 1:6; 5:8; 8:3-4 make it clear that God works in connection with the prayers of the saints. John knows that when a believer sins "the restoration is in many cases effected rather by the pleading of intercession with God than by pleading of expostulation with the offender."[40] Knowing that his intercession for the sinning brother is in accord with God's will, the intercessor has the glorious privilege of working with God in the fulfilment of His redemptive purposes. Thus

---

[36]Glen W. Barker, "I John," in *The Expositor's Bible Commentary* (Grand Rapids: Zondervan, 1981), 12:355.

[37]Brooke, p. 146; Plummer, p. 167; Lias, pp. 403-6; Bultmann, p. 87, notes 16.

[38]Plummer, p. 167.

[39]David M. Scholer, "Sins Within and Sin Without: An Interpretation of I John 5:16-17," in Gerald F. Hawthorne, ed., *Current Issues in Biblical and Patristic Interpretation* (Grand Rapids: Eerdmans, 1975), p. 240, note 53.

[40]Findlay, *Fellowship in the Life Eternal*, p. 403.

"Spirit-empowered, Bible-based praying is working with God at the very point where the action lies!"[41]

In the remainder of the statement, "and he shall give him life for them that sin not unto death" (*dōsei autō zōēn, tois hamartanousin mē pros thanaton,* or "he [God] shall give him life for [or "to"] them that sin") there also is some uncertainty as to the intended identity of "him" *(autō).* The pronoun may denote either the one interceding, or the one sinning. The literal rendering of Rotherham, "He shall ask and He will grant unto him life,–For them who are sinning not unto death," clearly implies that life is granted to the intercessor to be shared with those sinning. (Similarly ASV, RSV, and NEB). The KJV rendering, "he shall give him life for them that sin" implies that God gives life to, or through, the intercessor for those sinning. The NIV changes the grammatical construction to indicate that "him" refers to the one sinning: "God will give him life. I refer to those whose sin does not lead to death."[42] Under either view the notable change from the singular pronoun "him" *(autō)* to the articular plural participle "them that sin" *(tois hamartanousin)* enlarges upon the scope of such an effective prayer ministry, not only in this individual case but also in other similar instances. The assurance that God will give "life" to the sinning brother does not imply that he no longer possesses spiritual life. The reference is not to the original gift of life at regeneration but rather to the restoration and promotion of the life that sin is threatening. It results in a strengthening of the life already possessed (3:14; 5:11-13), prompting a fuller spiritual life and victory in Christ.

c. The suggested limitation on such intercession (v. 16c). John is well aware that the nature of the sin being committed can negate the effectiveness of the believer's intercession. John categorically declares, "There is a sin unto death" *(estin hamartia pros thanaton),* but he does not identify the individual thus guilty. He does not say that the individual thus guilty was a brother, nor is the sin identified. Without the article, the noun "sin" may denote some specific sin or a state of sin. Clearly it is a sin persisted in until it culminates in death. John apparently assumes that the observant believer will be able to distinguish between these two types of sin, but he offers no guiding criteria.

---

[41]D. Edmond Hiebert, *Working With God: Scriptural Studies in Intercession* (New York: Carlton Press, 1987), p. 122.

[42]The view that "him" *(autō)* refers to the one sinning seems supported by the comma placed in the Greek text after *zōēn* ("life") in the text of B.F. Westcott and F.J.A. Hort, *The New Testament in the Original Greek,* 2nd ed. (1881; reprint ed., New York: Macmillan Co., 1935); Nestle-Aland, *Novum Testamentum Graece,* 26th ed.; United Bible Societies, *The Greek New Testament,* 3rd ed.; and Tasker.

As to the intercessor's response to a case of "sin unto death," John simply remarks, "I do not say that he shall pray for it" (*ou peri ekeinēs legō hina erōtēsē,* literally, "not concerning this [sin] I say that he should make request"). The forward position of "for this" *(peri ekeinēs),* makes the reference to this sin emphatic. "The sin unto death is isolated and regarded in its terrible distinctness."[43] The distinctness of the sin at once raises the question concerning the intercessor's reaction. John states his own response negatively: "Not . . . I am saying that he should make request." He does not expressly prohibit intercession in the case, but Smalley notes that "the use of *ou* ('not') at a distance from *legō* ('I say,' or 'I command') implies that the dissuasion is mild."[44] The use of the singular "I say," only here in the epistle, suggests that John is offering his own feeling in the matter. Clearly the reaction is due to the nature of this sin, which John obviously believes was deliberate and self-willed. The effectiveness of intercessory prayer is limited by the mysterious power of self-determination with which God has endowed every human being. Here the use of the aorist-tense verb "pray" or "request" *(erōtēsē)* does not seem to have a meaning distinctly different from the verb "ask" *(aitēsei)* used earlier. In the context both verbs convey the thought of intercession. The singular subject "he" of both verbs suggests that the intercession John has in view is personal rather than a united congregational activity.

What then is this "sin unto death" for which intercession is not enjoined? Both the identity of the sin and the nature of the resultant death have been differently understood.[45] Used without a definite article, both nouns "sin" and "death" are qualitative rather than specific. Any suggestions as to their identity are best made in the light of the epistle as a whole.

One view is that "sin unto death" is a sin so serious "that God judges that sin with swift physical death."[46] Bruce expounds this view as follows:

> Elsewhere in the New Testament instances occur of sins which caused the death of the persons committing them, when these persons were church members. Ananias and Sapphira come to mind (Acts 5. 1-11); the incestuous man at Corinth is possibly another example, if he suffered 'the destruction of the flesh' in the literal sense (1 Cor. 5.5), and those other Corinthian

---

[43]Westcott, p. 192.

[44]Smalley, p. 301.

[45]For an elaborate discussion of views concerning the petitions, penalties, and types of sins see Brown, pp. 610-17.

[46]Hodges, p. 902.

Christians who are said to have 'fallen asleep' because of their profanation of the Lord's Supper (1. Cor. 11. 30) certainly provide further examples.[47]

This view assumes that those guilty of this fatal sin were believers and members of the local church; it was indeed the fact of their death that showed that they were guilty of "sin unto death." But since John does not explicitly prohibit intercession for those thus guilty, it would seem that he at least condones prayer for those who had thus died; this would involve intercession for the dead! The conditions within the church thus implied do not seem consistent with the spiritual state of the readers addressed since the departure of the false teachers from among them (2:19). The only other direct mention of "death" in this epistle is the double occurrence in 3:14, where its meaning clearly is spiritual, not physical death. And in 3:15 John pictures the murderous attitude that hatred produces as the very antithesis of "eternal life." The expression "unto death" in John 11:4 cannot be used as a parallel to support the view that John here means physical death, because the context is different. There the reference is to "sickness unto death"; here it is used of "*sin* unto death." In the New Testament, "death," whether used of physical or spiritual death, denotes a separation which is viewed as the penal consequence of sin.[48] Sin produces separation: in physical death the result is the separation of man's nonmaterial being from his physical body; in spiritual death the soul is separated from God; in eternal death the human being is banished from the presence of God. It seems clear that "death" here "refers to a spiritual rather than a physical condition; i.e., separation from the life which is only available in Christ."[49]

Accepting that John here refers to spiritual death, we still face the question of the identity of the sin that produces this separation from God. Since all sin, as regards its nature and tendency, moves "unto death," this is clearly a sin that is carried to its ultimate conclusion. As Jackman remarks,

> It is not the magnitude of the sin that prevents its pardon, as though there existed this one sin for which Christ's sacrifice was insufficient. Rather, it is the attitude and disposition of the sinner that excludes the possibility of forgiveness.[50]

---

[47]F. F. Bruce, *The Epistles of John* (Old Tappan, N.J.: Revell, 1970), p. 124. In his commentary Bruce does not explicitly commit himself to this view, but in his book *Answers to Questions* (Grand Rapids: Zondervan, 1973), p. 134, he does commit himself to this view.

[48]W. E. Vine, *An Expository Dictionary of New Testament Words with Their Precise Meanings for English Readers* (London: Oliphants, 1939), 1:276.

[49]Culpepper, p. 110.

[50]Jackman, p. 164.

In view of what John has said about the false teachers (2:18-23; 4:1-3; 5:10), it is clear that he has in view the persistent attitude of those who separate from the true Church and pervert or reject the apostolic message of redemption in Jesus Christ, the incarnate Son of God. In thus persistently rejecting the divine provision for forgiveness, they commit themselves to a spiritual disposition and course of conduct which can only be described as "sin unto death." Characterized by full and deliberate unbelief in the incarnate Redeemer, they are fatally guilty of sinning against the remedy.

   d. *The concluding warning and encouragement to intercessors* (v. 17). Without a connecting particle John abruptly terminates the subject of prayer and intercession by reminding the intercessor of two unacceptable attitudes toward sin. The double statement is the last reference to "sin" in the epistle. The assertion "all unrighteousness is sin" *(pas adikia hamartia estin)* raises a warning against any careless assumption that some forms of sin are inconsequential. The fact that there are sins "not unto death" does not minimize their seriousness. The term "unrighteousness" *(adikia)* portrays sin in its negative character as a departure from, or failure to measure up to, the divine standard of what is right. As Vine notes, it is "the comprehensive term for wrong, or wrong-doing, as between persons."[51] But the term should not be restricted to breaches of duty in social relations; it covers anything wrong, anything that involves unfairness, injustice, or unkindness. The enlightened conscience becomes aroused whenever such deviations are measured in the light of God's holiness and His revealed will for His own. The comprehensive assertion is a warning against and rejection of the claims of the Gnostics who maintained that their elite intellectual enlightenment and superior insights made them acceptable before God, and so they were indifferent to the moral demands for righteous living inherent in the gospel.

   The further assertion "and there is a sin not unto death" adds encouragement, prompting his readers to continue the practice of intercession for erring believers. The connecting "and" *(kai)* suggests that his readers must hold the two assertions of this sentence in proper balance. All sin is serious but not all is hopeless and beyond the reach of Christian intercession; this leaves a standing challenge to brotherly intercession. Such intercession for sinning believers is God's gracious provision in permitting His saints to work together with Him in furthering His redemptive purpose for their sinning brother.

C. The Certainties of the Christian Faith (vv. 18-20)

   Having spoken of the believer's confidence in connection with prayer and intercession, John next sets forth three ringing affirmations concerning

---

[51]Vine, 4:174.

the certainties of the Christian life. His triple declaration, each beginning with "we know," reasserts the realities set forth in the epistle. Findlay points out that the order of presentation is the order of experience: "St John's mind here travels up the stream, from the human to the Divine, from the present knowledge of salvation to the eternal counsels and character of God, out of which our being and salvation sprang."[52] John declares the believer's relationship to sin (v. 18), reasserts the crucial contrast between the believer and the world (v. 19), and again sets forth the reality of Christ's mission and its results (v. 20).

1. The Believer's Relationship to Sin (v. 18)

The threefold use of the verb "we know" *(oidamen)* in verses 18-20 suggests intuitive knowledge rather than the activity of acquiring knowledge. In this epistle the verb is always used in the plural, either in the first or second person, and thus relates to the corporate knowledge of true believers against the spurious claims of the heretics. The fact of human sin, which is touched on in each chapter of this epistle, plagues the life of the believer and is involved in the conflicts which mark the Christian life. (See the conflicts developed in Part 2.) In this verse John declares that the born-again believer does not practice sin, is being protected by Christ, and is secure from the re-enslaving efforts of Satan.

a. The believer and the practice of sin (v. 18a). Born-again believers collectively know "that whosoever is born of God sinneth not" *(hoti pas ho gegennēmenos ek tou theou ouch hamartanei,* literally, "that every one having been born of God not is sinning"). The construction *(pas* with the singular participle) places the assertion on the individual level but insists that there should be no exceptions to the stated rule. The rule applies to every one who "is born of God" *(gegennēmenos ek tou theou),* who has experienced the transforming reality of the new birth; he continues to be a born-again believer (see 2:9; 3:9; 5:1, 4). His new birth was not a passing experience, but the imparted new life continues to produce a spiritual change in him. In 3:9 John accounts for the change in the believer's conduct as due to the fact that God's "seed remaineth in him: and he cannot sin, because he is born of God." Here, as in 3:9, the present-tense verb, "sin," *(hamartanei)* portrays his characteristic practice. In 5:16 John notes that if a brother sins, his Christian brother will intercede for him; here he asserts that "whosoever is born of God sinneth not." This apparent contradiction illustrates the tension produced by sin in the believer. Plummer explains: "The one statement refers to possible but exceptional facts; the other to the habitual state. A child of God may sin; but his normal condition is one of resistance to sin."[53]

---

[52]Findlay, p. 416.
[53]Plummer, p. 169.

b. The believer and Christ's keeping (v. 18b). John continues his statement with the strong adversative "but" *(all')*, pointing to the dilemma in the believer's life produced by the presence of sin and the operation of the supernatural within. The real answer to his problem with sin lies in the fact that "he that is begotten of God keepeth himself" *(ho gennētheis ek tou theou tērei auton)*. The intended force of this statement is beset with difficulty.[54] The NASB rendering, "He who was born of God keeps him" (see also RV, ASV, NIV, NEB, etc.), contains two distinct changes from the KJV rendering, "he that is begotten of God keepeth himself." The first change depends upon the interpretation of the aorist passive participle *(ho gennētheis)* whereas the second change involves the problem of the pronoun, i.e., whether the original used a personal or a reflexive pronoun. The person intended in the unique expression "that is begotten" *(ho gennētheis)* is not immediately obvious. The King James rendering takes the aorist participle as denoting the born-again believer, but the NASB (and the other versions noted above) takes it as a reference to Jesus Christ. Having just used the perfect tense of the believer's birth in the preceding clause, the arresting change to the aorist tense here strongly suggests that a change in the one identified is intended. Both in his Gospel and in this epistle, John always uses the perfect tense to denote the born-again believer. To insist that the aorist tense here carries the same meaning seems arbitrary and confusing. Surely a change in meaning is intended by the unique expression here. Smalley remarks that "by using the same verb *(gennasthai,* 'to be born') to refer to Christ and the Christian, John may have wished to emphasize the identity of God's Son with his disciples (cf. 4:17); whereas the variation of tense . . . marks an ultimate difference in the two sonships (cf. John 5:26)."[55] Plummer notes that in "the Nicene Creed, 'begotten of the Father' *(ton ek tou Patros gennēthenta)* is the same form of expression as that used here for 'begotten of God' *(ho gennētheis ek tou theou)*."[56] As used of Christ, the aorist-tense participle has been differently understood. Thus Lias remarks that "the Son's generation is an eternal fact, incapable of alteration, addition, or completion"[57] whereas Smalley suggests that the aorist tense refers "to the specific event, in the past, of the birth of Jesus."[58] The former seems preferable, pointing to His eternal Sonship. In support of the view that the expression refers to Christ is the fact that the keeping or protection of the believer is a task that

---

[54]See Brown, pp. 620-22, for five different interpretations of this statement.
[55]Smalley, p. 303.
[56]Plummer, p. 170.
[57]Lias, p. 415.
[58]Smalley, p. 303.

the Fourth Gospel assigns to Christ (John 17:12). This fact is also found in 1 Peter 1:5, Jude 24, and Revelation 3:10. Burdick further asserts that "the concept of the believer keeping himself is not taught elsewhere in Scripture; in fact, it is quite contrary to what the Bible teaches on the subject."[59] The view that the reference is to Christ's keeping the believer establishes a striking contrast between the activity of Christ and "that wicked one" in the next clause. This interpretation demands that the pronoun denoting the one being kept cannot be the reflexive pronoun *(heauton)*. The manuscript evidence is divided between the reflexive and the personal pronouns and is not decisive.[60] When the scribes understood the aorist participles as a reference to the believer, they naturally changed the personal pronoun to the reflexive.

The verb rendered "keepeth" *(tērei)* has already occurred seven[61] times in connection with the believer's response to God's commandments with the meaning, "keep, observe, fulfil, pay attention to,"[62] but here in its last occurrence it is used with a personal object, "keeps him" (NASB) *(tērei auton)*. As Brooke notes, "With an accusative of the person *tērein* always has the sense in the N.T. of watching or guarding, in a friendly or hostile spirit."[63] In the present tense, the verb here describes Christ's continued action of preserving the believer from the dangers threatening him. Well aware of his own weaknesses and failures, the Spirit-guided believer can rejoice in the assurance that his own safekeeping does not depend solely upon his own efforts. "Our security is not our grip on Christ but His grip on us."[64] This, of course, does not imply that he can be indifferent to or relax his efforts to keep the commandments of God, but he knows that apart from the divine empowerment his own efforts would be ineffectual. He rejoices in the fact that "it is God who is at work in you, both to will and to work for His good pleasure" (Phil. 2:13 NASB).

c. The believer and the Satanic efforts (v. 18c). The added clause "and that wicked one toucheth him not" *(kai ho ponēros ouch haptetai autou)* sets forth our continuing need for Christ's protection. With "and" John sets side by side the rival supernatural realms contending for control over and possession of the individual human being. The title "that wicked one" *(ho ponēros)* underlines the malicious, evil-minded nature of the Devil as the

---

[59]Burdick, p. 393.

[60]For the manuscript evidence see United Bible Societies, *The Greek New Testament,* 3rd ed. On a scale A to D the editors rate the evidence for *auton* as C.

[61]1 John 2:3, 4, 5; 3:22, 24; 5:2, 3.

[62]Arndt and Gingrich, p. 822.

[63]Brooke, p. 149.

[64]David Smith, "The Epistles of St. John," in *the Expositor's Greek Testament* ([1897]; reprint ed., Grand Rapids: Eerdmans, n. d.), 5:199.

active enemy of the believer. As Morgan observes, "Ruined himself, his whole purpose and effort are to ruin others. Wickedness is the element in which he lives and delights."[65]

The words "toucheth him not" declare the comforting assurance that the Devil will fail in his efforts to recapture the believer. The verb "touch" *(haptetai)* denotes more than a superficial touch but rather suggests firm contact. In the middle voice it means "lay hold on" or "fasten to," and thus conveys the picture of the evil one seeking to fasten his grip on the believer; the present tense depicts his persistent effort. Although the verb may be used benevolently to bless, here it clearly conveys a hostile intention. Satan will assail the believer, but his slimy fingers will never regain an abiding grip on the redeemed soul. His attacks may be vicious and inspire fear, but the promise is that he will never destroy the true child of God. The security of the saint, even when he is tempted and sins, lies in the intercessory action of Christ on his behalf (cf. Luke 22:31-32).

2. The Contrast Between Believers and the World (v. 19).

John's second ringing certainty declares a decisive spiritual contrast: "We know that we are of God, and the whole world lieth in wickedness." True believers know that they belong to God and not to this world. This declared certainty challenges the readers to demonstrate that reality in their daily lives.

Believers have an abiding inner assurance concerning their spiritual origin: "We know that we are of God" *(oidamen hoti ek tou theou esmen,* more literally, "we know that out of God we are"). The author stresses the source of their new life. The verb "we are" asserts this relation as a fact, not a mere intellectual deduction. Brown notes that the expression implies "not only origin but a sense of belonging."[66] To be gripped with this certainty "is to be charged with a principle of righteousness that can dissolve every bond of iniquity, that breaks the power of worldly fear and pleasure and will make us, living or dying, more than conquerors."[67]

"And" adds the contrasting relationship that characterizes the world: "and the whole world lieth in wickedness" *(kai ho kosmos holos en to ponērō keitai).* The position of the adjective "whole" *(holos)* implies that the indicated relationship applies to all humans who belong to the world in its estrangement from God. The present-tense verb "lieth" *(keitai),* which basically means "to lie, recline," pictures the world as characteristically nonresistant to and passively dependent upon the power that grips the lost

---

[65]Morgan, p. 505.

[66]Brown, p. 622.

[67]Findlay, pp. 425-26.

masses of humanity; that power John identifies here as *tō ponerō,* which the KJV renders "in wickedness." This rendering interprets the articular noun as neuter, thus portraying the power dominating the world as an impersonal force. Since in verse 18 the term is clearly masculine, it is more probable that John here also uses the noun as masculine, "the wicked one." Thus Arndt and Gingrich render, "the world lies in (the power of) the evil one."[68] John did not say that the world is "of" (*ek,* "out of") the evil one, for the Devil is not the source of their being; he did not create them. He holds control over those in the world as a usurper, one "who controls it with tyrannical authority, organizing and orchestrating its life and activities to express his own rebellion and hatred against God."[69] Thus Jesus portrays the Devil as "the ruler of this world" (John 12:31 NASB; 14:30; 16:11).

It is a matter of lordship. For John there is no middle ground between these two spiritual masters and the realms which they head. As a free moral agent, man is free to choose his master, but he is not free to be without a master.

3. The Certainty Concerning Christ's Mission and Identity (v. 20)

The use of the particle "and" (*de,* better, "now, moreover") implies that something further and more fundamental is being added. This third assurance, the longest and most involved, is the ground and substance of the preceding two. John again asserts the Christian certainty that the Son of God has come (v. 20a), indicates the resultant gift of understanding (v. 20b), and expresses the resultant experiential realization of believers (v. 20c).

a. The assurance concerning the Son's coming (v. 20a). The opening clause, "we know that the Son of God is come" *(oidamen de hoti ho huios tou theou hēkei),* expresses the fundamental reality of the Christian faith. The title "the Son of God" reasserts the true deity of the one in whom Christian faith is centered whereas the verb "is come" asserts His historical appearance among men in incarnation. The verb *(hēkei,* a present-tense verb with the force of the perfect) expresses the finality of His appearing in incarnation. In contemporary Greek pagan usage this verb was used to record the solemn appearance of a god, and indeed John 1:14 portrays the solemn uniqueness of the incarnate Christ. The abiding reality of His incarnate appearing here on earth is essential for His present heavenly ministry (Heb. 2:17-18; 4:14-16).

b. The resultant gift of understanding (v. 20b). The message of Christianity is not only historically based but also involves personal experience: "and hath given us an understanding, that we may know him that is true." John's "and" *(kai)* serves to connect the historical and the experiential. The

---

[68] Arndt and Gingrich, p. 428.

[69] Jackman, p. 169.

perfect-tense verb, "hath given us an understanding" *(kai dedōken hēmin dianoian)*, marks the abiding nature of this gift of "understanding." This noun, which occurs only here in the Johannine writings, is a compound term *(dia,* "through," and *nous,* "mind," hence "a through mind"); it denotes the ability to pass beyond the external and superficial to discern and understand true reality. Involved is the mental ability to discern the true significance of the coming and person of the incarnate Son of God. This enlightenment also enables John and all true believers in Christ to see through and refute the heretical claims of the false teachers. It is the work of the Holy Spirit as God's "anointing" (2:27) that gives the believer this understanding.

John's statement adds that the chief objective of this gift of understanding is to lead us into a personal knowledge of God, "that we may know him that is true" *(hina ginōskōmen ton alēthinon).* The manuscript evidence is divided as to the mode of "know," indicative *(ginōskomen)* or subjunctive *(ginōskōmen).*[70] The manuscript evidence seems to support the indicative,[71] but the context suggests a purpose clause. Lias concludes, "If we read *ginōskomen,* we must interpret *in order that we may know, as in fact we do,* implying that the knowledge is both present and future."[72] Thus the unusual indicative expresses accomplished purpose; the Holy Spirit has brought to inner realization the divine intention that believers should come to know Him personally. As Jackman points out, "Understanding Christian truth is not a matter of mastering doctrinal formulations, important though they are, or of grasping philosophical ideas like those the gnostics propagated; but of meeting, knowing and submitting to the person who is truth, 'so that we may know him who is true.' "[73] John designates the person we have come to know as "him that is true" *(ton alēthinon,* "the true or real one").[74] It designates Him as the God who is genuine or real as opposed to the counterfeit gods of the heretics.

c. The union of believers with God (v. 20c). With a further "and" John adds that our knowledge of God results in our union with Him: "and we

---

[70]For the manuscript evidence see Nestle-Aland, *Novum Testamentum Graece,* 26th ed.

[71]In classical Greek *hina* was used with the subjunctive mode, but in Byzantine writers its use with the indicative was known. A. T. Robertson, *A Grammar of the Greek New Testament in the Light of Historical Research,* 5th ed. (New York: Harper & Brothers, 1914) concludes that *hina* with the indicative "occurs only three times in the N.T." but adds, "It is so common in later writers as not to surprise us in the N.T." (p. 984).

[72]Lias, pp. 419-20. Italics in original.

[73]Jackman, pp. 170-71.

[74]The manuscripts show some variant readings. Some add *theon* ("God") either before or after the adjective *alēthinon* whereas some scribes use the neuter *to elēthinon.* See United Bible Societies, *The Greek New Testament,* 3rd ed.

are in Him that is true, *even* in His Son Jesus Christ.'' The assertion "we are in Him that is true" *(esmen en tō alēthinō)* reaffirms that mystical union with God that John has repeatedly asserted (2:5, 24, 27-28; 3:24; 4:4, 12-13, 15-16). The relationship expressed by "in him" brings us back to the fellowship with God with which John begins the epistle (1:3).

The designation "in him that is true" seems naturally to refer to God the Father as in the preceding clause (cf. John 17:3), but the intended connection of the following clause, "in His Son Jesus Christ" *(en tō huiō autou Iēsou Christō)*, is differently understood. The KJV rendering, "and we are in him that is true, *even* in his Son Jesus Christ," refers the entire expression to Christ. Against this appositional identification of the phrase is the use of the expression "His Son." It seems better to accept "in His Son" as an explanation of the preceding phrase, indicating how this mystical union is brought about. Removing the comma and uniting the two phrases gives us John's explanation of how we are in the true God: "and we are in the true one in his Son, Jesus Christ" (literal rendering). *The Twentieth Century New Testament* renders: "and we are in union with the True God by our union with his Son, Jesus Christ."[75] Lenski supports this connection of the two clauses as follows:

> Only in this way are we in God. Apart from the Son no one is in God (John 14:6). He who denies the Son has not the Father (2:23). This is the burden of the entire epistle. This meaning cannot be eliminated at the climax. We are in the real One in Christ; no man is in God without Christ.[76]

We truly "know" God as we are "in His Son Jesus Christ." "The deepest level of awareness of God," Grayston adds, "is achieved only by intimate communion with the Son."[77]

John completes his statement of the third Christian certainty with the climactic assertion, "This is the true God, and eternal life" *(houtos estin ho alēthinos theos kai zōēn aiōnios)*. The divine being identified by "This" *(houstos)* is given a double designation; He is both "the true God, and eternal life." The second designation, used without the article, is closely joined to the first designation; He is both true deity and life eternal. In Him Godhood and eternal life are inseparably united. This fact distinguishes Him from all false gods.

---

[75]*The Twentieth Century New Testament, A Translation into Modern English* (Chicago: Moody Press, n.d.). The Jerusalem Bible renders as follows:
"We are in the true God,
  as we are in his Son, Jesus Christ."

[76]Lenski, p. 541.

[77]Kenneth Grayston, *The Johannine Epistles,* New Century Bible Commentary (Grand Rapids: Eerdmans, 1984), p. 147.

Grammatically the pronoun "This" may refer either to "him that is true" *(estin ho elēthinos)* or to Jesus Christ. Both views have their ardent advocates.[78] Proponents of the view that "This" refers to the Father advance varied arguments: (1) The pronoun here need not refer to the nearest antecedent but appropriately sums up all that has been said about God following the term "understanding." (2) The repetition involved in this view is characteristic of John. (3) John 5:26 states that the Father is the source of the life that is in the Son. (4) This is the designation of the Father in John 17:3.

Proponents of the view that the pronoun refers to Jesus Christ offer varied supporting claims: (1) The construction logically points to Jesus Christ as the nearest antecedent. (2) To make the clause refer back to the Father makes it repetitious and superfluous. (3) In this epistle (1:2; 5:12), as well as in the Fourth Gospel (11:25; 14:6), Christ is called the life. (4) As in the Fourth Gospel (1:1; 20:28), this view fittingly ascribes full deity to Jesus Christ both at the beginning and at the end of the epistle (1:2; 5:20). (5) A careful study of John 17:3 and 5:26 establishes that they do not necessarily demand the other view.[79] (6) This was the view held in the early Church. Athanasius (c. 296-373), in his controversy with Arius, used this statement to support the full deity of Jesus Christ, compelling Arius to maintain that the pronoun referred to the Father rather than to Jesus. Lenski tersely adds, "This Arian exegesis became that of all later anti-Trinitarians, of the old Socinians, of the English deists, of the German rationalists, etc."[80] Brown notes that "there is an uneasiness (sometimes unexpressed) among scholars about NT texts that call Jesus 'God,' " and calls this "an unwarranted uneasiness, especially for the Johannine writings where that description is solidly attested (John 1:1, 18; 20:28)."[81] Although even evangelical scholars sincerely differ as to the intended meaning here, that fact does not undermine the Biblical teaching concerning Christ's deity. As Plummer notes, "That S. John teaches the Divinity of Jesus Christ both in Epistle and Gospel is so manifest, that a text more or less in favour of the doctrine need not be the subject of heated controversy."[82] In view of the two possible interpretations here, Smalley suggests that "it is possible that the writer is once again being ambivalent in his confession."[83] Bennett, indeed, even

---

[78]For a list of scholars for either view see Brown, p. 625.

[79]See Lenski, pp. 544-45.

[80]*Ibid.,* p. 543.

[81]Brown, p. 626.

[82]Plummer, p. 172.

[83]Smalley, p. 308.

suggests that the reference may be "to the Godhead generally."[84] We accept a reference to Jesus Christ here as the true capstone of the epistle. Calling this "the clinching statement" of the epistle, Lenski asserts:

> Everything depends on his deity, and his deity means no less than this, that as the Father who is made known to us by him is the only real God (I Thess. 1:9), so also his Son Jesus Christ "is the real God" and eternal life. If the Son is less, if he is not the real God even as the Father is the real God, then this entire epistle and all that it declares about his blood, expiation, our fellowship with God, etc., are futile.[85]

D. The Final Warning Against Idols (v. 21)

John abruptly concludes the epistle with a warm-hearted warning: "Little children, keep yourselves from idols." The personal address "little children" *(teknia),* last used in 4:4, is an affectionate pastoral reminder of his personal concern for his readers in view of the dangers confronting them.

John's terse command "keep yourselves from idols" *(phulaxate heauta apo tōn eidōlōn)* sums up his spiritual concern for their safety. The exact phrase does not occur elsewhere in the New Testament. The aorist imperative carries a sense of urgency, "effectively keep yourselves," and the active voice with the reflexive pronoun "yourselves" stresses their personal responsibility in assuring their safety. The verb "keep" or "guard" *(phulaxate),* which occurs only here in 1 John and twice in the Fourth Gospel (12:25; 17:12), calls upon them to be alert like armed guards, ready to repulse every attack. In verse 18 John gives them the comforting assurance of God's keeping activity on their behalf; now he uses a different term to stress that they have a part in assuring their security. God works in and through the efforts of His saints in keeping them from harm (Phil. 2:12-13).

The warning to guard themselves "from idols" *(apo tōn eidōlōn,* "from the idols") is arresting. Because this is the only direct reference to idols in the epistle, interpreters have advanced varied views as to the intended reference.[86] One view is that the reference is to the pagan idols which held such a powerful place in the life and culture of that day. So understood, John was warning his readers against associations with the paganism around them. (Cf. Rev. 2:20.) Proponents of this view point out that elsewhere in the New Testament "the word is *invariably* used literally: Acts vii. 41, xv. 20; Rom. ii. 22; 1 Cor. viii. 4, 7, x. 19, xii. 2; 2 Cor. vi. 16; 1 Thess. i. 9; Rev. ix.

---

[84]W. H. Bennett, *The General Epistles, James, Peter, John, and Jude,* The Century Bible (London: Blackwood, Le Bas & Co., n.d.), p. 319.

[85]Lenski, p. 542.

[86]See Brown, pp. 627-28, for a discussion of no less than ten different views.

20.''[87] In support of this literal meaning Burdick asserts, ''John gives not the slightest hint that he is using the term in a figurative sense. It is only reasonable, therefore, to take the term literally.''[88]

But others hold that such a literal meaning seems inconsistent with the contents and scope of this epistle. They hold that a broad, nonliteral meaning is more probable. Thus Westcott notes,

> ''Idolatry'' (Col. iii. 5) and ''idolater'' (Eph. v. 5) have a wider sense in St Paul; and the context here seems to require a corresponding extension of the meaning of the term. An ''idol'' is anything which occupies the place due to God. The use of the definite article calls up all the familiar objects which fall under the title.[89]

But such a broad extension of the concept may well go beyond what John here had in mind.

It seems most probable that in giving this warning John had in mind the false teachers with their perverse view of the person and work of Jesus Christ. Repeatedly John has warned against corruption of the redemptive message in Christ and the perversion of the true identity of the incarnate Son of God. The reference to the true or real God in verse 20 seems to have prompted John to brand their fictional, humanly contrived conceptions of Christ as idols, placing them in the same category as the pagan images and the imagined gods they represented. So understood, Grayston characterizes this closing comment ''as a finally wounding blow against the dissidents' attachment to God.''[90] Their infatuation with their own views concerning the true God and His incarnate Son was indeed a new kind of idolatry. His verdict is equally valid today!

* * * * *

The King James Version, following the Textus Receptus, adds a ritualistic ''Amen'' to the epistle. It appears in later Greek manuscripts and the Clementine Vulgate but does not appear in the earliest manuscripts.[91] Concerning such a closing ''Amen'' in the various books of the New Testament, Brown remarks that it ''is genuine as part of the blessing in Gal. 6:18, and is debatable in II Peter 3:18. Elsewhere it is a liturgical addition, influenced by the custom of reading the Scriptures in church services.''[92]

---

[87]Plummer, p. 173. Plummer's italics.

[88]Burdick, pp. 397-98.

[89]Westcott, p. 197.

[90]Grayston, p. 148.

[91]For the textual evidence see Nestle-Aland, *Novum Testamentum Graece,* 26th ed. In the United Bible Societies, *The Greek New Testament,* 3rd ed., the editors leave off the *Amēn* and all manuscript references.

[92]Brown, p. 629.

17

An Introduction to Second and Third John

The two brief letters known as 2 and 3 John have the distinction of being the shortest books in the New Testament. They correspond "to the conventional brief length of a private letter which, at the time, would have been written on a single papyrus sheet of standard size (about 25 x 20 cm)."[1] They are precious examples of the correspondence that passed between local Christian congregations or individual believers during the stirring days of the latter part of the first century A.D. Their similarity in length, structure, and style justifies the description of them as "twin sisters." In dealing with introductory matters it will be convenient to set them side by side.

The Canonicity and Authorship of 2 and 3 John

1. External Evidence

In view of their brevity and the casual nature of these two letters, it is not surprising that they were among the New Testament writings which had the hardest struggle for canonical recognition. Eusebius listed them among the *antilegomena,* "the disputed books, although they are well known and approved by many" (*Eccl. Hist.* 3. 25). Though scanty, the external evidence is remarkably weighty.

Irenaeus (fl. c. 175–c. 195),[2] in his famous work *Against Heresies,* twice quotes from 2 John. Speaking about certain heretics, he writes, "John, the disciple of the Lord, has intensified their condemnation, when he desires us not even to address to them the salutation of 'good-speed,' " and then quotes 2 John 11 (1. 16. 3). In 3. 16. 8 he quotes 2 John 7-8 but makes the slip of

---

[1] Stephen S. Smalley, *1, 2, 3 John,* Word Biblical Commentary (Waco, Texas: Word Books, 1984), p. 314.

[2] The dates are those given in J. D. Douglas, ed., *The New International Dictionary of the Christian Church* (Grand Rapids: Zondervan, 1974).

quoting it as from the first epistle. "This slip of memory," D. Smith remarks, "only makes the attestation more effective. Irenaeus knew that it was a saying of St. John that he was quoting: the Second Epistle no less than the First was the Apostle's."[3]

Clement of Alexandria (c. 155–c. 220) in his extant works speaks of John's "longer Epistle," thus showing that he recognized at least one other and shorter epistle by John (*The Stromata, 2. 15*). Eusebius tells us that Clement in his *Hypotyposes,* or "Outlines," gave "abridged accounts of all the canonical Scriptures, not even omitting those that are disputed, I mean the book of Jude, and the other general epistles" (*Eccl. Hist.* 6.14).

Cyprian, bishop of Carthage (c. 200/210-258), makes no known quotations from these epistles himself; but in his account of a council at Carthage (A.D 256), he says that Aurelius, bishop of Chullabi, quoted 2 John 10-11 with the observation "John the Apostle laid it down in his Epistle" *(Concerning the Baptism of Heretics).* This suggests that these epistles "were received as apostolic and canonical in the North African church."[4]

The evidence of the Muratorian Canon, a fragmentary list of New Testament books known at Rome about A.D. 200, is somewhat ambiguous. First John is mentioned in connection with the Fourth Gospel, and later on it mentions "two epistles of the John who has been mentioned before." This has been taken to refer to 1 and 2 John, 3 John being thus omitted. But it seems more natural to understand this reference to "two epistles" as denoting 2 and 3 John. If so, that would show that these two epistles were regarded as canonical in Rome before the end of the second century.

Origen (c. 185–c. 254), an Alexandrian theologian, did not quote from these two epistles in his extant writings, but he knew of them. He expressed no personal opinion about them but did remark that "not all agree that they are genuine" (*Eccl. Hist.* 6:25). Westcott holds that Origen quotes 1 John in such a way as to "shew that the other Epistles were not familiarly known."[5]

Eusebius of Caesarea (c. 265–c. 339), in his famous *Historia Ecclesiastica* (A.D. 325), conscientiously placed these two epistles among the *antilegomena* in his list of canonical books (3:25). But in his *Demonstratio Evangelica* (3. 3) he appears "to be favourable to the Apostolic authorship; he speaks of them without qualification as S. John's."[6]

---

[3] David Smith, "The Epistles of St. John," in *The Expositor's Greek Testament* ([1897]; reprint ed., Grand Rapids: Eerdmans, n.d.), 5:159.

[4] Henry Alford, *The Greek Testament,* 4th ed. (London: Rivingtons, 1871), 4:182.

[5] Brooke Foss Westcott, *The Epistles of St. John, The Greek Text with Notes,* 3rd ed. (1892; reprint ed., Grand Rapids: Eerdmans, 1950), p. 331.

[6] Alfred Plummer, *The Epistles of S. John,* Cambridge Bible for Schools and Colleges (1883; reprint ed., London: Cambridge University Press, 1938), p. 52.

Jerome (c. 345–c. 419), noted Biblical translator, although testifying that 1 John was approved by all the churches and scholars as written by the Apostle John, yet ascribed 2 and 3 John to "John the Presbyter" instead (*De Viris Illustribus,* Chap. 9). Jerome's doubts concerning 2 and 3 John seem to be the doubts of the scholar rather than the prevailing view in the Church. The Council of Carthage (A.D. 397) definitely accepted these epistles as canonical.

The external evidence for the third epistle is considerably less than for the second. Its contents were less suitable for quotation; so it is less frequently mentioned. Goodspeed, who conceives of 2 and 3 John as covering letters for 1 John, holds that all three originally circulated as a corpus and that consequently the ancients referred to them differently as one, two, or three letters. He accordingly remarks, "These varied testimonies are not to be understood as meaning that one writer had one letter and another two, but that all possessed the full corpus of three letters, one long and two very short, and designated them differently."[7] If this view is correct, it would greatly strengthen the external evidence for both of these letters.

In summarizing the external evidence Plummer remarks, "It is apparent that precisely those witnesses who are nearest to S. John in time are favourable to the Apostolic authorship, and seem to know of no other view."[8] The fact that these two brief letters were not quoted more often by the ancient Church Fathers does not prove that they were ignorant of their existence or regarded them as unauthentic. The nature of their contents, generally unmarked by arresting features or unusual statements, offered slight occasion for their being quoted. The one passage in these two epistles that was most distinctive and arresting is 2 John verses 10-11, and it was just this passage that was most often quoted. Their brevity, as well as the fact that at least one, if not both, was a strictly private letter, naturally caused them to be less widely circulated and read than 1 John with its profound doctrinal teachings. We may agree with Law when he asserts, "The fact, therefore, that, in spite of such obstacles, these letters did become widely known and eventually attained to canonical rank is proof of a general conviction of the soundness of the tradition which assigned them to the apostle John."[9]

2. Internal Evidence

The contents of 2 and 3 John convey a strong impression that they are the product of the same pen. This is suggested by their close resemblance

---

[7]Edgar J. Goodspeed, *An Introduction to the New Testament* (Chicago: University of Chicago Press, 1937), p. 324.

[8]Plummer, p. 53.

[9]R. Law, "John, The Epistles of: The Second and Third Epistle," in *The International Standard Bible Encyclopedia* (Grand Rapids: Eerdmans, 1939), 3:1718.

in structure, style, phraseology, and tone of thought. Both open in the same manner: the writer identifies himself as "the elder"; the readers are indicated with the same formula; and both give expression to the writer's joy in relation to his readers. Both also close in almost identical ways: the assertion about having many other things to write; the promise of an impending visit; and the greetings to the readers. Characteristically Johannine expressions appear in both letters. Both speak of hospitality, the one of that which is forbidden, the other of that which is enjoined. Brooke concludes: "The similarity between them is too close to admit of any explanation except common authorship or conscious imitation. It would tax the ingenuity of the most skillful separator to determine which is the original and which the copy."[10]

The relationship of these letters to 1 John further makes it clear that all three must have come from the same hand. Second John bears the closer resemblance to the First. More than half of its contents are also contained in 1 John. Both of these letters have various phrases which recall, or are identical with, those of the first epistle.[11] Both also reveal the characteristic Johannine practice of emphasizing an idea by stating it both positively and negatively (2 John 9; 3 John 11). These similarities confront us with the alternative of accepting all three as coming from the same author or that these shorter writings are the product of conscious imitation. In support of the former, Burdick notes, "There is no telltale unnatural or strained employment of the terms or expressions as often results when one tries to use the style and vocabulary of another."[12] For the common reader, the most natural explanation is the view that all three writings are the work of the same author. This view "goes back to the early church and was held almost unanimously until the rise of modern critical scholarship."[13] Various recent scholars are critical of this view; some have suggested that "2 John and 3 John are not really letters but fictions."[14] But such a claim places a strain on common credulity. Recent scholarship has spoken quite extensively of a "Johannine school" which gathered around the Apostle John and that the various writings traditionally ascribed to the Apostle John were written by

---

[10]A. E. Brooke, *A Critical and Exegetical Commentary on the Johannine Epistles,* International Critical Commentary (New York: Charles Scribner's Sons, 1912), p. lxxiii.

[11]*Ibid.,* p. lxxiv.

[12]Donald W. Burdick, *The Letters of John the Apostle, An In-Depth Commentary* (Chicago: Moody Press, 1985), p. 415.

[13]*Ibid.,* p. 11.

[14]See Rudolf Bultmann, *The Johannine Epistles,* Hermeneia–A Critical and Historical Commentary on the Bible (Philadelphia: Fortress Press, 1973), p. 107, note 2, and the literature cited there.

various members of this school who drew upon and adapted materials received from the Apostle.[15]

The fact that the writer of 2 and 3 John identifies himself as "the elder" *(ho presbuteros)* has evoked much discussion and different views as to his true identity. It is held that this designation distinguishes the writer from the Apostle John. This view is based on the distinction which Eusebius made between John the Apostle and John the Elder based upon his interpretation of a somewhat confusing passage from Papias *(Eccl. Hist.* 3. 39). Under this view the writer was a member of the Johannine school who viewed himself as a bearer and transmitter of the apostolic tradition. But those interpreters who reject the view of Eusebius concerning two men named John at Ephesus[16] insist that there is nothing which makes it impossible to accept that the Apostle John himself could have used this designation to identify himself in writing these two letters. In calling himself "the elder," the author comes boldly forward in his own person, aware that his readers knew who he was and knew him well. He speaks with authority, sends his delegates to an established church, and feels that his presence, when he arrives, will be sufficient to put down opposition to his authority. He speaks and acts as one who is conscious of apostolic authority and is aware that his authority is known to his readers. The writer's identification of himself as "the elder" marks a position wholly exceptional. An ordinary elder, writing in his own person and not wishing to deceive, would hardly have called himself "*the* elder." There is no reason to hold that the term is here used to denote a local ecclesiastical position of authority. "The authority which the author claims is far greater than ever attached to the office of 'Presbyter'."[17] The ministry which "the elder" is seen as carrying on in these epistles–sending out deputies and receiving their reports, supervising a wide circle of churches, visiting them and giving them directions and guidance–is precisely the sort of ministry the Apostle John is known to have carried on from Ephesus in his later life.[18]

Just why John chose not to use his name cannot be said, but his use of the designation "the elder" is quite appropriate and distinctive. Its use marks out for him a position which would not necessarily have been suggested by the title "an apostle." Toward the close of the first century, the term "apostle" had become a common designation for just such messengers as are

---

[15]See Raymond E. Brown, *The Community of the Beloved Disciple* (New York: Paulist Press, 1979); Oscar Cullman, *The Johannine Circle* (Philadelphia: Westminster Press, 1975).

[16]See "The Elder John" under "Authorship" in the introduction to 1 John (pp. 14-16). See also Burdick, pp. 13-16.

[17]Brooke, pp. lxxv-lxxvi.

[18]See "John's Ephesian Ministry" in the introduction to 1 John (pp. 11-14).

mentioned in the third epistle. But this title was more definitive of his true position as the sole survivor of an earlier generation. Concerning the use of this title Smith says,

> The second generation of Christians used it of their predecessors, "the men of early days," who had witnessed the great beginnings. Thus, Papias uses it of the Apostles, and Irenaeus in turn uses it of Papias and his contemporaries. It was therefore natural that St. John, the last of the Apostles, the sole survivor of "the elder men," should be known among the churches of Asia as "the elder."[19]

John's use of this term would thus clearly and accurately identify his position of authority to his readers. In writing these letters, John clearly did not feel it necessary to use his personal name or make an open claim to apostolic authority. This is in accord with his practice in the Fourth Gospel and the first epistle.[20]

Again, it is objected that the author cannot be an apostle because it is inconceivable that an apostle should have been so opposed and defied as was the author by Diotrephes (3 John 9-10). "In such a conflict," Bornkamm insists, "the author would certainly not refrain from appealing to his apostolic status."[21] But if his self-designation "the elder" establishes his apostolic identity to the readers, his remark that he would deal with the deeds of Diotrephes upon arrival (v. 10) implies precisely such a use of his apostolic authority. Certainly the bold and malicious action of Diotrephes is astonishing. But the revelation of this surprising action cannot invalidate the evidence for the Johannine authorship of the epistle. The event simply shows that even leaders within apostolic churches were not always examples of worthy Christian conduct and holiness. Paul had his violent opponents; the opposition Paul experienced at Corinth should prepare us for an action such as this. As Farrar observes, "The history of the Church of Christ, from the earliest down to the latest days, teems with subjects for perplexity and surprise."[22]

3. Conclusion

The external evidence is by no means unfavorable to the view that John the Apostle wrote these letters; that was the view of those closest to the time of their composition. Later, as the circumstances that prompted their com-

---

[19]Smith, p. 160.

[20]John's use of his name in Revelation is determined by the fact that the book is modeled after the Old Testament prophetic books, where the name of the prophet to whom the prophecy was communicated is always given.

[21]Günther Bornkamm, *"presbus, presbuteros,"* in *Theological Dictionary of the New Testament,* ed. Gerhard Kittel (Grand Rapids: Eerdmans, 1964), 6:671.

[22]F. W. Farrar, *The Early Days of Christianity,* author's ed. (New York: Cassell, n.d.), p. 590.

position were forgotten, doubts concerning the true identity of "the elder" arose. The preponderance of the external evidence is in favor of their apostolic authorship.

The internal evidence is strongly in favor of the traditional view. The historical situation reflected in these brief letters harmonizes with our information concerning the closing years of John's life. The contents of these letters clearly point to Johannine authorship. We conclude with Salmon that "no account of the matter seems satisfactory but the traditional one, that the writer was the Apostle John."[23]

The Readers of 2 and 3 John

1. Second John

The second epistle is addressed to "the elect lady and her children." The exact meaning of this address is enigmatic and has given rise to varied interpretations. This diversity of interpretations is by no means of modern origin. The intended meaning of the writer's designation of the recipients still puzzles the interpreters. Westcott, indeed, concludes that "the problem of the address is insoluble with our present knowledge."[24] The interpretations fall into two general groups. The basic question is whether the words "the elect lady" *(eklektē kuria)* are to be taken figuratively or literally.

Those interpreters who understand the words figuratively divide into two groups. One view, as old as Jerome, is that this is a catholic epistle addressed to the Church as a whole under the figure of a woman. But under this view the reference to "your elect sister" in verse 13 is meaningless. Bultmann suggests that "the author conceived his writing as a 'catholic' letter, which the bearer would deliver to appropriate congregations from time to time."[25] But under such an encyclical view the reference to the "elect sister" (v. 13) should be in the plural, unless, indeed, "the elder" recognized only one other orthodox congregation!

The view of most interpreters who accept a figurative meaning for the term "elect lady" is that the reference is to a local church. In support of this view, reference is made to the uncertain allusion in 1 Peter 5:13. Conjectures as to the location of this local church have included Corinth, Jerusalem, Philadelphia, Ephesus, and Babylon. The ancient practice of referring to cities or collective organizations as feminine is well known. But there is nothing in this epistle to suggest this figurative meaning in naming its readers. In a highly figurative writing, such as the book of Revelation, such

---

[23]George Salmon, *An Historical Introduction to the Study of the Books of the New Testament,* 9th ed. (London: John Murray, 1904), p. 272.

[24]Westcott, p. 224.

[25]Bultmann, p. 108.

a usage might be justified and readily understood. But this epistle gives no hint of any figurative interpretation being intended. Rather, "the simplicity of the little letter precludes the possibility of so elaborate an allegory, while the tenderness of its tone stamps it as a personal communication."[26] As Farrar remarks, "A Church certainly might be called 'the bride of Christ,' but the word 'Lady' is nowhere applied to the Church, still less is there any trace of correspondence between Churches under the title of 'ladies.' "[27]

It seems most natural to take the simple words of the epistle to refer to an actual lady and her children. This view is favored by the simplicity of the letter, the writer's reference to having met some of her children (v. 4), the mention of her sister's children (v. 13), the reference to the elect lady's house (v. 10), as well as the analogy of the third epistle, which certainly is addressed to an individual. It is interesting to notice that the formula of address in both epistles is exactly the same.[28] We conclude that this letter *may* have been addressed to a church, but we do not think it probable. In the words of Burdick, "The principles of biblical interpretation would seem to direct one to adopt the most natural meaning of the passage, namely that an individual lady and her children were the intended receivers of the letter."[29]

But there is no agreement as to the exact significance of the address "to the elect lady" *(eklektē kuria)* among those who accept the personal interpretation of the designation. The Greek may be literally rendered "to an elect lady" or "to the elect lady."[30] But either of the two Greek terms have been taken as the personal name of the lady addressed. Clement of Alexandria took Eklektē *(eklektē)* to be the lady's personal name, thus holding that the term *eklektē* here was a proper name rather than an adjective, "elect, chosen." Law, as a modern representative of this view, suggests that the best rendering is "to the lady Eklektē."[31] But this seems untenable in the light of verse 13 where the term is clearly an adjective. Its position in verse 1, standing before the noun *kuria,* suggests that here also it is an adjective.

More probable is the view that the second term was the lady's personal name, "to the chosen Cyria" *(Kuria).* This was the view of Athanasius (c.

[26]Smith, p. 162.

[27]F. W. Farrar, *The Messages of the Books, Being Discourses and Notes on the Books of the New Testament* (New York: E. P. Dutton, 1897), p. 501.

[28]This similarity is made evident by comparing the two:
"The elder to the chosen lady and her children, whom I love in truth."
"The elder to the beloved Gaius, whom I love in truth."

[29]Burdick, p. 416.

[30]The first is the more literal and seems preferable. The second rendering is possible and intelligible without the definite article.

[31]R. Law, "Elect Lady," in *The International Standard Bible Encyclopedia* (Grand Rapids: Eerdmans, 1939), 2:925.

296-373) and is accepted as probable by many modern scholars. It is the rendering suggested in the margin of the ASV (1901). The name Cyria does occur in ancient documents. The difficulty with this translation is that if it is a proper name, based on the analogy of 3 John 1 ("unto Gaius the beloved"), the adjective "chosen" should stand after the proper name. (See also Rom. 16:5, 8, 9, 10, 12, 13 [Greek]). The name Cyria *(Kuria)* is the feminine of the common word for "Lord" *(kurios)*; it is the Greek equivalent of the Aramaic for Martha. This has led some to conjecture that the lady was Martha of Bethany, or even Mary the mother of our Lord. But as Farrar remarks, to make such conjectures "is to be guilty of the idle and reprehensible practice of suggesting theories which rest on the air, and are not even worth the trouble of a serious refutation."[32]

The rendering "to the chosen lady," or "to an elect lady," leaves open the question of the identity of this matron to whom the letter is addressed. That the Apostle John should write such a letter to a Christian lady and her family is nothing extraordinary. Women such as Priscilla, Lydia, and Phoebe played an important part in the life of the early churches. In Romans 16 Paul sent his personal greetings to a number of Christian women. All that we know about the lady to whom the Elder addressed this letter must be learned from its contents.

2. Third John

The third epistle is addressed "to the wellbeloved Gaius." About him we know nothing for sure beyond what is found in this brief communication. The name *Gaius*, which is the Greek equivalent of the Latin *Caius,* was one of the most common names in the Roman Empire. Farrar remarks, "So common was it that it was selected in the Roman law-books to serve the familiar purpose of John Doe and Richard Roe in our own legal formularies."[33] That Gaius was a man of sterling Christian character and highly esteemed by the Elder is obvious from the letter sent to him.

The Occasion for 2 and 3 John

1. Second John

The writing of 2 John was occasioned by the writer's knowledge that certain heretical teachers, posing as Christian missionaries, were planning to work in the Christian community where this Christian lady lived. John knew that she was a Christian lady, known for her hospitality, who made it a practice to entertain itinerant preachers visiting the community. Aware of the efforts of these false teachers to gain entrance to such homes to propagate

---

[32]Farrar, *Early Days of Christianity,* p. 589.

[33]*Ibid.,* p. 569.

their heretical teachings, he warns her not to welcome them into her home and thus encourage their efforts, lest she become a partaker of their sins. The letter was prompted by John's pastoral concern for his dear friends. Her Christian home, as a sanctuary of God's truth, must keep out all that was contrary to His revealed truth.

2. Third John

The third epistle was called forth by the report received by John from his missionaries concerning the high-handed action of Diotrephes in the church to which Gaius belonged. John had sent out messengers of the gospel to the surrounding territory and had commended them to the churches for hospitality and support. When they arrived at the church where Gaius lived, Diotrephes, an influential member, if not the leader, of the church, refused to receive them, spoke against the apostle himself, and opposed those who followed John's request. Gaius actively befriended these missionaries; upon their return to the church where John resided, they reported their experiences before the church. In response John wrote to Gaius, expressing his warm appreciation for his friendly reception of the missionaries and announcing his intention of a personal visit to deal with the trouble.

The Place and Date of 2 and 3 John

1. Place

These epistles offer no direct indications concerning the place from which they were written. The common assumption is that they were written from Ephesus while the Apostle John was formulating plans for a tour through the churches of the province.

2. Date

These letters offer no data to determine the date of their composition. Their close affinity to 1 John supports the assumption that they were written near the time of that epistle. This would suggest an early date of A.D. 80-81, or a later date of A.D. 97-98. The earlier date seems preferable.

The Purpose of 2 and 3 John

1. Second John

The primary purpose of this letter is to give warning against extending indiscriminate hospitality to traveling teachers whose soundness in the Christian faith is justly questionable. John's pastoral heart prompted him to impress upon this Christian lady the need to exercise spiritual discernment in manifesting Christian hospitality and love. Those who proved themselves to be "progressives" who did not abide in the doctrine of Christ were to be refused aid in their destructive work. A further purpose in writing was to commend this "elect lady and her children" for their loyalty to the truth that the apostle himself preached, by their continuing in the teaching which they had received.

2. Third John

The primary purpose of the Elder in writing this letter was to enlist the further good services of Gaius on behalf of the missionaries whom John was sending out. He strengthened his ties with Gaius by stressing his own deep love for him, by assuring him of his prayers for the prosperity and health of his dear friend, and by commending him for his open stand for the truth by showing hospitality to the missionaries John had already sent. John urges Gaius to continue the good work and also to learn a lesson from the unworthy example of Diotrephes. To encourage Gaius, the apostle announces that he will come personally and deal with the self-seeking Diotrephes. The letter to Gaius is in effect also a letter of recommendation for Demetrius, who apparently was the bearer of this letter and the leader of the missionary party John was sending out.

The Characteristics of 2 and 3 John

These brief letters show a remarkable similarity in structure, style, and tone of thought. Their salutation and conclusion are remarkably alike. Both epistles move in the realm of truth and love;[34] both present the Christian life as a walk in the truth.

These two letters provide an attractive picture of the Apostle John in his dealings with individuals. They are valuable illustrations of a free and intimate correspondence between Christians such as must have been very common in the early Church. They are not of crucial doctrinal importance, but they do give us a vivid glimpse into the closing years of the apostolic era with its troubles and triumphs.

Both epistles indicate the place and importance of Christian hospitality in the early Church. The second epistle warns against a false hospitality which would aid and further false teaching; it is a strong testimony against fellowship with apostasy. The third commends Christian hospitality to missionary brethren as the inviolable duty of individuals and of the church. It is distinctly the epistle of missionary obligation; such hospitality inculcates fellowship in and with the truth. In them John thus provides two safeguards for the Church. "Heresy and schism are the dangers to which it is perpetually exposed. St. John's condemnation of the spirit of *heresy* is recorded in the

---

[34]The noun "truth" *(alētheia)* occurs five times in 2 John and six times in 3 John; the adjective "true" *(alēthēs)* appears once in 3 John. The word "love" as a noun *(agapē)* occurs three times (2 John 3, 6; 3 John 6) and the verb *(agapaō)* occurs three times (2 John 1, 5; 3 John 1) and the adjective "beloved" *(agapētos)* occurs four times in 3 John (vv. 1, 2, 5, 11).

Second Epistle; his condemnation of the spirit of *schism* is written in the Third Epistle.''[35]

John's directive in the second epistle not to receive heretics into the house, nor bid them goodspeed, has frequently been felt to be too severe. But it would be a mistake to attribute this directive as unfortunate guidance, as simply due to John's personal zeal and fiery nature. These words of John contain a vitally needed corrective to our modern easy-going tolerance which will tolerate and even fellowship with open error for the sake of peace and organizational unity. Alford insists, ''It would have been infinitely better for the Church now, if this command had been observed in all ages by her faithful sons.''[36] But the comment of Farrar, alas, is also true:

> This text–torn from its context, servered from its historic meaning–has been terribly abused. It tells ill for the spirit of Christians that from the earliest days the one verse almost exclusively quoted from this Epistle of love by the Apostle of love has been a verse which has been perverted into a plausible excuse for religious hate.''[37]

The third epistle gives a vivid character portrayal of the three men which appear in it. The etchings are made with great psychological skill. Each man appears as a distinct individual; the presentation testifies to the writer's full knowledge behind the picture. His character delineations are lifelike and convincing.

---

[35]W. Alexander, ''The Third Epistle of John,'' in *The Speaker's Commentary, New Testament* (London: John Murray, 1881), 4:374. Italics in original.

[36]Henry Alford, *The New Testament for English Readers* ([1865-1872]; reprint ed., Chicago: Moody Press, [1958]), p. 1764.

[37]Farrar, *Messages of the Books,* p. 502.

18

An Outline Of Second John

I. The Salutation (vv. 1-3)
   A. The Writer (v. 1a)
   B. The Recipients (vv. 1b-2)
   C. The Assurance (v. 3)
II. The Message (vv. 4-11)
   A. The Occasion for the Letter (v. 4)
   B. The Appeal for Love and Obedience (vv. 5-6)
      1. The character and content of the appeal (v. 5)
      2. The nature and age of the commandment (v. 6)
   C. The Warning Against the False Teachers (vv. 7-9)
      1. The reason for the warning (v. 7)
      2. The statement of the warning (v. 8)
      3. The contrast between the heretics and true believers (v. 9)
   D. The Prohibition Against Aiding the Heretics (vv. 10-11)
      1. The statement of the prohibition (v. 10)
      2. The reason for the prohibition (v. 11)
III. The Conclusion (vv. 12-13)
   A. The Plans for a Coming Visit (v. 12)
   B. The Greetings from her Sister's Children (v. 13)

19

An Exposition of Second John

1 The elder unto the elect lady and her children, whom I love in the truth; and not I only, but also all they that have known the truth;

2 For the truth's sake, which dwelleth in us, and shall be with us for ever.

3 Grace be with you, mercy, *and* peace, from God the Father, and from the Lord Jesus Christ, the Son of the Father, in truth and love.

4 I rejoiced greatly that I found of thy children walking in truth, as we have received a commandment from the Father.

5 And now I beseech thee, lady, not as though I wrote a new commandment unto thee, but that which we had from the beginning, that we love one another.

6 And this is love, that we walk after his commandments. This is the commandment, That, as ye have heard from the beginning, ye should walk in it.

7 For many deceivers are entered into the world, who confess not that Jesus Christ is come in the flesh. This is a deceiver and an antichrist.

8 Look to yourselves, that we lose not those things which we have wrought, but that we receive a full reward.

9 Whosoever transgresseth, and abideth not in the doctrine of Christ, hath not God. He that abideth in the doctrine of Christ, he hath both the Father and the Son.

10 If there come any unto you, and bring not this doctrine, receive him not into *your* house, neither bid him God speed:

11 For he that biddeth him God speed is partaker of his evil deeds.

12 Having many things to write unto you, I would not *write* with paper and ink: but I trust to come unto you, and speak face to face, that our joy may be full.

13 The children of thy elect sister greet thee. Amen.

Second John clearly reveals the conventional three-part structure of an ordinary letter written during the first century A.D. It consists of an opening salutation (vv. 1-3), the message conveyed to the reader (vv. 4-11), and added personal comments and greetings in conclusion (vv. 12-13).

I. The Salutation (vv. 1-3)

The opening salutation of a first-century letter commonly followed a basic three-point formula: A to B, greeting. This common formula was used by Christians and non-Christians alike (cf. Acts 15:23; 23:26). Each part might be modified or expanded according to the circumstances and purposes of the writer. The contents of the salutation at once make it clear that this is distinctly a Christian communication. Each part of the salutation manifests distinctive characteristics and arouses intriguing questions of interpretation.

A. *The Writer (v. 1a)*

The writer does not conform to the usual practice of starting with his name but simply identifies himself as "the elder" *(ho presbuteros)*. In the New Testament epistles this enigmatical self-designation occurs only in the salutation in 2 and 3 John. Dodd notes that "it would be difficult to cite a precise parallel from known Greek correspondence of the period."[1] Its use in both of these letters without any further elaboration makes clear that the term, which implies a unique position of dignity and authority, was well known to the readers and would at once establish the writer's identity. The use of the definite article, "the elder," rather than "an elder" from some local congregation, at once indicates the unique position and authority of the writer. Orr well remarks that the writer's self-designation aptly points to "the simple and solitary dignity of the last surviving apostle of Christ."[2] The author's use of this unique designation and the conscious sense of authority in dealing with his readers in both of these short letters are in full agreement with the early church tradition concerning the closing years of the apostle John at Ephesus as the sole survivor of the twelve apostles. (See the discussion concerning authorship in the Introduction to First John and the Introduction to Second and Third John, pp. 3-16 and 275-81). The only known titles for these letters, "of John," support that view.

B. *The Recipients (vv. 1b-2)*

The designation of the recipients of this letter, "unto the elect lady and her children" *(eklektē kuria kai tois teknois autēs)*, likewise is unique and has sparked much discussion. Interpreters divide into two general groups. Those who understand the designation have figuratively taken it to mean

---

[1]C. H. Dodd, *The Johannine Epistles,* Moffatt New Testament Commentary (New York: Harper & Row, 1946), p. 155.

[2]R. W. Orr, "The Letters of John," in *A New Testament Commentary* (Grand Rapids: Zondervan, 1969), p. 623.

either the Christian Church as a whole or, more probably, some local church. Those who understand the designation as literally denoting an individual lady have taken either of the two Greek terms *(eklektē kuria)* as her personal name, with the second, Cyria, as the more probable. But most probable is the view that both terms are simply a courteous designation of the lady who is left unnamed. Since the letter apparently was personally delivered to the reader by John's messenger, the latter seems the most probable view. (For a fuller discussion see the Introduction to 2 and 3 John, pp. 281-83).

The two terms denoting the recipient, "unto the elect lady" *(eklektē kuria),* may be rendered with a definite article "the elect lady," but more probably the absence of the article is intended to convey a qualitative implication, described here as "an elect lady," recognized as among those "chosen" of God. The fact that John also uses this adjective of her sister in verse 13 indicates that both sisters were recognized as believers by grace, chosen out of the godless world around them as acknowledged members of the family of God. The contents of the letter make it obvious that the adjective "elect" was more than an expression of respect or flattery but is descriptive of their true spiritual status. The source of their election was God's grace, not human will (Eph. 1:4-5), but they had freely responded to God's call in their hearts and lives through the preaching of the gospel.

All that we know about this Christian lady must be gleaned from the letter written to her by John. Clearly she was some well-known Christian lady, apparently a widow, known for her exemplary character and Christian hospitality. She was probably a lady of some means, having a house large enough to entertain traveling preachers. It is probable that her house was the meeting place for the church in her community, according to the custom of those days when as yet there were no separate church buildings. She had a family of grown children, at least some of whom John had learned to know as devout Christians. She had a sister, perhaps now deceased, with whose children John was personally acquainted; he was in contact with them at the time of the writing of this letter and includes their greetings to their aunt. Her place of residence is unknown, but apparently she lived not too far from Ephesus, and John had previously visited her home. Beyond this, Scripture is silent about her. Cox remarks,

> In the very silence of Scripture and the early Ecclesiastical History there lies a lesson which touches us close home, and all the closer the less we live, or are likely to live, in the memory and on the tongues of men. . . . In all probability, they were simple inconspicuous folk, such as might be matched in any Christian church whether of this time or that. And yet, because they "walked in the truth" and "kept the commandment," John

loved them, and "all who knew the truth" loved them (ver. 1). . . . *On the like terms, we may have the same reward.*[3]

In adding "and her children" John makes clear that he deliberately includes the members of this "elect lady's" family. The fact that he had met at least some of her children (v. 4) indicates that they were grown and at times away from home in pursuit of their own activities. It reveals that John recognized and appreciated the importance of Christian family relationships.

The added words "whom I love in the truth" *(hous egō agapō en alētheia)* make clear John's personal feeling toward the recipients of his letter. "Whom" *(hous)* is masculine and embraces both the mother and her children of both sexes. Having referred to himself impersonally as "the elder," the writer now uses the emphatic personal "I" *(egō)* to stress his personal feeling of "love" *(agapō)* toward them. John's verb, which has been called "the characteristic word of Christianity," is not the term which denotes personal friendship and affection *(phileō)* but rather that high ethical love, characteristic of the nature of God Himself (1 John 4:8, 16), which is prompted to act by its desire to further the highest welfare of those loved. The plural pronoun "whom" makes clear that his love includes her children as well. It is a love operating in the realm of "the truth" *(alētheia)*. Although the KJV renders it "the truth," the noun here is used without the article. The term here could possibly simply mean "in reality." But the fact that in the remainder of his description of the recipients John twice uses it with the definite article, "the truth," rather suggests that John had in mind "the truth" as embodied in the Christian gospel, hence the KJV rendering. Lenski holds that "truth" without the article marks the love as qualitative, "never separated from the objective verity of the gospel."[4] It was a love prompted by their mutual adherence to the divine truth revealed in the incarnate Son of God.

The remainder of verse 1, "and not I only, but also all they that have known the truth," makes clear the scope and nature of this love for the recipients. Having already spoken of his own love for this lady, John now speaks for all true believers. The assertion "and not I only" *(kai ouk egō monos)* emphatically denies that this declared love for the readers is true of "the elder" alone; "but" *(alla)* strongly marks the contrasted reality, that "also all they that have known the truth" *(kai pantes hoi egnōkotes tēn alētheian)* share this love for the recipients. John's "all" insists that this is true without exception of those "that have known the truth." The articular perfect participle designates a distinct group characterized by having expe-

---

[3]Samuel Cox, *The Epistles of John* (1865; reprint ed., Minneapolis: Klock & Klock Christian Publishers, 1982), pp. 70-71. Italics by Cox.

[4]R.C.H. Lenski, *The Interpretation of the Epistles of St. Peter, St. John and St. Jude* (Columbus, Ohio: Wartburg Press, 1945), p. 558.

rientially come to know "the truth" and as a result are now in possession of it. It includes all orthodox believers, as opposed to the heretics, concerning whom John writes to warn this chosen lady. This love is connected with the knowledge of "the truth" *(tēn alētheian)* as embodied in the message of the self-revelation of God in the incarnate Christ.

The added words in verse 2–"For the truth's sake, which dwelleth in us, and shall be with us for ever"–make clear that "truth is the motivation as well as the context of all Christian love."[5] The expression "for the truth's sake" *(dia* with the accusative, "because of, for the sake of") explains why John and all orthodox believers feel this love for this chosen lady. Their relationship to "the truth" is experiential and abiding; it "dwelleth in us, and shall be with us for ever." John has just spoken of all those who "know the truth" as an objective reality; that truth is now appositionally portrayed as also indwelling the believer *(tēn menousan en hēmin,* literally, "the one abiding in us"). Christ's promise to His disciples in John 14:16-17 that the Holy Spirit, who is "the Spirit of truth," would abide in them is here applied to "the truth" itself. The indwelling Holy Spirit mediates the consciousness of the indwelling truth in the life of the believer, making it morally dynamic in life and character. This Spirit-vitalized indwelling of "the truth" in the life of the believer produces an intimate and ongoing relationship with the Father and the Son. It is the distinguishing mark of the true believer.

The concluding phrase, "and shall be with us for ever" *(kai meth' hēmōn estai eis ton aiōna),* "adds an important eschatological dimension."[6] The phrase "with us" stands emphatically forward to stress that the believer's relationship with "the truth" is not a temporal relationship. God's truth, embodied in Christ and vitalized in our hearts by the Holy Spirit, by its nature is unchanging; it "shall be with us for ever." "For ever" *(eis ton aiōna,* literally, "into the age") assures that this relationship will continue into the future age of eternity which has no end. (Cf. 1 John 2:17; 5:20). In saying "with us," John again unites himself with those who have this blessed assurance for the future. John's use of the future, "shall be" *(estai),* conveys an expression of assurance and future certainty. Although assured of its eschatological permanence, believers need again and again to grasp anew this truth as a living reality in personal experience.

C. The Assurance (v. 3)

The Elder's salutation concludes with a blessing, which in his hands is not a mere devout wish but becomes a ringing declaration. Skillfully John turns the traditional epistolary salutation into a strong testimony of Christian assurance.

---

[5]Stephen S. Smalley, *1, 2, 3 John,* Word Biblical Commentary (Waco, Texas: Word Books, 1984), p. 320.

[6]*Ibid.*

The unique formulation "Grace be with you, mercy, *and* peace" *(estai meth' hēmōn charis eleos eirēnē,* literally, "There will be with us grace, mercy, peace") seems to have been prompted by the preceding clause "and shall be with us for ever" (v. 2b). The future indicative verb "shall be," standing before the usual epistolary greeting, underlines that true believers will continue to experience these blessings. The KJV rendering,"grace be with you," does not adequately express this sense of assurance in the future indicative. No other New Testament epistle thus uses a future-indicative verb in the third part of an epistolary salutation. The Pauline Epistles all omit the traditional infinitive of greeting *(chairein,* cf. James 1:1) and leave the greetings without any expressed verb. In First and Second Peter and in Jude, the writers used a finite verb in the optative mode, "may be . . . multiplied" *(plēthuntheiē),* thus expressing a devout wish. The KJV designation of the recipients of the triple blessing, "with you" *(meth' humōn),* follows some late cursive manuscripts and some copies of the Vulgate; this usual and expected reading replaces the unusual and strongly supported reading "with us" *(meth' hēmōn).*[7] John's unique statement includes the writer in this assurance of the continuing presence of these triple blessings with true believers.

In all the New Testament epistolary greetings, "grace" *(charis)* is always named first, except in the epistle of Jude which uses "mercy, peace, and love." In the Christian life the reality of grace is foundational. Grace is the free and unmerited favor of God bestowed upon guilty and unworthy individuals in and through Jesus Christ. In his nine letters addressed to churches, Paul always used "Grace to you and peace," but in his letters to Timothy and Titus he used the triple formula, "grace, mercy, and peace." Strauss notes that the use of this triple formula here "lends added weight in favor of the argument that John wrote his Second Epistle to an individual and not to the Church."[8] The word "mercy" *(eleos),* which occurs only here in the Johannine writings,[9] denotes God's pity and compassion for those in trouble

---

[7]For the textual evidence see Nestle-Aland, *Novum Testamentum Graece,* 26th ed. (Stuttgart: Deutsche Biblestiftung, 1979). "With us" *(meth' hēmōn)* is the reading in the Greek texts of B.F. Westcott and F.J.A. Hort, *The New Testament in the Original Greek,* 2nd ed. (1881; reprint ed., New York: Macmillan Co., 1935); Alexander Souter, *Novum Testamentum Graece,* 2nd ed. (1947; reprint ed., Oxford: Clarendon Press, 1962); Kurt Aland et al., ed. *The Greek New Testament,* 3rd ed. (New York: United Bible Societies, 1975); Nestle-Aland; R.V.G. Tasker, *The Greek New Testament, Being the Text Translated in the New English Bible 1961* (Oxford; Cambridge: University Press, 1964); and Zane C. Hodges and Arthur L. Farstad, *The Greek New Testament According to the Majority Text* (Nashville: Thomas Nelson Publishers, 1982).

[8]Lehman Strauss, *The Epistles of John* (1962; reprint ed., Neptune, N.J.: Loizeaux Brothers, 1984), p. 148.

[9]The cognate verb "have mercy" *(eleeō)* does not occur in the Johannine literature.

and distress. "Peace,"as the third term in this Christian formula of greeting, flows from the experience of grace and mercy and denotes that inner sense of tranquility and well-being which is the sure result. Bengel tersely summarizes: "*Grace* removes guilt; *mercy,* misery; *peace* expresses a continuance in grace and mercy,"[10] and Westcott notes that "the succession 'grace mercy, peace' marks the order from the first motion of God to the final satisfaction of man."[11]

John notes that this triple blessing is received "from God the Father, and from the Lord Jesus Christ, the Son of the Father." The repeated use of the preposition "from" (*para* with the ablative) stresses the true source from which these three blessings enter human experience. The construction pictures them as flowing down upon us from alongside the divine presence. They are imparted to us "from God the Father, and from the Lord Jesus Christ." "The repetition of the preposition 'from' indicates the separate personality of Father and Son, while the titles used indicate their unity."[12] In the Pauline Epistles generally[13] these blessings are said to come "from God our Father" (*apo theou patros hēmōn*) as marking His personal relationship to His people. Here John's use of "from God the Father" (*para theou patros*) lays stress "upon the revelation of God in this absolute character."[14] These blessings flow not only from "God the Father" but also from "the Lord Jesus Christ,"[15] or "from Jesus Christ" (ASV). He is explicitly identified as "the Son of the Father" (*tou huiou tou patros*). This further identification makes clear the true nature of the person of Jesus Christ as the incarnate revelation of the Father. In this double identification of the source of these blessings, as Marshall observes, "God is given the title

---

[10]John Albert Bengel, *New Testament Word Studies,* trans. Charlton T. Lewis and Marvin R. Vincent (1864; reprint ed., Grand Rapids: Kregel, 1971), 2:817.

[11]Brooke Foss Westcott, *The Epistles of St. John, The Greek Text with Notes,* 3rd ed. (1892; reprint ed., Grand Rapids: Eerdmans, 1950), p. 225.

[12]Fred L. Fisher, "II John," in *The Biblical Expositor, The Living Themes of the Great Book* (Philadelphia: A. J. Holman Co., 1960), vol. 3, *The New Testament,* p. 452.

[13]See Romans 1:7; 1 Corinthians 1:3; 2 Corinthians 1:2; Ephesians 1:2; Philippians 1:2; Colossians 1:2; 1 Timothy 1:2; Titus 1:4; Philemon 3.

[14]Westcott, p. 226.

[15]The KJV, following the Textus Receptus, reads "the Lord Jesus Christ" (*Kuriou Iēsou Christou*). For the textual evidence see the United Bible Societies, *The Greek New Testament,* 3rd ed. Metzger explains the the editors' omission of *kuriou* as follows: "Since it is more likely that copyists would have added rather than deleted such a word, the Committee preferred the shorter text, which is supported by good representatives of both the Alexandrian and the Western types of text (A B 81 1739 vg cop^sa)." Bruce M. Metzger, *A Textual Commentary on the Greek New Testament* (London, New York: United Bible Societies, 1971), p. 721.

which had taken on a new significance for Christians in the light of the revelation of Jesus as his Son; 'father' was a word already used in the Old Testament and in Judaism to describe God, but only in Christianity was the thought of God's personal, loving relationship to the individual developed."[16]

In concluding his assurance John reminds his readers that this triple blessing will be operative in their lives "in truth and love" *(en alētheia kai agapē)*. He thus reminds his readers that "these three virtues (grace, mercy and peace) flourish in an environment where truth and love prevail."[17] The combination of "truth and love" occurs only here in the New Testament. They belong together in Christian faith and experience. Westcott remarks,

> Truth and love describe an intellectual harmony and a moral harmony; and the two correspond with each other according to their subject matter. Love is truth in human action; and truth is love in regard to the order of things.[18]

For a vital Christian life the two must be kept in balance. Bruce asserts, "Where 'truth and love' coexist harmoniously, we have a well-balanced Christian character."[19] Truth and love must also be kept in balance for a vital Christian fellowship to flourish in a Christian community. A united adherence to the revealed truth is essential when the Christian community is faced with the falsehood of heretical teachers or when it encounters open attack upon its faith from an unbelieving world. The active love of believers toward one another will unite them in spiritual unity and demonstrate to the world that they are indeed one body in Christ.

II. The Message (vv. 4-11)

The Elder's message contains personal encouragement and specific warning (vv. 4-11). He begins his message to this chosen lady with an expression of gratitude at having met some of her devout children (v. 4). This leads to an appeal to the readers to continue their commendable practice of love and obedience to God's commandments (vv. 5-6). John is also aware that the readers are facing the deceptive effort of the false teachers and warns them against the subtle impact of their work (vv. 7-9). Highly appreciative of this matron's practice of hospitality, John feels constrained explicitly to prohibit such hospitality when the false teachers come to her home; he directs

---

[16]I. Howard Marshall, *The Epistles of John,* New International Commentary on the New Testament (Grand Rapids: Eerdmans, 1978), p. 64.

[17]Simon J. Kistemaker, *Exposition of the Epistle of James and the Epistles of John,* New Testament Commentary (Grand Rapids: Baker, 1986), p. 376.

[18]Westcott, p. 226.

[19]F. F. Bruce, *The Epistles of John* (Old Tappan, N.J.: Revell, 1970), p. 139.

her not to receive them into her home nor to give them encouragement in their work (vv. 10-11).

A. *The Occasion for the Letter (v. 4)*

John begins with an expression of personal joy caused by his encounter with certain members of this elect lady's family. His remark "I rejoiced greatly that I found of thy children walking in truth" corresponds to the opening thanksgiving that Paul expresses in most of his letters.[20] The expression "I rejoiced greatly" *(echarēn lian)*, which occurs also in 3 John 3, recalls his initial joy upon meeting them. The aorist passive verb *(echarēn,* "I was made to rejoice") recalls the joyful occasion, and the added adverb "greatly" *(lian,* "very much, exceedingly") underlines the depth of the joy which the occasion produced.

The occasion for the joy was "that I found of thy children walking in truth" *(hoti heurēka ek tōn teknōn sou peripatountas en alētheia,* more literally, "because I have found of your children walking in truth"). The perfect-tense verb *(heurēka,* "I have found") records the abiding sense of joy produced by that encounter. Plummer remarks that the verb does not imply "that there had been any *seeking* on the part of the Apostle, still less that there had been any *examination* as to the rightness of their conduct."[21] John does not indicate where the encounter took place but rather stresses its joyous impact. Certainly it is a report that should comfort and thrill the heart of this pious mother. D. Smith thinks that John's use of the term "of thy children" *(ek tōn teknōn)* is "a tenderer word than 'sons,' *(huiōn)*" and implies close family ties.[22] The expression "of thy children" *(ek tōn teknōn sou)* has been differently understood. Some interpreters, especially those who hold that the letter is addressed to a local church, understand John to imply that what he is reporting is not true to all the members of the church, since some had already been contaminated by the heresy he warns against. Then the expression implies a divided church, a condition which the writer could hardly have described as making him feel "very glad" (NASB). John's use of the preposition *ek* has a partitive force, implying that he had met only part of the children. John's expression, as Burdick notes, "does not necessarily mean that her children were not all faithful. It may mean that John had come in contact with some, but not all, who were 'walking in

---

[20]See Romans 1:8; 1 Corinthians 1:4-8; Philippians 1:3-5; Colossians 1:3-7; 1 Thessalonians 1:2-4; 2 Thessalonians 1:3; Philemon 4-5.

[21]Alfred Plummer, *The Epistles of S. John,* Cambridge Bible for Schools and Colleges (1883; reprint ed., London: Cambridge University Press, 1938), p. 177. Italics in original.

[22]David Smith, "The Epistles of St. John," in *The Expositor's Greek Testament* ([1897]; reprint ed., Grand Rapids: Eerdmans, n.d.), 5:201.

truth.' ''[23](*peripatountas en alētheia*). Their daily round of activities marked them as living "in" the sphere of "truth." This is the fifth occurrence of the term in the first four verses of the letter. Used without the article, the term characterizes their habitual course of life as committed to the truths and the moral standards embodied in the orthodox Christian faith. Their lives reveal the reality of their living union with Jesus Christ.

John explicitly underlines the faithful nature of their conduct by his assertion that they walked "as we have received a commandment from the Father" (*kathōs entolēn elabomen para tou patros,* more literally, "even as commandment we received from alongside the Father"). John's expression makes clear that for the believer such conduct is not an option but a divine commandment. The adverb "as" (*kathōs, "just as"*) marks the close conformity of their conduct to the commandment received "from the Father" as stressing the ultimate source of the command. God the Father is the true source of the revelation brought by the incarnate Son. Their daily conduct revealed their love-prompted obedience to the commandment they had received. John does not define the nature of that commandment, but clearly both "truth and love" (v. 3) were reflected in their conduct. From the character of their conduct, John thankfully recognizes that they willingly conformed their lives to the commandment they had accepted as believers in Christ Jesus.

B. The Appeal for Love and Obedience (vv. 5-6)

Following his comment about the past (v. 4), John turns to practical exhortation in view of present circumstances. "And now" (*kai nun*) is transitional, marking the turn to present concerns. John states the character and content of his appeal (v. 5) and then clarifies the nature and age of the duty enjoined (v. 6).

1. The character and content of the appeal (v. 5). In saying "and now I beseech thee, lady" (*kai nun erōtō se, kuria*), his verb, "I beseech" (*erōtō*), conveys a sense of dignity and authority as he addresses his polite personal request to this respected "lady" (*kuria*).[24] Before he expresses his request, he indicates that what he is asking is not something new which he is setting forth under his own authority: "not as though I wrote a new commandment unto thee" (*ouch hōs entolēn graphōn soi kainēn,* literally, "not as a commandment writing to you new"). In placing the term "new" at the end of his negation, he insists that he is not like the heretics who customarily

---

[23]Donald W. Burdick, *The Letters of John the Apostle* (Chicago: Moody Press, 1985), p. 422.

[24]"To use *kuria* as a style of address was then a mark of respect, expressing the higher station of the one thus addressed." Werner Foerster, *"kuria,"* in *Theological Dictionary of the New Testament,* ed. Gerhard Kittel (Grand Rapids: Eerdmans, 1964), 3:1095.

insisted on offering something new. The contrasting "but" *(alla)* at once makes clear that what he has in mind is not a "new" commandment; rather, it is "that which we had from the beginning" *(alla hēn eichomen ap' archēs)*. In saying "we have had" *(eichomen)*, John unites himself with all true believers who have accepted this as an original part of the apostolic message. He had received this command from Jesus Himself (John 13:34; 15:12, 17) at the beginning of the Christian era.

The obligation in view is "that we love one another" *(hina agapōmen allēlous)*. While "that" *(hina)* points to the content of the command, the notion of purpose is not absent from the statement. As Blair remarks, "God's commandments are not given to be believed; they are to be obeyed."[25] The present-tense verb "love" calls for the characteristic practice of a selfless love that seeks the welfare of others above one's own desires. Such love is the present, continuing obligation of believers, while the reciprocal pronoun "one another" insists that it must be mutually operative among believers. Each believer must express as well as be the recipient of such love. The mutual practice of this love among believers "offers the clearest test of the truthfulness of the confession and the sincerity of the obedience given to God's commands."[26] It produces the soil in which false teaching cannot grow.

2. *The nature and age of the commandment* (v. 6). John next explains that the love he is talking about is the love that prompts obedience to God's commands: "And this is love" *(kai hautē estin hē agapē*, literally, "and this is the love"), namely, the love whose nature is "that we walk after his commandments" *(hina peripatōmen kata tas entolas autou*, "in order that we may be walking according to his commandments"). In verse 5 John speaks about a "commandment" and about "love." Now he reverses the terms to stress that true Christian love is living according to God's commandments. In the Christian life, love and obedience are inseparably related. As Plummer asserts: "Love divorced from duty will run riot; and duty divorced from love will starve."[27] Where there is no obedience to God there is no true love for Him. Conversely, it is true "that love must clothe itself in forms of obedience; and that obedience to law becomes perfect liberty when inspired by love."[28] Christian love is revealed when we walk according to God's commands.

---

[25]J. Allen Blair, *The Epistles of John: Devotional Studies on Living Confidently* (Neptune, N.J.: Loizeaux Brothers, 1982), pp. 214-15.

[26]Glen W. Barker, "2 John," in *The Expositor's Bible Commentary* (Grand Rapids: Zondervan, 1981), 12:363.

[27]Plummer, p. 179.

[28]Cox, p. 80.

In verse 5 John connects this love with the singular "commandment," but in verse 6 he employs the plural "commandments" *(tas entolas)*. Marshall notes that any apparent difficulty is solved "when we grasp that *'the command'* is that we should love one another, while 'the commands' are the detailed requirements which unfold the structure of this central command."[29] God's varied commands give guidance to love's obedience under the varied and diverse circumstances that the Christian encounters. The present-tense verb "walk" *(peripatōmen,* "walk around") is figurative of daily life with its diverse round of activities, while the preposition "after" *(kata* with the accusative, "down along the line of") suggests that these commandments mark out the path to be followed under these varied circumstances.

In reverting to the singular, "This is the commandment" *(hautē hē entolē estin),* John notes that these various commandments are in reality all gathered up in this one basic command of mutual love. This God-like love is the governing reality for victorious Christian living. The parenthetical remark "as ye have heard from the beginning" *(kathōs ēkousate ap' archēs)* recalls that they had heard this reality proclaimed from the beginning of their Christian life. John feels no hesitancy in repeating this fact; he is well aware of the truth of the old maxim, "Repetition is the mother of learning." When confronted with new and strange ideas, we are often prone to forget those fundamental truths which wrought a fundamental change in our lives when first we heard and accepted them.

John's purpose in recalling these old truths is "That. . . ye should walk in it" *(hina en autē peripatēte).* The change to the second-person plural subject in the verb reminds the readers of their duty personally to put into practice the things they have so frequently heard. The pronoun "in it" *(en autē)* may refer either to the commandment or to love. Both views are advocated. The rendering of the Vulgate implies that the reference is to the commandment, and some modern interpreters, such as Houlden and Wilder,[30] accept that view. Bultmann asserts, "Whether the *en autē* ('in it') in this clause refers to the commandment or to love is uncertain, but makes no difference."[31] But Westcott holds that "in it" means *"in love,* which is the main subject of the sentences."[32] Plummer agrees that the reference is to love and supports this view as follows:

---

[29]Marshall, p. 67.

[30]J. L. Houlden, *A Commentary on the Johannine Epistles,* Harper's New Testament Commentaries (New York: Harper & Row, 1973), p. 145; Amos N. Wilder and Paul W. Hoon, "The First, Second, and Third Epistles of John," in *The Interpreter's Bible* (New York: Abingdon Press, 1957), 12:305.

[31]Rudolf Bultmann, *The Johannine Epistles,* Hermeneia–A Critical and Historical Commentary on the Bible (Philadelphia: Fortress Press, 1973), p. 111.

[32]Westcott, p. 228.

S. John speaks of walking *in (en)* truth, *in* light, *in* darkness; but of walking *according to (kata)* the commandments. S. Paul speaks both of walking *in* love (Eph. v. 2) and *according to* love (Rom. xiv. 15). Neither speaks of walking *in* commandments: and in Luke i. 6 a different verb is used. Moreover the context here is in favour of 'in it' meaning in love.[33]

We accept the latter view as the intended meaning.

Barker notes that John's argument here is intentionally circular:

> The test of love is obedience to God's commands, and the test of obedience is whether one "walks in love." . . . Love of God that does not result in obedience to the Word of God cannot be the love that is God's gift in Jesus Christ. . . . Obedience that does not lead to the life of love in which we love one another even to death is not obedience offered to God. Not to love means to remain in darkness (1 John 2:11) and in death (1 John 3:14). Hatred of one's brother can never be defended as obedience to God.[34]

C. The Warning Against the False Teachers (vv. 7-9)

The opening "for" *(hoti)* of verse 7 marks the connection with verses 5-6 and introduces the reasons for the call for mutual love which John has just made. John now "turns from the true believers to the false teachers, from the wheat to the tares."[35] He points out the tragic fact which prompts his warning against the false teachers (v. 7), declares the duty of his readers in the face of the danger (v. 8), and states the contrasting results produced by these antithetical positions. (v. 9).

1. The reason for the warning (v. 7). John's appeal for mutual love and obedience on the part of his readers is prompted by sad reality: "for many deceivers are entered into the world" *(hoti polloi planoi exēlthon eis ton kosmon)*. The unity of believers in mutual love and obedience will enable them to recognize and resist these deceptive false teachers. John's statement of the presence of these deceivers recalls the facts announced in 1 John 2:18-19; 4:1-6. John's reference to "many deceivers" indicates that they constitute a widespread movement and present a real danger to believers. The term "deceivers" *(planoi)* characterizes them by their basic activity as intentionally seeking to deceive and lead astray the unwary. They are so dangerous because they "lead to wrong action, and not only to wrong opinion."[36] They cannot rest until they have ensnared others in their error.

---

[33]Plummer, p. 179.

[34]Barker, p. 363.

[35]J.R.W. Stott, *The Epistles of John,* Tyndale New Testament Commentaries (Grand Rapids: Eerdmans, 1964), pp. 208.

[36]Westcott, p. 228.

John further characterizes these deceivers as those who "are entered into the world" (*exēlthon eis ton kosmon,* literally, "have gone out into the world"). The expression may simply recall the fact that they withdrew from the orthodox church (1 John 2:18-19) and as such are seeking to deceive those who remained. More probably John's expression implies that they view themselves as carrying out a special mission. Thus Stott suggests that "it seems more likely that the language is deliberately reminiscent of the mission of Christ and of His Apostles. Christ was being aped by antichrist."[37] So understood, these deceivers are motivated by a demonic mission. Smalley depicts the contrasts: "Whereas the orthodox followers of Jesus are sent out into the world to preach the truth, the heretics went out, as itinerant emissaries of the devil, to teach error and gain converts for their own cause."[38]

To make clear their apostate nature John applies the christological test: "who confess not that Jesus Christ is come in the flesh" (*hoti mē homologountes Iēsoun Christon erchomenon en sarki).* This appositional description of the "many deceivers" presents them as a distinct group, marked by the fact that they deliberately "confess not that Jesus Christ is come in the flesh." The negative *(mē)* with the present-tense participle portrays their practice of openly avoiding a direct denial of the incarnation, but they were subtle enough to counterfeit that basic apostolic teaching through the teaching they brought. What a professed Christian teacher deliberately refuses to acknowledge in dealing with doctrinal matters may be just as revealing as what he openly rejects. The refusal of these false teachers to acknowledge that Jesus Christ "is come in the flesh" (*erchomenon en sarki,* better, "as coming in flesh," NASB) was in fact a repudiation of that concept. In 1 John 4:2 John's use of the perfect tense, "that Jesus Christ has come in the flesh" (NASB), sets forth the fact of the incarnation as an abiding historical reality. Here his use of the present tense indicates that these heretics deny the possibility of the incarnation. In either case the basic error of the heretics was their refusal to accept the permanent union of the divine and the human natures in Jesus Christ. John never speaks of Christ coming "into the flesh" *(eis ton sarka);* he either speaks of Him coming "in the flesh" (here and 1 John 4:2) or that He "became flesh" *(sarx egeneto;* John 1:14, NASB). To have said that Christ "came *into* flesh" would have opened the door to Cerinthian Gnosticism. Cerinthus, a late contemporary of John at Ephesus, taught that Jesus was a mere man but that the divine Christ came upon Him at His baptism and empowered His ministry but left Him before His death on the cross. Such teaching blatantly denies the reality of the incarnation and dissolves the doctrine of the atonement. Here the use of the present

---

[37]Stott, p. 208.
[38]Smalley, p. 328.

tense to deny the possibility of the incarnation may imply a repudiation of Docetic Gnosticism. Because they held that "flesh" was inherently evil, Docetic Gnostics claimed that Christ only seemed to have a human body and that such a union of the divine and the human was inherently impossible. They insisted that the divine Christ never became incarnate in human flesh. They held that the apostolic teaching concerning the incarnate Christ was a misapprehension of His real nature. Some, such as Dodd, suggest that the present tense, "Jesus Christ coming in the flesh," is a denial of Christ's return "in the flesh."[39] Then, as Orr suggests, "the heretics were taking the logical next step in denying the personal return of the Lord Jesus at the end of the age."[40] But the context relates to the nature of Christ's first coming and does not support such a future reference in the present participle here.

Having spoken of the heretics as a group, John next individualizes: "This is a deceiver and an antichrist" *(houtos estin ho planos kai ho antichristos).* The demonstrative pronoun "this" *(houtos,* "this one") stresses that this is the true identity of every individual belonging to this group. The definite article with both nouns, "the deceiver and the antichrist," stresses that he personally embodies the characteristics conveyed by both of these terms. The former term mainly portrays his relation to men as seeking to deceive them and lead them astray from the truth in Christ; the latter stresses his personal rejection of the incarnate Christ and his desire to replace Him with a "christ" of his own devising. Plummer notes that this devastating portrayal "completes the series of condemnatory names which S. John uses in speaking of these false teachers; liars (1 John ii. 22), seducers (1 John ii. 26), false prophets (1 John iv. 1), deceivers (2 John 7), antichrists (1 John ii. 18, 22; iv. 3; 2 John 7)."[41] As Fausset observes, these many antichrists "who in a degree fulfil the character, are forerunners of the final personal Antichrist, who shall concentrate in himself all the features of previous Antichristian systems."[42]

2. The statement of the warning (v. 8). Having set before his readers the dangerous picture, John no longer politely asks but rather issues an emphatic warning to insure their safety: "Look to yourselves, that we lose not those things which we have wrought, but that we receive a full reward." In using the present imperative, "look to yourselves" *(blepete heautous,* or "watch yourselves"), John lays upon them the standing duty to place themselves

---

[39]Dodd, p. 149.

[40]Orr, p. 623.

[41]Plummer, p. 181.

[42]A. R. Fausset, "The Second General Epistle of John," in Robert Jamieson, A. R. Fausset, and David Brown, *A Commentary, Critical and Explanatory, on the Old and New Testaments,* American ed. (Hartford, Conn.: S. S. Scranton, Co., n.d.), vol. 2, *New Testament,* p. 539.

under continuous guard. Issued without any connecting particle, the command is solemn and forceful. While not unmindful of God's care for His own, John reminds them of their personal duty ever to be watchful, to keep an eye on themselves.

John graphically states the danger confronting them: "that we lose not those things which we have wrought, but that we receive a full reward" *(hina mē apolesēte ha ērgasametha, alla misthou plērē apolabēte).* The Greek manuscripts show much variety in the expressed subject of these three verbs. On the basis of the manuscript evidence, it is commonly accepted that the subject for the first and third verbs is the second person plural: "that *you* may not lose" and "that *you* may receive a full reward." But for the middle verb, the evidence is divided, either "which *you* have wrought" or "which *we* have wrought."[43] While the evidence for reading "which we have wrought" is not strong, the editors of the United Bible Societies Greek text believed that this was more probably the correct reading. The editors preferred the first-person plural "we" on two grounds: (1) *transcriptional:* the first-person plural more readily explains the other reading; the scribes would be more likely to make all three verbs read alike; (2) *internal:* "the delicate nuance ('. . . that you do not destroy the things which we, apostles and teachers, wrought in you') is more likely to be due to the author than to copyists."[44]

If the reading "which you have wrought" is accepted, then John is warning his readers that they must be on guard lest they destroy their own accomplishments; if they yield to these false teachers they will thereby destroy the spiritual growth they have experienced through their acceptance of the true apostolic message. (The NIV uses "you" with all three verbs). If "you" is accepted as the subject for the first and third verbs and "we" as the original subject of the middle verb (so the NASB), John's appeal is twofold. He first of all makes a delicate and touching appeal to their personal affection for the Elder himself; if they fall prey to the false teachers John reminds them that they will be destroying "what *we* have accomplished," namely, the spiritual results of the missionary workers in bringing the gospel to them. But more probably this "we" is intended to be more inclusive, uniting the efforts of the readers with those of the apostolic messengers. As Hodges observes,

> The author's touch was both delicate and humble. He regarded himself as a co-laborer with his readers and their loss would be shared by him if they

---

[43]For the evidence see United Bible Societies, *The Greek New Testament,* 3rd ed.
[44]Metzger, p. 721.

did not effectively resist the false doctrine. The antichrists were a threat to the work of the Lord in which he and they were mutually engaged.[45]

John further makes an eschatological appeal: if they remain true to the apostolic message, the contrasted result will be "that we receive a full reward" *(alla misthon plērē apolabēte)*. The adversative "but" *(alla)* points to the resultant contrast in that future day. If they prove themselves faithful laborers who faithfully stay with the task until the end, assuredly they will not experience loss but rather "we"–understood in an inclusive sense–will receive a "full reward." Since salvation is wholly by grace (Eph. 2:8-9), there is no thought here of meriting their salvation through their faithfulness. As Smalley notes, "The image is drawn from the area of employment, since 'reward' *(misthon)* is the term for a workman's wage (cf. Matt. 20:8; Jas. 5:4)."[46] The expression "a full reward" *(misthon plērē,* "a reward in full" or "a reward that attains the full possibility") looks forward to the final outcome for the faithful believer (Rev. 3:11). In view is that future day when "we must all appear before the judgment seat of Christ, that each one may be recompensed for his deeds in the body, according to what he has done, whether good or bad" (2 Cor. 5:10 NASB). Their full reward will be affected in that day if they yield to these deceivers and antichrists (cf. 1 Cor. 3:11-15). In that future day, as a further expression of His grace, God will reward present faithfulness and obedience to His commands. It is another instance of John's appeal to the hope of the future to stimulate present faithfulness (cf. 1 John 2:28).

3. The contrast between the heretics and true believers (v. 9). John sets forth the present contrast between the heretics and the true believers in the form of a striking antithetical parallelism:

> Any one who goes too far and does not abide in the teaching of Christ
>   does not have God:
> The one who abides in the teaching,
>   he has both the Father and the Son (NASB).

He thus sets in contrast the fundamental characteristic of each group as well as their resultant spiritual status.

The heretics are portrayed as a distinct group marked by a positive and a negative characteristic activity: "Whosoever transgresseth, and abideth not in the doctrine of Christ." "Whosoever" *(pas ho,* literally, "every one who")* asserts that these two features without exception mark every one in this group. The use of one article governing two present-tense participles

---

[45]Zane C. Hodges, "2 John," in *The Bible Knowledge Commentary, New Testament* (Wheaton, Ill.: Victor Books, 1983), p. 907.

[46]Smalley, p. 331.

(pas ho proagōn kai mē menōn) makes clear that all these heretics are marked by the same positive-negative activities.

Their positive feature is "whosoever transgresseth" *(pas ho proagōn)*. The manuscript evidence is divided concerning the verb used here. The KJV reading, "transgresseth," follows the Textus Receptus which reads *parabainōn,* "to go alongside of," as departing from the true line, hence "transgresseth." The manuscript evidence for this reading is later and not as strong as the evidence for the alternative reading *proagōn,* "going forward, advancing."[47] The nature of the heretics' advancement is made clear by the following negative, "and abideth not in the doctrine of Christ."

John's positive designation of them, which he may well have drawn from the claims of the heretics themselves, presents them as self-professed progressive thinkers. "The verb *proagōn,* as used here," Burdick notes, "speaks of professed progress, reflecting the Gnostic claim to have progressed to a higher understanding of God, of the human predicament, and of the secret way of salvation from the predicament."[48] John is not opposed to spiritual growth and increasing understanding in the truths of the gospel. The kind of progress he is opposed to is the professed progress which "abideth not in the doctrine of Christ." He is condemning "an advancement which involves desertion of first principles; and such an advancement is not progress but apostasy."[49] As professed progressive thinkers these individuals claimed to have found a system of thought that went beyond God's revelation in Christ. Such progress beyond the revelation in Christ, however, was not spiritual advancement but a fatal plunge into spiritual darkness. This follows from the fact that he no longer adheres to "the doctrine of Christ" which he once professed to accept. The genitive "of Christ" *(tou Christou)* may be understood either as an objective genitive or as a subjective genitive. Smith accepts the genitive as objective and understands the expression to mean "the teaching which recognizes Jesus as the Christ."[50] But others, such as Westcott, view the genitive as subjective, as denoting "the doctrine which Christ brought, and which He brought first in His own person, and then through His followers (Hebr. ii. 3)."[51] The reference is to the self-revelation in Christ as received and reported by His chosen followers. This is the only place in the Johannine Epistles where the term "Christ" *(tou Christou,* "the Christ") is used alone without the noun "Jesus." It points

---

[47]For the evidence see Nestle-Aland, *Novum Testamentum Graece,* 26th ed.

[48]Burdick, p. 427.

[49]Plummer, pp. 181-82.

[50]Smith, p. 202.

[51]Westcott, p. 230.

to His messianic identity as the agent of God's revelation to mankind. John is concerned about the preservation of the true teaching given by Christ to His disciples and as proclaimed by them. He hangs the validity of Christianity upon the truthfulness of that message.

John views the departure from this divinely revealed message as fatal; the inevitable result is that such a one "hath not God" (*theon ouk echei,* literally, "God not he has"). In spite of his professed advanced knowledge concerning God and His nature, he does not possess the true God as his own God, "does not possess Him in his heart as a Being to adore, and trust, and love."[52] His brilliant advanced speculation about God fails to bring him into a personal relationship with God. He who rejects the Son who revealed the Father cannot have the Father whom Christ came to reveal. Stott well asserts, "To deny the Son is to forfeit the Father. This is as true today of all non-Christian religions as it was of Cerinthian Gnosticism in the first century."[53]

Dodd expresses the fear that "the writer has incautiously expressed himself in terms which might seem to stigmatize any kind of 'advance' as disloyalty to the faith, and so to condemn Christian theology to lasting sterility."[54] But this is to misread John's true concern in combating the heretics. John certainly agreed with Peter concerning the Christian need to "grow in grace, and *in* the knowledge of our Lord and Saviour Jesus Christ" (2 Pet. 3:18). But he is strongly opposed to any "advance" which moves beyond and so perverts the revelation in Christ. For theology to be vital the believer must grow in his understanding and experience of the revelation given in Christ. But Christian growth must remain true to the revelation in Christ, for "no interpretation of Christianity is true which eliminates Redemption or obscures the glory of the Cross."[55]

The positive side of John's antithesis is "He that abideth in the doctrine of Christ, he hath both the Father and the Son" (*ho menōn en tē didachē, houtos kai ton patera kai ton huion echei*). John identifies the true believer as "he that abideth in the doctrine of Christ," marking him as remaining true to the apostolic message concerning the incarnate Christ. His continued adherence to the truth in Christ does not imply that his spiritual life is fixed and sterile; rather, the truth to which he adheres motivates and vitalizes his character and conduct. But unlike the heretics, his growing Christian experience "is rooted in the historical events of the incarnation and the atonement, the revelation and redemption which were finished in Christ."[56]

---

[52]Plummer, p. 182.

[53]Stott, p. 211.

[54]Dodd, p. 150.

[55]Smith, p. 203.

[56]Stott, p. 211.

His faithful adherence to the authentic message of Christianity assures that "he hath both the Father and the Son." The demonstrative pronoun rendered "he" (*houtos,* "this one") marks that this is specifically true of the one just identified; it is not true of the one who abandons the authentic Christian revelation. His adherence to "the doctrine" assures that he possesses "both the Father and the Son." "It is impossible to separate the Father and the Son in Christian experience."[57] The change from the abstract "God" to the personal term "Father" points to the intimate family relationship he experiences through the Son. The divine self-revelation through the incarnate Son assures that "our fellowship *is* with the Father, and with His Son Jesus Christ" (1 John 1:3).

D. The Prohibition Against Aiding the Heretics (vv. 10-11)

Having identified the heretics, John next offers practical instructions to protect his readers against personal contamination from them. He issues his prohibition against aiding the false teachers (v. 10) and adds his reason for the prohibition (v. 11).

1. The statement of the prohibition (v. 10). John's prohibition is motivated by his concern for the personal safety of his beloved friends. The setting for the application of his forceful prohibition is clearly stated: "If there come any unto you, and bring not this doctrine." The opening "if" *(ei)* with the indicative assumes that the condition portrayed is actually occurring. It seems that the Elder has learned that some of these heretical traveling missionaries were making a tour through the area where this "elect lady and her children" lived. Such peripatetic philosophers or religious teachers were a familiar phenomenon in the Roman world, and John knew that the Christian matron to whom his prohibition is directed was well known for her hospitality toward traveling Christian missionaries. The scene John has in view is not the arrival of some passing traveler who hopes to find needed shelter and entertainment in the home of this gracious matron. The verb "come" *(erchetai)* denotes the purposeful arrival of a traveling missionary with the intention of procuring an opportunity to propagate his message. The added description "and bring not this doctrine" at once makes clear the situation John has in view. The application of the prohibition is determined by the kind of message he brings. The Third Epistle of John makes it clear that it was an accepted duty of believers to welcome and aid missionaries of the Christian gospel. But that obligation did not apply to the propagator of a heretical, Christ-rejecting message. The established fact that he does not bring "this doctrine," the teaching about Christ as set forth in

---

[57]Marshall, p. 73.

verse 9, places him under John's prohibition. It implies that his identity as a false teacher is known.

John orders that when such a heretical teacher arrives, "receive him not into *your* house, neither bid him God speed." The present imperatives mark this as a standing practice. She must not open her home to such an individual and thus provide him the opportunity to spread his pernicious views, either among the members of the family or to the house-church that might be assembled. Such a refusal to open her home to these heretics was an effective way to frustrate the spread of heresy. John insists that the propagation of heresy must not be encouraged but rather resisted. As Blair notes, "This is not a denial of the love of God, but an application of it to protect innocent victims from heresy."[58]

At first sight it might seem that the second element in the prohibition, "neither bid him God speed" (*kai chairein autō mē legete,* rendered "or welcome him" in the NIV), should more properly have been mentioned before receiving him into the house. The Greek term rendered "bid him God speed" (*chairein*) was used as a warm expression of greeting upon arrival and in the New Testament generally has this meaning (cf. Acts 15:23; 23:26; James 1:1). But here and in 2 Corinthians 13:11, it seems rather to refer to an affectionate expression of farewell. As a formula of greeting the infinitive *chairein,* which basically means "to rejoice," was an expressed desire that the traveler, upon arrival, might experience joy upon having attained his destination; used upon departure, it expressed the desire for a pleasant journey by the traveler. In either case the term implied approval of the one so addressed. The term was used among Christians as a token of Christian brotherhood. The KJV rendering "God speed," a contraction of "God speed you," indicates a wish for the God-promoted success of the one so addressed. For a true believer thus to greet a heretical teacher upon arrival or departure would be to express sympathy and encouragement to an individual intent on destroying the very faith that the believer holds dear. It would be an act utterly inconsistent with his own faith and Christian efforts.

2. The reason for the prohibition (v. 11). With his connective "for" (*gar*) John at once declares his reason for this prohibition: "for he that biddeth him God speed is partaker of his evil deeds." For the believer it would be a non-Christian and dangerous course of action. In thus encouraging the heretical teacher he becomes a "partaker of his evil deeds" (*koinōnei tois ergois autou tois ponerois*). The verb rendered "is partaker" (*koinōnei,* "to share in common, to have fellowship with") declares the great evil involved. This verb, which occurs only here in the writings of John, "implies more than participation in the definite acts. It suggests fellowship with the character of which they are the outcome."[59] Trapp notes that by disregarding the Elder's prohibition, the believer becomes a partaker in the heretic's evil deeds in three ways: "1. By his sinful silence and dissimulation. 2. Next, by confirming the sinner in his evil way. 3. Lastly, by offence given to others."[60] By such an action he would share in a fellowship the very opposite of that set forth by John in 1 John 1:3, 7. By his tolerance he shares in the heretic's "evil deeds" (*tois ergois autou tois ponērois,* literally, "in the deeds of him, the evil ones"). The noun rendered "deeds," or "works," includes not only what the heretic teaches but also what he achieves through his efforts. John stresses the "evil," or vicious, nature of those deeds by placing the adjective with the repeated article at the very end of his sentence. This adjective *(tois ponērois)* is the term John uses in designating the Devil as "the wicked one" (1 John 2:13-14; 3:12; 5:18-19). It was in the light of this tragic possibility that the Elder commands his beloved readers, "Watch yourselves, that you might not lose what we have accomplished" (v. 8 NASB).

John's stern prohibition must be seen in the light of the occasion he had in mind. It states the needed Christian reaction when confronted with the efforts of one furthering soul-destroying heresy. It does not restrict the practice of hospitality and Christian love when no heretical proselyting intentions are involved. Today some are inclined to regard the Elder's prohibition as too harsh and offensive and "decline to accept the Presbyter's ruling here as a sufficient guide for Christian conduct."[61] Unfortunately this prohibition has at times been appealed to by certain Christian groups when no teachings destructive of Christianity were involved. But today there is the danger that the Church "is too ready to profess doubt even as regards the centralities of the gospel and too ready to tolerate dissent from the faith once and for all handed down to the people of God."[62] In a day when there is a diminishing sense of the danger of open heresy, the tendency is to tolerate known heresy for the sake of unity.

It has been noted that in issuing this prohibition to his readers the Elder gives no directives as to any efforts that should be made to counteract the false views of these traveling missionaries or win them, back to the orthodox faith. But obviously John does not consider those to whom this letter was addressed sufficiently trained and prepared to deal successfully with these aggressive false teachers. If they engaged in open discussion with them it was likely that they would be taken in and deceived by their deadly devia-

---

[59]Westcott, p. 231.

[60]John Trapp, *Trapp's Commentary on the New Testament* (1865; reprint ed., Evansville, Ill.: Sovereign Grace Book Club, 1958), p. 735.

[61]Dodd, p. 152.

[62]Marshall, p. 75.

tions from the orthodox faith. These false teachers had rejected the efforts of the orthodox leaders and had withdrawn from the church (1 John 2:18-19), and John did not anticipate that they could be won back by those to whom he wrote. John's concern was rather to shield his readers from the subtle efforts of these practiced deceivers and antichrists (v. 7).

III. The Conclusion (vv. 12-13)

The conclusion in verses 12-13 is strikingly similar to the conclusion in 3 John. The fact that "the conclusion of the letter is virtually verbally identical with the closing of 3 John" elicited the following skeptical comment of Bultmann: "As a consequence, one cannot resist the suspicion that it is an imitation."[63] But Wilder, who likewise questions the apostolic authorship of these epistles, expresses a positive reaction: "The phrases closely resemble those in III John 13, with just enough difference to reassure us that no copyist or imitator is at work."[64] We accept these similarities as evidence that the same individual wrote them, while the differences aptly reflect the diverse historical conditions he was confronting when he composed them.

Having nearly filled his sheet of papyrus paper with what he had written, the Elder terminates his letter with his announcement of an impending visit (v. 12) and appends personal greetings from "the children of thy elect sister" (v. 13).

A. *The Plans for a Coming Visit (v. 12)*

These closing remarks may appear somewhat formal, but they do reflect the warm personal feelings of the writer. His reference to the brevity of his letter leads to an announcement of his plans to visit the recipients.

The Elder explains the brevity of his letter: "Having many things to write unto you, I would not *write* with paper and ink." His remark "having many things to write unto you" *(polla echōn humin graphein)* assures his readers that there are still many things on his mind that he desires to share with them. The forward position of "many things" *(polla)* stresses that various matters have not been touched on which are still on his mind. We do not know what they were, but clearly they were related to John's concern regarding the danger from the coming of the heretical teachers.

Mention of these many things which still called for discussion leads John to offer a twofold explanation for the brevity of his letter. There was, first of all, his personal decision not to deal with these matters in writing: "I would not *write* with paper and ink" *(ouk eboulēthēn dia chartou kai melanos,* literally, "not I wished through paper and ink"). The compressed

---

[63]Bultmann, p. 115.

[64]Wilder and Hoon, p. 307.

expression implies that a verbal designation such as "to write" or "to do so" needs to be added. "Paper and ink" refer to the standard writing materials in common use in the Mediterranean world of that day (cf. 3 John 13). The word "paper" *(chartou)* indicates his use of a sheet of papyrus rather than the more expensive parchment (2 Tim. 4:13) made of leather. Papyrus paper was made from the papyrus plants which flourished in Egypt. Cut into desired lengths, the pitch of the papyrus stalks, as narrow strips, were laid side by side, and then another layer of strips was placed over them at right angles; then the two layers were united by being moistened and placed under pressure; frequently some glue was added. After the dried sheet was rubbed smooth, it was ready for use. Generally, apparently as here, only the side where the strips ran horizontally was used for writing. For longer documents sheets of papyrus were pasted together. In New Testament times the "ink" *(melanos,* literally "black") was made of vegetable soot mixed with gum and moistened as needed, but better grades of ink were made of nutgalls, sulphate of iron, and gum.[65]

It has been suggested that the writer's decision not to write more is probably "a sign of the failing powers of an old man, to whom writing is serious fatigue."[66] But his added reference to his plans to visit the readers indicates that the author did not consider himself too old to travel. In view of the available modes of travel in those days, one wonders whether the writer would not find such a trip equally exhausting.

Instead of writing more, John explains "but I trust to come unto you, and speak face to face." He has decided that it is more desirable to discuss these other matters with them personally. His expression "I trust to come unto you" *(elpizō genesthai pros humas)* implies that the decision has been made, but the plans are not yet fully formalized. Although the aorist infinitive rendered "to come" *(genesthai,* literally, "to become") was often used as the equivalent of the regular verb "to come" *(elthein),* its use here seems to refer to the resultant personal presence with them on arrival. His words give no clue as to where the readers lived.

His hope is that upon arrival they will "speak face to face" (*stoma pros stoma lalēsai,* literally, "mouth to mouth to speak"). The expression denotes the intimate relationship made possible by personal encounter. Clearly John believes that such communication will be more effective than through writing. In support Stott comments, "Spoken words are less easily misunderstood than written words, because it is not only by language that the speaker conveys his meaning, but by the tone of his voice and the expression on his

---

[65]See S. Barabas, "Ink," and E. M. Blaiklock, "Papyrus," in *Zondervan Pictorial Encyclopedia of the Bible* (Grand Rapids: Zondervan, 1975, 1976), 3:279 and 4:589-90, respectively.

[66]Plummer, p. 184.

face.''[67] But Miller, while accepting that such oral communication is preferable at any time, yet points to the resultant benefit to us from the fact that he did write:

> But what would we have done without the permanent record contained in the letters of the apostles? Writing has an abiding value which conversation and oral ministry have not, however excellent these are at the time. We thank God for the inspired Scriptures.[68]

John is assured that upon his arrival they will welcome him, with the result "that our joy may be full" *(hina hē chara hēmōn*[69] *peplērōmenē ē)*. If we accept the reading "your joy," John refers to the effect his presence will have on his readers. If "our joy" is accepted as the original reading, John expresses his confidence that his presence with them will produce completed joy both for him and them. (On "our joy," see 1 John 1:4.) The reference is to a joy which is "more than the simple gratification which naturally comes from the reunion with old friends."[70] Lenski notes that the original, here rendered "may be full" *(peplērōmenē ē)*, is not a periphrastic construction but that the perfect participle is predicate to the verb; he renders "that your joy may be as having been filled."[71] John has in view the joy that is the result of Christian fellowship among believers; as fellow believers they will experience that joy in full measure with him.

B. The Greetings from Her Sister's Children (v. 13)

The Elder ends his letter with a personal remark to "the elect lady" to whom the letter is sent: "The children of thy elect sister greet thee" *(Aspazetai se ta tekna tēs adelphēs sou tēs eklektēs)*. Clearly they were in personal touch with the Elder when he wrote, for they asked him to convey their greetings to their aunt. It is generally assumed that those sending their greetings were members of the church at Ephesus where John resided. No greetings are included from the sister herself. She apparently resided in another place or perhaps had died. John's reference to her as "thy elect

---

[67]Stott, p. 215.

[68]John Miller, *Notes on James, I and II Peter, I, II and III John, Jude, Revelation* (Bradford, England: Needed Truth Publishing Office, n.d.), p. 98.

[69]The Greek manuscripts are divided between "your" *(humōn)* and "our" *(hēmōn)* in the pronoun used. Textual critics are not agreed on which is the original. For the evidence see the United Bible Societies, *The Greek New Testament*, 3rd ed. The majority of the editors of this Greek text favor the reading "our" *(hēmōn)* not only because of its good textual support but also because they believe it "is quite in harmony with the author's generous spirit in associating himself with his readers (cf. *hēmōn* in 1 Jn. 1.4)." Metzger, p. 722.

[70]Dodd, p. 153.

[71]Lenski, pp. 571-72.

sister" (*tēs adelphēs sou tēs eklektēs,* literally, "the sister of you, the elect") makes clear that she too is a chosen believer, one of God's elect in Christ, a fact confirmed by the solid Christian character of her children at Ephesus. Clearly John is grateful for the Christian training these two sisters had given their children. Burdick suggests that "it may be that these children were the ones who had informed John concerning their aunt's mistaken application of the principle of Christian love."[72] Then they agreed with John's prohibition to her (v. 10). John's use of the singular pronoun "greet thee" *(aspazetaise)* makes clear that their greetings are sent to their aunt personally.

Those who interpret the indicated recipients in verse 1 ("the elect lady and her children") figuratively, as denoting a local church and its members, also understand this reference to "the children of thy elect sister" figuratively of a local church. But since in verse 13 the sister does not appear personally, only her children, then, for consistency, we must conclude that the church at Ephesus did not officially support John's position, but only individual members of the church did so. It seems better to understand the designations in verse 1 and here literally to denote individual mothers and their children. Strauss remarks that "this personal note adds to an already lovely little letter."[73]

---

[72]Burdick, p. 431.
[73]Strauss, p. 155.

20

An Outline of Third John

I. The Salutation (vv. 1-4)
   A. The Writer (v. 1a)
   B. The Recipient (v. 1b)
   C. The Prayer (vv. 2-4)
      1. The statement of the prayer (v. 2)
      2. The reason for the prayer (vv. 3-4)
         a. The reports concerning Gaius (v. 3)
         b. The joy because of the reports (v. 4)
II. The Message (vv. 5-12)
   A. The Obligation to Support the Missionaries (vv. 5-8)
      1. The commendation of Gaius's ministry to the missionaries (vv. 5-6a)
      2. The nature of Gaius's further ministry to the missionaries (v. 6b)
      3. The explanation concerning the missionary obligation (vv. 7-8)
         a. The portrayal of the missionaries (v. 7)
         b. The missionary obligation of the believers (v. 8)
   B. The Opposition of Domineering Diotrephes (vv. 9-10)
      1. The letter of John to the church (v. 9a)
      2. The refusal of Diotrephes to cooperate (v. 9b)
      3. The dealing with Diotrephes upon John's arrival (v. 10a)
      4. The delineating of the deeds of Diotrephes (v. 10b)
   C. The Personal Lesson from the Circumstances (v. 11)
   D. The Testimony to Demetrius (v. 12)
III. The Conclusion (vv. 13-14)
   A. The Brevity of the Letter and John's Impending Visit (vv. 13-14a)
   B. The Benediction upon the Reader (v. 14b)
   C. The Mutual Greetings of Friends (v. 14c)

21

An Exposition of Third John

1 The elder unto the wellbeloved Gaius, whom I love in the truth.

2 Beloved, I wish above all things that thou mayest prosper and be in health, even as thy soul prospereth.

3 For I rejoiced greatly, when the brethren came and testified of the truth that is in thee, even as thou walkest in the truth.

4 I have no greater joy than to hear that my children walk in truth.

5 Beloved, thou doest faithfully whatsoever thou doest to the brethren, and to strangers;

6 Which have borne witness of thy charity before the church: whom if thou bring forward on their journey after a godly sort, thou shalt do well:

7 Because that for his name's sake they went forth, taking nothing of the Gentiles.

8 We therefore ought to receive such, that we might be fellowhelpers to the truth.

9 I wrote unto the church: but Diotrephes, who loveth to have the pre-eminence among them, receiveth us not.

10 Wherefore, if I come, I will remember his deeds which he doeth, prating against us with malicious words: and not content therewith, neither doth he himself receive the brethren, and forbiddeth them that would, and casteth *them* out of the church.

11 Beloved, follow not that which is evil, but that which is good. He that doeth good is of God: but he that doeth evil hath not seen God.

12 Demetrius hath good report of all *men,* and of the truth itself: yea, and we *also* bear record; and ye know that our record is true.

13 I had many things to write, but I will not with ink and pen write unto thee:

14 But I trust I shall shortly see thee, and we shall speak face to face. Peace *be* to thee. *Our* friends salute thee. Greet the friends by name.

Third John is the shortest book in the New Testament, about a line shorter than 2 John,[1] its "twin sister." Each letter filled a single sheet of ordinary papyrus paper. Both are precious examples of Christian correspondence which passed between local churches and individuals in the early Church. They reveal the problems encountered by a vigorously growing Christian faith. These letters center on the conflicts and triumphs experienced in connection with the coming of varied traveling missionaries who presented themselves in the local churches. They shatter any notion that things in the first century churches were ideal, or nearly so.

The messages of these two letters complement each other. In both, the basic concern is connected with the extension of the true faith and the question of giving aid to traveling missionaries. Second John speaks of the kind of people from whom aid is to be withheld; 3 John relates to those to whom Christian aid is to be extended. It is in connection with this obligation that three individuals, in three distinct roles, are named in 3 John.

The structural outline of 3 John is not as obvious as the simple three-part outline of 2 John.[2] The last two verses of 3 John naturally form the epistolary conclusion,[3] but it is not so obvious as to how far the opening salutation extends before the epistolary message begins.[4] Verse 1 contains the usual epistolary designation of the writer and reader, but it lacks the

---

[1] "Counting the letters, and allowing 36 letters for the ancient line, gives for 2 John 32 lines, for 3 John not quite 31 lines." Theodor Zahn, *Introduction to the New Testament,* trans. from the 3rd German ed. (Edinburgh: T. & T. Clark, 1909), 3:38. It is also the shortest on the basis of a word count: "In the 21st edition of the Nestle Greek NT it has 219 words, as compared with 245 in II John, 355 in Philemon, and 457 in Jude." Raymond E. Brown, *The Epistles of John,* The Anchor Bible (Garden City, N.Y.: Doubleday & Co., 1982), pp. 727, note 1.

[2] Robert W. Funk, "The Form and Structure of II and III John," *Journal of Biblical Literature* 86 (1967): 424-30.

[3] Most of our English versions follow the numbering in the Textus Receptus of this concluding paragraph as verses 13-14. But a few English versions—such as the RSV, TEV, and Living Bible—follow the numbering in the Greek editions of B. F. Westcott and F.J.A. Hort, *The New Testament in the Original Greek,* 2nd ed. (1881; reprint ed., New York: Macmillan Co., 1935); *Novum Testamentum Graece,* 26th ed. (Stuttgart: Deutsche Bibelstiftung, 1979); and Kurt Aland et al., ed., *The Greek New Testament,* 3rd ed. (New York: United Bible Societies, 1975) in numbering this paragraph as verses 13-15.

[4] There is no unanimity among the editors of the Greek text, nor in our English versions, concerning the number of recognized paragraphs in 3 John. The number of paragraphs ranges from five to eight. The commonly accepted paragraphs are 1, 2-4, 5-8, 9-12, and 13-14, following the Textus Receptus. Others divide vv. 9-12 into two paragraphs (9-10 and 11-12) or even three (9-10, 11, 12). Nestle-Aland, *Novum Testamentum Graece,* 22nd ed. (New York: American Bible Society, 1956) make vv. 2-8 one paragraph, but in their 26th edition (Stuttgart: Deutsche Bibelstiftung, 1979) they again mark these verses as two paragraphs. English versions and the commentators naturally reflect this diversity.

usual epistolary greeting; however, verse 2 continues with the conventional epistolary health-wish for the reader. Although some interpreters accept that the body of the letter proper begins with verse 3, verses 3-4 are generally accepted as closely connected with verse 2 as giving the writer's reason for his prayer for the reader. Accepting this close connection, verses 3-4 are preferably viewed as part of the epistolary salutation.

It seems most natural to accept verses 5-12 as constituting the body of the letter. This portion naturally falls into several distinct parts. Under this grouping of its contents, 3 John also has the usual three parts: the opening salutation (vv. 1-4), the epistolary message (vv. 5-12), and the epistolary conclusion (vv. 13-14).

I. The Salutation (vv. 1-4)

In accepting the first four verses as the opening salutation, this portion consists of three parts of very unequal length. The first part, identifying the writer, receives no expansion (v. 1a); the second part, naming the reader, receives some expansion (v. 1b); the third part, setting forth the writer's prayer for the reader, receives considerable expansion (vv. 2-4). The structure of the opening salutation underlines the writer's deep love and warm concern for the reader.

A. The Writer (v. 1a)

Instead of giving his name, the writer simply identifies himself as "the elder" *(ho presbuteros)*. Its use in these twin epistles indicates that the writer feels assured that the designation will readily identify him to his readers. He obviously feels no need further to identify himself or to enhance his position. Only in 2 and 3 John does this opening designation for the writer of an epistle occur. The use of such symbolic designations seems to be a Johannine trait; in the Gospel of John the writer refers to himself as "the disciple whom Jesus loved" (20:2; 21:7, 20), and he never gives the name of the mother of Jesus. No epistolary self-identification occurs in 1 John.

In itself the term "elder" *(presbuteros)* is simply an adjective indicating comparative age, someone older than another individual (cf. Luke 15:25). If that were its intended force we would need to imagine Gaius and his friends as referring to the writer as "the Old Man" and that the writer good-naturedly applied the affectionate nickname to himself. But any view that the term here is simply a designation of age is inconsistent with the position of unquestioned authority which the writer assumes in these letters. His attitude and words bespeak a conscious position of great ecclesiastical dignity.

Used in the plural, "the elders" is a common New Testament designation for the officials in the Jewish synagogues and the Christian churches. But the tone and contents of these letters indicate that "the elder," or "the presbyter," was more than just one of the elders of a local church. The writer of this letter may have served as a recognized elder in the local church where he resides,[5] but the designation *"the* elder" points to the uniqueness of his position. As Sawtelle points out, "There is an air of authority, a supervising interest, and a certain absoluteness in the teaching of our Epistle, as well as in that of the preceding one, which most powerfully suggests an apostolic, rather than *merely* presbyterial, origin."[6]

The suggested apostolic identity of the writer is in accord with early church tradition which portrays the Apostle John as spending the later years of his life at Ephesus, from which, as his center, he carried out an extensive ministry of evangelism and supervision over the churches in the surrounding region.[7] The title ascribed to these epistles is in our earliest manuscripts, identifying them as "of John" *(Iōannou),* weighty testimony to their supposed origin. The view that the author of the three documents identified as "of John" was indeed the Apostle John goes back to the early church and was almost unanimously held until the rise of modern critical scholarship.

Those who reject apostolic authorship for these epistles propose to identify "the elder" as a leading "member of the Johannine circle which was responsible for the Gospel and all the letters of John," who "may be called 'John' for convenience."[8] This "John the Elder," as distinct from John the Apostle, was recognized as an important member of the Johannine community, consisting of the apostle's disciples and adherents, in that he was "a bearer and deliverer of the apostolic tradition."[9] This distinction between John the Apostle and John the Elder is rooted in the proposal by Eusebius in his *Ecclesiastical History* (A.D. 325) that there were two men at Ephesus by the name of John whom tradition has confused. Scholarly opinion has been, and still is, sharply divided concerning the validity of the distinction advocated by Eusebius. (See the Introduction to 1 John under "The Elder John," pp. 14-16.) We accept the traditional view that "the elder" who wrote 2 and 3 John was indeed the Apostle John.

That the Apostle John in his old age should identify himself as "the elder" is quite appropriate and distinctive. Toward the close of the first

---

[5]So Donald W. Burdick, *The Letters of John the Apostle, An In-Depth Commentary* (Chicago: Moody Press, 1985), pp. 14-15. Compare 1 Peter 1:1 with 5:1 of that same epistle.

[6]Henry A. Sawtelle, "Commentary on the Epistles of John," in *An American Commentary on the New Testament* (1888; reprint ed., Philadelphia: American Baptist Publications Society, n.d.), p. 77.

[7]See the Introduction to 1 John under authorship (p. 11-14).

[8]Stephen S. Smalley, *1, 2, 3 John,* Word Biblical Commentary (Waco, Texas: Word Books, 1984), p. 317. See also Raymond E. Brown, *The Community of the Beloved Disciple* (New York: Paulist Press, 1979).

[9]L. Coenen, "Bishop, Presbyter, Elder," in *The New International Dictionary of New Testament Theology,* ed. Colin Brown (Grand Rapids: Zondervan, 1975), 1:200.

century, when the term "apostle" had become a common designation for just such messengers as are mentioned in this epistle, his self-chosen designation as "the elder" distinguishes his true position as the sole survivor of the original Christ-chosen apostolic band. Its use in these two brief letters would at once make clear to the readers his true identity and position. This conviction concerning the identity of the writer of 2 and 3 John assured their admission into the New Testament canon.

B. The Recipient (v. 1b)

The recipient of 3 John is identified as "the wellbeloved Gaius." As addressed to a single individual, it is thus strictly a personal letter. Its grouping with the "general epistles" is due to its close connection with 1 John. Nothing further is known with certainty about this Gaius beyond what can be learned from this letter.

Three men by the name of Gaius appear in the New Testament in connection with the life of Paul: *Gaius of Corinth,* whom Paul baptized at Corinth (1 Cor. 1:14) and who was Paul's host when he wrote the letter to the Romans (Rom. 16:23); *Gaius of Macedonia,* mentioned in Acts 19:29 in connection with the Ephesian riot as one of Paul's companions in travel; and *Gaius of Derbe,* mentioned in Acts 20:4 as one of the church-appointed bearers of the collection for the saints at Jerusalem. Commentators have offered various conjectures seeking to identify the recipient of John's letter with one or another of these three men. Trapp assumes his identity with the Gaius of Corinth in describing the recipient as "a rich Corinthian, rich in this world and rich in good works" and characterizes him as "a rare bird, at Corinth especially."[10] But surely the trait of Christian hospitality was not so rare in the early church as to assure this identification. Also, the time element is against it. Bengel, who is favorable to the identification, well points out that Gaius "either migrated from Achaia to Asia, or John sent this letter to Corinth."[11] Neither is probable.

Others suggest that the recipient of this letter is to be identified with the Gaius of Macedonia (Acts 19:29), whom, according to a tradition found in the *Apostolic Constitutions* (7. 46. 9), dated around A.D. 370, John appointed as the bishop of Pergamum. Ogilvie, in view of this tradition, believes that this identification is assured in view of "the geographical proximity, coupled with Gaius's experience and growth in Christ in Roman Asia."[12] Findlay,

---

[10]John Trapp, *Trapp's Commentary on the New Testament* (1865; reprint ed., Evansville, Ind.: The Sovereign Grace Book Club, 1958), p. 735.

[11]John Albert Bengel, *New Testament Word Studies,* trans. Charlton T. Lewis and Marvin R. Vincent (1864; reprint ed., Grand Rapids: Kregel, 1971), 2:820.

[12]Lloyd John Ogilvie, *When God First Thought of You, The Full Measure of Love as Found in 1, 2, 3 John* (Waco, Texas: Word Books, 1978), p. 194.

on the basis of this tradition, argues that both 2 and 3 John were sent to Pergamum.[13] But Brooke thinks that this late tradition "is of too slight historical value to guide our conjectures as to the recipient of this Epistle."[14] Generally interpreters agree that the Gaius to whom the Elder wrote this letter is not to be identified with any of the men by that name who were associated with Paul.

The name "Gaius" *(Gaios),* the Greek equivalent of the Latin *Caius,* was common in the Graeco-Roman world and was "as distinctive as John in the English."[15] Bruce points out that "it was one of the eighteen names from which Roman parents could choose a *praenomen* for one of their sons."[16] As such it was a personal and individual name used to distinguish brothers in the same family. The name suggests that the recipient of this letter "himself was a former pagan, although the Johannine community obviously included others . . . who were Jewish Christians."[17]

We do not know where Gaius lived, but it was apparently in the Roman province of Asia, some distance from Ephesus. The letter does not make clear whether Gaius was an official in his local church, but clearly he was a man of integrity and influence in the church.

The apposititional designation "the wellbeloved" *(tō agapētō)* depicts the warm and affectionate regard in which Gaius was held by John and fellow believers. The KJV rendering "wellbeloved," only in verse 1, intensifies the warmth. This articular adjective, following his name, describes "this man as highly regarded among brethren because he was in good stead with God."[18] The fact that John uses this designation three more times (vv. 2, 5, 11) in addressing Gaius directly clearly marks this as "a letter of commendation and encouragement."[19] John's use of this adjective, which was rare in non-Christian Greek but common in the New Testament,[20] de-

[13]George C. Findlay, *Fellowship in the Life Eternal, An Exposition of the Epistles of St John* (1909; reprint ed., Grand Rapids: Eerdmans, 1955), pp. 306-7.

[14]A. E. Brooke, *A Critical and Exegetical Commentary on the Johannine Epistles,* International Critical Commentary (New York: Scribner's 1912), p. 182.

[15]James Hope Moulton and George Milligan, *The Vocabulary of the Greek Testament* (1930; reprint ed., London: Hodder and Stoughton, 1952), p. 120.

[16]F. F. Bruce, *The Epistles of John* (Old Tappan, N.J.: 1970), p. 147.

[17]Smalley, p. 344.

[18]Lehman Strauss, *The Epistles of John* (1962; reprint ed., Neptune. N.J.: Loizeaux Brothers, 1984), p. 160.

[19]Manford George Gutzke, *Plain Talk on the Epistles of John* (Grand Rapids: Zondervan, 1977), p. 116.

[20]The adjective *agapētos* occurs nine times in the Synoptic Gospels, each time of the Father's relation to the Son; once in Acts (15:25); twenty-eight times in the epistles of Paul; once in Hebrews (6:9); and twenty-three times in the General Epistles. It does not occur in 2 John.

scribes Gaius as the recipient of a love which was motivated by their mutual experience of God's love (1 John 4:11, 19).

In adding "whom I love in the truth" *(hon egō agapō en alētheia),* John underlines his own participation in this affectionate regard for Gaius. His "I" *(egō)* stresses John's personal, active love for Gaius, but it need not imply that John thus deliberately set himself in contrast to any gainsayers of Gaius, as Westcott suggests.[21] The assertion that John loves Gaius "in the truth," although without the definite article, cannot mean that his love for him is genuine rather than in pretense; such a meaning could only arouse the suspicion of Gaius. John's use of the term "truth" is never merely casual, and the term here denotes the fact that his love operates within the circle of those who know and practice the truth. His love for Gaius is "that love which is the only fitting relation between us who are of the truth."[22]

C. The Prayer (vv. 2-4)

In this personal note to his dear friend, John omits the customary opening greeting in the salutation. Wilder notes that 3 John is strictly a letter from one individual to another, and as such "our best parallel in the NT for the formula of address in such a letter is found in Acts 23:26, which includes the customary 'greeting' *(chairein)* absent here."[23] Instead of the simple "greeting" (James 1:1), or the more elaborate Pauline formula, "Grace to you and peace," John addresses Gaius anew with an expressed prayer for him. The addition of such a prayer-wish for the reader was a conventional Hellenistic practice, prompting Funk to declare that its use "marks this letter as the most secularized in the N.T."[24] But clearly John was not expressing a mere conventional health-wish but was giving personal utterance to a heartfelt prayer for Gaius.

This prayer for the reader is to be taken as a part of the epistolary introduction; verse 2 is best taken with verse 1 as constituting one paragraph. The prayer is undergirded in verses 3-4 by the writer's reason for his prayer.

1. The statement of the prayer (v. 2). His warm assertion, "Beloved, I wish above all things that thou mayest prosper and be in health, even as thy soul prospereth," expresses his comprehensive desire for Gaius. The direct address, "beloved" *(agapēte),* so early in the epistle is unique and reveals

---

[21]Brooke Foss Westcott, *The Epistles of St. John, The Greek Text with Notes,* 3rd ed. (1892; reprint ed., Grand Rapids: Eerdmans, 1950), p. 235.

[22]Neil Alexander, *The Epistles of John,* Torch Bible Commentaries (New York: Macmillan, 1962), p. 161.

[23]Amos N. Wilder and Paul W. Hoon, "The First, Second, and Third Epistles of John," in *The Interpreter's Bible* (New York: Abingdon Press, 1957), 12:308.

[24]Funk, "The Form and Structure of II and III John," p. 430.

John's loving outreach toward his friend. The love conveyed by this term "is the God-given bond uniting the Christian brothers and constituting their deepest obligation to each other."[25] This assurance of John's love can only encourage and strengthen Gaius for what lies ahead. This love, which is wholly connected with the truth, will sustain him as he encounters the opposition of self-seeking arrogance and false teaching.

The verb "I wish" *(euchomai)* in early non-Biblical Greek was "the most comprehensive term for invocation to the deity," having the force of "I pray, ask, vow," but with the passing of time its force in secular expression came to denote no more than "I wish."[26] The King James Version here renders it "I wish," but obviously John's words convey more than conventional good wishes. Clearly his personal good wishes for Gaius found definite expression in explicit prayer for him.

John's prayer for Gaius is inclusive: "I wish above all things that thou mayest prosper and be in health, even as thy soul prospereth." The phrase "above all things"[27] *(peri pantōn,* better "concerning all things") refers not to the intensity of John's own desire for Gaius but rather, emphasized by its forward position, to the full scope of the prosperity John desires for Gaius. The expression stands in antithesis to the soul prosperity of Gaius. Ogilvie observes that love-prompted "graciousness is wholistic: it is concerned about a person's emotional, physical, and relational life."[28]

John's request for Gaius is expressed by two infinitives: "that thou mayest prosper and be in health" *(se euodousthai kai hugiainein).* The scope of the first is general, the second specific. Both are in the present tense and combine "the elements of progress and vigour."[29] The first verb *(euodouomai),* which occurs elsewhere in the New Testament only in Romans 1:10 and 1 Corinthians 16:12, literally means "to be led along a good road." Thus Trapp rhetorically expresses the request, "that thou mayest make a good voyage of it, and come safe and sane to thy journey's end."[30] But here, as elsewhere in the New Testament, the usage is metaphorical; John is not thinking of a literal journey for Gaius. His request for Gaius is that he may

---

[25]J. L. Houlden, *A Commentary on the Johannine Epistles,* Harper's New Testament Commentaries (New York: Harper & Row, 1973), p. 151.

[26]Heinrich Greeven, *"euchomai, euchē,"* in *Theological Dictionary of the New Testament,* ed. Gerhard Kittel (Grand Rapids: Eerdmans, 1964), 2:775-78.

[27]The rendering "above all things" in the KJV does not give the meaning of the phrase. So understood, the preposition should be *pro,* "before." The reference is not to John's own desires but to the prosperity desired for Gaius.

[28]Ogilvie, p. 195.

[29]Westcott, p. 236.

[30]Trapp, p. 735.

"prosper" or "be successful," but the use of the passive implies "an agency in the prosperity above that of Gaius himself."[31] The second term, "and be in health" *(kai hugiainein),* expresses a specific aspect of the general prosperity just prayed for. Although in the Pastoral Epistles this verb is used metaphorically of correct doctrine, here, as in the Gospels and Acts, the term is used literally, "to be in good health." John was concerned about the physical health of Gaius for a very practical reason. In the words of Lenski, "John would not want to send his missionaries to a sick man's home and to burden a sick man with lodging them and outfitting them for the next stage of their journey."[32] Since Gaius was putting first the Kingdom of God (cf. Matt 6:33), John had no hesitancy in praying for his physical welfare. Clearly John had no sympathy for the Gnostic depreciation of the physical body.

The added words "even as thy soul prospereth" *(kathōs euodoutai sou hē psuchē)* state the measure for the desired physical well-being of Gaius. John's words were a confident assertion of the soul-prosperity of Gaius. The expression does not imply that Gaius was in poor health. Assured of the inner, spiritual progress and well-being of Gaius, John desires that Gaius may experience physical well-being in the same measure. This was important for the further services John expects Gaius to render. The order is noteworthy: the spiritual is the standard of measurement for the physical! How many today, even among those who profess the name of Christ, would be willing to have this standard applied to them? Clearly John knew his man! Strauss remarks,

> We may deduce from this verse that sound physical health does not always accompany sound spiritual health. The Church is beset with many and varied dangers from without, but none are so damaging right now as the spiritually sick saints within.[33]

2. *The reason for the prayer* (vv. 3-4). The opening "for" of verse 3 marks a close connection between verses 2 and 3. John assures Gaius that he has ample reason for his unique prayer request. His assurance is grounded in the reports he had received concerning Gaius (v. 3) as well as his own joyous reaction to those reports (v. 4).

a. *The reports concerning Gaius* (v. 3). Before telling Gaius about the nature of the reports received concerning him, John mentions his own response to them: "I rejoiced greatly, when the brethren came and testified of the truth that is in thee." His opening words, "I rejoiced greatly" *(echarēn*

---

[31]Sawtelle, p. 78.

[32]R.C.H. Lenski, *The Interpretation of the Epistles of St. Peter, St. John and St. Jude* (Columbus, Ohio: Wartburg Press, 1945), pp. 578-79.

[33]Strauss, p. 161.

lian), record the historical fact of his joyous reaction. The aorist tense may denote a single occasion, but in view of the present tenses in the remainder of verses 3-4, the aorist tense seems best taken as simply reporting the fact of his joy, while what follows makes clear that such was his personal reaction on several occasions. Two present-tense participles, in the genitive absolute construction, picture those repeated occasions: "when the brethren came and testified of the truth that is in thee" *(erchomenōn adelphōn kai marturountōn sou tē elētheia,* more literally, "brethren coming and bearing witness to your truth").

Those bringing the reports are simply identified as "brethren," a common New Testament designation for fellow believers. The term may simply denote Christians who knew Gaius, men whose business had taken them to the place where the writer lived. More probably the reference is to missionaries under John's supervision who, upon their arrival at his place, had been hospitably entertained by Gaius (cf. vv. 5-8) and had returned to make their report to John. Under either view we have a passing glimpse of the stream of travelers between the churches in the region which enabled John to keep informed concerning their spiritual condition.

John tells Gaius that upon arrival these brethren "testified of the truth that is in thee" *(marturountōn sou tē alētheia,* "testifying to thy truth"), implying that they had objective evidence that Gaius possessed "the truth." In the Johannine Epistles this term is used to denote doctrinal truth (1 John 2:21-23) as well as appropriate Christian behavior (1 John 1:6; 2:4; 3:18-19). The implication is that these brethren had witnessed Gaius giving open expression of his adherence to the truth of the Christian message as well as supporting and defending it in daily conduct. The fact that he possessed "the truth" showed that he had a living faith, and this brought forth "love" in the life of Gaius (v. 6).

One may understand the last clause of verse 3 ("even as thou walkest in the truth") in two different ways. The NASB rendering, "*that is,* how you are walking in truth" *(kathōs su en alētheia peripateis),* may be construed as an example of indirect discourse, as giving expression to what the brethren reported about Gaius.[34] Or the clause may be rendered "even as thou walkest in truth" (KJV, ASV) as expressing John's own conviction about Gaius. Under this view the words further present John's own evaluation of Gaius, indicating that the reports were in harmony with John's own knowledge of the faith and conduct of Gaius. The suggestion of Fausset that

---

[34]Then *kathōs* has the force of *pōs,* "as." See William F. Arndt and F. Wilbur Gingrich, *A Greek-English Lexicon of the New Testament* (Chicago: University of Chicago Press, 1957), p. 392.

"even as" *(kathōs)* carries an implied "contrast to Diotrephes (v. 9)"[35] is not obvious, since neither Diotrephes, or others who oppose Gaius, have yet been mentioned. "Walkest" *(peripateis)* employs a familiar Biblical metaphor picturing the whole round of the activities of an individual's life. The present tense depicts the characteristic daily conduct: "you continue to live according to the truth" (NIV). "In the truth" *(en alētheia,* "in truth") without the article is qualitative, describing his conduct as characterized by truth.

b. *The joy because of the reports* (v. 4). The joy already mentioned in verse 3 is now substantiated and enlarged upon in verse 4: "I have no greater joy than to hear that my children walk in truth." It is the Elder's supreme joy to know that those who are members of the churches under his supervision are committed to the truth of the gospel and are molding their lives by its teachings. This renewed reference to his joy indicates the profound joy John feels. His statement, "I have no greater joy than to hear" *(meizoteran*[36] *toutōn ouk echō charan,* very literally, "greater than these things I have no joy"), stresses that no gift from God made him feel richer or more joyful than reports like those concerning Gaius. John's life was rich in joys, but the joy produced by such reports was unsurpassed. Instead of "joy" *(charan),* some manuscripts here have a variant reading, "grace" *(charin).*[37] Westcott accepts "grace" as the preferred reading since "it expresses the divine favour in a concrete form."[38] But textual critics generally evaluate this reading as scribal modification, a substitution of a more familiar form. Grayston stamps this reading as "a desperate scribal effort to introduce a more theological word into the Epistle."[39] Metzger points out that the reading "joy" *(charan)* is preferable as more Johannine and as strongly supported by the manuscript evidence.[40]

The concluding clause, "to hear that my children walk in truth" *(hina akouō ta ema tekna en tē alētheia peripatounta),* is epexegetical, expanding on and explaining what it was in the reports that caused John such joy. In classical Greek the conjunction *hina* with the subjunctive mode expressed

---

[35]A. R. Fausset, "The First General Epistle of John," in Robert Jamieson, A. R. Fausset, and David Brown, *A Commentary, Critical and Explanatory, on the Old and New Testaments,* American ed. (Hartford, Conn.: S. S. Scranton, Co., n.d.), vol. 2, *New Testament,* p. 540.

[36]In form, *meizoteran* is a double comparative, "greaterer," comparable in formation to our English "lesser." Such forms were employed when the comparative force of the usual form was fading.

[37]For the textual evidence see United Bible Societies, *The Greek New Testament,* 3rd ed.

[38]Westcott, p. 237.

[39]Kenneth Grayston, *The Johannine Epistles,* New Century Bible Commentary (Grand Rapids: Eerdmans, 1984), pp. 159.

[40]Bruce M. Metzger, *A Textual Commentary on the Greek New Testament* (London, New York: United Bible Societies, 1971), p. 723.

purpose, and Ebrard holds that the expression here involves "the idea of a wish."[41] But in Hellenistic Greek the construction was often used with the force of an explanatory infinitive. John is not saying that he wishes to hear these things about Gaius; rather, he is explaining what it is in the reports that gives him such joy. He finds his supreme joy in reports that any of "my children walk in truth."

One may understand the expression "my children" *(ta ema tekna)* in two senses. Paul frequently uses the term of his own converts (1 Cor. 4:14; Gal. 4:19; Phil. 2:22; 1 Tim. 1:2; Philem. 10), and it is possible that the term here implies that Gaius had been brought to faith in Christ through the work of John. It is also possible that the Elder uses the term "my children" to denote those who are under his spiritual care, believers for whom he feels a warm fatherly affection and a sense of responsibility as their spiritual mentor. This broader view seems more probable here. Under either view, the use of the possessive pronoun *(ema)* stresses the closeness of the relationship; he regards and treasures them as his own.

These children manifest their oneness with John in that they "walk in truth" *(en tē alētheia perpatounta),* ordering their daily lives in the light of God's truth. It reveals that they had not merely accepted "the truth" of the gospel intellectually but had assimilated it into their very being as a living power operating in every area of their lives. Such reports concerning his dear people always produce joy in the heart of a Christian leader.

II. The Message (vv. 5-12)

The central message which John writes to convey, verses 5-12, relates to the Elder's concern for the furtherance of the gospel amid the circumstances in which Gaius found himself. In verses 5-8 he deals with the missionary obligation in relation to the life and activities of Gaius, and in verses 9-10 he refers to the opposition of Diotrephes to John's missionary program. In view of this contrasting situation, John offers Gaius some practical advice (v. 11) and adds a warm testimonial to Demetrius, the bearer of the letter (v. 12).

A. The Obligation to Support the Missionaries (vv. 5-8)

In turning to the immediate occasion for this letter, the Elder again addresses Gaius as "beloved" *(agapēte),* the third use of this warm epithet in the first five verses. Stimulated by the reports just mentioned (v. 3), John's heart is aglow with love for this lovable man. He commends Gaius for his services to the missionaries (vv. 5-6a), indicates the nature of the further

---

[41]John H. A. Ebrard, *Biblical Commentary on the Epistles of St. John,* trans. W. B. Pope (Edinburgh: T. & T. Clark, 1860), p. 398.

services desired on their behalf (v. 6), and explains the missionary obligation of fellow Christians toward such workers (vv. 7-8).

1. The commendation of Gaius's ministry to the missionaries (vv. 5-6a). "Beloved, thou doest faithfully whatsoever thou doest to the brethren, and to strangers" (v. 5). The commendation is prompted by the reports of the returning missionaries and John's assurance that Gaius would be showing the same hospitality to the missionaries being sent out. Clearly Gaius is a householder of some means.

The words, "thou doest faithfully" *(piston poieis)* are literally "a faithful thing you are doing." Lenski calls the present tense "an epistolary present"[42] whereby the writer places himself at the side of Gaius as he acts to receive the missionaries. More probably the present tense is a complement to Gaius, indicating that the expected hospitality is in keeping with his established practice, which John highly appreciates. He characterizes it as "a faithful thing," an act becoming a faithful man. His hospitality demonstrates his loyalty to the message proclaimed by John and his missionaries. Gaius is acting in harmony with the faith that was in him, revealing himself as a "good and faithful servant" (Matt. 25:21). This interpretation takes the adjective *(piston)* in its usual passive sense, "trustworthy, dependable, faithful." Westcott holds that the meaning is rather " 'thou makest sure'; that is, such an act will not be lost, will not fail of its due issue and reward."[43] But most interpreters think that this explanation is improbable here.[44] John is concerned with strengthening Gaius in his course of action which will now be more difficult because of the stance of Diotrephes (v. 9).

The added words "whatsoever thou doest" *(ho ean ergasē,* "that which you may have done") are indefinite, leaving open the time of the completion, not the fact of the hospitality. The use of the verb here rendered "doest" *(ergasē)* implies that toilsome effort will be involved, while the aorist tense simply looks as it as an accomplished whole. The use of the conditional form may imply that the hospitality might express itself in varied forms and ways.

It was their status as "brethren" that established the claim of these missionaries upon the brotherhood for support. According to the KJV text, Gaius showed hospitality "to the brethren, and to strangers" *(eis tous adelphous kai eis tous zenous),* designating two groups. This is the reading of the Textus Receptus. Then the two groups in view are "the travelling preachers as 'the brothers,' while also asserting that Gaius' hospitality did not stop there but extended also to 'strangers' (probably esp. Christians) who hap-

---

[42]Lenski, p. 582.

[43]Westcott, pp. 237-38.

[44]I. Howard Marshall, *The Epistles of John,* New International Commentary on the New Testament (Grand Rapids: 1978), p. 85, note 2; Smalley, p. 349.

pened to be in the vicinity.''[45] But the reading in the ASV, "toward them that are brethren and strangers withal,'' based on a variant Greek text *(eis tous adelphous kai touto zenous),* identifies the recipients of his hospitality as one group given a double designation, "brethren and strangers.'' Most modern critical editors agree that this latter reading, which unites the two nouns under one article, is to be accepted as better attested.[46] Then the words *kai touto,* "and this,'' further describe the missionaries as brethren who were strangers to Gaius when they first arrived, thus enhancing the hospitality of Gaius. Westcott thinks that this emphasis "seems to imply that it had been made the occasion of unjust blame.''[47] Some probably felt that thus to befriend traveling preachers who were locally unknown and unapproved was dangerous (cf. the situation in 2 John). But clearly Gaius had done so because the missionaries carried the commendation of John himself.

John now informs Gaius that upon their return to the place where John lived, these missionaries "have borne witness of thy charity'' (v. 6a). "Have borne witness,'' rendering an aorist-tense verb *(emarturēsan),* most naturally refers to a definite occasion when these missionaries recounted their personal experience of "thy charity'' *(sou tē agapē,* "thy love''), an expressive Johannine summary of the hospitality shown them by Gaius. The term "charity'' no longer conveys the full force of the original to the modern English reader. John was not simply thinking of the hospitality of Gaius as a benevolent act of good will toward these needy individuals. Rather, his kindly and hospitable action on their behalf was motivated by his own experience of the love of Christ, expressing itself in Christlike conduct. Burdick points to the expression as confirmation that "in the epistles of John, love is never mere sentiment or verbalization. Instead it is action.''[48]

These reports were given, not merely to John personally, but "before the church'' *(enōpion ekklēsias),* in the presence of the local assembly where John resided, probably Ephesus. Acts 14:26-27 records an instance of such a report by missionaries returning to their home church. "The church'' *(ekklēsias),* used without an article, clearly has a local "congregational'' force, somewhat like our English "in church'' or "before the assembly'' (cf. Matt. 18:17).[49] These reports concerning Gaius were appreciated by John

---

[45]Zane C. Hodges, "3 John,'' in *The Bible Knowledge Commentary, New Testament* (Wheaton, Ill.: Victor Books, 1983), pp. 912-13.

[46]For the manuscript evidence see Nestle-Aland, *Novum Testamentum Graece,* 26th ed.

[47]Westcott, p. 238.

[48]Burdick, p. 451.

[49]This is the first of only three occurrences (vv. 6, 9, 10) of the word "church'' in the Johannine epistles. It does not occur in the Fourth Gospel. It occurs twenty times in Revelation, nineteen times in the first three chapters.

and the assembly as evidence that his was indeed a living faith (cf. v. 3). "Always and everywhere that man is to be highly esteemed in the Church, who combines firm conviction with a generous heart."[50]

2. The nature of Gaius's further ministry to the missionaries (v. 6b). Highly appreciative of what Gaius has been doing, John adds his desire for the further services of Gaius on behalf of these traveling missionaries: "whom if thou bring forward on their journey after a godly sort" (*hous kalōs poiēseis propempsas axiōs tou theou,* more literally, "whom nobly you will do, having sent forward worthily of God"). The relative "whom" *(hous)* makes clear that the missionaries whose report John mentions were planning another visit to that region and would need the aid of Gaius. The use of the future, "thou shalt do," shifts the thought from the past to the future. This use of the future tense was a recognized idiom expressing a polite request by the writer.[51] Without explicitly stating his request, John declares his assurance that Gaius will continue the noble course he has already adopted. That further action John characterizes as "well" *(kalōs),* that is nobly or beautifully done.

Gaius would lodge the missionaries and would also "bring forward on their journey after a godly sort." The term "bring forward on their journey" *(propempsas)* was something of a technical term in regard to the missionary activities of the early church (cf. Acts 15:3; 20:38; 21:5; Rom. 15:24; 1 Cor. 16:6; Titus 3:13). It involved not only a warm send-off but also the supplying of the varied needs of the travelers for the next stage of their journey. The action of the aorist participle (*prōpempsas,* "having sent forward") is simultaneous with that of the future verb "thou shalt do," but implies the completion of the varied aspects involved in that sending.

The phrase "after a godly sort" (*axiōs tou theou,* literally, "worthily of God") would remind Gaius of the spiritual character of his hospitality. The genitive "of God" may mean the way God, whose messengers the missionaries are, should be treated (cf. Matt. 10:40), or, as Smalley states it, "worthily from God's point of view,"[52] as receiving His approval. The former seems preferable, but the genitive may well involve both ideas; certainly a service that is worthy of being rendered to God Himself receives His approval and blessing. Here is the standard by which every activity of the believer should be measured.

3. The explanation concerning the missionary obligation (vv. 7-8). With "because that" *(gar)* John sets forth why the support of the missionaries is

---

[50]Donald Fraser, *Synoptical Lectures on the Books of Holy Scripture, Romans–Revelation* (New York: Robert Carter & Brothers, 1876), p. 243.

[51]Moulton and Milligan, pp. 522-23.

[52]Smalley, p. 350.

so important. He portrays the true character of these missionaries (v. 7) and states the resultant missionary obligation of fellow believers (v. 8).

a. *The portrayal of the missionaries* (v. 7). The words "for his name's sake they went forth" (*huper tou onomatos exēlthan,* "on behalf of the Name they went forth") stress that their missionary activities were motivated by "the Name." The KJV reading, "for his name's sake," follows the Textus Receptus reading, *tou onomatos autou.* The personal pronoun, however, lacks manuscript authority.[53] They were not individuals engaged in private business pursuits, but men who had initiated their journey in order to further the cause of "the Name." This absolute use of "the Name" implies that no ordinary human being is meant. Some, such as Bengel,[54] have taken the Name to be the ineffable Name of Yahweh, or Jehovah, whereby God revealed Himself to His people Israel. But in this context it is natural to understand a reference to Jesus Christ, not directly mentioned elsewhere in 3 John. Such an absolute use of "the Name" to denote Jesus Christ occurs in the history of the early Church (Acts 4:12; 5:41; 9:16, 21), appears in the letters of Paul (Rom. 1:5; Phil. 2:9), and would certainly be familiar to the Johannine churches. Plummer notes that this expression is also "common in the Apostolic Fathers; Ignatius, *Eph.* iii., vii; *Philad.* x.; Clem. Rom. ii., xiii.; Hermas, *Sim.* viii. 10, ix. 13, 28."[55] "The Name" summarizes the saving message which the missionaries proclaimed. That Name is the inspiration for the life and outreach of the Christian Church and provides the highest motive for cooperation by believers in its dissemination.

"Taking nothing of the Gentiles" (*mēden lambanontes apo tōn ethnikōn*) reveals the deliberate principle of operation adopted by these missionaries. The negative with the present active participle (*mēden lambanontes*) makes clear that it was their choice not to receive any financial support from "the Gentiles" (*ethnikōn*) whom they sought to evangelize. The word "Gentiles" is not the noun rendered "Gentiles" or "nations" (*ethnōn*)[56] but an adjective[57] which expresses the characteristic of,[58] thus indicating individuals

---

[53]For the manuscript evidence see Nestle-Aland, *Novum Testamentum Graece,* 26th ed.

[54]Bengel, 2:821.

[55]Alfred Plummer, *The Epistles of S. John,* Cambridge Bible for Schools and Colleges (1883; reprint ed., London: Cambridge University Press, 1938), p. 189.

[56]The Textus Receptus reading, *tōn ethnōn,* lacks adequate support. For the textual evidence see Nestle-Aland, *Novum Testamentum Graece,* 26th ed.

[57]The adjective *ethnikos* elsewhere in the New Testament occurs only in Matthew 5:47; 6:7; 18:17. The adverb *ethnikōs* appears in Galatians 2:14.

[58]Bruce M. Metzger, *Lexical Aids for Students of New Testament Greek* (Princeton, N.J.: Author, 1955), p. 56; A. T. Robertson and W. Hersey Davis, *A New Short Grammar of the Greek Testament for Students Familiar with the Elements of Greek* (New York: Harper & Brothers, 1935), p. 176.

belonging to the pagan world, who, being without the knowledge of the revelation in Christ Jesus, lived in moral and spiritual darkness. Brown notes that this adjective here "refers to the non-Christian Gentile (since there is no reason to think that the Presbyter is excluding support from Gentile *Christians*)."[59] The missionaries have decided not to receive material assistance from unconverted Gentiles to avoid any misunderstanding of the nature of their message or their personal motive in proclaiming it. There were numerous peripatetic street-preachers of various religious and philosophical cults who avariciously solicited funds from their audiences. Deissmann cites an inscription of a man, calling himself "the slave" of his Syrian goddess, who boasted that he never returned from his begging journeys with less than seventy bags of money for his deity.[60] The missionaries "kept themselves totally free from profiting by the resources of the world" and thereby "proved that they sought the best good of the Gentiles, not their own things."[61]

b. *The missionary obligation of the believers* (v. 8). With his words "we therefore" *(hēmeis oun)* John at once proceeds to state the missionary obligation in view of the situation just described in verse 7. With his emphatic "we" John unites himself with true believers in contrast to the non-Christians around them, while the conjunction "therefore" *(oun)* calls attention to the resultant obligation resting upon the believers.

The obligation is "we ought to receive such" *(opheilomen hupolambanien tous toioutous)*. "We ought" *(opheilomen)* does not denote a legal obligation imposed upon believers upon joining the church. It is rather a moral obligation that arises out of our mutual relationship in Jesus Christ. The present tense marks this as a standing obligation. The duty is "to receive such" men because of our common commitment to the work of Christ. The compound present active infinitive rendered "to receive" *(apolambanein)* declares the continuing activity. The manuscript evidence for this stated duty is divided between two readings. The KJV rendering "to receive" follows the Textus Receptus *apolambanein,* but the better attested reading is *hupolambanein,* "to undertake" or "support," which conveys the picture of receiving, supporting, and protecting the missionaries.[62] Brown notes that this reading "makes excellent sense" and introduces a word-play upon the verb rendered "taking" *(lambanontes)* in verse 7.[63] The missionaries are

---

[59]Brown, *The Epistles of John,* p. 713.

[60]Adolf Deissmann, *Light from the Ancient East* (London: Hodder and Stoughton, 1910), p. 109.

[61]William Kelly, *An Exposition of the Epistles of John the Apostle* (1905; reprint ed. Oak Park, Ill.: Bible Truth Publishers, 1970), p. 415.

[62]G. Delling, *"hupolambanō,"* in *Theological Dictionary of the New Testament,* ed. Gerhard Kittel (Grand Rapids: Eerdmans, 1964), 4:15.

[63]Brown, *The Epistles of John,* p. 713.

going out "taking nothing" from unbelievers (v. 7); believers therefore have the moral obligation to "undertake" for them.

The designation of the recipients of this support as "such" individuals *(tous toioutous)* broadens the picture beyond the immediate scene; John states a missionary principle which is applicable to the missionary work of the Church as a whole. As Burdick notes, "The article *tous* serves to point out the particular persons John has in mind, and the qualitative correlative demonstrative pronoun speaks of their characteristics, namely, they were the kind of persons who made it a point on their missionary journeys to take no support from unbelievers."[64] John's directive is consistent with the modern practice of the settled churches in providing the support of missionaries abroad. It is not incompatible with a "tentmaking" ministry on the part of the missionary himself (cf. Acts 18:1-4).

Acceptance of this obligation also has deep significance for those supporting the missionaries; it offers effective realization of a spiritual goal, namely, "that we might be fellowhelpers to the truth" *(hina sunergoi ginōmetha tē alētheia)*. One should not press John's statement to mean that the members of these churches had not been helping the missionaries. Often the verb here *(ginōmetha)* is the practical equivalent of the ordinary verb "to be" *(eimi)*, but with *hina* it means "that we may prove to be." In accepting the truth of the gospel, his readers had already allied themselves with the cause of the missionaries; to act upon this obligation will enable them to live out what they already are. It is consistent with the Johannine emphasis that the internal realities of the Christian faith must prove themselves in external conduct. In supporting the missionaries, fellow-believers demonstrate that they themselves are "fellow-workers with the truth" (NASB).

It is not certain whether the compound noun "fellowhelpers" *(sunergoi)* pictures them as co-workers with the missionaries or with "the truth" as embodied in the Christian gospel. Used without a preposition, "the truth" *(tē alētheia)* may be differently understood. (1) It may be the dative of personal relationship. Paul always uses the expression "fellow-worker" of the persons who worked with him in the cause of the gospel (Rom. 16:3, 9, 21; Phil. 2:25; Col. 4:11; Philem. 24). So understood, the meaning here is that by helping the missionaries they are co-workers with the missionaries "for the truth" (ASV, NIV, NKJV, Jerusalem Bible) or "to the truth" (KJV). Thus Lenski renders, "that we may be joint workers (with them) for the truth."[65] Sawtelle remarks, "The supporter of the missionary of the cross is himself a missionary. He who goes and he who sends are one in the work

---

[64]Burdick, p. 452.
[65]Lenski, p. 584.

of the Great Commission."[66] (2) Or the case of "the truth" may be viewed as locative, "in the truth" (RSV). Then the meaning may be that as co-workers they labor in the sphere of the truth, guided and directed thereby. (3) Or the case may be the associative-instrumental, picturing them as working in association "with the truth" (NASB, Rotherham, Goodspeed). Brown holds that "the evidence favors the connotation of 'cooperation with' " the truth.[67] Then "the truth," already at work among men, is practically personified,[68] and "the thought is of partnership with what the truth accomplishes in people's hearts and lives."[69] All three views make good sense, but we lean toward the third view as the most probable. But whatever the precise relationship, it is clear that "the truth" of the gospel must control the relationship. The proclamation of heresy, rather than the truth of the gospel, by any missionary negates the obligation John presents. This positive appeal for support of the missionaries must be held in balance with the prohibition expressed in 2 John (vv. 7-10).

B. The Opposition of Domineering Diotrephes (vv. 9-10)

The opposition to John portrayed in verses 9-10 forms the most surprising part of this letter. That any Christian should so act toward the last surviving apostle is generally felt to be the most weighty item in the internal evidence against apostolic authorship. Plummer replies,

> But from the very first the N.T. is full of the saddest surprises. And those who accept as historical the unbelief of Christ's brethren, the treachery of Judas, the flight of all the Disciples, the denial of S. Peter, the quarrels of Apostles both before and after their Lord's departure, and the flagrant abuses in the Church of Corinth, with much more of the same kind, will not be disposed to think it incredible that Diotrephes acted in the manner here described even toward the Apostle S. John.[70]

This sad scene helps us to understand why John so highly valued the attitude and actions of Gaius. But it is not wholly clear how the scene relates to Gaius himself. It is not certain whether Gaius and Diotrephes were members of the same assembly or members of neighboring house-churches; probably the former. The stance of Diotrephes obviously made the course of Gaius more difficult, but how or to what extent his opposition had been personally directed against Gaius is not clear.

---

[66]Sawtelle, p. 81.

[67]Brown, *The Epistles of John,* p. 714.

[68]But any suggestion that "the truth" is to be fully personified as denoting Christ Himself as the Truth incarnate goes beyond any suggestion in the context.

[69]Hodges, p. 913.

[70]Plummer, pp. 190-91.

In recounting the opposition of Diotrephes, John refers to his letter to the church (v. 9a), mentions the refusal of Diotrephes to cooperate (v. 9b), asserts that he will deal with Diotrephes upon his arrival (v. 10a), and elaborates on the hostility of Diotrephes (v. 10b).

1. The letter of John to the church (v. 9a). "I wrote unto the church," or "I wrote something to the church" (NASB) *(eprapsa ti tē ekklēsia),* is best understood as referring to a note to the church where Diotrephes lived. "I wrote" simply records the past fact, while *ti,* "something" (not found in the Textus Receptus), suggests its modest size. The reference cannot be to either 1 or 2 John, because the problem raised here is not alluded to in either of them. It apparently was a brief letter, now lost, requesting assistance for the missionaries being sent out by John. If so, it is not improbable that Diotrephes suppressed the letter.

2. The refusal of Diotrephes to cooperate (v. 9b). "But Diotrephes, who loveth to have the preeminence among them, receiveth us not" records the sad scene. "But" *(alla),* the stronger of two Greek adversative conjunctions, contrasts the request of John expressed in his letter and the refusal of Diotrephes to cooperate with the Elder. The name Diotrephes, which means "nourished by Zeus," occurs only here in the New Testament. Its pagan implications suggest that he had a Greek background, but nothing beyond what is here recorded is known about him.

In the original, John characterizes the man morally before recording his name: literally, "the one loving to be first among them, Diotrephes" *(ho philoprōteuōn autōn Diotrephes).* The articular present participle *(ho philoprōteuōn),* "who loveth to have the preeminence," characterizes the persistent desire of this man to be first in all matters relating to the assembly. The compound participle, found only here in the New Testament, portrays an ambitious, self-seeking, power-hungry individual who aggressively sought to be at the head of things and to rule over others. Whatever his position in the church, John's picture makes it clear that he was able to exercise a good deal of power in the assembly. He was motivated by an aggressive passion to be in charge. Unfortunately, the spirit of Diotrephes has survived to the present day. A.T. Robertson tells of writing an article on Diotrephes for a denominational paper. He adds, "The editor told me that twenty-five deacons stopped the paper to show their resentment against being personally attacked in the paper."[71]

The consuming desire of Diotrephes revealed that in his heart he did not give the Lord Jesus Christ the first place in everything (Col. 1:18), nor was he deterred by Christ's condemnation of such a self-seeking spirit (Matt.

---

[71]A. T. Robertson, *Word Pictures in the New Testament* (Nashville: Broadman Press, 1933), 6:263.

20:26-28; 23:6; Luke 22:24-27). Stott well observes that "the motives governing the conduct of Diotrephes were neither theological, nor social, nor ecclesiastical, but moral. The root of the problem was sin."[72]

The self-centered response of Diotrephes to John's letter is briefy stated: he "receiveth us not" (*ouk epidechetai hēmas,* "does not accept us," in the sense of refusing to recognize John's authority). The NASB rendering, "does not accept what we say," is an understandable paraphrase. The fact that Diotrephes "receiveth us not" was demonstrated in his refusal to comply with John's request in the letter presented by his missionaries. Clearly the writer of this letter possessed and exercised an authority which he naturally expected to be recognized and acted upon by the churches to which his missionaries came with his letter. But Diotrephes was an exception. The present tense denotes his persistent refusal to acknowledge that authority. John's "us" *(hēmas)* is not an editorial plural but indicates that the action of Diotrephes did not involve John alone; it also involved the missionaries who worked under John's authority.

Diotrephes' professed reason for this rejection of John's authority is not indicated.[73] One suggestion is that the reason was doctrinal. Lenski holds that "Diotrephes barred out John's missionaries in order to let the roaming Gnostic emissaries in."[74] But there is no direct indication that Diotrephes was guilty of supporting heresy. The problem presented by the presence of heretical teachers is clear from 1 and 2 John. If Diotrephes did favor the Gnostic teachers in opposition to John's missionaries, John could hardly have failed to mention this crucial doctrinal issue. More natural is the view that the problem was basically a matter of ecclesiastical authority. In view of the self-seeking motive of Diotrephes just laid bare, it seems natural that he desired to establish the autonomy of his local church to enhance his own authority. He regarded John's missionaries as unknown intruders whose presence and claims upon the church were unwanted and must be rejected. John regarded the stance of Diotrephes as an egocentric lust for power which prompted him to challenge the writer's apostolic authority.

3. The dealing with Diotrephes upon John's arrival (v. 10a). The phrase "wherefore" *(dia touto,* "because of this")* looks back to what has just been said. The stance of Diotrephes makes it necessary for John to come and deal personally with the situation: "if I come, I will remember his deeds" *(ean elthō, hupomnēsō autou ta erga).* The conditional statement,

---

[72]J.R.W. Stott, *The Epistles of John,* Tyndale New Testament Commentaries (Grand Rapids: Eerdmans, 1964), pp. 226.

[73]For a full discussion of the possible reasons for the hostility of Diotrephes, see Brown, *The Epistles of John,* pp. 717-18, 732-39; Smalley, pp. 354-57.

[74]Lenski, p. 586.

"if I come," does not throw doubt upon his decision to come but rather denotes uncertainty concerning the time and circumstances which will enable him to come (cf. 1 John 2:28 for a similar construction). That he expects to make the trip is clear from verse 14, but the time when he would be able to come John leaves in the hands of God.

When John does arrive, he will confront Diotrephes: "I will remember his deeds which he doeth" *(hupomnēsō autou ta erga ha poiei)*. The future indicative verb, "I will remember" *(hupomnēsō)*, implies that John is resolved to confront the self-seeking Diotrephes. The only other Johannine occurrence of this compound verb is in John 14:26 where we have Christ's promise that the coming Holy Spirit will "bring to your remembrance all that I said to you" (NASB). Such a bringing to mind of the past may be either a blessing or a judgment, depending upon what is recalled. John will confront Diotrephes with "his deeds which he doeth," letting them speak for themselves. These persistent deeds in words and action will reveal his true motives and character. Since his deeds were public knowledge, an open exposure before the assembly seems implied.

Hodges remarks that John's "assertion should probably be taken as an understatement . . . with the manifest implication that Diotrephes' works would be dealt with appropriately."[75] His announcement is not prompted by vindictiveness but by his zeal for the cause of the Lord's church. He clearly sees that the course of Diotrephes only weakened the true church and made easier the spread of doctrinal error. Dodd suggests that the very preservation of this letter is in favor of the conclusion that John's authority was vindicated.[76]

4. The delineating of the deeds of Diotrephes (v. 10b). The deeds of Diotrephes are vividly portrayed: "prating against us with malicious words: and not content therewith, neither doth he himself receive the brethren, and forbiddeth them that would, and casteth *them* out of the church." Grammatically, two participles delineate the "deeds" of Diotrephes, "prating against us" and "not content therewith." The second participle is unfolded by three finite clauses. This recital of his deeds will clearly establish his guilt.

The attacks of Diotrephes upon John and his missionaries were verbal: "prating against us with malicious words" *(logois ponērois phluarōn hēmas,* "with wicked words prating against us"–Rotherham). The order makes prominent that his instruments of attack were verbal deeds. The adjective "malicious" *(ponērois)* marks his attacks as vicious and injurious in their nature. Plummer notes that in 1 John this adjective is used to characterize

---

[75]Hodges, pp. 912-13.

[76]C. H. Dodd, *The Johannine Epistles,* Moffatt New Testament Commentary (New York: Harper & Row, 1946), p. 165.

the Devil (1 John 2:13-14; 5:18-19).[77] The present participle "prating against" *(phluarōn)* portrays repeated assertions and unveils the utter nullity of his charges. The verb, which occurs only here in the New Testament,[78] means "to talk nonsense." In secular Greek it was used of one who was "an idle babbler," one talking like a fool.[79] Diotrephes deliberately attempted to undermine John's authority by resorting to unfounded slander.

A second participle further portrays the reaction of Diotrephes: "and not content therewith" *(kai mē arkoumenos epi toutois,* "and not satisfied with these things"). The present-tense participle marks his continuing feeling of discontent; his slanderous charges did not allay his feeling of antagonism against John and his missionaries. This persistent feeling of enmity found further expression, enumerated in three finite verbs.

His hostility found expression against John's missionaries: "neither doth he himself receive the brethren" *(oute autos epidechetai tous adelphous).* It was his set policy not to receive them into his home, nor to allow them to minister to the assembly. The use of the emphatic personal pronoun "himself" *(autos)* points to his personal leadership in this matter. He treated John's missionaries in the very way John had bidden true believers to respond to the heretical teachers (2 John 10-11).

Diotrephes' hostility also lashed out against loyal members in the assembly: "and forbiddeth them that would" *(kai tous bouloumenous kōluei,* literally, "and those wishing he forbids"). His wrath also vented itself against "them that would," those desiring to carry out John's request. The verb "forbiddeth" *(kōluei)* when used in relation to persons may denote a verbal prohibition or the use of actual restraints or hindrances to prevent what is prohibited. If the former, the reference is to the stern prohibitions he promulgated; if the latter, he aggressively acted to keep them from welcoming the missionaries. When members did not comply with his prohibitions, Diotrephes took further action, "and casteth *them* out of the church" *(kai ek tēs ekklēsias ekballei,* "out of the assembly he doth cast out"–Rotherham). John's strong verb "casteth out" *(ekballei)* may denote violent physical action against them, but more probably the thought is that of excommunicating them from the church.

The verbs used of Diotrephes in verse 10 are all in the present tense and have been interpreted in two different ways. Some, such as Burdick[80] and

---

[77]Plummer, p. 191.

[78]The cognate adjective occurs in 1 Timothy 5:13.

[79]Henry George Liddell and Robert Scott, *A Greek-English Lexicon,* 7th ed. (Oxford: Clarendon Press, 1890), p. 1683; Moulton and Milligan, p. 673.

[80]Burdick, pp. 456-57.

Lenski,[81] understand the meaning here to be conative, depicting what he was attempting to do. Others, such as Smalley[82] and Brown,[83] understand the present tense to indicate what was actually occurring. Accepting that the reference is to actual expulsion from the church, Brown suggests that "the action may have involved Diotrephes' instigating community action against them and not necessarily expelling by personal fiat."[84] Under either meaning, Diotrephes was in open rebellion against the authority of John.

This picture of Diotrephes leaves uncertain the precise ecclesiastical position of this domineering individual. He has been variously viewed as a bishop, the leading presbyter of his church, a domineering deacon, or even an ambitious layman who demanded that things be done in his way. Whatever his actual position, John's picture reveals an "ambitious, arbitrary, pragmatical, jealous, self-seeking, place-hunting, rule-or-ruin, hard talking man."[85] It offers a standing warning that even among the people of God there can be those whose "self-love vitiates all relationships."[86]

C. The Personal Lesson from the Circumstances (v. 11).

In verse 11 John reminds Gaius of the lesson to be learned from the unhappy circumstances recounted in verses 9-10. Those circumstances also provide the setting for the recommendation given to Demetrius in verse 12.

In turning back directly to Gaius, John for the third time addresses him as "beloved" (see vv. 1, 5). The transition is abrupt, made without any transitional particle. It undoubtedly was a relief for John to turn from the deeds of domineering Diotrephes to offer some loving advice to Gaius. The crisis created by Diotrephes constituted a challenge to Gaius concerning his own response. The desired course of action set before him is stated both negatively and positively: "follow not that which is evil, but that which is good." The imperative leaves no other option open to Gaius.

Usually the negative with the present imperative *(mē mimou)* is used to prohibit the continuation of an action already in progress.[87] This would assume that Gaius was already imitating the evil exemplified by Diotrephes,

---

[81]Lenski, p. 588.

[82]Smalley, p. 358.

[83]Brown, *The Epistles of John,* p. 720.

[84]*Ibid.*

[85]Sawtelle, p. 82.

[86]Stott, p. 228.

[87]H. E. Dana and Julius R. Mantey, *A Manual Grammar of the Greek New Testament* (1927; reprint ed., New York: The Macmillan Co., 1967), pp. 300-302; F. Blass and A. DeBrunner, *A Greek Grammar of the New Testament and Other Early Christian Literature,* trans. and rev. Robert W. Funk (Chicago: University of Chicago Press, 1961), pp. 172-73.

but this interpretation is clearly inconsistent with his action commended in verses 5-8. The expression here simply prohibits a practice without implying that it was already being done: it is a warning, "Don't be doing it!" Burdick suggests that "it may be that John was merely reflecting Gaius' tendency to be too easily influenced by Diotrephes' evil ways."[88] But John well knew the infectious nature of evil and was anxious to steer Gaius away from any danger. "John feels so full of abhorrence towards it that he must exhort all, even the good Gaius, against it, against all its influence."[89] John is intent on urging Gaius to continue the course of action for which he is already known. Even good men need encouragement in an hour of crisis. When faced with evil, they can always learn from it what not to do.

The verb "follow" *(mimeomai),* appearing only here in the Johannine books, conveys the picture of observing a course of action and then copying it ourselves. As Stott observes, "It is natural for us to look up to other people as our model and to copy them. This is all right, the Elder seems to be saying, but Gaius must choose his model carefully."[90] Paul uses the term in connection with persons to be imitated (2 Thess. 3:7, 9), and the author of Hebrews used it to urge imitation of "the faith" of Christian leaders (Heb. 13:7). Here John is concerned with adopting a characteristic conduct.

The Elder urges Gaius to discriminate between "that which is evil" and "that which is good" *(to kakon alla to agathon)* and to choose accordingly. The strong adversative particle *alla* ("but") sets the two over against each other in a typical Johannine antithesis. "That which is evil" *(to kakon)* is abstract, "the evil thing." The example of Diotrephes is clearly in the background, but the expression generalizes anything which is characterized as "evil." This adjective, appearing only here in the Johannine epistles,[91] denotes that which is morally bad or evil. In its intrinsic character it is the direct opposite of "the good" *(to agathon),* that which is morally and spiritually beneficial. An example of what is evil appears just before this exhortation, while an example of what is "good" follows in the next verse.

John's appeal to Gaius is undergirded by two axiomatic statements: "He that doeth good is of God: but he that doeth evil hath not seen God." "The author may be citing a proverb, but it is immediately baptized with Johannine meaning."[92] The asyndeton sets forth the stark realities. The use of the

---

[88]Burdick, p. 457.

[89]Sawtelle, p. 83.

[90]Stott, p. 228.

[91]It also occurs in John 18:23 and Revelation 2:2; 16:2. Elsewhere John uses *ponēros,* which denotes that which is vicious and destructive: John 3:19; 7:7; 17:15; 1 John 2:13, 14; 3:12; 5:18, 19; 2 John 11; Revelation 16:2.

[92]Robert Kysar, *I, II, III John,* Augsburg Commentary on the New Testament (Minneapolis: Augsburg, 1986), pp. 145.

articular participle construction in this double statement portrays these contrasting realities as embodied in habitual personal conduct. But the assertions are general, with no particular individual in view. The order of the antithesis in the second half of the verse reverses the order in the first half, thus creating a chiasmus, evil : good – good : evil.

The clause "He that doeth good is of God" *(ho agathopoiōn ek tou theou estin)* pictures an individual who is characterized as engaged in "gooddoing." His habitual practice reveals his character, establishing that he "is of God," has been born "out of God" *(ek tou theou).* He has been brought into a living union with the true God who has revealed Himself in His Son, Christ Jesus. The believer's characteristic "good-doing" does not produce his new birth but is the moral test demonstrating that the relationship has been established through faith. This test is often insisted upon in 1 John (e.g., 2:3-6, 28-29; 3:4-10; 5:18).

The opposite is also true: "but he that doeth evil hath not seen God" *(ho kakopoiōn ouch heōraken ton theon).* "But" has weak textual support and is best omitted; the asyndeton strengthens the contrast. That individual whose habitual conduct is characterized as "evil-doing" *(kakopoiōn)* gives moral proof that he has never experienced a transforming vision of the true God; a living encounter with the living God produces an effective change in character, manifesting itself in a new manner of living. A person practicing sin lacks a vital understanding of the nature of God as revealed in Jesus Christ (John 1:18; 14:9). In the words of Hodges, "Evil never arises from a real spiritual perception of God but is always a product of darkness of heart and blindness toward Him."[93] Clearly John invites Gaius to evaluate the scene confronting him in the light of this test of character. Stott observes, "Perhaps in this generalization John has Diotrephes in mind and thus obliquely indicates that he questions whether Diotrephes is a true Christian at all."[94] Certainly he was not one who was fit to have "the preeminence among them" (v. 9).

D. The Testimony to Demetrius (v. 12)

John appends the strong testimony to Demetrius in verse 12 without any connecting particle or further identification of the recipient. Obviously his Christian life was vital and impressive. The close sequence of this testimony to verse 11 implies that this well-known Christian personally exemplified the good that Gaius was urged to imitate. Gaius could follow his example with confidence.

---

[93]Hodges, p. 914.

[94]Stott, p. 228.

The name Demetrius *(Dēmētrios),* which means "belonging to Demeter," or Ceres, the goddess of agriculture and rural life,[95] implies that he came from a pagan family. It was a common Greek name but occurs elsewhere in the New Testament only in Acts 19:24, 38 of the silversmith in Ephesus who stirred up a riot against Paul in that city. Although the proposed identification of these two men is of comparatively modern origin, some recent interpreters, such as William Alexander, insist that "the conjecture has nothing in the least improbable."[96] He thinks that the very vehemence of the silversmith's language against Paul betrayed an inner sense of the possible truth of his teaching that "gods made with hands are not gods *at all"* (Acts 19:26 NASB). Both are clearly associated with Ephesian surroundings. Barclay notes that if the identification is accepted "his early opposition was still a black mark against him."[97] This would help explain why John gives him this strong testimony. While this identification is admittedly possible, there is no historical evidence to support it. This is a conjecture that would be pleasant to believe. Even less probable is the conjecture that Demetrius is to be identified with Demas (an abbreviated form of the name Demetrius), who once was one of Paul's co-workers but left Paul because he loved this present world (Col. 4:14; Philem. 24; 2 Tim. 4:10). All that we know about this Christian brother named Demetrius whom John commended must be gathered from John's words here, and we are left with many unanswered questions.

The stated testimony to Demetrius is threefold. First, there is the general testimony of those who know him: "Demetrius hath good report of all *men."* John's assertion "Demetrius hath good report" *(Dēmētriō memarturētai,* literally, "To Demetrius it has been witnessed") marks that the testimony given him had an abiding quality. The perfect-tense verb indicates that the testimony was given over a period of time and still has abiding validity. The verb, a favorite term in the Johannine literature, means "to bear witness to, to confirm." When used alone, as here, it always implies a testimony that is decidedly favorable, "to speak well or approvingly of" (cf. Luke 4:22; John 3:26; Acts 13:22). The verb is commonly used of bearing witness to Christ and His gospel, but here it relates to an individual member of the Christian community.

---

[95]Liddell and Scott, p. 338.

[96]W. Alexander, "The Third Epistle of John," in *The Speaker's Commentary, New Testament* (London: John Murray, 1881), 4:381. Ogilvie firmly accepts the identification and uses it to develop a strong sermonic appeal, pp. 201-6.

[97]William Barclay, *The Letters of John and Jude,* Daily Study Bible, 2nd ed. (Philadelphia: Westminster Press, 1960), p. 178.

This testimony to Demetrius was given "of all *men*" *(hupo pantōn),* which Burdick describes as "hyperbole, not exaggeration," since "John desires to emphasize the widespread character of the testimony."[98] The sweeping expression includes all those acquainted with Demetrius and especially the Christian community at Ephesus. Their commendation of him was uniform. Bruce suggests that the scope of the term may be even wider: "we cannot exclude the probability that, in terms of the qualifications for a 'bishop' specified in 1 Tim. 3: 7, he was 'well thought of by outsiders.' "[99]

Further, the testimony to Demetrius was given "of the truth itself" *(hupo autēs tēs alētheias),* an unusual expression which has evoked much discussion. The articular designation, "the truth," is specific–not just truth as an abstract quality but the revealed truth as embodied in the gospel. The use of the personal pronoun "itself" *(autēs)* personifies the term. But how is this personification to be understood? Some, such as Bruce, accept the full personification implied and hold that " 'the Truth' is here personal, denoting our Lord (cf. John 14. 6) and that we should translate: 'the Truth Himself.' "[100] Others, such as Plummer, hold that " 'the Truth' is the Spirit of truth (I John v. 6) which speaks in the disciples" and that it was "the Spirit, who guided and illuminated them in their estimate."[101] But Smalley thinks that such a full personification of "the truth" here "seems abrupt and out of place, occurring as it does between the entirely human testimony of 'everyone' on the one hand, and of the presbyter himself on the other."[102] More probable is the view that "the truth itself" denotes "the revealed corpus of truth . . . personified as a witness to Demetrius' character."[103] The apostolic faith, now preserved for us in the recorded revelation in the Scriptures, so manifestly governed the faith and conduct of Demetrius that this truth could be cited as a clear witness to his genuineness.

To this double testimony, which reached into the past with its continuing impact in the present, John adds his own testimony: "yea, and we *also* bear record" *(kai hēmeis de marturoumen).* This threefold witness establishes the testimony to Demetrius as wholly trustworthy (cf. Deut. 19:15). Until Gaius has opportunity to evaluate the character of Demetrius for himself, he can fully rely upon this threefold testimony.

John's emphatic "we" *(hēmeis)* can be taken to denote those around John at Ephesus. Those who do not accept apostolic authorship for the epistle

---

[98]Burdick, p. 458.

[99]Bruce, p. 155.

[100]*Ibid.*

[101]Plummer, p. 193.

[102]Smalley, p. 361.

[103]Burdick, p. 459.

take the writer to mean "that Gaius knows the truth of the Presbyter's testimony because the Presbyter is part of the Johannine School–the quality of the testifier and not the object of the testimony is what Gaius knows."[104] But others, such as Sawtelle who accepts apostolic authorship, suggest that John's "we" implies "some reminiscence perhaps of apostolic associates, whose voices he knew would be with him could they speak."[105]

The added comment "and ye know that our record is true" is a further appeal for full acceptance of the writer's testimony concerning Demetrius. The plural "ye know" follows the reading of the Textus Receptus *(oidate),* but the plural is not well attested.[106] The plural was apparently introduced by the scribes to conform to the plural in John 21:24. The singular "you know" *(oidas)* makes clear that the remark was addressed to Gaius personally. His contacts with John have assured Gaius that the testimony of John is "true" *(alēthēs),* is qualitatively true and no lie; it is wholly trustworthy. Sawtelle remarks that such a self-testimony "is natural as coming from John the apostle (John 19:35; 21:24), but unnatural for another."[107]

John is obviously intent upon setting Gaius fully at ease concerning this man Demetrius. But his words do not explain precisely how Demetrius was related to the situation of Gaius. Some have conjectured that Demetrius was a member of the church of Diotrephes who "had felt the wrath of Diotrephes. Perhaps he is the person who had been punished by this powerful leader in the church."[108] But if Gaius personally knew Demetrius, such a strong testimony given him by John seems unnecessary. This testimony to Demetrius seems better understood as directly related to John's missionary concern which is central to this letter. He seems most naturally to be the bearer of this letter. Palmer thinks that "John's very strong endorsement of him seems too extensive for an individual who is simply the carrier of the epistle."[109] But the recommendation is fully consistent with the view that Demetrius as the bearer of the letter from John was himself the leader of the new group

---

[104]Brown, *The Epistles of John,* p. 724.

[105]Sawtelle, p. 84.

[106]For the textual evidence see Nestle-Aland, *Novum Testamentum Graece,* 26th ed. The singular *(oidas)* is the reading in the Greek texts of Westcott and Hort, Alexander Souter, *Novum Testamentum Graece,* 2nd ed. (1947; reprint ed., Oxford: Clarendon Press, 1962); United Bible Societies, *The Greek New Testament,* 3rd ed.; Nestle-Aland, and R.V.G. Tasker, *The Greek New Testament, Being the Text Translated in the New English Bible 1961* (Oxford; Cambridge: University Press, 1964).

[107]Sawtelle, p. 84.

[108]Earl F. Palmer, *1, 2, 3 John, Revelation,* The Communicator's Commentary (Waco, Texas: Word Books, Publisher, 1982), p. 90.

[109]*Ibid.*

of missionaries John was sending out. For effectiveness in their ministry it was essential that they be assured hospitality from Gaius. In view of the turbulence produced by Diotrephes, John believes it necessary to provide Demetrius with a letter of recommendation. Such letters of recommendation were common in the early Christian Church (cf. Acts 18:27; Rom. 16:1-2; 1 Cor. 16:3).

III. The Conclusion (vv. 13-14)

The marked similarity between the endings of 2 and 3 John is obvious and suggests that similar endings characterized the numerous notes which John wrote (cf. v. 9) in supervising the work of the missionaries sent out from Ephesus. But the differences in these two endings make it clear that his words were not rote formulas; he carefully shaped his concluding words to the actual situation being dealt with.

In concluding his letter to Gaius, the Elder comments on the brevity of his letter and indicates an impending visit (vv. 13-14a), pronounces his benediction upon the recipient (v. 14b), and directs the exchange of mutual greetings between friends (v. 14c).

A. The Brevity of the Letter and John's Impending Visit (vv. 13-14a)

As in 2 John, the writer comments upon the brevity of the present note as related to his anticipated visit: "I had many things to write, but I will not with ink and pen write unto thee: But I trust I shall shortly see thee, and we shall speak face to face" (vv. 13-14a).

"I had many things to write" *(polla eichon grapsai soi)* points back to the various matters still on his mind which he felt needed to be communicated when he began to write. The use of the first-person singular "I" in contrast to the first person plural "we" in verse 12 has drawn comment. Brown seeks to account for the change as simply due to use of stereotyped formula,[110] but Smalley more aptly holds that the shift occurred because "the presbyter wished to strike a personal and individual note at the end of his missive."[111] The remainder of the conclusion makes it clear that John valued the personal touch between Christian friends.

John's use of the imperfect tense, "I had many things" *(polla eichon),* looks back to the time he sat down to write. As he began there were numerous matters on his mind which he felt might appropriately be communicated to Gaius; the aorist infinitive "to write" *(grapsai)* simply refers to these varied matters as a whole. "But" *(all')* serves to mark a contrast between his previous inclination and his present decision: "but I will not with ink and

---

[110]Brown, *The Epistles of John,* p. 724.
[111]Smalley, p. 362.

pen write unto thee.'' His use of the present tenses, ''I will not . . . write''
(ou thelō . . . graphein), marks his present unwillingness to go on writing
the other matters ''with ink and pen'' *(dia melanos kai kalemou,* literally,
''with black and a reed''), the common instruments used in written com-
munications. In 2 John 12 the mention of ''paper and ink'' refers to the
papyrus sheets commonly used for such letters.

The writing was inscribed with ''ink'' *(melanos),* the substantival usage
of the adjective meaning ''black.'' The term denotes the pigmented fluid
used in writing on papyrus, generally composed of powdered charcoal,
lampblack, or soot, mixed with gum and water. ''Pen'' *(kalamos)* is the
common term meaning ''reed'' or ''stalk''; only here in the New Testament
does the term refer to the reed-pen as indicating the plant from which the
pen was made. For writing purposes the reed was cut to a suitable length,
sharpened to a point and split like a quill-pen. The use of such writing
materials did not readily lend themselves to rapid production. Having dealt
with his central concern to assure hospitality for the missionaries being sent
out, John decided that the other matters, apparently of a more delicate and
personal nature, would better be dealt with orally upon his arrival.

John's decision not to write more calls for further comment, introduced
by the connective particle *de,* rather than *alla* just before; *de* indicates that
what is now added is different from but consistent with his stated decision.
The clause ''But I trust I shall shortly see thee'' *(elpizō de eutheōs se idein)*
announces the hope of an impending visit, yet he speaks with caution. ''I
trust'' indicates that he is actively planning such a visit yet cannot say for sure
when the way will open up for it. His anticipated arrival will be ''shortly''
(autheōs), with no long interval between his letter and his own arrival. The
adverb means ''immediately'' and in James 1:24 it is so rendered in the
NASB and NIV and as ''straightway'' in the KJV and ASV. Lenski insists
that ''shortly'' in our versions is not exact enough; he holds that John ''will
follow on the heels of his missionaries; they will scarcely have left Gaius
and have gone forward before John hopes to arrive and to attend to Diotrephes.''[112] The stance of Diotrephes is creating a crisis and John believes
it urgent to take personal action.

The added words ''and we shall speak face to face'' hold out the assurance of personal fellowship with Gaius upon arrival. It will enable them to
converse ''face to face'' *(stoma pros stoma,* literally, ''mouth to mouth''),
implying oral discussion. In such a personal encounter with Gaius, his beloved friend, John will be able to ''pour out his thoughts, without the limits
or restraints of paper and pen, and inscribe them on Gaius' heart with the

---

[112]Lenski, pp. 592-93.

vividness which personal intercourse, the look of the face, and the tones of the voice are so well fitted to produce."[113]

B. The Benediction upon the Reader (v. 14b)

Uttered without any connecting particle, John's benediction, "Peace *be* to thee" *(Eirēnē soi),* indicates his deep concern for the spiritual welfare of Gaius personally, for the pronoun is singular. Instead of the common epistolary "farewell" *(errōse,* literally, "be strong"; Acts 15:29), John uses "a Jewish blessing (cf. Num. 6:26), which had been given a new content for Christians from its use by Jesus (cf. John 20:19, 21, 26; see also John 14:27)."[114] Knowing that the position of Gaius might well become more difficult in the days ahead, John pronounces on him "the internal peace of the conscience, the fraternal peace of friendship, the supernal peace of glory [Lyra]."[115] Used without a verb, the words are exclamatory, expressing a fact rather than a mere wish. For John this "peace is not, as with us, a negative term meaning the absence of war, but rather the positive presence of blessing."[116] It is that state of spiritual well-being which flows from the experience of reconciliation and forgiveness. It begins with the believer's experience of reconciliation with God through faith in Christ Jesus and inevitably reflects itself in the believer's manward relations.

C. The Mutual Greetings of Friends (v. 14c)

John informs Gaius, "Our friends salute thee" *(aspazontai se hoi philoi),* better "the friends greet thee," denoting the friends with John. This was not a formal greeting from the congregation where John resided; rather, the greetings were sent by individuals with John who associated themselves with the position of the Elder and supported his request for the hospitality of Gaius toward the missionaries being sent out. The rendering "our friends" (KJV) implies that Gaius and John had a number of mutual friends in the church where John resided. But there is no word for "our" in the original; "the friends" *(hoi philoi)* denotes fellow-believers and need not imply that Gaius was personally acquainted with all of them. Burdick points out, "This is the only place in the NT that fellow Christians are called 'friends,' although Jesus employed the term to refer to those for whom He was about to give His life (John 15:13)."[117] Elsewhere in the New Testament this

---

[113]Sawtelle, p. 84.

[114]Smalley, pp. 363-64.

[115]Quoted in Henry Alford, *The New Testament for English Readers* ([1865-1872]; reprint ed., Chicago: Moody Press, [1958]), p. 1768.

[116]Leon Morris, "3 John," in *The New Bible Commentary,* rev. ed. (Downers Grove, Ill.: InterVarsity Press, 1970), p. 1273.

[117]Burdick, p. 460.

relationship of mutual affection and friendship between believers is expressed by the term "brethren." But John believes that Christian brotherhood should be characterized by warm mutual affection and personal care. Hodges remarks, "The use of the term 'friends' twice in these closing statements is perhaps one final reminder to Gaius that Christians in every place are or should be a network of friends who are ready to help one another whenever the need arises."[118]

John also directs Gaius to extend his own greetings to the various friends with him: "Greet the friends by name." These friends are those who have kept aloof from the rebellion of Diotrephes and have confirmed their loyalty to God's truth and mission. In extending John's greetings to them Gaius would have a ready opportunity to share the contents of this letter with each of them. The directive that they be greeted "by name" *(kat' onoma)* does not prove that they were only a scant number. This individual approach with greetings from John would tend to unite them with John when he arrived to deal with Diotrephes. Ward aptly remarks, "Such individualisation is not only tactful in its encouragement to loyalty; it is the mark of the pastoral heart."[119] Like the Good Shepherd who "calleth his own sheep by name" (John 10:3), "S. John as shepherd of the Churches of Asia would imitate the Good Shepherd and know all his sheep by name."[120] For John the oneness of believers in the Christian brotherhood did not minimize his high regard for individual worth and the cultivation of warm personal friendships. As Palmer remarks, "This note of human worth and belovedness is the final stroke of the book."[121]

---

[118]Hodges, pp. 914-15.

[119]Ronald A. Ward, *The Epistles of John and Jude. A Study Manual* (Grand Rapids: Baker, 1965), p. 72.

[120]Plummer, p. 195.

[121]Palmer, p. 91.

Bibliography

Biblical Text

The Greek Text

Aland, Kurt, Matthew Black, Bruce M. Metzger, and Allen Wikgren. *The Greek New Testament.* 1st ed. American Bible Society, British and Foreign Bible Society, National Bible Society of Scotland, Netherlands Bible Society, Württemberg Bible Society, 1966.

Aland, Kurt, Matthew Black, Carlo M. Martini, Bruce M. Metzger, and Allen Wikgren. *The Greek New Testament.* 3rd ed. United Bible Societies, 1975.

Hē Kainē Diathēkē. The New Testament. The Greek Text Underlying the English Authorized Version of 1611. London: Trinitarian Bible Society, 1977.

Hodges, Zane C., and Arthur L. Farstad. *The Greek New Testament According to the Majority Text.* Nashville: Thomas Nelson Publishers, 1982.

Nestle, Eberhard. *Hē Kainē Diathēkē. Text with Critical Apparatus.* 1904. Reprint. London: British and Foreign Bible Society, 1951.

Nestle, Erwin, and Kurt Aland, ed. *Novum Testamentum Graece.* 22nd ed. New York: American Bible Society, 1956.

Nestle, Erwin, and Kurt Aland. *Novum Testamentum Graece.* 26th ed. Stuttgart: Deutsche Biblestiftung, 1979.

Scrivener, F. H. *Hē Kainē Diathēkē. Novum Testamentum Textus Stephanici A.D. 1550.* London: Cantabrigiae, Dieghton, Bell Et Soc, 1867. (The Textus Receptus)

Souter, Alexander. *Hē Kainē Diathēkē. Novum Testamentum.* 1947. Reprint. Oxford: University Press, 1962.

Tasker, R.V.G. *The Greek New Testament, Being the Text Translated in the New English Bible 1961.* Oxford: University Press, 1964.

Westcott, Brooke Foss, and Fenton John Anthony Hort. *The New Testament in the Original Greek.* 2nd ed. 1907. Reprint. New York: Macmillan Co., 1935.

English Versions

American Standard Version. *The Holy Bible Containing the Old and New Testaments*. New York: Thomas Nelson & Sons, 1901.

The Amplified Bible. Grand Rapids: Zondervan, 1965.

The Everyday Bible, New Century Version. Fort Worth, Texas: Worthy Publishing, 1987.

Good News for Modern Man: The New Testament in Today's English Version. New York: American Bible Society, 1966.

Goodspeed, Edgar J. *The New Testament, An American Translation*. Chicago: University of Chicago Press, 1923.

Jerusalem Bible. *The New Testament of the Jerusalem Bible*. Reader's edition. Edited by Alexander Jones et al. 1966. Reprint. Garden City, N.Y.: Doubleday & Co. 1969.

King James Version. *The Holy Bible Containing the Old and New Testaments*. Nashville: Holman Bible Publishers, 1979.

The Living Bible Paraphrased. Wheaton, Ill.: Tyndale House Publishers, 1971.

Moffatt, James. *The New Testament, A New Translation*. Rev. ed. New York: Hodder & Stoughton, n.d.

Montgomery, Helen Barrett. *The New Testament in Modern English*. Philadelphia: Judson Press, 1924.

New American Bible, The New Testament. Washington, D.C.: Publications Office, United States Catholic Conference, 1977.

New American Standard Bible. Carol Stream, Ill.: Creation House, 1971.

New English Bible. Oxford and Cambridge: University Press, 1961, 1970.

New International Version. *The Holy Bible Containing the Old Testament and the New Testament*. Grand Rapids: Zondervan, 1978.

New King James Bible, New Testament. Nashville: Royal Publishers, 1979.

Revised Standard Version. *The Holy Bible, Containing the Old and New Testaments*. Philadelphia: A. J. Holman Co., 1962.

Revised Version. *The New Testament of Our Lord and Saviour Jesus Christ Translated Out of the Greek, A.D. 1881*. New York: Harper & Brothers, 1881. (English Revised Version)

Rotherham, Joseph Bryant. *The Emphasized New Testament*. 1878. Reprint. Grand Rapids: Kregel Publications, 1959.

The Twentieth Century New Testament. A Translation into Modern English. Reprint. Chicago: Moody Press, n.d.

Verkuyla, Gerrit, ed. *The Modern Language Bible, The New Berkeley Version*. Grand Rapids: Zondervan, 1969.

Weymouth, Richard Francis. *The New Testament in Modern Speech*. Revised by James Alexander Robertson. 5th ed. New York: Harper and Brothers, 1929.

Grammars, Lexicons, Word Studies

Abbott-Smith, G. *A Manual Greek Lexicon of the New Testament,* 3rd ed. Edinburgh: T. & T. Clark, 1937.

Arndt, William F., and F. Wilbur Gingrich. *A Greek-English Lexicon of the New Testament and Other Early Christian Literature.* Chicago: University of Chicago Press, 1957.

Blass, F., and A. Debrunner. *A Greek Grammar of the New Testament and Other Early Christian Literature.* Translated and revised by Robert W. Funk. Chicago: University of Chicago Press, 1961.

Cremer, Herman. *Biblico-Theological Lexicon of New Testament Greek.* Translated from the German by William Urwick. Reprint. Edinburgh: T. & T. Clark, 1954.

Dana, H. E., and Julius R. Mantey. *A Manual Grammar of the Greek New Testament.* New York: Macmillan Co., 1967.

Liddell, Henry George, and Robert Scott. *A Greek-English Lexicon.* 7th ed. Oxford: Clarendon Press, 1890.

Louw, Johannes P., and Eugene A. Nida, ed. *Greek-English Lexicon of the New Testament Based on Semantic Domains.* 2 vols. New York: United Bible Societies, 1988.

Metzger, Bruce M. *Lexical Aids for Students of New Testament Greek.* Princeton: Published by the author, 1955.

————. *A Textual Commentary on the Greek New Testament.* London, New York: United Bible Societies, 1971. [A companion volume to United Bible Societies, *The Greek New Testament,* 3rd ed., 1975.]

Moulton, James Hope, and George Milligan. *The Vocabulary of the Greek Testament Illustrated from the Papyri and Other Non-Literary Sources.* 1930. Reprint. London: Hodder and Stoughton, 1952.

Moulton, W. F., and A. S. Geden. *A Concordance to the Greek Testament.* 3rd ed. 1926. Reprint. Edinburgh: T. & T. Clark, 1950.

Robertson, A. T. *A Grammar of the Greek New Testament in the Light of Historical Research.* 5th ed. New York: Richard H. Smith, 1914.

Robertson, A. T., and W. Hersey Davis. *A New Short Grammar of the Greek Testament.* 1931. Reprint. New York: Harper & Row, 1935.

Trench, Richard Chenevix. *Synonyms of the New Testament.* 1880. Reprint. Grand Rapids: Eerdmans, 1947.

Vine, W. E. *An Expository Dictionary of New Testament Words with Their Precise Meanings for English Readers.* 4 vols. London: Oliphants, 1939.

New Testament Introductions

Allen, Willoughby C., and L. W. Grensted. *Introduction to the Books of the New Testament,* 3rd ed. Edinburgh: T. & T. Clark, 1936.

Goodspeed, Edgar J. *An Introduction to the New Testament*. Chicago: University of Chicago Press, 1937.
Guthrie, Donald. *New Testament Introduction*. Rev. ed. Downers Grove, Ill.: Inter-Varsity Press, 1970.
Hiebert, D. Edmond. *An Introduction to the New Testament*. Vol. 1. *The Gospels and Acts*. Chicago: Moody Press, 1975.
Moffatt, James. *An Introduction to the Literature of the New Testament*. 3rd ed. 1918. Reprint. Edinburgh: T. & T. Clark, 1949.
Robert, A., and A. Feuillet. *Introduction to the New Testament*. Translated from the French. New York: Desclee Company, 1965.
Salmon, George. *An Historical Introduction to the Study of the Books of the New Testament*. 9th ed. London: John Murray, 1904.
Scroggie, W. Graham. *Know Your Bible, A Brief Introduction to the Scriptures*. Vol. 2. *The New Testament*. London: Pickering & Inglis, n.d.
Zahn, Theodor. *Introduction to the New Testament*. Translated from the 3rd German ed. 3 vols. Edinburgh: T. & T. Clark, 1909.

Books on the Epistles of John

Alexander, Neil. *The Epistles of John*. Torch Bible Commentaries. New York: Macmillan, 1962.
Alexander, W. "The First Epistle General of John," and "The Third Epistle of John." In *The Speaker's Commentary, New Testament*. Vol. 4. London: John Murray, 1881.
Alford, Henry. *The Greek Testament*. 4th ed. 4 vols. London: Rivingtons, 1871.
———. *The New Testament for English Readers* [1865-1872]. Reprint. Chicago: Moody Press [1958].
Augustine. *Ten Homilies on the First Epistle of John*. Translated by H. Browne. *Nicene and Post-Nicene Fathers of the Christian Church*. 1st series. Reprint. Grand Rapids: Eerdmans, 1974.
Barclay, William. *The Letters of John and Jude*. Daily Study Bible. Philadelphia: Westminster Press, 1958.
Barker, Glen W. "1 John," "2 John," and "3 John." In *The Expositor's Bible Commentary*. Vol. 12. Grand Rapids: Zondervan, 1981.
Bengel, John Albert. *New Testament Word Studies*. Translated by Charlton T. Lewis and Marvin R. Vincent. 2 vols. Originally published as *Gnomen of the New Testament*, 1864. Reprint. Grand Rapids: Kregel, 1971.
Bennett, W. H. *The General Epistles, James, Peter, John, and Jude*. The Century Bible. London: Blackwood, Le Bas & Co., n.d.
Blair, J. Allen. *The Epistles of John: Devotional Studies on Living Confidently*. Neptune, N.J.: Loizeaux Brothers, 1982.
Blaney, Harvey J.S. "The First Epistle of John." In *Beacon Bible Commentary*. Vol. 10. Kansas City, Mo.: Beacon Hill Press, 1969.

Boice, James Montgomery. *The Epistles of John.* Grand Rapids: Zondervan, 1979.

Brooke, A. E. *A Critical and Exegetical Commentary on the Johannine Epistles.* International Critical Commentary. New York: Charles Scribner's Sons, 1912.

Brown, Raymond E. *The Epistles of John.* The Anchor Bible. Garden City, N.Y.: Doubleday & Co., 1982.

Bruce, F. F. *The Epistles of John.* Old Tappan, N.J.: Revell, 1975.

Bultmann, Rudolf. *The Johannine Epistles.* Hermeneia–A Critical and Historical Commentary on the Bible. Philadelphia: Fortress Press, 1973.

Burdick, Donald W. *The Letters of John the Apostle, An In-Depth Commentary.* Chicago: Moody Press, 1985.

Calvin, John. *Commentaries on the Catholic Epistles.* Translated by John Owen 1855. Reprint. Grand Rapids: Eerdmans, 1948.

Candlish, Robert S. *The First Epistle of John.* 1871. Reprint. Grand Rapids: Zondervan, n.d.

Clark, Gordon H. *First John, A Commentary.* Phillipsburg, N.J.: Presbyterian and Reformed, n.d.

Cox, Leo G. "First, Second, and Third John." In *The Wesleyan Bible Commentary.* Vol. 6. Grand Rapids: Eerdmans, 1966.

Cox, Samuel. *The Epistles of John.* 1865. Reprint. Minneapolis: Klock & Klock Christian Publishers, 1982. (Reprint bound in one volume with James Morgan, *The Epistles of John* [q.v.].)

Culpepper, R. Alan. *1 John, 2 John, 3 John.* Knox Preaching Guides. Atlanta: John Knox Press, 1985.

Dammers, A. H. *God Is Light, God Is Love, A Running Commentary on the First Letter of John.* New York: Association Press, 1963.

Dana, H. E. *The Epistles and Apocalypse of John.* Kansas City, Kan.: Central Seminary Press, 1947.

Dodd, C. H. *The Johannine Epistles.* Moffatt New Testament Commentary. New York: Harper & Row, 1946.

Drummond R. J., and Leon Morris. "The Epistles of John." In *The New Bible Commentary.* Grand Rapids: Eerdmans, 1953.

Ebrard, John H. A. *Biblical Commentary on the Epistles of St. John.* Translated by W. B. Pope. Edinburgh: T. & T. Clark, 1860.

Everest, Quinton J. *Messages from 1 John.* South Bend, Ind.: Your Worship Hour, 1982.

Fausset, A. R. "The First General Epistle of John," "The Second General Epistle of John," and "The Third General Epistle of John." In Robert Jamieson, A. R. Fausset, and David Brown, *A Commentary, Critical and Explanatory, on the Old and New Testaments.* American ed. Vol. 2. *New Testament.* Hartford, Conn.: S. S. Scranton Co., n.d.

Findlay, George C. *Fellowship in the Life Eternal, An Exposition of the Epistles of St John.* 1909. Reprint. Grand Rapids: Eerdmans, 1955.

Fisher, Fred L. "II John." In *The Biblical Expositor, The Living Themes of the Great Book.* Vol. 3. *The New Testament.* Philadelphia: A. J. Holman Co., 1960.

Gibbon, J. M. *Eternal Life, Notes of Expository Sermons on the Epistles of S. John.* London: Richard D. Dickinson, 1890.

Gingrich, Raymond E. *An Outline and Analysis of the First Epistle of John.* Grand Rapids: Zondervan, 1943.

Grayston, Kenneth. *The Johannine Epistles.* New Century Bible Commentary. Grand Rapids: Eerdmans, 1984.

Gutzke, Manford George. *Plain Talk on the Epistles of John.* Grand Rapids: Zondervan, 1977.

Haupt, Erich. *The First Epistle of St. John. A Contribution to Biblical Theology.* Translated by W. B. Pope. Edinburgh: T. & T. Clark, 1893.

Hobbs, Herschel H. *The Epistles of John.* Nashville: Thomas Nelson Publishers, 1983.

Hodges, Zane C. "1 John," "2 John," and "3 John." In *The Bible Knowledge Commentary, New Testament.* Wheaton, Ill.: Victor Books, 1983.

Houlden, J. L. *A Commentary on the Johannine Epistles.* Harper's New Testament Commentaries. New York: Harper & Row, 1973.

Jackman, David. *The Message of John's Letters.* The Bible Speaks Today. Downers Grove, Ill.: Inter-Varsity Press, 1988.

Kelly, William. *An Exposition of the Epistles of John the Apostle.* 1905. Reprint. Oak Park, Ill.: Bible Truth Publishers, 1970.

King, Guy H. *The Fellowship, An Expositional Study of 1 John.* 1954. Reprint. Fort Washington, Pa.: Christian Literature Crusade, 1971.

Kistemaker, Simon J. *Exposition of the Epistle of James and the Epistles of John.* New Testament Commentary. Grand Rapids: Baker, 1986.

Kysar, Robert. *I, II, III John.* Augsburg Commentary on the New Testament. Minneapolis: Augsburg, 1986.

Laurin, Roy L. *First John, Life at Its Best.* 1957. Reprint. Grand Rapids: Kregel, 1987.

Law, Robert. *The Tests of Life.* Edinburgh, T. & T. Clark, 1909.

Lenski, R.C.H. *The Interpretation of the Epistles of St. Peter, St. John and St. Jude.* Columbus, Ohio: Wartburg Press, 1945.

Lias, John James. *An Exposition of the First Epistle of John.* 1887. Reprint. Minneapolis: Klock & Klock Christian Publishers, 1982.

McDowell, Edward A. "1-2-3 John." In *The Broadman Bible Commentary.* Vol. 12. Nashville: Broadman Press, 1972.

Marshall, I. Howard. *The Epistles of John.* New International Commentary on the New Testament. Grand Rapids: Eerdmans, 1978.

Miller, John. *Notes on James, I and II Peter, I, II and III John, Jude.* Bradford, England: Needed Truth Publishing Office, n.d.

Moody, Dale. *The Letters of John.* Waco, Texas: Word Books, 1970.

Moorehead, William G. *Catholic Epistles–James, I and II Peter, I, II, III John, and Jude.* Outline Studies in the New Testament. New York: Revell, 1908.

Morgan, James. *The Epistles of John.* 1865. Reprint. Minneapolis: Klock & Klock Christian Publishers, 1982.

Morris, Leon. "3 John." In *The New Bible Commentary.* Rev. ed. Downers Grove, Ill.: Inter-Varsity Press, 1970.

Ogilvie, Lloyd John. *When God First Thought of You, The Full Measure of Love as Found in 1, 2, 3 John.* Waco, Texas: Word Books, 1978.

Orr, R. W. "The Letters of John." In *A New Testament Commentary.* Grand Rapids: Zondervan, 1969.

Palmer, Earl F. *1, 2, 3 John, Revelation.* The Communicator's Commentary. Waco, Texas: Word Books, Publisher, 1982.

Pentecost, J. Dwight. *The Joy of Fellowship.* Grand Rapids: Zondervan, 1977.

Plummer, Alfred. *The Epistles of S. John.* Cambridge Bible for Schools and Colleges. 1883. Reprint. London: Cambridge University Press, 1938.

Ross, Alexander. *The Epistles of James and John.* New International Commentary on the New Testament. Grand Rapids: 1954.

Sawtelle, Henry A. "Commentary on the Epistles of John." In *An American Commentary on the New Testament.* 1888. Reprint. Philadelphia: American Baptist Publications Society, n.d.

Smalley, Stephen S. *1, 2, 3 John.* Word Biblical Commentary. Waco, Texas: Word Books, 1984.

Smith, David. "The Epistles of St. John." In *The Expositor's Greek Testament.* [1897]. Reprint. Grand Rapids: Eerdmans, n.d.

Stott, J.R.W. *The Epistles of John.* Tyndale New Testament Commentaries. Grand Rapids: Eerdmans, 1964.

Strauss, Lehman. *The Epistles of John.* 1962. Reprint. Neptune, N.J.: Loizeaux Brothers, 1984.

Trapp, John. *Trapp's Commentary on the New Testament.* 1865. Reprint. Evansville, Ind.: The Sovereign Grace Book Club, 1958.

Van Gorder, Paul R. *Lessons from First John.* Grand Rapids: Radio Bible Class, 1978.

Vine, W. E. *The Epistles of John, Light, Love, Life.* Grand Rapids: Zondervan, n.d.

Ward, Ronald A. *The Epistles of John and Jude. A Study Manual.* Grand Rapids: Baker, 1965.

Westcott, Brooke Foss. *The Epistles of St. John, The Greek Text with Notes.* 3rd ed. 1892. Reprint. Grand Rapids: Eerdmans, 1950.

White, R.E.O. *Open Letter to Evangelicals, A Devotional and Homiletic Commentary on the First Epistle of John.* Grand Rapids: Eerdmans, 1964.

Wiersbe, Warren W. *Be Real*. Wheaton, Ill.: Victor Books, 1972.

Wilder Amos N., and Paul W. Hoon. "The First, Second, and Third Epistles of John." In *The Interpreter's Bible*. Vol. 12. New York: Abingdon Press, 1957.

Williams, George. *The Student's Commentary on the Holy Scriptures, Analytical, Synoptical, and Synthetical*. 5th ed. London: Oliphants, 1949.

Williams, R. R. *The Letters of John and James*. Cambridge Commentary on the New English Bible. Cambridge: University Press, 1965.

Other Books

Brown, Raymond E. *The Community of the Beloved Disciple*. New York: Paulist Press, 1979.

Bruce, F. F. *Answers to Questions*. Grand Rapids: Zondervan, 1973.

Cullman, Oscar. *The Johannine Circle*. Philadelphia: Westminster Press, 1975.

Culpepper, R. Alan. *The Johannine School: An Evaluation of the Johannine-School Hypothesis Based on an Investigation of the Nature of Ancient Schools*. Society of Biblical Literature Dissertation Series. No. 26. Missoula, Mont.: Scholars Press, 1975.

Deissmann, Adolf. *Light from the Ancient East*. London: Hodder and Stoughton, 1910.

Douglas, J. D., ed. *The New International Dictionary of the Christian Church*. Grand Rapids: Zondervan, 1974.

Enroth, Ronald. *The Lure of the Cults and New Religions*. Downers Grove, Ill.: Inter-Varsity Christian Fellowship, 1987.

Farrar, F. W. *The Early Days of Christianity*. Author's ed. New York: Cassell, n.d.

———. *The Messages of the Books, Being Discourses and Notes on the Books of the New Testament*. New York: E. P. Dutton, 1897.

Fraser, Donald. *Synoptical Lectures on the Books of Holy Scripture, Romans–Revelation*. New York: Robert Carter & Brothers, 1876.

Greenlee, J. Harold. *Introduction to New Testament Textual Criticism*. Grand Rapids: 1964.

Hiebert, D. Edmond. *Working With God: Scriptural Studies in Intercession*. New York: Carlton Press, 1987.

Hogg, C. F., and W. E. Vine. *The Epistles to the Thessalonians, with Notes Exegetical and Expository*. 1914. Reprint. Grand Rapids: Kregel, 1959.

Hunt, Dave. *The Cult Explosion*. Irvine, Calf.: Harvest House Publishers, 1980.

Hunt, Dave, and T. A. McMahon. *The Seduction of Christianity, Spiritual Discernment in the Last Days,* Eugene, Ore.: Harvest House Publishers, 1985.

Johnstone, P. J. *Operation World, A Handbook for World Intercession.* Bromley, Kent, England: STL Publications, 1978.

Marrs, Texe. *Dark Secrets of the New Age, Satan's Plan For a One World Religion.* Westchester, Ill.: Crossway Books, 1987.

Martin, Ralph P. *New Testament Foundations: A Guide for Christian Students.* Vol. 2. *The Acts, The Letters, The Apocalypse.* Grand Rapids: Eerdmans, 1978.

Nash, Ronald H. *Christianity and the Hellenistic World.* Grand Rapids: Zondervan, 1984.

Newman, J. H. *Parochial and Plain Sermons.* London: Longman's, 1896.

Ramsay, W. M. *The Church in the Roman Empire Before A.D. 180.* New York: G. P. Putnam's Sons, 1919.

Robertson, A. T. *Word Pictures in the New Testament.* Vol. 7. Nashville: Broadman Press, 1933.

Scholer, David M. "Sins Within and Sins Without: An Interpretation of I John 5:16-17." In *Current Issues in Biblical and Patristic Interpretation,* edited by Gerald F. Hawthorne, pp. 230-46. Grand Rapids: Eerdmans, 1975.

Westcott, Brooke Foss. *A General Survey of the History of the Canon of the New Testament.* London: Macmillan, 1870.

Dictionary, Encyclopedia, and Periodical Articles

Bietenhard, H. "Name, *Onoma.*" In *The New International Dictionary of New Testament Theology,* edited by Colin Brown. Grand Rapids: Zondervan, 1976, 2:648-55.

Bornkamm, Günther. "*presbus, presbuteros.*" In *Theological Dictionary of the New Testament,* edited by Gerhard Kittel. Grand Rapids: Eerdmans, 1964, 6:651-80.

Coenen, L. "Bishop, Presbyter, Elder." In *The New International Dictionary of New Testament Theology,* edited by Colin Brown. Grand Rapids: Zondervan, 1975, 1:188-201.

Delling, G. "*hupolambanō.*" In *Theological Dictionary of the New Testament,* edited by Gerhard Kittel. Grand Rapids: Eerdmans, 1964, 4:15.

Foerster, Werner. "*kuria.*" In *Theological Dictionary of the New Testament,* edited by Gerhard Kittel. Grand Rapids: Eerdmans, 1964, 3:1095.

Funk, Robert W. "The Form and Structure of II and III John." *Journal of Biblical Literature* 86 (1967):424-30.

Greeven, Heinrich. "*euchomai, euchē.*" In *Theological Dictionary of the New Testament,* edited by Gerhard Kittel. Grand Rapids: Eerdmans, 1964, 2:775-78.

Günther, W. "*nikaō.*" In *The New International Dictionary of New Testament Theology,* edited by Colin Brown. Grand Rapids: Zondervan, 1975, 1:650-52.

Hiebert, D. Edmond. "Satan." In *Zondervan Pictorial Encyclopedia of the Bible*. Grand Rapids: Zondervan, 1975, 5:282-86.

Law, R. "Elect Lady." In *The International Standard Bible Encyclopedia*. Grand Rapids: Eerdmans, 1939, 2:925.

———. "John, The Epistles of." In *The International Standard Bible Encyclopedia*. Grand Rapids: Eerdmans, 1939, 3:1711-20.

Schniewind, Julius. *"apangellō."* In *Theological Dictionary of the New Testament,* edited by Gerhard Kittel. Grand Rapids: Eerdmans, 1964, 1:64-67.

Stählin, Gustav. *"hamartanō, hamartēma, hamartia."* In *Theological Dictionary of the New Testament,* edited by Gerhard Kittel. Grand Rapids: Eerdmans, 1964, 1:293-96.

Scripture Index

Scripture Index

*Boldfaced passages represent the consecutive passages of this commentary. The successive subdivisions under each section are not listed in the index; these subdivisions are listed when referred to in other sections.

*Boldfaced passages represent the consecutive passages of this commentary. The successive subdivisions under each section are not listed in the index; these subdivisions are listed when referred to in other sections.

Subject Index